Three Sons of Abraham

How three Jewish followers of Jesus influenced the formation of the modern Messianic Jewish movement

Kelvin Crombie

ALL RIGHTS RESERVED

No part of this publication may be used or reproduced without permission from the author.
First published in 2013.

Contacts details:
Heritage Resources, PO Box 565, Mundaring, WA, 6073, Australia
Email: kjcrombie09@bigpond.com; sales@heritageresources.com.au
Website: www.heritageresources.com.au

Crombie, Kelvin
Three Sons of Abraham

ISBN: 978-0-9873630-2-2

Artwork:
Cover design by Minuteman Press, Midland, Western Australia.
Typesetting by Mike Lockhart, Print Publishing, Western Australia.

Printed in Great Britain by Imprint Digital, Exeter..

Visuals on the front and back cover are courtesy of Conrad Schick Library and Archive, Christ Church, Jerusalem and CMJ UK, Eagle Lodge.

Published by Heritage Resources.

Table of Contents

			Page
Acknowledgements			vii
Introduction			ix
Chapter	1	Father Abraham had many Sons	1
Chapter	2	Dispersion and Rejection	7
Chapter	3	Reformation and Restoration	21
Chapter	4	The Puritan Stream	27
Chapter	5	The Pietist and Moravian Streams	38
Chapter	6	The Evangelical Stream	52
Chapter	7	Joseph Levi and the New Covenant	63
Chapter	8	Joseph Frey and the (London) Missionary Society	74
Chapter	9	Jewish ministry within the Missionary Society	81
Chapter	10	The Parting of the Way	90
Chapter	11	The London (Jews) Society	97
Chapter	12	The Movements of Joseph Wolff	106
Chapter	13	Palestine Place and *Benei Abraham*	110
Chapter	14	The Anglican Society	114
Chapter	15	Frey to America and Wolff in Rome	122
Chapter	16	New Pastures	127
Chapter	17	Wolff goes to Jerusalem	137
Chapter	18	Alexander in Plymouth	146
Chapter	19	Wolff goes East	155
Chapter	20	Alexander and Wolff meet in Ireland	160
Chapter	21	The Mediterranean and Germany	168
Chapter	22	Consolidation in London	177
Chapter	23	Wolff's Epic Journey	182
Chapter	24	Frey, Alexander and Wolff's Varied Ministries	191
Chapter	25	Is this the time for Israel's Restoration?	201
Chapter	26	The Jerusalem Bishopric	213
Chapter	27	Alexander to Jerusalem	232
Chapter	28	Alexander in Jerusalem	251
Chapter	29	Wolff Returns to Bokhara	272
Chapter	30	Consolidation in Jerusalem	280
Chapter	31	A Hebrew Protestant 'Church' for Jerusalem	291
Chapter	32	The Deaths of Alexander, Frey and Wolff	302
Chapter	33	The Legacy of Frey, Wolff and Alexander	311
Selected Bibliography			319

Joseph Frey

Joseph Wolff

Michael Solomon Alexander

Acknowledgements

Special thanks are due to those who administer the various archives accessed for this project, namely the London Society Archives at SOAS in London; the CMJ Archives at the Bodleian Library in Oxford and Conrad Schick Library at Christ Church in Jerusalem; St. Anthony's College in Oxford; Lambeth Palace Archive and Kings College in London.

Due to the tyranny of distance I have had to lean quite heavily upon research for my previous publications, particularly those associated with CMJ. This has been particularly so for the life of Bishop Alexander and I have pulled quite heavily upon *A Jewish Bishop in Jerusalem*. The reader may notice some overlap.

There have been some invaluable secondary sources that I have utilised, and to each of the following researchers, historians and authors I give special thanks: Rev James Parkes (*Conflict between the Church and the Synagogue*); Iain Murray (*The Puritan Hope*); Christopher Clark (*The Politics of Conversion*); Mel Scult (*Millennial Expectations and Jewish Liberties*); Hugh Hopkins (*A Sublime Vagabond*); Dr. Stephen Orchard (*English Evangelical Eschatology 1790-1850*, unpublished thesis); D. Eichhorn (*Evangelizing the American Jew)*; Albert Hyamson (*The British Consulate in Jerusalem*).

Many thanks are owed to those who have helped with the research, editing and proof reading, especially Rev. Cyril Pritchard, Roy Saunders, Alison Marchant, Peter and Kathy Booth and Chris Moxon. As always my wife Lexie has been extremely supportive, as well as helping out with the editing. Special thanks also to Eileen Alvis and Mary Pinkess for their support and encouragement.

Although not directly involved with this project thanks must also be given to Rev. David Pileggi of Christ Church Jerusalem, who has been supportive of my writing projects during more than twenty years, as well as being the custodian of the Conrad Schick Library and Archive.

Special thanks also to Rev. Alex Jacob of CMJ UK who had the vision for this project. When Alex initially asked me to write up the story of the *Benei Abraham* I was somewhat reluctant. My apprehension grew when following a visit to the Bodleian Library I became quite despondent as there were just so few original sources about the *Benei Abraham*.

For some time I had felt that Joseph Frey needed to receive more acknowledgement for his contribution to the establishment of CMJ as well as being a pioneer in the modern Hebrew Christian movement. I then began to ponder about writing the story of *Benei Abraham* through the lens of Frey. Then the idea grew of also including Joseph Wolff and Michael Solomon Alexander in the story line. It was while voicing out some other possibilities that Jane Moxon from CMJ suggested the idea of writing the story, as *Three Sons of Abraham*.

Thus, as always, there are many contributors other than the actual author, and to each of these I give thanks. This work could not have been completed without each of the above stated – and others whose names do not appear above.

Introduction

Few people within the world-wide Church would have heard of the *Benei Abraham*, or even of Joseph Frey. Some may have heard of Joseph Wolff, as he is regarded as one of the foremost evangelists of the last two hundred years, while others again have probably heard of Michael Solomon Alexander, the rabbi who became the first Anglican-Protestant bishop in Jerusalem. More people, though, would have heard of Jews who believe in Jesus, Messianic Jews, and the Hebrew Christian-Messianic Jewish movement.

How many though, who have heard of the modern day Messianic movement know about its origins, or its significance, if any, for the Church of today.

We might well ask is there any significance today in there being a movement of Jewish followers of Jesus? Some might contend that surely in Christ there is neither Jew nor Gentile, therefore why all the concern about a Jew who believes in Jesus. Some might even contend that once a Jewish person comes to faith in Jesus then he or she has to leave all that Jewish tradition behind.

Despite one's attitude towards the status of a Jewish person when they become a disciple of Jesus, today a Jewish follower of Jesus, generally speaking, *does* believe there is significance in their Jewishness and that they should not have to leave all their Jewish tradition behind. The Gentile Christian should be willing to take heed of this reality or fact, as perhaps there is something spiritually beneficial in it for them, and for the Gentile dominated Church.

A Jewish person who becomes a disciple of Jesus is often faced with three obstacles and challenges; the enemy of our souls, who hates seeing anyone transfer from the kingdom of darkness to the Kingdom of Light; from their own people, who will often say that once you believe in the *Goyish* (Gentile) Jesus then you are no longer one of us, no longer Jewish; and from some within the Church who will say, or think, that when you become a follower of Jesus then you are no longer Jewish, you are now one of us and that your Jewish identity is of no future significance.

That there is now a vibrant movement of over 100,000 Jewish followers of Jesus (by whatever name they prefer to use to describe themselves) means there is a tremendous challenge both to the Jewish community and to the predominantly Gentile Church. In the past they have been ignored or overlooked. But no longer.

Most Christians are familiar enough with the history of the Church to know that at the very beginning there were some serious conflicts within national Israel between those who followed Jesus as Lord and Messiah (known as 'the Way', or the 'Nazarenes' or, as I often describe them, as 'Messianic Israel'[1]) and those who did not.

Most Christians will know that at a certain time the synagogue forced such Jewish followers of Jesus out – never to return.

If this is the case, how is it that today we are confronted by a movement of over 100,000 Jewish people who follow Jesus; Jewish people who clearly identify themselves as Jews and who have not 'converted' to becoming Gentile.

The starting point for where a collective group of Jewish followers of Jesus began to understand their distinctive Jewish identity could be traced to a gathering of forty-one Jewish followers of Jesus in a room (perhaps it was even an *upper room*) in the East End of London on 9 September 1813, whereupon they formed the *Benei Abraham*, the Sons or Children of Abraham.

If this really is the beginning point of this modern day phenomenon known as the Hebrew Christian-Messianic Jewish movement, then the question arises: how did those forty-one Jewish disciples of Jesus get to that point?

There were four main streams within Gentile Christianity which led up to it. Two of these streams were from Germany, which were the Pietist movement within the Lutheran Church and the Moravian Church; and two from Britain, which were the Puritans and the Evangelicals.

This book which looks very briefly at the birth of the modern Messianic Jewish movement, will provide a quick overview of the historical circumstances which saw the divergence of 'Messianic Israel' from national Israel in the first and second centuries and how this movement then became Gentile Christianity.

Then a brief analysis will be provided of developments within the Gentile Church, focusing upon those four streams, which then led to the formation of the *Benei Abraham*. Within this analysis we will observe just how pivotal those pioneering efforts were within the German Church.

The core of this book centres around the lives of the three German-born Jewish followers of Jesus; Joseph Frey, Joseph Wolff and Michael Solomon Alexander – three sons of Abraham according to the flesh.

Joseph Frey was the main architect not just of the *Benei Abraham* but of the establishment of a British-based movement desirous of taking the message of Jesus to other Jewish people. The role of Joseph Frey has perhaps been under-emphasised, partly because he may not have finished well. Regardless of how this man finished, there is little doubt that he was pivotal in the pioneering stages of the modern Messianic movement.

---

1 The term 'Messianic Israel' is not found in the Scriptures. I employ this term to describe the remnant within national Israel.

Frey was the embodiment of the German streams, and when he went to England in 1801 he linked up with the British missionary and Restorationist movement, itself the embodiment of the Puritan and Evangelical streams. He was definitely the man for the time.

The two other German Jews, Joseph Wolff and Michael Solomon Alexander built upon the foundation laid by Joseph Frey.

Wolff had an extraordinary life before finally entering into covenant with Jesus, and an even more extraordinary life afterwards when he set out to be a modern day Francis Xavier – albeit a Jewish one. Wolff it would be safe to say, was the pioneer evangelist to the Jewish people in the broad region from Constantinople (Istanbul) through to Calcutta (Kolkata); from Bokhara (Bukhara) through to Yemen. His story and particularly his love for Jesus are truly inspirational.

Alexander was most definitely a man for the times. Had he lived a generation before or after he did, then Michael Solomon Alexander may have been just a name on a birth certificate. As it was he came to the fore when the British movement for the restoration of Israel was at its zenith, driven by Lord Shaftesbury and the Evangelicals; and when Prussian ambitions for establishing an evangelical witness in Jerusalem were at their very beginnings, a movement driven by King Frederick William IV and Chevalier Bunsen.

It is often difficult when looking at an historical subject such as this not to project 21st century concepts and understandings back into the text. For instance, today, there is much less of a problem for a Jewish follower of Jesus openly identifying themselves as a Messianic Jew. But in 1813 that journey was only just beginning. Thus we cannot be critical if at that initial point a Jewish follower of Jesus was still somewhat reticent, even unsure of their identity as a Jew who followed Jesus. It is important for us to try and absorb the context of the period.

At the outset of this book I need to emphasize that although the *Benei Abraham* (and the parent body the 'London Jews Society') was the beginning point in the movement, other streams merged with it, such as Joseph Rabinowitz and his movement of Jewish followers of Jesus from Kishinev. The end result of all these streams is that today there is a wide and broadly running river; a river which cannot be stopped.

This book tells only part of this wonderful story. There are many other very fine books written on the subject, and more importantly, there are many more living testimonies of this story – more than 100,000 of them![2]

2 Debbie Rodgers is currently writing *Bond of Union* which will be an adjunct to this volume, and which looks primarily at the history of the Hebrew Christian-Messianic Jewish movement from 1866 onwards.

May I strongly encourage one and all to jump into this river; a river wherein a Jew who follows Jesus retains the national identity that God gave them, and a Gentile background follower of Jesus likewise retains the national identity that God gave to them.

It could be that within this river, which has come together because of the confluence of many streams, there is spiritual life and vitality for the world-wide Church.

Chapter 1

Father Abraham had many sons

Father Abraham had not just three sons, but many. Two of them, Ishmael and Isaac, however, took pre-eminence over all the others.

When God first spoke to Abraham (or as he was then known, Abram) He gave him many promises; promises that would be fulfilled only if Abram left his homeland and went to the land of Canaan. Of these many promises, four stand out:
- that a nation would come forth from him
- that the land of Canaan would be given to this nation
- that there would be blessings for those who blessed him and curses for those who cursed him
- that all the families or nations on earth would be blessed through him (Genesis 12: 1-3)

Abram obeyed and went to the land of Canaan, whereupon God then confirmed all those previously stated promises in the most tangible way then known in antiquity – the cutting of a covenant. The context of the covenant cutting ceremony, however, related to the actual granting of the land (see Genesis 15), but it can be inferred that all of the promises previously given were also included.[1]

In eastern society, once a covenant has been cut between two entities and then ratified by the swearing of an oath, those conditions (promises) could not be broken. In the case of the covenant between God and Abraham, only God swore on oath, as Abraham was asleep when that part of the ceremony associated with the swearing of the oath took place. It was now incumbent upon God, not Abraham, to fulfill those promises. God's very character is associated with the keeping of this covenant and the promises it contained.

The covenant with Abraham did not cease at his death, but was transferred to his son. Which son? To the eldest as was expected? No. The covenant was not transferred to Ishmael, the eldest son, but to the son of promise, Isaac, and then to Isaac's second born son, Jacob (who later became known as Israel). From Jacob the covenant promises were transferred collectively to the sons of Israel, who in turn became the nation of Israel.

It was to this collective seed or nation of Israel that God then entered into covenant, initially in the Sinai and then later on the banks of the Jordan

[1] See Genesis 15, and *In Covenant with Jesus*, by this author, for further details.

River.[2] Moses was the representative Hebrew in this covenant. This was not an adjunct to the covenant with Abraham, but was a different covenant altogether, complete with different conditions, which engendered different promises for obedience and curses for disobedience.

The physical seed of Abraham lived thereafter in the land of Canaan, which then became known as the land of Israel. Yet encompassed within this collective seed, the nation of Israel, there would come one individual seed of Abraham, one promised in fact many centuries before Abraham even lived, one promised to Adam and Eve. This individual seed would restore mankind to their rightful position as God's regents on earth. (See Genesis 3: 15)

That original position had been squandered by Adam and Eve and usurped by the adversary, Satan. God then promised an individual seed who would redeem mankind to that original position. All creation waited in anticipation of this coming seed, this 'second Adam.' (Romans 5:14; 1 Corinthians 15:45)

This coming promised One would enter into Israel through one family, so God then entered into covenant with another representative Israelite named David. The promised individual seed was to come through David's line and would become the King of Israel.

Many centuries after Abraham, Moses and David, a prophet arose named Jeremiah, through whom God promised a new covenant to the collective nation of Israel:

"Behold, the days are coming," declares the LORD, "when I will make a new covenant with the house of Israel and with the house of Judah, not like the covenant which I made with their fathers in the day that I took them by the hand to bring them out of the land of Egypt, My covenant which they broke, although I was a husband to them," declares the LORD.

"But this is the covenant which I will make with the house of Israel after those days," declares the LORD, "I will put My law within them, and on their heart I will write it; and I will be their God, and they shall be My people.

And they shall not teach again, each man his neighbor and each man his brother saying, 'Know the LORD,' for they shall all know Me, from the least of them to the greatest of them," declares the LORD, "for I will forgive their iniquity, and their sin I will remember no more."

Thus says the LORD, Who gives the sun for light by day,
And the fixed order of the moon and the stars for light by night,
Who stirs up the sea, so that its waves roar; The LORD of Hosts is His name:

"If this fixed order departs from before Me," declares the LORD,

---

2 This is what I term the 'Sinai-Mosaic Covenant.'

"Then the offspring[3] of Israel shall also cease
From being a nation before Me forever." (Jeremiah 31: 31-36, NAS)[4]

The God of Israel was declaring that one day there would be a new covenant with the nation of Israel, a covenant whereby there would be forgiveness of sins; and a new covenant whereby Israel would come 'to know Him'- that is have a personal relationship with Him; and that all Israel (a large collective number) would know Him.

The implementation of such a covenant, though, would require a representative Israelite, just as previously Abraham, Moses and David had all been representatives in covenants between God and Israel.

The people of Israel now waited for this coming One, the King Messiah, the one whom Jeremiah also called THE LORD OUR RIGHTEOUSNESS, (Jeremiah 23: 6; cf Isaiah 9: 6-7) - a very special king. Micah the prophet even prophesied that this king would be born in Bet Lehem (Bethlehem) in Judah. (Micah 5: 2)

The prophets wrote of a coming time when Israel and the nations would live in universal peace and harmony: the King Messiah reigning over redeemed Israel and over the nations of the world, was the hope of Israel. (Psalm 2; Isaiah 2:4; 9: 6-7; 11: 1-2, 6-10; 25: 6-8; Zechariah 12 and more). One prophet, Isaiah, also prophesied of a man who would come to Israel who would be perfect, and yet who would die for the transgressions of the nation – and yet who would also see the light of the day. (Isaiah 52: 13 – 53: 12)

Institution of the New Covenant
Many centuries after the ministries of Isaiah, Jeremiah and Micah a baby boy named *Yeshua* (Hebrew = Saviour) was born in Bet Lehem. The angel Gabriel, as well as the Gentile magi from the East all acclaimed Him as the king. (Luke 1: 30-33; Matthew 2: 2) Then when baby Jesus was dedicated at the Temple in Jerusalem an aged man named Simeon took him into his arms and proclaimed these words:

> "Lord now you are letting your servant depart in peace, according to your word;
> for my eyes have seen your salvation;
> Which you have prepared before the face of all peoples,
> A light to bring revelation to the Gentiles,
> And the glory of your people Israel." (Luke 2: 29-32, NKJV)

---

3 Jeremiah 31: 36, 'the offspring of Israel' = 'the seed of Israel.'
4 In addition, they could have recalled Exodus 24: 8, "This is the blood of the covenant which the LORD has made with you according to all these words".

Yeshua ben Yosef (Jesus the son of Joseph) grew up in Nazareth in the Galilee and about the year 30 AD began to call others to follow Him (as was normal for itinerant rabbis of that time) and began proclaiming, 'Repent for the Kingdom of Heaven is at hand.'

Rabbi *Yeshua* (Jesus the teacher) then ate a Passover meal with His followers in an upper room in Jerusalem about the year 33-34 AD. When He raised the third cup of wine He proclaimed these profound words:

> "This cup is the new covenant in my blood, which is poured out for you." (Luke 22: 20, NIV). "This do, as often as you drink it, in remembrance of Me." (1 Corinthians 11: 25, NKJV)[5]

These words related to that profound prophecy of Jeremiah. But, in accordance with traditional customs, for a covenant to be instituted there would need to be the cutting of a sacrifice. Shortly after Jesus had brought His Jewish followers into covenant relationship with Himself, He became the sacrifice for the institution of this covenant when He was publicly executed on a stake outside the walls of Jerusalem. (Isaiah 52:12-53: 13)

Although executed and pronounced dead, Jesus, in accordance with His own declaration, (Matthew 17: 23) was raised from the dead three days later. He then spent forty days with His followers (disciples), teaching and reinforcing to them the principles of the Kingdom of God (Heaven). These principles were communicated by Jesus mostly (but not exclusively) through one language, Hebrew, and through one culture, the Jewish culture of first century Israel.

Ten days before the festival of *Shavuot* (Weeks), Jesus walked to the Mount of Olives whereupon His followers asked Him a very relevant question:

> "Lord, will you at this time restore the kingdom to Israel?" (Acts 1: 6, RSV)

To this question Jesus answered:

> "It is not for you to know times or seasons which the Father has fixed by his own authority. But you shall receive power when the Holy Spirit has come upon you; and you shall be my witnesses in Jerusalem, and in all Judea and Samaria, and to the end of the earth." (Acts 1:7-8, RSV)

Jesus did not tell them that God's kingdom purposes for the nation of Israel had ended. Such would be impossible in view of the very principles of covenant, and would be contrary to the many prophetic utterances relating to a time of universal peace *on earth*. Instead Jesus merely reminded His followers of His

---

5 See also Matthew 26: 28; Mark 14:24.

priority call for them – and those who came after them. This priority call was for them to be witnesses of Him, and of His resurrection.

This proclamation was not to be local, it was to be to the ends of the earth; not just to the nation of Israel, but to all nations. This call was for 'Messianic Israel', the remnant within national Israel, to invite the nations, the Gentiles, into the covenant relationship between God and Israel.

To be such a witness, though, would require divine intervention and help.

The coming of the Holy Spirit
Such divine intervention then occurred on *Shavuot*, when Jesus' followers were visited by an outpouring of God's Spirit. Thereafter many more from the nation of Israel became part of 'Messianic Israel', the remnant within the nation.

Not long afterwards though, 'Messianic Israel' was confronted by reality – God really did intend to do that which He had always said He would do: that Israel was to be a light to the nations. God's plan was universal, not local. God's plan was for the Gentiles of the world to also participate in this new dynamic movement.

God revealed in a vision to Peter, one of Jesus' followers, that the Gentiles were not to be regarded any longer as 'unclean.' (Acts 10: 28) Immediately after this, Peter received a call to visit a Roman centurion named Cornelius in Caesarea – a Gentile. Peter obeyed the call and during his first meeting the Spirit of God fell upon those Gentiles, in similar manner to how He fell upon the Jewish people at *Shavuot* (Pentecost). This was a totally new and extraordinary event for Jewish people to observe.

There had always been Gentile converts to the nation of Israel, but this was a completely new way for the Gentiles to be 'grafted in'. Until this event in about the year 34-35 AD, if a Gentile wanted to leave being a pagan or heathen, or even a 'God-fearer'[6] they would go through an accepted period of conversion according to the tenets of Judaism, which would culminate in a *mikve* – a full immersion in water and for a male, the rite of circumcision.

At Caesarea, Gentile Romans entered into covenant with Jesus and were filled with the Holy Spirit – without going through the normal procedure. Later following the journeys of Paul and Barnabas, more Gentiles entered into 'Messianic Israel' in like fashion.

This new way was what Paul would call a 'mystery' (Ephesians 3: 1-6; also Col 1: 24-27; Rom 16: 25-26) - the 'mystery' of how God would allow Gentiles to become part of Israel, albeit as members of the Commonwealth of Israel, without converting to Judaism. This 'mystery' would mean that Gentiles, formerly heathens and without hope in the world and strangers to the covenants

---

6 A 'God-fearer' was a Gentile who attended synagogue and other Jewish observances but had not gone through the full conversion process.

of promise, would now also be reckoned as sons and daughters of Abraham – not by natural birth, but by faith. The sons and daughters of Abraham by faith, though, were not heirs to all the promises given to Abraham. They were 'grafted in' through one promise, 'that all families on earth would be blessed through Abraham.' They would, nevertheless, be recipients of those promises which were to be found 'in Jesus.'

Sons of Abraham by faith did not mean, therefore, that they would replace the natural sons. That would be an impossibility, as the natural sons were recipients of the promises of Abraham. Being a natural son of Abraham though, did not guarantee automatic entrance into the Kingdom of God, as both Jesus and John the Baptist had made very clear. Entrance into the Kingdom of God was only by being born again of the Spirit. (John 3)

There were many opponents within national Israel, and even within 'Messianic Israel' to this new way. It was due to this opposition that the Jewish leaders of the Messianic movement called for a meeting in Jerusalem. There the Jewish leaders, with James the brother of Jesus taking the lead, confirmed what had already been happening, and declared authoritatively that Gentile followers of Jesus did not have to convert to the Judaism of the time, but merely had to observe four *mitzvoth*, four commandments. (See Acts 15)

As could be expected the new Gentile followers of Jesus were ecstatic and extremely thankful for this magnanimous and very generous decision by the Jerusalem Jewish leaders. Everything augured well for the spread of the Messianic message and for harmonious relations between the Jewish and Gentile followers of Jesus, with each understanding and respecting the position and role of the other. Jesus was to bring revelation to the Gentiles, and also to be the glory of His people, Israel; His followers were to be known as His body, His bride, the *one new man* comprised of the Jew and the Gentile. (Ephesians 2: 11-22)

Chapter 2

Dispersion and Rejection

The dispersion of the message of Jesus

This new way for Gentiles to become attached to Israel without going through the normal conversion process was fraught with many dangers. Israel, despite its national shortcomings, had experienced God for some two thousand years. Apart from the God-fearers, many of these new Gentile followers of Jesus had little knowledge or understanding of Israel's collective history with God. It is understandable that many Jewish people, including Saul (Paul), would have concerns about this 'mystery.'

Paul in his letter to the New Covenant community in Rome wrote three whole chapters dealing with the relationship between the Gentiles and national Israel. Concerning national Israel which had not accepted Jesus as Lord and Messiah, he stated:

> … Did they stumble so as to fall beyond recovery? Not at all! Rather, because of their transgression salvation has come to the Gentiles to make Israel envious …
>
> I am talking to you Gentiles … For if their rejection is the reconciliation of the world, what will their acceptance be but life from the dead? …
>
> If some of the branches have been broken off, and you, though a wild olive shoot, have been grafted in among the others and now share in the nourishing sap from the olive root, do not boast over those branches. If you do, consider this: You do not support the root, but the root supports you. You will say then, "Branches were broken off so that I could be grafted in." Granted. But they were broken off because of unbelief, and you stand by faith. Do not be arrogant, but be afraid. For if God did not spare the natural branches, he will not spare you either …
>
> As far as the gospel is concerned they are enemies on your account; but as far as election is concerned, they are loved on account of the patriarchs, for God's gifts and his call are irrevocable. (Romans 11: 11, 13, 15, 17-21, 28-29, NIV)

Paul specifically wanted to address the attitude of Gentile spiritual arrogance. He also wanted the Roman Gentile Christians (and all Gentile Christians since) to know that national Israel would one day experience a great revival and would be saved:

> I do not want you to be ignorant of this mystery, brothers, so that you may not be conceited: Israel has experienced a hardening in part until the full number of the Gentiles has come in. And so all Israel will be saved …
> (Romans 11: 25-26, NIV)

National Israel might then have been living outside of a New Covenant relationship with God, but, as Jeremiah had stated, one day they would all know Him from the least of them to the greatest of them; that would be a revival worth praying for and anticipating!

Despite Paul's corrective teaching and exhortations, though, Gentile arrogance towards national Israel (the natural branches) did increase. This process was greatly assisted by a growing antagonism from within national Israel towards 'Messianic Israel' and later even towards the Gentile Church before it was legally recognized, as well as historical events which took place.

The rejection of 'Messianic Israel' by national Israel

From the very beginning of Jesus' ministry there was contention within Israel between those who confessed Jesus as Lord and Messiah and those who did not. Initially the matter was an inter-Jewish disagreement. But when national Israel observed how easily the Gentiles were being permitted to join the Messianic movement (which was invariably known as 'the Way' or 'the Nazarenes') resentment and animosity intensified.

This tension, though, was just one of many such tensions in Israel at that time. The predominant concern was with the ruling Roman authority. Rome was a pagan nation and many Jewish people could not accept that a nation in covenant with God could be subservient to a pagan entity.

These national tensions boiled over when a revolt broke out against Rome in 66 AD. Although only a small number of Jewish people actually wanted to physically fight Rome, very soon the conflict engulfed the entire nation.

Many of the Jewish followers of Jesus left Jerusalem about 68 AD and went to Pella on the other side of the Jordan River. This move did not augur well for their relationship with the mainstream Jewish population.

In their absence Jerusalem was surrounded by the Roman forces. One rabbi, Yochanan Ben Zakai, then foresaw that Jerusalem would be captured and destroyed, along with the Temple, and the people would be led away into slavery. Ben Zakai managed to get out of Jerusalem and ultimately made his way to Yavne near the coast where he laid the foundations for a Judaism without Jerusalem, without the Temple, without the priesthood and dispersed with many of the people from the land.

When the Jewish Revolt finally ended (Jerusalem in 70 AD and in the land 73

AD) a new reality existed in the land of Israel. The Sadducean party, alongside the Zealots, the Sicarii and the Essene groups, had all ceased to exist. The main group left was the Pharisaic party, whose leader now was Rabbi Yochanan Ben Zakai and the academy at Yavne.

Ben Zakai's new Jewish religious system in time became known as Orthodox, Rabbinic or Talmudic Judaism. Many of the traditions of Israel which had developed over many centuries were then in time written down and codified, in addition to fresh interpretations of the Scriptures. These writings became known as the *Talmud*, a combination of two distinct sets of writings, the *Mishnah* and the *Gemara*. The Jewish people henceforth subscribed not so much to the teachings of the Bible, but more-so to those of the *Talmud*.

This new stream of Judaism (which henceforth was synonymous with the national life of Israel) desired sole authority over the lives of the Jewish people. One way in which this was done was to make an addition to the *Shemoneh Esreh*, the Eighteen Benedictions. These Benedictions, often referred to as 'the Prayer', were recited three times daily in the synagogue. Prior to 90 AD the thirteenth benediction, known as the *Birkat HaMinim*, was basically a curse against the *minim* – heretics – as well as apostates (*meshumaddim*). If any heretic was in the synagogue they would not recite these words against themselves.

In about 90 AD some words were added to this benediction, which specified the followers of the Nazarene.[1] Although Jewish followers of Jesus could still have attended synagogue, yet for all intents and purposes this benediction made it much more difficult for them to do so. The battle lines had been drawn in the sand by the mainstream Jewish leadership.

The Bar Kochba Revolt and its consequences
Jewish resentment against Roman control continued to simmer in the land of Israel. Another revolt broke out in the year 132 AD. This revolt was led by Simon Bar Kosiba, who was proclaimed as the Messiah by the great Rabbi Akiva, and his name thereafter became Bar Kochba – 'Son of the Star', a Messianic entitlement.

To the Jewish followers of Jesus, Bar Kochba was a false messiah, and so they could not fight under his banner. Some Jewish followers of Jesus received harsh treatment from Bar Kochba's followers as a result, and the separation lines between national Israel and 'Messianic Israel' grew wider.

Once again the mighty Roman forces triumphed. Tens of thousands of Jewish people were killed, and Jerusalem was captured in 135 AD. Many more thousands of Jewish people were then led away into Roman slavery.

The Romans destroyed Jerusalem and upon its ruins they rebuilt a new pagan

---

1 Wilson, M. *Our Father Abraham*, (Grand Rapids, 1989) p. 65. *Notrzrim* in Hebrew could mean either Nazarene or *Netzer*, branch.

city known as *Aelia Capitolina*. They renamed the land of Israel *Syria Palestina* – in an attempt to erase the Jewish connection. Jewish people, including Jewish followers of Jesus were forbidden to live in the region in and near to Jerusalem. Many still lived in the Galilee, which now became the centre of Jewish life.

The vibrant Messianic Jewish community which had been centred in Jerusalem now ceased to exist. Until this point there had been fifteen leaders of the Jerusalem 'Church', beginning with James the brother of Jesus. This entity now disappeared, ejected from Jerusalem – seemingly never to return.

Although Simon Bar Kochba was shown to be a false messiah, Jewish followers of Jesus were still not fully accepted into the life of national Israel because they acknowledged Jesus as the Messiah. The separation between the two communities was now seemingly irreversible.

The dispersion of the Jewish people

A Jewish *diaspora* had been in existence since the national dispersion of Israel to Babylon in the sixth century BC. During the intervening centuries Jewish people moved throughout the Eastern Mediterranean and Middle East region. This movement intensified during the Greek and subsequent Roman periods, with Jewish communities existing over a wide area.

Following the two failed Jewish revolts more Jewish people were dispersed throughout the Roman and Gentile world, while Jewish life in the land of Israel existed primarily in the Galilee.

The hope of a restored national Israel was kept alive by the teachings of the rabbis. Yet, from a pragmatic perspective the likelihood of national Israel ever becoming an independent nation again in the land, centred upon Jerusalem, was very remote – and would require a mighty miracle.

The Gentile Church rejects its Hebraic-Jewish roots

Following the destruction of Jerusalem the leadership of the Messianic-Christian movement moved away from David's City and became located at various other centres within the Roman Empire, namely Antioch, Alexandria, Constantinople and Rome. A geographical move heralded also a philosophical move.

Two historical developments converged which caused a separation and rejection of 'Messianic Israel' from its Hebraic-Jewish roots and foundations. Due to the growing number of Gentiles entering into 'Messianic Israel' without having to go through any form of official conversion to Judaism, the character of this movement inevitably changed. Many of these new converts from paganism may have had no understanding at all of Israel's long history and heritage with God.

Then, as the antipathy of national Israel towards 'Messianic Israel' intensified, Gentile followers of Jesus (Christians) began to be further disassociated from

Israel. Throughout the Roman Empire, Gentile Christians witnessed how the Jewish nation had twice been severely defeated, destroyed and dispersed by Rome. In addition, the icon of Jewish national life, the Temple in Jerusalem, had been destroyed. By the mid-2nd century AD the Jewish connection was becoming an embarrassment to many Gentile Roman Christians.

A number of these Gentile Christians became leading theologians and leaders, often referred to as the Church Fathers. The writings and sayings of these men were regarded as of great importance by the growing Gentile component within the Church. These Church Fathers, all Gentiles, mostly came from pagan and Greco-Hellenic backgrounds.

They looked at Israel's recent history and present situation and began to deduce that national Israel was under God's curse. The main reason for this judicial curse they claimed was because the nation had rejected and crucified Jesus. This act was also called *deicide* – the murder of God. The Jewish people were being collectively accused of the murder of Jesus – regardless of the fact that it was God's will for Jesus to die; that Jesus Himself stated that no-one takes His life but that He gives it up of His own will; that the Roman governor alone had the authority to kill Jesus; and that the purpose of Jesus dying was for the salvation of humankind – Gentile as well as Jew.

About the year 160 AD Justin Martyr, who had been heavily influenced prior to his conversion by Greek philosophical thought, wrote *Dialogue with Trypho, the Jew*. On one occasion Justin said to Trypho concerning the Scriptures, that 'David sung them, Isaiah preached them, Zechariah proclaimed them, and Moses wrote them. Are you acquainted with them, Trypho? They are contained in your Scriptures, or rather not yours, but ours…'[2] This comment indicates that the Scriptures which had once belonged exclusively to the Jewish people, now belonged to the Gentile Church.[3] It was just a short step away from the belief that the Gentile Church was actually going to replace national Israel altogether and become the 'new Israel.'

The trend adopted by Justin Martyr continued to grow, leading by degrees away from Jerusalem, and closer to Rome; away from a Hebraic understanding of the Scriptures, and more to a Greco-Hellenic understanding of them. Other Fathers from this period wrote similarly, including Cyprian, the Bishop of Carthage, who wrote *Three Books of Testimonies against the Jews*; Hippolytus, a theologian in Rome who wrote *Expository Treatise against the Jews*; and theologian Tertullian who wrote *Against the Jews*. These and other treatises and Homilies projected a collective negativity towards the Jewish people.[4]

One Father, Origen, from Alexandria, was heavily influenced by Greek philosophical thought. Origen was committed to an allegorical interpretation

---

2 Justin Martyr, *Dialogue with Trypho the Jew*, Chapter 29. www.earlychristianwritings.com
3 Wilson, ibid, p. 89.
4 Wilson, ibid, p, 95.

of Scripture, especially the Old Testament, and divorced many passages from their historical, earthly context. As a result many of the unfulfilled prophecies of the Old Testament were spiritualised and were seen to be fulfilled in the 'new Israel', the Gentile Church, and not by the 'old' Israel.[5]

Another was Marcion, who in time was ostracized by the broader Church leadership but whose teaching had an influence upon the emerging Gentile Church. Marcion saw a definite distinction between the God of the Jews and the Old Testament from the Father of Jesus, as expressed in the New Testament. His desire was to jettison the Old Testament altogether.[6]

Ironically, despite definite negative attitudes towards the Jewish people, many of these early Church Fathers held to a future fulfilment of the earthly period of peace and tranquillity - like any Jewish follower of Jesus of the time. This belief system was known as *Chiliasm* (Greek = thousand). Justin Martyr wrote:

> But I and others, who are right-minded Christians on all points, are assured that there will be a resurrection of the dead, and a thousand years in Jerusalem, which will then be built, adorned, and enlarged, the prophets Ezekiel and Isaiah and others declare.[7]

This thousand year period which the Apostle John wrote about in Revelation 20 seemed to equate to the prophetic picture of Isaiah and the prophets of a period of peace and tranquillity on earth, and with a rebuilt Jerusalem at the centre! Such a picture always gave hope to the Jewish followers of Jesus; that He would return and fully establish His kingdom reign in Jerusalem over redeemed Israel. The hope of national Israel was for the Messiah, the perfect Son of David, to come and establish his reign over Israel and the nations – from Jerusalem.

Not all of the early Church Fathers, though, accepted this future perspective as did Justin Martyr.

Gentile Christianity recognized in the Roman Empire
The progression of 'Messianic Israel' away from its Hebraic foundations increased rapidly from the beginning of the fourth century. In 313 AD Emperor Constantine basically recognized Christianity as an official religion in the Roman Empire. This now placed the Gentile Church legally on a par with Judaism.

Then in 325 AD Constantine, in an effort to bring unity within his vast empire and especially between discordant Christian groups, convened a gathering of Church leaders at Nicea. Over 200 'bishops' or leaders participated - none of whom were Jewish followers of Jesus!

5 Wilson, ibid, pp. 95-95, 97, 168.
6 Wilson, ibid, pp. 96, 108-110.
7 Justin Martyr, Chapter 80.

The Council of Nicea made many unifying decisions, but in the process it also further severed Gentile Christianity from its Jewish parent. The time for remembering the death and resurrection of Jesus, the central event in the New Covenant community calendar, was officially changed from the Jewish Passover to a week after Passover. Later the name was changed from Passover to Easter. This decision was a major factor in officially separating Gentile Christianity from its Hebraic roots and thus from national Israel.

In 380 AD Emperor Theodosius declared that Christianity would be the official religion of the Roman Empire. Now Church and State were very closely connected, and the Gentile Church had political power. Until this point there had been an ideological tussle between two monotheistic faiths, Judaism and Christianity. Now one of them, Christianity, was the official faith of the Roman Empire.

Countless residents of the Roman Empire henceforth entered into the Roman Church, most of whom probably would not have had a genuine conversion experience and who would not have been filled with the Spirit of God. This decision might have assisted the Roman Empire from an administrative perspective, but it would have negative spiritual effects upon the true Church.

Life henceforth became more challenging for Jewish people living within the Roman Empire. The monotheistic faith which had been its main competitor for some three hundred years, was now the official religion of the Roman Empire. Thereafter Judaism and the Jewish people would be tolerated, but they would be in a subservient position to the Roman or Established Church.

The administration of the official Roman Church was vested primarily in the bishops or patriarchs of the principal Roman cities, Constantinople, Antioch, Alexandria – and Rome, whose bishop became known as the Pope.

Only three decades after this historic decision, Rome was invaded and sacked by the Goths in 410 AD. A shock wave went throughout Europe. The one institution that withstood this great trauma was the Church, and thereafter the influence of the Roman Catholic Church and the Pope further increased, as he was seen as God's *Vicar* or representative on earth.

Chrysostom and Augustine
During this same general period two prominent Church Fathers arose who furthered the separation between the Roman Gentile Church and its Hebraic foundations; John Chrysostom and Augustine of Hippo.

John Chrysostom (347-407) was a leader in Antioch and then became the Archbishop of Constantinople. He was a profound writer, and one of his writings was a Homily entitled *Adversus Judaeos* (Against the Jews). Although John's purpose in this Homily was to keep his flock from attending synagogue and Jewish festivals, his rhetoric and language was negative in the extreme against the Jewish people. Within this book he stated:

> But do not be surprised that I call the Jews pitiable. They really are pitiable and miserable ... [8]
> ... But when God forsakes a people, what hope of salvation is left? When God forsakes a place, that place becomes a dwelling of demons.[9]
> ... No Jew adores God.[10]
> ... the Jews ... live for their bellies, they gape for the things of this world, their condition is not better than that of pigs or goats because of their wanton ways and excessive gluttony.[11]
> ... the synagogue ... Must you not despise it, hold it in abomination, run away from it?
> Again the Jews, the most miserable and wretched of all men ...[12]

Church historian Rev. James Parkes stated that Chrysostom's 100 page Homily against the Jewish people 'has left us the most complete monument of the public expression of the Christian attitude to the Jews in the century of the victory of the Church. In these discourses there is no sneer too mean, no gibe too bitter for him to throw at the Jewish people. No text is too remote to be able to be twisted to their confusion ... no blasphemy too startling for him to employ ... Dealing with the Christians, no text which deals with forgiveness is forgotten: dealing with the Jews only one verse of the New Testament is omitted: 'Father, forgive them, for they know not what they do'.[13]

Chrysostom's writings and attitude exacerbated existing negative attitudes towards Jewish people, and these sentiments were taken seriously by those who followed him. It is not hard to see how Jewish people henceforth were often acquainted with devil-worship, and even of the anti-Christ system.[14] Unfortunately Chrysostom took words from Scripture, including from Jesus Himself, which were words of rebuke for those *within Israel* whose hearts were not turned to God, and then turned these words, which were from an internal Jewish debate, into a condemnation for the entire nation of Israel.

The Church Father who was to have the greatest influence upon the Roman Catholic Church was Augustine, the Bishop of Hippo. In his book *Contra Faustum* which he began to write in 397 AD, Augustine wrote that the Jewish people were to be protected (like Cain) and to remain within the Roman Empire

---

8 John Chrysostom, *Adversus Iudaeos*, ('Homilies against the Jews') Homily 1.2.1.www.preteristarchive.com
9 Chrysostom, ibid, Homily 1.3.1
10 Chrysostom, ibid, Homily 1.3.2
11 Chrysostom, ibid, Homily 1.4.1
12 Chrysostom, ibid, Homily IV, 1.
13 Parkes, J. *The Conflict of the Church and the Synagogue*, (Cleveland, 1964), p. 163.
14 Scult, M, *Millennial Expectations and Jewish Liberties*, (Leiden, E.J. Brill, 1978), p. 11.

as a witness of the truth of Christianity. He wrote:

> So ... the continued preservation of the Jews will be a proof to believing Christians of the subjection merited by those who, in the pride of their kingdom, put the Lord to death.[15]

Thomas McDonald summarized Augustine's reasons why they were to be protected: 'The Jews are to be kept alive and protected for ... they are under the mark of Cain, they are a scriniaria[16] which carries the holy texts of the Christians, their continued blindness fulfills Biblical prophecy, and their existence helps spread Christianity.'[17]

Robert McEachnie stated of Augustine's attitude that, 'Despite his belief in their divine protection, unlike other apocalyptic teachers, Augustine did not believe the Jews would convert to Christianity; rather, like many gentiles, they would largely be passed over for salvation.'[18]

The Augustinian approach then to the Jewish people, as McEachnie states, was that they were to be tolerated and protected within the Christian world, but could never be equal citizens, and would basically be the slaves of Christianity.[19]

In the wake of the destruction of Rome by the Goths in 410 AD Augustine began writing his major treatise, *De Civitate Dei* (The City of God). Here he reiterated many of his previous comments about the Jewish people. In Chapter 46 of Book 18, he alludes to Romans 11:11, 'their offense is the salvation of the Gentiles', and in reference to the dispersion of the nation of Israel, Augustine states that the Jewish people are 'witnesses among the nations to the prophecies which were sent before concerning Christ.'[20]

The heart of *City of God* was dedicated to revealing a distinction between the city of earth and the city of God; between the earthly and the heavenly. Nowhere did Augustine make this distinction as clear as his exposition on the millennium based on Revelation 20. Initially Augustine held to a belief that Jesus would return and reign with the saints on earth, a belief held by the *Chiliasts*. Then he came into contact with some who maintained an extreme view on this

---

15 Augustine, *Contra Faustum*, Book 12. 12. www.newadvent.org/fathers
16 An archivist, one who retains the original source.
17 Thomas McDonald, St Augustine and the Jews, www.patheos.com
18 Robert McEachnie, University of Florida, review of Paula Fredriksen, *Augustine and the Jews: A Christian Defense of Jews and Judaism*, (New Haven/London: Yale University Press, 2010) www.bmcr.brynmawr.edu
19 Robert McEachnie, University of Florida, review of Paula Fredriksen, *Augustine and the Jews: A Christian Defense of Jews and Judaism*, (New Haven/London: Yale University Press, 2010) www.bmcr.brynmawr.edu
20 Augustine, *City of God*, Book 18, Chapter 46. www.newadvent.org/fathers. Also, when referring to Psalm 59: 11, Augustine reiterated that the Jewish people needed to be protected within the Roman Empire.

point, and he changed his viewpoint on the millennium.[21] Thereafter Augustine maintained that there was to be no earthly period of peace and harmony, stating:

> Those who, on the strength of this passage, have suspected that the first resurrection is future and bodily, have been moved, among other things, specially by the number of a thousand years, as if it were a fit thing that the saints should thus enjoy a kind of Sabbath-rest during that period, a holy leisure after the labors of the six thousand years since man was created ... But, as they assert that those who then rise again shall enjoy the leisure of immoderate carnal banquets, furnished with an amount of meat and drink such as not only to shock the feeling of the temperate, but even to surpass the measure of credulity itself, such assertions can be believed only by the carnal. They who do believe them are called by the spiritual Chiliasts, which we may literally reproduce by the name Millenarians.[22]

The result of Augustine's theology was that the millennium as written by the Apostle John referred to Jesus reigning through the Church - the Roman Catholic Church. It was a spiritual millennium – there would be no physical millennial period, no physical reign of the King Messiah on earth. This view was contrary to the sentiments and writings of the Hebrew prophets; contrary to the hopes of the people of Israel; contrary to the beliefs of the early Jewish followers of Jesus; and contrary to the beliefs of numerous early Church Fathers.

No future hope for Israel

This perspective meant there would be no future purpose for national Israel – if Jesus was reigning on earth now through the Gentile (Roman Catholic) Church, then there would be no need of a future earthly reign of Jesus the Messiah over a restored Israel. Thus there was no future purpose for the nation of Israel – except to be scattered throughout Christendom and to be a witness of the supremacy of the Gentile Church.

Such an attitude was not surprising considering the manner in which most of the Church Fathers had began to 'spiritualize, typologize, and christologize' the Old Testament text.[23] In other words during these centuries various of the Gentile Church Fathers had re-interpreted vast portions of the Scriptures so that they no longer had the same meaning as they had to Jesus and the early Messianic movement in Jerusalem. Professor Wilson summed up this movement, 'Accordingly, Irenaeus, Origen, Augustine, and others developed a system of allegorical exegesis that had the disastrous effect of wrenching the

---

21 Frank A James III, 'Augustine's Millenial Views' in *Christian History Institute*, Issue 15, www.christianhistoryinstitute.org
22 Aurelius Augustine, *City of God*, Book 20, Chapter 7. www.thriceholy.net
23 Wilson, ibid, p. 97.

biblical text from its plain historical meaning.'[24]

Not only were the Scriptures very often divorced from their Hebraic and land of Israel context, but when they were ultimately translated into Latin they only became accessible to a small and elite group of people. The ordinary Church members never had the opportunity of reading the Scriptures for themselves.

The combined teachings of the Church Fathers, were that Jewish people were a living testimony of those who disobeyed God; that they were a people without hope; that there were no promises concerning them living again in the land of Israel; that the nation of Israel was under God's curse; and that the role of national Israel had now been taken over completely by the Roman Catholic Church.

The unfortunate consequences

The combination of Gentile Christianity becoming the official state religion of the Roman Empire and the oft-times severe condemnations against the Jewish people by the Church Fathers boded ill for the Jewish communities scattered throughout Europe.

Despite toleration, acceptance and protection by some Gentile rulers in some locations on some occasions, Jewish communities were often subjected to discrimination, forced conversion to the Roman Catholic Church, persecution, exile (from France in 626, England in 1290 and Spain in 1492) and massacres. One such massacre was at York in England in 1190.

Corporate persecution against the Jewish people climaxed during the period of the Crusades, beginning in 1096 AD. As the Crusader armies marched towards the 'Holy Land' to battle the infidel Muslims, they persecuted and massacred Jewish people along the way, particularly in Germany. At this time and thereafter numerous Jewish people moved further eastwards, into Poland and Russia.

Throughout Europe most Jewish people lived in impoverished ghettos. Whenever a monarch, or other leader, or even the people, sought a scapegoat because of problems within their society, it was often the Jewish people who were the collective victim. Mobs would then rampage into these poorly defended ghettos.

Such rampages, unfortunately, often occurred during the period of Easter, often following a sermon which accused the Jews of killing Jesus. Several other pitiful excuses for the massacre and pillage of the Jewish people were the blood libel and 'desecrating the host'.

Jewish people were accused of kidnapping and killing Christian children and using their blood for the Passover meal. Once this false rumour was spread the inflamed mobs would fall upon any unsuspecting Jewish person, and often upon

24 Wilson, ibid, p. 97.

entire communities. Many such events happened in England and in Germany.

In 1215 Pope Innocent III convened a gathering at Rome, named the Fourth Lateran Council, which almost 500 patriarchs and bishops, as well as some 900 other clergy attended. One of the numerous decrees passed at this Council declared that the wafer and wine used in the Eucharist (Communion) actually turned into the body and blood of Jesus. This Roman Catholic doctrine is known as 'Transubstantiation'.

Jewish people were often accused of stealing the elements, or of purchasing them, especially the bread (or wafer), in order 'to break it or seethe it, and to stick needles into it or transfix it, whereupon it began to bleed.'[25]

In 1243 the Jewish community at Belitz near Berlin was accused of 'desecrating the host', and the entire community was rounded up 'and burned on the spot.'[26] The *Jewish Encyclopaedia* stated that such events occurred very often thereafter, including:

> ... in 1290, at Paris; 1294, at Laa, in Austria; 1298, at Röttingen, near Würzburg, and at Korneuburg, near Vienna; 1299, at Ratisbon; 1306, at Saint-Pälten; 1325, at Cracow; 1330, at Güstrow; 1337, at Deggendorf; 1338, at Pulka; 1370, at Enghien (see Brussels); 1388, at Prague; 1399, at Posen; 1401, at Glogau; 1410, at Segovia; 1420, at Ems; 1453, at Breslau; 1478, at Passau; 1492, at Sternberg, in Mecklenburg-Schwerin; 1510, at Berlin; 1514, at Mittelberg, in Alsace.[27]

Life for Jewish people at the turn of the 16th century

Daily life for Jewish people spread wherever they were under the yoke of Christendom, was therefore extremely precarious. With some exceptions, the general perspective of the Gentile Church towards the Jewish people was that they were the Christ killers, the killers of God (*deicide*), and thereby the recipients of the curses of God. Mel Scult wrote in his book *Millennial Expectations and Jewish Liberties*, that the Jewish people during this period were often collectively equated with the anti-Christ.[28]

Under this dark system of theology there seemed little hope whatsoever for a restoration of the Jewish people - restoration to a life of equality, and to their ancient homeland.

One possibility for a Jewish person to escape this seemingly hopeless situation was to believe in Jesus. But if a Jewish person did choose willingly to follow Jesus during that period they would be totally cast away from their own Jewish

---

25 Jewish Encyclopaedia, (1906), *Host: Desecration of*, www.jewishencyclopedia.com
26 Ibid.
27 Ibid.
28 Scult, ibid, p. 11. Scult himself is drawing upon Joshua Trachtenberg, *The Devil and the Jews*, (New York, 1961).

community. They would be viewed as *meshumaddim* – apostates and traitors. In addition they could never be guaranteed full acceptance into the Gentile Church, where they would often still be classified as second class, and would be expected to completely separate themselves from their Jewish heritage.

A sample of this attitude is given here, of a confession that Jewish people were forced to take in Toledo in Spain, upon their baptism:

> "I do here and now renounce every rite and observance of the Jewish religion, detesting all its most solemn ceremonies and tenets that in former days I kept and held. In future I will hold no rite or celebration connected with it, nor any custom of my past error, promising neither to seek it out nor to perform it. Further do I renounce all things forbidden or detested by Christian teaching, and:
> (here follows the Nicene Creed)
> In the name of this Creed … I promise that I will never return to the vomit of Jewish superstition. Never again will I fulfill any of the offices of Jewish ceremonies to which I was addicted, nor ever more hold them dear. I altogether deny and reject, the errors of the Jewish religion … shun all intercourse with other Jews and have the circle of my friends only among honest Christians." [29]

Another example was from the Church in Constantinople. Rev James Parkes states that upon baptism a Jewish person had to, '… confess and denounce verbally the whole Hebrew people, and forthwith declare that with a whole heart and sincere faith he desires to be received among the Christians. Then he must renounce openly in the church all Jewish superstitions, the priest saying, and he or his sponsor if he is a child, replying in these words':[30]

> "I renounce all customs, rites, legalisms, unleavened breads and sacrifices of lambs of the Hebrews, and all the other feasts of the Hebrews, sacrifices, prayers, aspersions, purifications, sanctifications and propitiations and fasts, and new moons and Sabbaths, and superstitions, and hymns and chants, and observances and synagogues, and the food and drink of the Hebrews; in one word I renounce absolutely everything Jewish, every law, rite and custom, and above all I renounce Antichrist, whom all the Jews await in the form and figure of Christ; and I join myself to the true Christ and God …"[31]

---

29 Parkes, ibid, Appendix Three, 'Professions of faith extracted from Jews on Baptism', p. 395. Original source, Visigothic Professions , *Leg. Vis.* 12.3.14.
30 Parkes, ibid, p. 397.
31 Parkes, ibid, Appendix Three, 'Profession of Faith, from the Church at Constantinople', p. 397. Original source, *Assemani*, Cod. Lit., I, p. 105.

These statements were representative of the general attitude of Christendom towards Jewish people who wanted to follow Jesus. There can be little doubt that under the existing ecclesiastical system in Europe, dominated as it was by the Roman Catholic Church, and its close association with the political system, dominated as it was by the Holy Roman Empire and national monarchs, there seemed little chance of the Jewish people ever being restored to their God-given heritage.

There was only one hope for the Jewish people: European society and especially the Roman Catholic Church needed to undergo considerable change and reformation.

Chapter 3

Reformation and Restoration

The Reformation begins

Such a change and reformation did happen the moment that John Wyclif in England in the fourteenth century and John Huss in Bohemia in the fifteenth century began to challenge the false doctrines of the Roman Catholic Church. Their efforts were then built upon by Martin Luther in Germany and John Calvin in France and Switzerland in the sixteenth century.

When Luther nailed his 95 Theses on the church door at Wittenberg in 1517 which seriously challenged the false doctrines of the Roman Church, the reformation of the Church in Europe began in earnest. With this reformation the seeds of Israel's restoration were also sown.

The main consequences of the Protestant Reformation were:

- The Scriptures were translated into the vernacular language, such as English, German, French and Dutch, thereby giving many people the opportunity of reading the Bible for themselves and not having to rely any longer upon the perspective held, and propagated by, the established Roman Church.
- This perspective also led to a deeper desire to know the original languages in which the Scriptures were written. Many people began learning Hebrew, which resulted in closer contact between Jewish people and some of the reformers and theologians.
- One particular outcome of the wider distribution of the Scriptures was an awareness, at least with some, that there was a future for the Jewish people. One Scripture in particular seemed to arouse the attention of many reformers: Romans 11: 26, 'all Israel shall be saved.' The Reformation was the greatest revival for hundreds of years, yet Paul also alluded to an even greater end time revival which was closely associated with a national revival of the Jewish people.
- The Reformation and associated events resulted in cataclysmic events in Europe. Many saw in these events the signs of the times signalling the end of the age. There was now more consideration given to the prophecies relating to the future.
- When the established Roman Catholic Church opposed and then renounced the reformers and their doctrinal positions, Christendom in the West became irrevocably divided. In the process the other side, whether it be the Roman Catholic Church, or the Protestant Church,

were often seen as 'the theological enemy' - and thereby replaced the Jewish people from the unenviable position they had held for over a thousand years as the theological enemy.

Antipathy towards Rome

As the Protestant movement grew and consolidated it came under terrible persecution from the Roman Catholic Church. To the Protestants the Roman Catholic Church and particularly the Pope became synonymous with the Anti-Christ system. Such an attitude is expressed by Luther who wrote in 1520:

> I am practically cornered, and can hardly doubt any more that the Pope is really the Anti-Christ, whom the world expects according to general belief, because everything so corresponds to the way of his life, words and commandments.[1]

Among the Reformers there 'was the unanimous belief', wrote Iain Murray 'that the Papal system is both the 'man of sin' and the Babylonian whore of which Scripture forewarns (2 Thess 2; Rev 19). In the conviction of sixteenth-century Protestants, Rome was the great Anti-Christ, and so firmly did this belief become established that it was not until the nineteenth century that it was seriously questioned by evangelicals.'[2]

As Luther and other Reformers now considered the Pope to be the Anti-Christ and the entire Roman Catholic system to be in error, then the severe judgment of the Church, that the Jewish people were the servants of the devil, dissipated. There was no longer the need to treat the Jewish people in such a hostile way as the Roman Catholic Church had in the previous centuries. This more lenient attitude towards the Jewish people is somewhat evidenced in some of Luther's early writings.

Prior to the Reformation some attempts had been made to bring the Jewish people into the Gentile Church by violence and coercion. These efforts invariably failed. Luther then at the beginning of his ministry determined to establish a new *modus operandi*, a new approach towards the Jewish people. In one of his earlier writings, *Dass Jesus Christus ein geborener Jude sei*, ('That Jesus Christ was Born a Jew') written in 1523, he stated:

> Our fools the Popes, Bishops, Sophists and Monks – The crude asses' heads have hitherto so treated the Jews that anyone who wishes to be a good Christian would almost have had to become a Jew. If I had been a Jew and had seen such dolts and block-heads govern and teach the Christian faith, I

---

1 Martin Luther, *Sammtliche Schriften*, ed. By J. G. Walch, (St. Louis, 1881-1910) XXI, 234, quoted in Mel Scult, *Millennial Expectations and Jewish Liberties*, (Leiden, E.J. Brill, 1978), p. 13. Luther also wrote *Dass Jesus Christus ein geborener Jude sei* which went even further in advocating showing kindness to the Jewish people. Others, such as Joachim de Fioris, John Wycliff and John Huss held similar views.
2 Murray, I. *The Puritan Hope*, p. 41.

would sooner have become a pig than a Christian.[3]

Luther, it would appear, gave some consideration to the place of the Jewish people in the end of the age, although he did not advocate, from Romans 11:26, that all the Jewish people would be saved. He did seem to believe, however, that a great number would turn to the Messiah, especially now that ecclesiastical pressure from the Roman Catholic Church had been taken away from them. This is probably the context for a publication in 1532, the English title being *The Signs of Christ's Coming and the Last Days*. In this publication he stated:

> ... for the Jews must needs remain as a 'sign' to the very last day; and though some of them be converted into Christ, yet their generation shall not end but some shall still remain in the world till Christ shall come.[4]

Luther's change of attitude

Towards the end of his life, however, and after about twenty years of adopting a positive attitude and seeing that the Jewish people were not responding to his overtures, Luther's attitude towards them changed. In 1543 he wrote a vitriolic anti-Jewish book entitled *Von den Juden und ihren Lugen* ('On the Jews and their Lies') which was on a par with Chrysostom's *Against the Jews*.

In this book Luther outlined seven points concerning the Jewish people:

1. First to set fire to their synagogues or schools and to bury and cover with dirt whatever will not burn, so that no man will ever again see a stone or cinder of them. This is to be done in honor of our Lord and of Christendom, so that God might see that we are Christians, and do not condone or knowingly tolerate such public lying, cursing, and blaspheming of his Son and of his Christians ...
2. Second, I advise that their houses also be razed and destroyed. For they pursue in them the same aims as in their synagogues. Instead they might be lodged under a roof or in a barn, like the gypsies. This will bring home to them that they are not masters in our country, as they boast, but that they are living in exile and in captivity, as they incessantly wail and lament about us before God.
3. Third, I advise that all their prayer books and Talmudic writings, in which such idolatry, lies, cursing and blasphemy are taught, be taken from them.
4. Fourth, I advise that their rabbis be forbidden to teach henceforth on pain of loss of life and limb ...
5. Fifth, I advise that safe conduct on the highways be abolished completely for the Jews. For they have no business in the countryside,

---

3 Martin Luther. *Dass Jesus Christus ein geborener Jude sei*, in Luther's Works, American Edition, XLV, p., 200. Quoted in Mel Scult, ibid, p. 14.
4 Martin Luther, *The Signs of Christ's Coming and the Last Days*, (London, 1661), pp. 5-10. (Quoted in Scult, ibid, p. 15)

since they are not lords, officials, tradesmen, or the like. Let them stay at home ...

6. Sixth, I advise that usury be prohibited to them, and that all cash and treasure of silver and gold be taken from them and put aside for safekeeping. The reason for such a measure is that, as said above, they have no other means of earning a livelihood than usury, and by it they have stolen and robbed from us all they possess. Such money should now be used in no other way than the following: Whenever a Jew is sincerely converted, he should be handed one hundred, two hundred, or three hundred florins, as personal circumstances may suggest. With this he could set himself up in some occupation for the support of his poor wife and children, and the maintenance of the old or feeble. For such evil gains are cursed if they are not put to use with God's blessing in a good and worthy cause.

7. Seventh, I commend putting a flail, an ax, a hoe, a spade, a distaff, or a spindle into the hands of young, strong Jews and Jewesses and letting them earn their bread in the sweat of their brow, as was imposed on the children of Adam (Gen 3[:19]}. For it is not fitting that they should let us accursed Goyim toil in the sweat of our faces while they, the holy people, idle away their time behind the stove, feasting and farting, and on top of all, boasting blasphemously of their lordship over the Christians by means of our sweat. No, one should toss out these lazy rogues by the seat of their pants.[5]

In the following years Luther wrote several more anti-Jewish publications including *Warning against the Jews* which was released in 1546, not long before his death. Luther's pronouncements concerning the Jewish people were taken seriously by some secular as well as ecclesiastical leaders, and in some parts of Germany the Jewish people were expelled and dealt with harshly. This was not the case, though, everywhere.

As the writings of Luther were very much revered in Germany following his death in 1546, a negative attitude towards the Jewish people was often to be found within the established Lutheran Church.

Reformed Christianity

The other great reformer, John Calvin (1509-1564) had a different life experience with the Jewish people. Whereas Luther had much physical contact with Jewish people, Calvin throughout his life had much less such contact.

One of the harshest statements that Calvin made in his many writings was

---

5 Luther, M. *On the Jews and their Lies*, (1543, Translated by Martin H. Bertram, 1971), Section XI, www.humanitas-international.org. This book was reprinted by the Nazi Party in the 1930's and prominently displayed at the Nuremberg Rallies. See Christopher Clark, *The Politics of Conversion*, (Oxford, 1995), p. 1.

in the treatise "Ad Quaestiones et Objecta Judaei Cuiusdam Responsio," (*A Response To Questions and Objections of a Certain Jew*), where he wrote, '*Their [the Jews] rotten and unbending stiffneckedness deserves that they be oppressed unendingly and without measure or end and that they die in their misery without the pity of anyone*'.[6]

It would seem though that Calvin held to a basic theological position which held out no future hope for the nation of Israel. He, like other Reformers, held close to the position advocated by Augustine, and seemed to believe that the Church was now the new Israel. But he never adopted the harsh and negative attitude towards the Jewish people that Luther did, although in one of his writings he did state, "I have had much conversation with many Jews: I have never seen either a drop of piety or a grain of truth or ingenuousness – nay, I have never found common sense in any Jew."[7]

The Reformation in Britain

When King Henry VIII began to officially break away from Rome in 1533, the English Church entered into the Reformation (of which John Wyclif had been the herald), albeit in somewhat different circumstances to the Continental experience. Henry's new Church of England, though, still needed much internal reformation.

Those who felt it their duty to purify the English Church of all Roman and Papal vestiges were called the Puritans. Under Henry's son Edward (1547-1553) they furthered this internal reformation, but Queen Mary (1553-1558) restored the English Church back to Roman Catholicism. These Protestant reformers, the purifiers, were severely persecuted.

Many Puritans took refuge in Europe, including in Calvin's Geneva. Two of these were Martin Bucer and Peter Martyr, teachers from Cambridge and Oxford. While in Geneva these refugee British reformers compiled a new English Bible which was named the Geneva Bible in 1560. In the notes for Roman 11:26 they wrote, 'He sheweth that the time shall come that the whole nation of the Jews, though not every one particularly, shall be joined to the church of Christ.'[8] Here was a beginning of restoration.

Consequences of the restoration of the Scriptures

If one considered that the end of the age was imminent and that the Jewish people would be nationally 'converted,' then the question for the Reformers, was: how would they be 'converted?' Now more than ever before there was tremendous interest in how the prophecies relating to the future would be fulfilled.

6 Excerpt from "Ad Quaestiones et Objecta Judaei Cuiusdam Responsio," (*A Response To Questions and Objections of a Certain Jew*) by John Calvin; The Jew in Christian Theology, Gerhard Falk, McFarland and Company, Inc., Jefferson, NC and London, 1931. Found in, www.yashanet.com.
7 Calvin's commentary of Daniel 2:44–45 translated by Myers, Thomas.*Calvin's Commentaries*. Grand Rapids, MI: Eerdmans, 1948. Quoted in Lange van Ravenswaay 2009, p. 146. www.wikipedia.johncalvin.
8 Murray, ibid, p. 41.

Some 'on the outer fringe of orthodox Protestantism' wrote Murray 'drew out of its grave' (as a Puritan later complained against them) the belief common among some of the early Fathers, that Christ would appear and reign with his saints a thousand years in Jerusalem before the Judgment. From their emphasis on the word 'thousand' (Greek, *chilias*; Latin *mille*), taken from Revelation chapter 20, they were anciently called 'chiliasts' or 'millenaries.'[9]

Calvin, a disciple of Augustine in many regards, stated that this perspective is 'too puerile to need or to deserve refutation.'[10] Calvin's attitude is best summed up by William Masselink, who wrote:

> The decline [of the Chiliast belief] can largely be ascribed to the extension of Christianity to the Gentile countries and also to the unbroken prosperity which the Church then enjoyed. The Gnostic philosophy of this period and the Alexandrian school with its allegorical interpretations of the Scripture were also a great detriment to the progress of Chiliasm.
>
> By far the most important figure of this period was the great church father Augustine, whose far reaching influence also in this matter extended beyond the Reformation, as his views in this were in the main, accepted by the four great reformers of the sixteenth century.[11]

The Reformation may have come to Europe and Britain, but by the mid 1500's there was still little to reveal that there would be any specific interest in the Jewish people; either by way of encouraging them to enter into a personal covenant relationship with Jesus, or of their being accepted as fellow citizens and not as second-class residents of the region under the control of Christendom, either the Roman or Protestant variety.

The seed may have been planted but it still needed to be watered.

---

9 Murray, ibid, p. 40.
10 Calvin, J. *The Institutes of the Christian Religion*, Book III, ch xxv, 5. Quoted in Murray, ibid, p. 40.
11 Masselink, W. *The History of Chiliasm*, www.the-highway.com.

Chapter 4

The Puritan Stream

Restorationism begins

When Elizabeth replaced Mary as Queen of England, she re-introduced Protestantism. The Puritans then continued the task of purifying the English Church, which was now a *via media*, (middle road) mostly Protestant in theology but with Catholic trappings including episcopacy (bishops).

Numerous theological books were now produced, including one in 1568 by Peter Martyr, entitled a *Commentary upon Romans*. Martyr's commentary upon Romans 11 and especially verse 26, 'all Israel shall be saved' probably 'prepared the way' wrote Murray 'for a general adoption amongst the English Puritans of a belief in the future conversion of the Jews.'[1]

Thereafter numerous books, articles and pamphlets were written on the subject of the Jewish people and their role in the revival the Puritans then believed they were part of. Many also speculated on how the unfulfilled prophecies relating to the end and of the Jewish restoration would occur. Mel Scult wrote concerning this new found interest:

> The English, more than any other people, became intoxicated with the new Hebraism of the Reformation ... Their enthusiasm for the 'Holy Word' meant in part a heightened expectation of the destruction of Anti-Christ (i.e. the Pope) and the coming of Christ a second time. Expositions of the millennium took many forms and involved many people.
>
> Some of these millennialists maintained that the conversion of the Jews was a pre-requisite for the second coming of Christ. The millennialists in question were quite unique in their confidence that the conversion was within the foreseeable future and that it was to include almost all the Jews.[2]

During this period the Geneva Bible was still very much in use, and that marginal note, as well as Peter Martyr's work, prompted others to write specifically about the Jewish people. Perhaps the first was Hugh Broughton, a student of Martyr. Broughton even proposed going to the East to speak about Jesus to the Jewish people, and of translating the New Testament for their benefit.

But Broughton's zeal for the cause was thwarted by the English bishops, whom he had previously 'offended', Murray states, 'by his Puritan leanings.'[3]

---

1 Murray, ibid, p. 42.
2 Scult, ibid, p. 18.
3 Murray, ibid, p. 42.

Murray concluded about Broughton's vision, 'This early possibility of a mission to the Jews was thwarted by the Church authorities, but Broughton's writings ... stimulated further study of the whole question.'[4]

Broughton was followed by Francis Kett, a Cambridge educated writer and physician who in 1585 published *The Glorious and Beautiful Garland of Man's Glorification Containing the Godly Misterie of Heavenly Jerusalem*, in which he had a section dealing with "the notion of Jewish national return to Palestine."[5]

Then in 1590 Andrew Willett stated in a treatise entitled *Calling of the Jews* that the term Israel in the Bible must be taken literally as referring to the people of Israel, and that before the return of Jesus the Jewish people would be restored to their homeland.[6] He took his lead from Romans 11:26 - 'all Israel shall be saved'. Willett did not agree that this was referring to a few individuals through history as Calvin and Melanchton had believed, but 'the whole nation of the Jews.'[7] The whole nation of the Jews, he stated, must be 'taken in the litterall sense, for the nation and people of Israel.'[8] Willett further stated: 'Toward the ende of the world, before the coming of Christ, the nation of the Jews shall be called.'[9]

At this point no Jewish people lived in England. One of the first to advocate that Jewish people should be permitted to return to England was Leonard Busher, in his book *Religious Peace: or a plea for Liberty of Conscience*. Busher stated of the Jewish people, that they:

> ... shall inhabit and dwell under His majesty's dominion, to the great profit of his realms and their furtherance in the faith (i.e. their conversion) ... for Christ hath commanded to teach all nations and they (i.e. the Jews) are the first.[10]

A short time later theologian Thomas Draxe wrote a treatise in 1608 which drew attention to the future 'conversion' of Israel.[11] Draxe saw no physical restoration, stating that although the whole body of the Jews in general will be called 'they are likely never to recover their land for they have no such promise.'[12]

The following year, 1609, Thomas Brightman published his fundamental book, *Apocalypsis Apocalypseos* (*Revelation of the Revelation*), the English edition of

---

4 Murray, ibid, p. 42.
5 www.kettmiller.mysite.wanadoo-members.co.uk/Page7.html.
6 See M. Verete, *The Restoration of the Jews in English Protestant Thought 1790-1840*. Middle East Studies, Frank Cass Publishers, (London, January 1972), p. 15.
7 Quoted in Verete, ibid, p. 15.
8 Verete, ibid, p. 15.
9 Verete, ibid, p. 15.
10 Leonard Busher, *Religious Peace: or a Plea for Liberty of Conscience*, (London, 1614), p. 38. Quoted in Scult, ibid, p. 19. Busher, like many Puritan writers, had to leave England when the established authorities disagreed with their stand, and lived for many years in Holland.
11 Pragai, M. *Faith and Fulfilment: Christians and the Return to the Promised Land*, (London, 1985), p. 13.
12 Quoted in Verete, ibid, p. 15.

which was published in Amsterdam in 1615. Brightman predicted the future overthrow of the Antichrist, who he (and numerous others) associated with Rome. He also added that this would be followed by the overthrow of the Ottoman Turk to be followed by the 'Calling of the Jews' and their restoration to the land of Israel.[13] Edward E. Hindson wrote:

> Brightman believed that the conversion of the Jews meant the "full restoring of the Jewish nation" and a literal Kingdom on earth. Brightman even went so far as to predict an unholy alliance of the apostate Roman Church (antichrist) with the Mohammadean Turks (false prophet) against restored Israel at the time of the end.[14]

William Perkins wrote only two years later, 'The Lord saith, *All the nations shall be blessed in Abraham*: Hence I gather that the nation of the Jews shall be called, and converted to the participation of this blessing: when, and how, God knows: but that it shall be done before the end of the world we know.'[15]

These writings, and many others, were followed in the year 1621 with the appearance of *The World's Great Restauration, or the Calling of the Jews, and (with them) of all the Nations and Kingdoms of the earth, to the faith of Christ* by Sir Henry Finch, a Member of Parliament and a lawyer, who was also well versed in Hebrew. Finch also made it very clear that such a physical restoration to Israel was linked to having a personal relationship with Jesus the King Messiah. He wrote:

> ... out of all the places of thy dispersion, East, West, North and South, HIS purpose is to bring thee home again and to marry thee to Himself by faith for evermore. Instead that thou wast desolate and forsaken, and sattest as a widow, thou shalt flourish as in the dayes of thy youth, nay, above and beyond thy youth.[16]

Finch's picture of a restored Israel living in millennial glory, with the nations of the world paying homage to this restored Israel was not appreciated by King James I. He had Finch put into prison in 1621 until he recanted of this 'treasonable' position. James could see no place for any other ruler than himself and his dynasty.

It was possibly Finch's book more than any other until this point in time which produced guidelines for interpreting the prophetic Scriptures and in particular the prophecies of the Old Testament. He stated clearly that wherever the names

---

13 See also Verete, ibid, p. 15.
14 Thomas Brightman, *A Revelation of the Revelation,* Leyden, 1616, pp. 557-9; 851-2; 932-3. Quoted in www.conservativeonline.org/journals/01_03_journal/1997v1n3_id01htm. Accessed August 2006. Brightman's Latin edition was published in Frankfurt in 1609.
15 Perkins, W. *A Commentarie upon the first five chapters of the Epistle to the* Galatians, 1617. Quoted in Murray, ibid, p. 42.
16 Sir Henry Finch, *The World's Great Restauration, or the Calling of the Jews, and (with them) of all the Nations and Kingdoms of the earth, to the faith of Christ.* Quoted in Pragai, ibid, p. 15.

Israel, Jerusalem, Judah, Zion were mentioned, these applied to the physical components not to the so-called 'spiritual Israel' the Gentile Church. Finch, like Brightman and Willet before him, also stated his belief in a future physical restoration of Israel to her land as prophesied by Ezekiel, Hosea, Zephaniah, Isaiah, Daniel and John.[17]

A man regarded as one of England's greatest Bible translators of the period, Joseph Mede, wrote a renowned book *Clovis Apocalyptica* (The Key of the Revelation) in 1627. Although not strictly relating to the subject of the restoration or the Latter Days, Mede did nevertheless heavily stress the need to interpret the Bible literally and not symbolically.[18]

While expositing the Book of Revelation Mede stated: 'The Jews ... shall possess the holy land again.'[19] In the preface to this book, Dr. Twisse wrote: 'When the time comes for the calling of the Jews ... then ... they shall gather themselves together from all places towards the land of Canaan.'[20]

Quite a common factor with these early writers was the belief in the personal return of Jesus to earth, with some also advocating a return of scattered Israel to the land, although there were certain discrepancies in the relationship between these two events. Most, however, were in basic agreement that these events would occur in connection with the decline of the Roman Catholic Church.

Much of their exegesis for this belief came from the books of Revelation and Daniel, especially Daniel chapter seven, where four successive beasts are revealed, depicting the four successive kingdoms of Babylon, Persia, Greece and Rome. Following the fall of the last kingdom, Rome, an everlasting Kingdom would be established.

Many of these Puritan writers viewed the Roman Empire being represented in their time by the Roman Catholic Church and the Holy Roman Empire (comprised mostly of Austria, the numerous German entities and France, but the Puritans viewed France as being the principal nation making up this Empire). France was the protector nation of the Roman Catholic Church, so they never had a high view of France. They viewed the Pope, being the head of the Roman Catholic Church, as the Antichrist.

These views, or components of them, were adhered to by other writers and theologians of the Puritan period, in both England and Scotland. By the 1640's their basic line of reasoning concluded that in the 'last days' these vestiges of

---

17 Verete, ibid, p. 16.
18 Joseph Mede, *The Key of the Revelation*, 2nd edition, 1650. (See Verete, footnote 27). It seems the first edition was printed in Latin, and then in 1643 the first English edition was printed in London by R.S for Phil Stephens. Mede was Professor of Greek at Christ's College, Cambridge.
19 Joseph Mede, *The Key of the Revelation*, 2nd edition, 1650, pp. 120-121. (See Verete, footnote 27).
20 Joseph Mede, *The Key of the Revelation*, 2nd edition, 1650, preface. In another work, entitled *Works*, 3rd Edition, 1672, Book III, pp. 603-4, Mede stated that Jesus is on his throne in heaven, but 'shall appear and be visibly revealed from heaven especially for the calling and gathering of his ancient people ... the whole nation of the Jews.'

the Roman Empire would receive a crippling blow, which would lead then to the restoration of Israel and the return of Jesus.[21]

The period of the Puritan Commonwealth

A Civil War broke out in 1642 between those dedicated to Parliamentary rule against King Charles I, who was determined to impose a theocratic rule over Parliament. The Parliamentarians finally won the Civil War and King Charles was executed in 1649. The Commonwealth of England was then proclaimed and Oliver Cromwell became the Lord Protector. It was a period of much political turmoil in England, out of which grew a number of extremist groups.

The most prominent of these was the Fifth Monarchy Men (or Fifth Monarchists), who were strongly millennialist. Their name came from a belief based upon Daniel chapter 2 which spoke of there being four kingdoms (Assyrian, Babylonian, Greek and Roman). These would be followed by a fifth kingdom, the reign of a returning Jesus, the 'Golden Age' or millennium. They believed they would reign with Jesus during this period, but were to prepare society beforehand for the returning Jesus. This would mean using both political and social means to achieve their goal.[22]

This period, known as the Interregnum, permitted matters relating to the Jewish people – of their restitution to England, and ultimate complete restoration, to be openly explored. The news of the execution of King Charles was greeted with enthusiasm by the émigré Puritan community in Holland. Ebenezer and Joanna Cartwright had already sent a petition to Cromwell in January 1649 seeking for the repealing of the Act of Parliament which banned the Jewish people from living in England in 1290. As believers in the Bible, they saw the future restoration of Israel to her land, and desired for Britain (and Holland[23]) to be part of this process.[24]

Although Cromwell took no immediate interest in the matter, the leading rabbi in Amsterdam, Menasseh Ben Israel wrote a book entitled *The Hope of Israel*. In 1650 he published an English edition, dedicated it to the English Parliament and thereupon embarked upon a campaign for a Jewish re-admission to England.

Ben Israel surmised that once the Jewish people had been dispersed 'to the ends of the earth' as stated in Daniel 12:7, then the Messianic Age could begin. This process could not begin if there were no Jewish people living in England. His book was widely circulated in England, where there was considerable

---

21 Verete, ibid, p. 18.
22 www.exlibris.org/nonconform/engdis/fifthmonarchists.html
23 See www.ahram.org.eg/acpss/eng/ahram/2004/7/5/SPAP4.HTM, and www.nmhschool.org/tthornton/mehistorydatabase/christian_persecution_of_the_jew.htm
24 Pragai, M. *Faith and Fulfilment: Christians and the Return to the Promised Land,* (Valentine Mitchell, London, 1985), quoting SUTRO Branch, California State Library, San Frisco: Photostat from the original, pp. 1-2. Also Don Patinkin, 'Mercantilism and the Readmission of the Jews to England.' Jewish Social Studies, Vol. 8. July 1946, pp. 161-78; and Cecil Roth, England in Jewish History (London, Jewish Historical Society of England, 1949), p. 7. See also, Scult, ibid, p. 24.

interest in anything Jewish and Hebraic.

Although having stated to Parliament on one occasion that 'God will bring the Jews home to their station from the isles of the sea, and answer their expectations as from the depths of the sea'[25] Cromwell at this stage was unable to act upon the requests of the Cartwrights and Menasseh Ben Israel. As the head of a sovereign nation any decisions concerning the Jewish people needed to be done with strategic, economic and geo-political factors in mind. Cromwell wanted to induce Jewish merchants from Amsterdam to come to England, so he invited Ben Israel to come to England.

In December 1655 Cromwell summoned a Conference at Whitehall to discuss the general question of Jewish readmission. Those present included lawyers, clergy and leading merchants. Although there were definite economic advantages in having Jewish merchants living in England, numerous members of the clergy and merchants were not agreeable. It would seem that there was still considerable suspicion and jealousy towards the Jewish people. In addition the terrible medieval lie that the Jewish people used Christian blood for the Passover began to be spread about; as well as the rumour that they were behind a conspiracy to take over control of the country.[26]

Cromwell ultimately had to call the Whitehall Conference to an end, and began working towards allowing Jewish people to return unofficially, which happened in 1657. In the years thereafter, especially after the restoration of the Crown in 1660, more Jewish people did return, in a somewhat quiet manner and without any formal legal recognition to do so.

Numerous Puritan supporters of readmission also stated that blessings would accrue to England following such a move. In connection to the blessings to be accrued, Iain Murray wrote of the Puritan theology:

> The future of the Jews had a decisive significance for them because they believed that, though little is clearly revealed of the future purposes of God in history, enough has been given us in Scripture to warrant the expectation that with the calling of the Jews there will come far-reaching blessing for the world. Puritan England and Covenanting Scotland knew much of spiritual blessing and it was the prayerful longing for wider blessing, not a mere interest in unfulfilled prophecy, which led them to give such place to Israel.[27]

Rev Stephen Sizer also stated: 'Puritan eschatology was essentially postmillennial and, based on Romans 9-11, believed the conversion of the Jews would lead

---

25 Stated to the Barebones Parliament on 4 July 1653. See Todd Endelman, *The Jews of Britain*, (Berkely, University of California Press, 2002), p. 22.
26 See William Hughes, *Anglo Judaeus* (London, 1656), pp. 39-40. Quoted in John M. Yeats, *The Rise of British Missions to the Jews 1808-1818*, (unpublished dissertation, Southwestern Baptist Theological Seminary, no date), p. 40.
27 Murray, ibid, pp. 59-60.

to future blessing for the entire world.'[28] It would seem therefore that the environment in England at the time of the re-admission was much influenced by millenarian thinking.

The theological environment by the late 1650's is perhaps best summarized in the Westminster Directory of Public Prayer, issued by the Reformed Church in Britain, in 1658:

> To pray for the propagation of the gospel and kingdom of Christ to all nations; for the conversion of the Jews, the fulness of the Gentiles, the fall of Antichrist, and the hastening of the second coming of our Lord; for the deliverance of the distressed churches abroad from the tyranny of the antichristian faction, and from the cruel oppressions and blasphemies of the Turk.[29]

Mel Scult summarizes the situation in Britain concerning the Jewish people at the end of this dramatic period:

> By 1660 then we see that a new attitude toward the Jew had solidified in the minds of many English Protestants. Many of them no longer believed that the Jew was the devil or the anti-Christ, but was again God's Chosen people who are to play a key role in the drama of God's historical plan. They also believed that the positive prophecies of the Old Testament refer to Israel of the Flesh and not to the Christian Church ... and that Christians are very much in debt to the Jews who have been the keepers of the 'word' throughout History. Some maintained that those who persecute the Jews will eventually be held accountable for their actions.[30]

Through the Puritan influence there had been a major paradigm change within the Church in Britain concerning the Jewish people. Whereas previously they were regarded as agents of the devil, and at best that a small remnant would be saved, now many believed they would all, or a large number, be saved or 'converted.'[31] Some now also envisioned a restoration of the Jewish people to their ancestral land, either before or after their national repentance and turning to Jesus.[32]

Interest in the Jewish people after the Restoration of the Monarchy

Shortly after the death of Cromwell the Monarchy was restored in 1660 under

---

28 Sizer, S. *Christian Zionism: Road-map to Armaggedon?* (Leicester, 2004), p.28.
29 'Of Public Prayer before the Sermon' in Westminster Directory of Public Prayer, Agreed Upon By The Assembly Of Divines At Westminster, With The Assistance Of Commissioners From The Church Of Scotland, As A Part Of The Covenanted Uniformity In Religion Betwixt The Churches Of Christ In The Kingdoms Of Scotland, England, And Ireland: With An Act Of The General Assembly, And Act Of Parliament, Both In Anno 1645, Approving And Establishing The Said Directory. Quoted in http://presbyterianreformed.org/worship.htm.
30 Scult, ibid, p. 34.
31 Although this was a widespread belief, it was best propounded by Henry Finch, *Restoration, Aphorism #7;* Moses Wall, *Considerations*, p. 59; Sadler, *Rights*, p. 48. See Scult, ibid, p. 32, footnote 59.
32 See Brightman, *Revelation*, p. 811; Finch, *Restoration, Dedication*; Wall, *Considerations*, p. 54.

Charles II. The period of the Puritan Commonwealth had now ended. The restored Monarchy and Government dealt harshly with radical Non-Conformist (or Dissenting) groups including the Fifth Monarchists. The Established Church, the Church of England, was also now restored to a position of pre-eminence, and henceforth also moved against any views known to be of Puritan in origin or propagated by the Puritans. The interest in Israel's restoration now dissipated. But it was not completely eclipsed - a remnant of interest remained. Some who did write about Israel's restoration and the Jewish place in the future were the great Puritan writer, John Milton who alluded to Israel's restoration in his *Paradise Regained*[33], Samuel Lee who in 1677 wrote *Israel Redux, or the Restauration of Israel*[34], and a Puritan from Boston Massachusetts named Increase Mather.

Mather who was at one time President of Harvard College in Boston wrote the *Mystery of Israel's Salvation* in 1669, and later in 1692 he wrote *A Dissertation Concerning the Future Conversion of the Jewish Nation*. Mather echoed much of what English Puritans had previously stated, that the large majority of the Jewish people would be 'converted', and that this would be a world-shaking event; the Pope is the Anti-Christ; and that the Jewish people are still God's chosen people.[35]

One of the most profound books on the subject written at that time was by a French Huguenot exile in Holland named Pierre Jurieu. In 1687 the English version of his book entitled *The Accomplishments of the Scripture Prophecies* appeared in London. In it Jurieu predicted, amongst other matters, that a revolution would occur in France that would have long-term effects. Jurieu also had an address entitled *To the Nation of the Jews* and stated:

> I confess the hopes they conceive of a *Kingdom of the Messiah*, which shall be chiefly for them, is built upon express and unquestionable *Prophecies*: that even their *Ierusalem* (sic) should be *rebuilt*, and that *they* shall be again gathered together in their own Land.[36]

Some European Protestants looked to England as being the vessel by which Israel's restoration would occur. One of these was a Danish Pietist named Holger Paulli, who believed that Israel's restoration would precede the return of Jesus. Paulli wrote considerably on this subject and sent his treatises to the monarchs of England and France, and even travelled to England in 1695. There he personally met with King William III and addressed the English monarch as

---

33 John Milton, *Paradise Regained*, (1671)
34 Samuel Lee, *Israel Redux or the restauration of Israel*, 1677, pp. 84-100. Quoted in Verete, ibid p. 17.
35 Increase Mather, *The Mystery of Israel's Salvation*, (Boston, 1669), pp. 7-8, 22, 49-51. Quoted in Scult, ibid, p. 37.
36 Jurieu, P. *The Accomplishment of the Scripture Prophecies*, (London, 1687), pp. 2-3. Copy in British Library, London.

Cyrus.[37]

King William may not have done anything for the Jewish people, but the interest in them continued to grow into the new century, due to their role in the forthcoming culmination of world history, the millennium and so forth.

The Age of Reason

The eighteenth century witnessed the beginning of what could be called the Enlightenment or the Age of Reason, a period during which there were many who opposed established Christianity and challenged the authority of the Bible. Many of these were known as Rationalists and Deists. They were thinkers and even theologians who reacted to the religious fundamentalism of the previous period, and tried to rationalize life, including religion and the Bible.

Religion was often divested of its 'spiritual' dynamic. It was seen that man through his knowledge, achievements and inventions could change society and thereby achieve the same results as that of the proposed spiritual millennium. The Age of Reason saw no centrality for the Jewish people, Israel's restoration, nor even of a returning Jesus.

Interestingly two men of repute, who belonged to the rationalist school, wrote of Israel's restoration during this period. One was John Locke, who published his *Paraphrase and Notes on the Epistle of Saint Paul* in 1707. Commenting on Romans 11:26, '... and so all Israel shall be saved', Locke wrote:

> It is plain that the salvation that St. Paul in this discourse concerning the matter of the Jews, and the gentile worlds in gross, speaks of, is not eternal happiness in heaven, but he means by it the profession of the true religion here on earth ... it is evident that being saved is used here by the apostle in this sense. That all the Jewish nation may become the people of God again by taking up the Christian profession may be easily conceived. But that every person of such a Christian nation shall attain eternal salvation in heaven, I think nobody can imagine to be intended here.[38]

The other was Sir Isaac Newton, who wrote his *Observations Upon the Prophecies of Daniel and the Revelation of St. John,* which was published in 1733 after his death. Newton wrote concerning Daniel 11:25:

> The commandment to return (to Palestine) ... may perhaps come forth not from the Jews themselves, but from some other Kingdom friendly to them, and precede their return from captivity and give occasion to it ... thus the return from the captivity and the coming of the Messiah and his Kingdom are

---

37 Pragai, ibid, pp. 15-16. Cyrus was the king of Persia who permitted the Jewish people to return to the land of Israel after the Babylonian exile. Restorationists were constantly looking for a modern day Cyrus.
38 John Locke, *Paraphrase and Notes on the Epistle of Saint Paul,* (London, 1823), p. 357. Quoted in Scult, ibid, p. 44.

described in Daniel ... the manner I know not. Let time be the interpreter.[39]

The excessive millennialism of the Fifth Monarchists and other similar groups, resulted in numerous detractors and opponents to those advocating anything connected to the Jewish people. One such detractor was Rev. George Hicks, chaplain to the Duke of Lauderdale, whose *Peculium Dei* printed in 1681, strongly castigated anyone advocating that the Jewish people are God's chosen people and that there should be a special interest upon the Jewish people and their conversion.[40]

Another was Richard Baxter who in 1691 wrote a pamphlet entitled *The Glorious Kingdom of Christ Described and Vindicated, Against the Bold Asserters of a Future Calling and Reign of the Jews and 1,000 Years Before the Conflagration,* in which he stated that the millennium had already passed, as too had the time of Israel's conversion, which he equated with the period of the Jewish Revolts of the first and second centuries, during which many Jewish people became followers of Jesus.[41]

Peter Allix, an Anglican was another and he wrote in 1707 that it was not possible to use Old Testament prophecies to relate to the Second Coming of Jesus, and that many Christians were mis-using the Book of Revelation. Allix wrote up nineteen rules to assist in interpreting Old Testament prophecies that would basically exclude all eschatological interpretations.[42]

By the early decades of the eighteenth century, despite the crackdown on extremist millennialism after the Restoration in 1660, and numerous opponents to any conversionist and restorationist theories, there was still an awareness of Israel and the Jewish people within the church in England. Most of this interest was more academic, with speculation upon how to properly interpret the various Old Testament unfulfilled prophecies concerning Israel's restoration, and Romans chapters 9 – 11.

This period was very important in the progression of thinking in Britain concerning the Jewish people. What had once been the domain of just a few Christian scholars had now become the domain of a much larger number. Although there does not seem to have been much active involvement in introducing Jesus as Messiah to the Jewish people living in England itself, the Puritans, nevertheless, introduced a stream into British Christianity which aided

---

39 Isaac Newton, *Observations Upon the Prophecies of Daniel and the Revelation of St. John*, (1733). Quoted in Scult, ibid, p. 45, who cites Franz Kobler, 'Isaac Newton and the Jews,' *New Judea*, December 1942, p. 44.
40 George Hicks, *Peculium Dei – A Discourse About the Jews as the Peculiar People of God*, (London, 1681), p. 23 Quoted in Scult, ibid, p. 47.
41 Richard Baxter, *The Glorious Kingdom of Christ Described and Vindicated, Against the Bold Asserters of a Future Calling and Reign of the Jews and 1,000 Years Before the Conflagration*, (London, 1691), p. 54. See Scult, ibid, p. 48.
42 See Peter Allix, *Two Treatises: I, A Confutation of the Hopes of the Jews Concerning the Last Redemption, II, An Answer to Mr. Whiston's Late Treatise on Revelation*, (London, 1707). Quoted in Scult, p. 51.

in arousing an interest in the Jewish people.

In Germany, where our story must now turn, tangible events were now occurring whereby many Christians were in fact taking the message of Jesus as Messiah back to the Jewish people. These events in turn would then converge with that Puritan stream.

Chapter 5

The Pietist and Moravian Streams

Aftermath of Thirty Years' War
The main issue facing the Church and the Jewish people in Germany in the seventeenth century was the Thirty Years War which took place between the years 1618-1648, and its aftermath. No-one was exempt from this terrible conflict.

At the conclusion of the War the Holy Roman Empire (of which Germany was part) remained intact, and Germany became a conglomeration of hundreds of small political entities, some of which had Roman Catholicism as the official religion, many had Lutheranism, a few had Reformed Christianity – and some were a combination.

The Jewish people must have been bemused by the ecclesiastical battle between the competing mainstream Churches - being told on one hand that Jesus was the Prince of Peace, and on the other hand witnessing so-called followers of Jesus massacring each other.

Rays of Hope
In the aftermath of this conflict there were signs of revival within the mainstream Lutheran Church. Despite the negativity generated by Luther and some of his successors, there were many who retained a positive attitude towards the Jewish people. A few German universities emphasised learning Hebrew and attaining an awareness of Judaism.

One academic, Johann Christoph Wagenseil of Altdorf, wrote a small booklet entitled *Hoffnung der Erlosung Israels (Hope of Israel's Redemption)* in which he wrote that it is fruitless to try and coerce the Jewish people into accepting Christianity, and that it is imperative that a new attitude of kindness be shown towards them.[1] He wrote:

> It is firstly the great persecution which the Jews suffer from us, above all in the German countries, which repels them from the Christian religion ... They are pushed and beaten; the people throw stones and filth at them in

---

1 J. C. Wagenseil, *Hofnung der Erlosung Israelis, oder Klarer Beweis der annoch bevorstehenden, und, wie es scheinet, allgemach-herannahenden Juden-Bekehrung, sammt unvorgreifflichen Gedanken, wie solche nacht Verleihung Gottlicher Hulffe zu befordern,* (Nuremberg and Altdorg, 1707). Quoted in Clark, ibid, pp. 11-12. Clark stated that Wagenseil also wrote *Tel Ignae Satanae,* (The Fiery Darts of Satan) in which he had some harsh words for the Jewish people. Wagenseil after reading *Toldoth Yeshua* became convinced that Jewish people were blaspheming Jesus, Mary and the teachings of Christianity.

the summer and snowballs in the winter. The [Christians] smear a piece of pork flesh about the mouths of the Jews when they are off their guards ... The children pull at their clothes, the adults at their beards. They go into the synagogues to mock them and even there will not let them be or finish their prayers. Who could find the words to express the insults, mockery, and annoyance the Jews must suffer every day?[2]

Wagenseil in his earlier years advocated a Christian witness to Jewish people, as he sensed 'that a mass conversion of the Jews was to be expected and might even be close at hand.'[3]

The mid years of the seventeenth century witnessed a rapid increase in millenarian thinking in Germany. One such advocate was the Huguenot, Jean de Labadie, who in 1667 wrote *L'Idee d'un bon Pasteur et d'une bonne Eglise* (The Reform of the Church through the Pastorate) in which he described 'the conversion of Israel as issuing in a golden age for the Church on Earth.'[4]

Labadie wrote this book at a time of much upheaval within the Jewish world, as shortly before, in 1666 Sabbatai Zevi had proclaimed himself as messiah in Smyrna in Turkey. When becoming aware of this event, Labadie then wrote, also in 1667, his *Jugement charitable et juste sur l'etat present des Juifs*, in which he stated that the Jewish people would become so disillusioned by this false messiah that they would be converted en-masse.[5] Indeed Sabbatai Ben Zvi was a false messiah and many Jewish people were disillusioned – but there was no mass repentance and turning to Jesus.

Shortly afterwards, another Huguenot theologian named Pierre Jurieu, whose work had already made an impact in England, had his book *The Accomplishment of the Scripture Prophecies* published in Germany.[6]

Labadie and Jurieu were only two of a number of *Chiliast* or pre-millenialist writers and theologians of the time. Mainline or orthodox Lutheran Christianity though was basically opposed to these views. Such is evident in Article XVII of the Augsburg Confession of the Lutheran Church from 1530, which under the heading 'Of Christ's Return to Judgment' stated: 'They condemn also others who are now spreading certain Jewish opinions, that before the resurrection of the dead the godly shall take possession of the kingdom of the world, the

---

2 Wagenseil, *Hofnung*, ibid, pp. 104-5. Quoted in Clark, ibid, p. 12. In *The Fiery Darts of Satan* Wagenseil firmly condemned the accusation that Jews used the blood of Christians for the Passover meal, stating 'even the stones must be moved to pity by the way in which the Jews have been harassed, tormented, and killed in their thousands on account of this accursed falsehood.' J. C. Wagenseil, *Tela Ingae Satanae*, (Altdorf, 1681), p. 131. Quoted in Clark, ibid, p. 12.
3 Clark, ibid, p. 17. From Wagenseil, ibid, p. 119.
4 Jean de Labadie, *L'Idee d'un bon Pasteur et d'une bonne Eglise*, (1667). Found in J. Wallmann, 'Das Collegium Pietatis', in M. Greschat (ed), *Zur neueren Pietismusforschung* (Darmstadt, 1977), p. 222. Quoted in Clark, ibid, p. 17.
5 Clark, ibid, p. 17.
6 Jurieu, P. *The Accomplishment of the Scripture Prophecies*, ii, p. 310.

ungodly being everywhere suppressed.'

Although there was some sympathy towards the Jewish people, for the most part Luther's final attitude towards the Jewish people seemed to be more predominant. Such an attitude is perhaps evident in the writings of Johann Jakob Schudt in his *Judische Merckwurdigkeiten* or 'Jewish Curiosities', written in 1714, who although stating some positive things about the Jewish people, also stated:

> Since I am not writing for the gratification of the Jews ... I can be frank about my opinion, for I believe and assert, along with Luther and many other theologians, that we Christians cannot with good conscience permit the Jews their synagogues and public religious observances, nor their rabbis, who only strengthen them in their unbelief. We can only permit each his own private religious observance at home.[7]

For the most part there was, Christopher Clark maintains, a great deal of ambiguity amongst German theologians and clergy toward the Jewish people.[8] Even the academic interest in Hebrew and the *Talmud* was accompanied by a deep seated suspicion of becoming too attached to Jewish traditions, as that may lead to Christians apostatizing to Judaism.

Clark states that, 'From the 1650's ... adherence to the doctrine of a prophesied conversion of the Jews came to be associated with the extremism of the chiliastic fringe.'[9] One of the strongest voices against the millennialist-chiliast approach was theologian Johann Dannhauer.

The restoration begins - Esdas Edzard and Phillip Spener
One man who was actively involved in assisting Jewish people was Esdas Edzard. Edzard had studied under the renowned Hebraist Johann Buxtorf in the University of Basel in the early 1650's. He then moved to Hamburg and opened an institute there in 1656 to provide Christian instruction and livings for Jewish followers of Jesus, thereby becoming probably the pioneer of practical assistance to the Jewish people. Edzard was not only interested in the spiritual needs of the new disciple, he also made efforts to train these men in new trades, even insisting that they learn a trade before being baptised.

During the following half a century numerous Protestant Christians, from other German states as well as from overseas, visited and also attended rabbinical studies at Edzard's institution. Lutherans such as Philipp Jakob Spener and August Hermann Francke were amongst those who visited Edzard's institution.

Spener had begun his education in theology at Strasbourg under Johann

---
7 J. J. Schudt, *Judische Merckwurdigkeiten (Frankfurt/Main, 1714)*, I, pt 1, Vorrede. Quoted in Clark, ibid, p. 13.
8 Clark, ibid, p. 12.
9 Clark, ibid, p. 18.

Dannhauer, a strong opponent of millennialism, but he then continued his studies at Basel under Johann Buxtorf. During this period he visited Geneva and had contact with Jean de Labadie, the renowned millennialist.

A devout Lutheran, Spener was disillusioned by the spiritual deadness of the German Lutheran Church and desired for a revival and return to a pure form of Christianity. Spener henceforth became the founder of a reform movement within the German Lutheran Church, known as 'Pietism.'

In his quest for a purer Christianity, Spener declared that the Jewish reluctance to 'convert' en-masse to Christianity was due not so much to the natural antipathy of the Jewish people to the message of Jesus, but to the behaviour they witnessed in Christians and Christianity as a system. He alluded particularly to the unfulfilled prophecy of Romans 11 as proof that Christianity was not doing its job. He wrote *Pia Desideria* in 1680, stating:

> If we look at the Holy Scripture, we need not doubt that God has promised a better state of the Church on Earth. We have, firstly, the heartfelt prophecy of St Paul and the mystery revealed to him (Romans 11:25,26), of how Israel shall become blessed after the fullness of the heathens shall be gone in, so that a great part, if not all, of the hitherto stubborn Jews shall be converted to the Lord.[10]

Some Lutherans responded to Spener that Paul's words had already found fulfillment in the past, with one critic stating that Spener was liable to be labeled a 'chiliast' by adopting or voicing these views.[11] In later editions Spener included a list of the Christian leaders who held similar views, and also quoted from the earlier writings of Luther, and stated that many of these earlier sentiments and writings of Luther had been omitted in later editions of the great reformer's works.

Perhaps the greatest aspect of Spener's views and position was his conviction that Christians had a responsibility to love the Jewish people, and to present Jesus as Messiah to them. Whether the Jewish people responded or not was really a matter for the Lord to deal with – but Christians could no longer neglect this responsibility.[12] In his book *Letzte theologische Bedencken,* written in 1711, he stated:

> The duty of Christian love obliges all Christians to contribute what they can with prayer and just and gentle behaviour towards the good of this people,

---

10 P.J. Spener, *Pia Desideria: Oder herzliches Verlangen nach gottgefalliger Besserung der wahren evangelischen Kirchen* (Frankfurt/Main, 1680). Quoted by Christopher Clark, "The Hope of Better Times:" Pietism and the Jews, in *Pietism in Germany and North America, 1680-1820,* edited by Jonathon Strom, Hartmut Lehman, and James Van Horn Melton, (Ashgate Publishing, 2009) p, 251.

11 A. Calov to P.J. Spener, 11 October 1675, cited in D. Blaufuss, 'Zu Philipp Jakob Spener und seinen Kritiken', *Pietismus und Neuzeit*, 14 (1988), p. 95. Quoted in Clark, ibid, p. 25.

12 See Clark, ibid, p. 26.

and to take every opportunity to address them in friendship and to inform them of our religion.[13]

Spener's attitude was somewhat controversial amongst German clergy as there was an instinctive fear of the 'Judaizing' of Christianity.[14]

He was also a realist and attested to the difficulties of attaining to such a lofty cause, maintaining that it was often stated that many Jewish 'converts' were insincere, and 'converted' for socio-economic reasons. Spener understood that the socio-economic dynamics which caused many Jewish people to live in poverty also needed to be changed, so that those who were sincere in their belief would come forward. At that time the majority of Jewish people in Germany were confined to peddling and small trading.

Spener bridged the gap between mission and eschatology, as his eschatology and especially his views on millennialism (*chiliasm*) were not extreme. Although many of his ideas about ministry to Jewish people may not have been uniquely his, yet it was Spener who integrated them all together for the first time. He saw a link between the failure of the church to provoke the Jews to jealousy, which would lead to Israel's collective conversion, and the shadow that was upon the Church. He therefore placed Romans 11 into the centre of his move for reform in the German Lutheran church.

The reform movement initiated by Spener did not have widespread support, especially from within the more orthodox branch of the Lutheran Church. It was close to being officially banned, but was saved by King Frederick III of Brandenburg. The Court at Brandenburg was Calvinist or Reformed, while much of the population remained Lutheran, so the King[15] saw Pietism as an unorthodox and mild form of Lutheranism, and a bridge between the two Protestant confessions. In time Pietism itself became the adopted confession of Brandenburg-Prussia and was the conduit of many state-initiated projects of reform. Thereafter more Lutherans of Pietist leanings received prominent positions in Prussian society.

August Hermann Francke
One of those who benefitted from this new found favour was August Hermann Francke,[16] a long time friend of Spener. Francke arrived in Halle in 1692, and shortly afterwards established a network of Christian charitable institutions based upon Pietist principles – rebirth, illumination, self-denial. These initiatives were encapsulated into the *Francke Stiftung* (Foundation) which Francke established in 1695.

Most prominent of Francke's initiatives was a school for the poor, and later for

---

13 P. J. Spener, *Letzte theologische Bedencken* (Halle, 1711), 1, pt 1, p. 286. Quoted in Clark, ibid, p. 15.
14 Schudt, ibid, I, pt. 2, bk. Vi, ch. Xxix, p. 117. Quoted in Clark, ibid, p. 16.
15 At that stage he was only the Protector, and was crowned King in 1701.
16 Francke was born at Lubeck in 1663 and died in 1727.

orphans, whereby education and accommodation were provided free of charge. The Pietists felt a call to assist all who were disenfranchised and impoverished. Most of the Jewish people in Halle, in Prussia, and indeed throughout Germany and nearby Poland, fell into this category.

Two of Francke's students later established important ministries in Germany, both of which incorporated the Jewish people. One student was Johann Callenberg[17] while the other was Nicholas Louis (later Count) Zinzendorf.[18] Both were influenced by the life and teachings of Francke and before him of the theology and lifestyle of Phillip Spener. The Pietist movement was a vital stream within Gentile Christianity which in different ways played a role in the initial formation of the London Jews Society and the *Benei Abraham*.

Zinzendorf and the Moravians

Nicholas Zinzendorf was born in 1700 in Dresden and Spener was one of his sponsors. Nicholas' father, the Count George Louis, was a fond admirer and acquaintance of Spener. From a very young age, wrote his biographer Rev. August Gottlieb Spangenberg, Nicholas was imbibed with a deep love for the Lord Jesus, while also being an admirer of Luther's 'Small Catechism.'[19]

Zinzendorf was sent to study under Francke at Halle at the age of ten, and although much esteemed by Francke, he encountered great difficulties adjusting to boarding school.[20] Such harsh lessons learned at Halle assisted him when he went to study law at the University of Wittenberg.[21] Nicholas, however, only wanted to study divinity.

At the age of nineteen Zinzendorf while in Dusseldorf, when viewing the painting *Ecce Homo* in the picture gallery, was struck by the accompanying words: 'All this I have done for thee; what doest thou for me?'[22] Challenged by these words, Zinzendorf thereupon saw his lifelong calling – working for the Lord, and then returned to Halle in 1721 and offered his services to Francke.

Zinzendorf by this time had concluded that the death of Jesus on the Cross and his resurrection was the essence of true Christianity, and that individuals needed to have a personal experience with Jesus. He subsequently found himself back at the estate of his grandmother at Hennersdorf, whereupon he quickly put into action some of the spiritual disciplines he had learned and developed since his time in Halle, most prominently the daily devotional meetings. But his family's desire was for him to enter the government of Saxony, in Dresden, which he finally, very reluctantly, agreed to do, in late 1721.

In 1722 Zinzendorf purchased a new estate at Bertholdsdorf which he

17 Callenberg, 1694-1760, is sometimes classified as the real father of modern Jewish missions.
18 Nicholas Ludwig, Count Zinzendorf, was born in Dresden in 1700. He died in 1760 at Herrnhut.
19 August Gottlieb Spangenberg, *The Life of Count Zinzendorf*, (London, 1838), p. 3.
20 Spangenberg, ibid, pp. 7-8.
21 Spangenberg, ibid, p. 11.
22 Spangenberg, ibid, p. 15.

envisaged would be used for the work of God. Shortly later he met a young Bohemian man, Christian David, who had recently become a disciple of Jesus. Zinzendorf's zeal for the Lord and sympathy for those oppressed because of their faith impressed the young Bohemian. At that very time many Christians in Bohemia and Moravia were suffering duress because of their personal faith in Jesus, and were seeking a refuge away from the control of the Roman Catholic Church.[23]

Christian David returned to Moravia, told the people about Zinzendorf, and in June 1722 two families accompanied David to Zinzendorf's new estate. There they built a small house, the first of many, and the little community that became known as Herrnhut began. This move laid the foundations of a new world missionary enterprise, an enterprise which drastically affected not only English Christianity, but also the life of a young Jewish man named Joseph Levi.

At this point Zinzendorf only desired to assist in transforming the inner spiritual life of the Lutheran Church - he was not at all interested in beginning a new movement. In the following years a community of like-minded believers gravitated to the Count's estate at Herrnhut, as more Moravian refugees and exiles joined them. The leaders of the community were all Pietistic Lutherans, and they, particularly Zinzendorf, desired to mold the new arrivals more into this Lutheran mold. But after some time the Moravians realized this mold just did not suit them completely. There were just too many different practices. Consequently a serious rift developed in 1727.

Then in the midst of this communal crisis, in August 1727, there was a visitation by the Holy Spirit who thoroughly transformed the struggling community. This visitation was manifested by prophecies, visions, *glossalalia* (speaking in different tongues) and healings. Thereafter Zinzendorf realized that his life vocation was to disciple and nurture this vibrant young covenant community.

Development of the Moravian stream
Zinzendorf had concluded that the only way forward was to allow the Moravians to worship God in the way that was natural for them. So he drew up some congregational regulations, called together the community, made a covenant with them before the Lord, and a new era began at Herrnhut. From that time onwards there was great blessing and anointing upon the Moravian Church.

---

23 The Moravian Church had its beginnings under a Roman Catholic priest named John (Jan) Huss. Hus wanted the Church to be restored to 'pure' Christianity, and in particular wanted: the liturgy to be in the language of the people; lay people being able to receive both elements of the communion; the elimination of indulgences; and the abolition of the idea of purgatory. Hus was ultimately condemned by the Roman Catholic Church and burned at the stake in 1417.

Some of Huss's followers made a compromise with the Roman Catholic authorities, but many did not and these became known as the Bohemian Brethren or 'Unity of the Brethren.' These were persecuted by the counter-Reformation groups during the Thirty Years War (1618-1648). Many of the followers had to leave, or go 'underground,' Many remained in Moravia. See www.wikipedia.org/wiki/Moravians_(religion).

D. W. Bebbington in his book *Evangelicalism in Modern Britain* wrote that the Moravians, 'Under Zinzendorf's guidance ... were reorganized in 1727 as the renewed Unity of the Brethren and became a dynamic missionary force.'[24]

Already in 1727 the Moravians had made four missionary journeys out of Herrnhut. This was the beginning of a new journey for this fledgling movement. News of what the Lord was doing with this small community quickly spread – even to England.[25]

Further missionary journeys were made to Stockholm and England in 1728, and then in 1732 missionaries were sent to work in Greenland and amongst the Afro-Americans in the West Indies. During the 1730's the Moravians also established a congregation in London. The miracle of Herrnhut was now being spread around the globe. This was the real birth of world-wide missions.

From the outset this movement included the Jewish people. Johann Leonhard Dober was sent to minister to the Jewish people in the Netherlands in 1738, and in 1739 they had in their liturgy a regular prayer for the national repentance of the Jewish people. J. E. Hutton in his book *History of the Moravian Church* states:

> For some years the Brethren conducted a mission to the Jews. For Jews the Count had special sympathy. He had vowed in his youth to do all he could for their conversion ... he made a practice of speaking about them in public on the Great Day of Atonement; and in their Sunday morning litany the Brethren uttered the prayer, "Deliver Thy people Israel from their blindness; bring many of them to know Thee, till the fulness of the Gentiles is come and all Israel is saved." The chief seat of this work was Amsterdam, and the chief workers Leonard Dober and Samuel Leiberkühn. The last man was a model missionary. He had studied theology at Jena and Halle; he was a master of the Hebrew tongue; he was expert in all customs of the Jews; he was offered a professorship at Königsberg; and yet, instead of winning his laurels as an Oriental scholar, he preferred to settle down in humble style in the Jewish quarter of Amsterdam, and there talk to his friends the Jews about the Christ he loved so deeply. His method of work was instructive. He never dazed his Jewish friends with dogmatic theology. He never tried to prove that Christ was the Messiah of the prophecies. He simply told them, in a kindly way, how Jesus had risen from the dead, and how much this risen Jesus had done in the world; he shared their hope of a national gathering in Palestine; and, though he could never boast of making converts, he was so beloved by his Jewish friends that they called him "Rabbi Schmuel."[26]

---

24 Bebbington, D. *Evangelicalism in Modern Britain*, (London, 1989), p.39.
25 Spangenberg, ibid, p. 98.
26 Hutton, J. *History of the Moravian Church,* Book 2, Chapter 6, in www.ccel.org/ccel/hutton/moravian.html

The beginnings of world-wide missions, springing forth from a student of Francke and admirer of Spener, included God's call of taking Jesus to the Jew first. (Romans 1: 16) The Moravian movement was another important stream within Gentile Christianity which led to those future key events in London.

The *Institutum Judaicum*

Johann Callenberg, another Pietist Lutheran, studied under Francke at the University of Halle. Callenberg was acquainted with Arabic, Hebrew, Yiddish and Judaism and was obviously an attentive student for Francke often mentioned in class the need to establish a missionary work among the Jewish people.[27]

Shortly after Francke died in 1727 Callenberg, in an effort to publish a missionary pamphlet in Yiddish, raised funds and published it himself. Other works followed, and shortly afterwards he not only owned a printing press, but was registered by 1732 under the name of *Institutum Judaicum*.

There were three categories of work at the *Institutum Judaicum*, as stated in a pamphlet by Callenberg:

1. The establishment of a Printing Press
2. A Provision for Proselytes and Catechumens
3. The appointment of Students as traveling Missionaries to the Jewish Nation.[28]

The printing press was intended to print and distribute Christian tracts and pamphlets in many languages. Numerous of these were printed in Yiddish, for Jewish people in central Europe, and others in Hebrew for Jewish people elsewhere. Such materials were taken by Christian travellers to many different locations.

The second component of the work, involvement with the Jewish disciples, involved people who were unable to provide for themselves. Rejected by the Jewish community for 'apostasizing,' and not being completely accepted by the Christian community, they were often caught between the two. Callenberg assisted as best he could, but the needs were often greater than his capability to help. Relating to this situation Callenberg's pamphlet stated, as quoted in 1813 in the *Jewish Repository*:

> ... the great obstruction to the conversion of the Jews was the destitute condition of the proselytes: several of whom, traveling, came to him with great complaints of the straits to which they were reduced by turning Christians; that the conduct of too many of them hardened the Jews against the Christian religion, and Christians against the Jewish nation; that care

---

27 Clark, ibid, p. 48.
28 John Henry Callenberg, *A short account of an Essay to bring the Jewish nation to the Knowledge and Practise of the Truth of the Gospel, etc*, (Halle, 1734). Quoted in *Jewish Repository*, January 1813, p. 1.

was taken to enquire into the motives of their turning Christians, and the occupation they should choose for their livelihood; also that they should obtain present supply, and be assisted in a way of maintaining themselves in time to come; and that numbers residing at Halle met every Lord's-day evening at his house, with other Christians, to hear from God's Word exhortations suitable to their condition.[29]

Although unable to accommodate many of those Jewish followers of Jesus requesting help at the *Institutum*, Callenberg endeavoured to ensure Jewish disciples could live a worthy life after baptism, although the *Institutum* itself did not perform baptism as that was the function of the Church. Callenberg understood the need of assisting Jewish disciples in finding employment, or where necessary, of helping to train them in a new profession. Most Jewish males who showed an interest in Callenberg's message belonged to the small itinerant peddler category. Any new professions taught, therefore, would not be linked to trading, but instead would be linked to a craft of the hand or agriculture. This endeavour of the *Institutum* was associated not only with the spiritual conversion of the Jewish person, but a social conversion as well.[30]

This matter was important in Germany. Many Christians were very suspicious of the motives behind why a Jewish person would 'convert.' It was felt by some opponents and skeptics that only someone of a base character would 'convert' or change 'religion', and that they were doing it purely for monetary reasons. There were cases of baptismal swindling, of a person going to different locations and being baptised, receiving the benefits there for a time, and then moving on.[31]

This is the background for the *Institutum's* desire to ensure that baptism was synonymous with the new disciple being able to earn his own bread. This would also facilitate an orderly transition into German 'Christian' society. Despite this, on numerous occasions even if a Jewish follower did make an honest living, he still was not always fully accepted by his fellow Gentile Christians.

There did not seem to be much by way of an encouragement for Jewish disciples to retain their Jewish identify, and even to form any sort of a Jewish believers fraternity. Had there been such a fraternity, under the umbrella perhaps of the *Institutum* for the sincere Jewish followers of Jesus to be able to meet and relate to each other, then perhaps they might have fared better.

Callenberg, though, had given the matter some thought. In 1735 he had actually conceived the idea of setting up farming colonies for 'Jewish Christians'. He realized there were tremendous changes for a Jewish person when they accepted Jesus as Lord and Messiah,[32] that such a person was leaving a community of

---

29 *Jewish Repository*, 1813, p. 43.
30 Clark, ibid, p. 55.
31 Callenberg, *Zehnte Fortsetzung* (Halle, 1735), p. 241. Quoted in Clark, ibid, p. 61.
32 Clark, ibid, p. 65.

like-minded people, and entering into another community of which they had virtually no commonality at all. This was an issue which would confront future generations of Jewish followers of Jesus.

The third component of Callenberg's *Institutum* was active missionary work. This was probably the most effective aspect of his ministry. It began when a former divinity student while travelling and speaking to Jewish people about Jesus, came across some of Callenberg's pamphlets, and then in 1730 offered his services to undertake this travelling work under Callenberg's supervision. Ultimately Callenberg employed students of theology for a period of 2-3 years and they travelled the length and breadth of central Europe, as well as touching upon northern Europe and even the Eastern Mediterranean, and supplied detailed accounts of their travels.[33]

Callenberg himself wrote of their task:

> Their chief care in their travels is to acquaint themselves with the Jews in a decent manner; to discourse with them about divine truths; to disperse the little treatises, printed here, amongst them; to forward the above-mentioned care of the proselytes; and to keep a constant journal of all that is worthy of any notice.
>
> They have opportunity of conversing with the Jews in their walks and in the public houses where they lodge, or of visiting the Jews in their own houses. They frequent their synagogues, where they always have their Bibles before them. What necessaries they want in their travels, they buy of the Jews; and go to them when they have occasion to change their money. They speak with them in their own Jewish-German dialect. They acquaint them with what Jewish-German books they carry about them. This soon paves the way, without much preamble, to a familiar and edifying conference with them, and though they always accost them in a civil, modest, and humble manner, yet they never flatter them, but exert their zeal, when they find it necessary.[34]

Callenberg envisaged a world-wide mission, and even communicated with the *Society for the Promotion of Christian Knowledge* in London. In this he hoped that the *Institutum's* publications could be distributed further aboard into Asia, Africa and America by English diplomats and merchants who were part of Britain's worldwide enterprise of the time. In the 1734 pamphlet quoted in the *Jewish Repository*, it is stated:

> The English Translation of our account of the undertaking in favour of the Jews, is printed for the service of English Merchants in remote parts of the world, who may be willing to give our Books and Pamphlets, to be

---

33 See Clark, ibid, p. 50. Many of these accounts are still present at the *Francke Institutum* in Halle today.
34 *Jewish Repository*, 1813, p. 45.

transmitted gratis by us, to the Jews.³⁵

Callenberg's enterprise existed upon donations from the public, not from the state or state church. All financial transactions were then made public, in periodic Reports, which also contained reports from the missionaries in the field, as well as commentaries by Callenberg himself and by other Christian authorities. These Reports were sent by Callenberg to interested and sympathetic supporters in different locations, including in England.

The *Institutum Judaicum* encountered numerous obstacles during its existence, both from the Christian and Jewish communities as well as from the State authorities. They were charting new waters, and as could be expected made mistakes. But they also left a rich legacy, a legacy which would be passed onto future generations.

Following Callenberg's death in 1760 the *Institutum* gradually declined and by 1771 was only a shadow of its former self. Yet despite its weakening, the *Institutum* had alerted many pious German Christians of the need to pray for the nation of Israel.

It was at this very time that one Jewish man who was to be greatly influenced by the efforts and prayers of the German Pietist and the Moravians streams, was soon to enter into the world.

Birth of Joseph Samuel Levi

On 21 September 1771 Joseph Samuel Levi was born at Mainstockheim near Kitzingen in the province of Franconia. Joseph's father, Samuel Levi, was 'a respected Rabbi, of eminent devotion, wholly retired from the world, giving up himself entirely to the study of the Jewish religion.'³⁶ Joseph and his four brothers were taught during the week by a tutor and received a strict Talmudic upbringing and 'every Saturday' Joseph later wrote, 'we were examined by our father in what we had learned during the week.'³⁷ At the age of six, Joseph 'could perfectly read the five books of Moses in Hebrew'.³⁸ At the age of thirteen he was admitted into the congregation, the observance known as *bar mitzvah*, 'Son of the Commandment.'

From a very young age Joseph and his brothers were educated with a strong attitude against Christianity. He wrote:

> Our tutor took every opportunity to impress us with prejudices and hatred against the Christian religion. Whilst explaining the five books of Moses, he mentioned in every place the *opinions* of Christians, raised *objections* against

---

35 *Jewish Repository*, 1813, p. 1.
36 *Evangelical Magazine*, 1806, p. 3.
37 Joseph Frey, *Judah and Israel, or The Restoration and Conversion of the Jews and the Ten Tribes* (London, 1837) p. 60.
38 *Evangelical Magazine*, ibid, p. 3.

them, and endeavoured to establish us in all the *Jewish errors*. On the evening preceding the 25th of December it being supposed that Jesus Christ was born on that evening, the Jews do not study anything sacred, but our teacher always made us read a little book called "Toldoth Jeshu," i.e the generation of Jesus; which contains the most horrid blasphemies, and is calculated to fill any person who believes it, with prejudice, disgust, and hatred against Jesus and his followers.[39]

This practise of the Jewish teachers, Levi stated, was even more apparent in his case, as his mother's brother had become a follower of Jesus, and his mother was 'a most inveterate enemy to Christianity'.[40] The Jewish boys in the village were so aware of this that when there were quarrels between them and the Levi boys and in particular with Joseph 'who was always the wildest' they taunted Joseph and his brothers shouting, "Let them alone, they will certainly turn Christians, as their uncle did."[41]

Joseph's mother was so upset by her brother's decision that she closely watched the conduct of her sons to ensure they received no Christian exposure. To 'embrace the Christian religion', Joseph wrote 'brings greater reproach upon the family than if all the children had been guilty of the worst of crimes; and the person who believes the Christian religion, becomes the object of their utmost abhorrence. One of the names by which such a person is called, is Meshummad, from the root Shamad, which signifies to destroy; and to this name they generally add *Yemach shemo vesichro;* ie let his name and memory be blotted out.'[42]

The Enlightenment flourishes and the *Institutum Judaicum* closes

During this very period of the 1770's the Enlightenment flourished in Germany, providing limited opportunities for Jewish people to leave the confines of the ghetto and enter into German society. In addition new state laws were enacted by King Frederick William II in 1786 thereafter affecting financial contributions to the work of the *Institutum*.

The financial giving decreased to such an extent that by 1791 the Provincial Government of Magdeburg made plans to dissolve the *Institutum*. The final act of dissolution took place in July 1792.

That same year saw the birth of a new missionary enterprise in England, itself the culmination of a fifty year 'Evangelical' or 'Pietist' awakening within the British Church, and which brought with it a new period of world-wide

---

39 Frey, *Judah and Israel*, pp. 60-61.
40 Frey, *Judah and Israel*, p. 61.
41 Frey, *Judah and Israel*, p. 61.
42 Frey, *Judah and Israel*, p. 62. *Yemach shemo vesichro* translates into the acronymn *Yeshu*, which many Jewish people even until today use when referring to Jesus, whose Hebrew name is actually *Yeshua*.

mission. Like its German counterparts, this new period of world-wide mission also involved the Jewish people and was in fact heavily influenced by both the Pietist and Moravian streams within German Christianity.

Chapter 6

The Evangelical Stream

Wesley and the Moravian influence

Simultaneous with the initiatives of Zinzendorf and Callenberg, an evangelical awakening was happening in Britain. This awakening is associated mostly with three individuals; George Whitefield and the brothers John and Charles Wesley.

In 1735 John Wesley accepted a commission to go to Savannah, Georgia in America to be a parish priest. Aboard the same ship were twenty-six Moravian Christians who were en-route to join the pioneer Moravian settlement of Ebenezer close to Savannah.[1]

Interestingly, in an accompanying ship there was a group of Protestants who had been expelled from Austria, victims of the Counter-Reformation in parts of Europe where the Roman Catholic Church was regaining control where Protestants had once either ruled or had freedom of religion. The ministers of this group of persecuted Protestants had been trained at the University of Halle which was, wrote Thomas Bebbington:

> … the centre of the Lutheran movement that most affected Evangelical origins: Pietism. Philip Spener had written in 1675 the manifesto of the movement, *Pia Desideria*, urging the need for repentance, the new birth, putting faith into practice and close fellowship among true believers. His disciple August Francke created at Halle a range of institutions for embodying and propagating Spener's vision … Francke's writings were to take their place in the spiritual biographies of Whitefield and both Wesleys. Pietism had already achieved in Lutheranism a great deal of what these men were to undertake in the English-speaking world.[2]

John Wesley in particular was greatly challenged by the lives and testimonies of the Moravian Christians and when, after two years, he returned to England he attended a Moravian meeting in Aldersgate Street. It was here on 24 May 1738 while he was listening to a reading of Luther's rendering of the book of Romans that, Wesley stated, "I felt my heart strangely warmed." Suddenly he knew that Jesus had saved him from the law of sin and death. "It pleased God," he wrote later, "to kindle a fire which I trust shall never be extinguished."[3] Two weeks later he himself preached at the Moravian assembly on the theme of

---

1 Bebbington, ibid, p. 39.
2 Bebbington, ibid, p. 39.
3 www.chi.gospelcom.net/GLIMPSEF/Glimpses/glmps163.shtml

personal salvation by faith and faith alone.[4]

Thereafter Wesley became closely attached to the Moravian congregation at Fetter Lane in London, and even visited Herrnhut in late 1738. Upon his return he began formulating hymns and even rules by which the society could work in London.

The association of both the Wesleys and Whitfield with non-Anglican religious societies, especially the Moravians, was not well received by the Anglican hierarchy and many parish churches were closed to them. So from 1739 they began speaking to audiences in the open air. From this point the Evangelical revival of eighteenth century Britain truly began.

The message proclaimed by Wesley and Whitefield was very basic: justification by faith alone in the atoning work of Jesus on the Cross. This was a message which much of Britain was waiting to hear. The Established Church was spiritually dry at the time, just as the Lutheran Church had been in Germany which gave rise to the Pietist movement.

The Baptist congregations and other Non-Conformist or Dissenting denominations were mostly affected by this spiritual awakening, with membership in their congregations increasing dramatically. Although Wesley never intended to sever his relationship with the Established (Anglican) Church, they basically severed their relationship with him, and his followers became known as Methodists.[5]

This Evangelical awakening would be another important stream within Gentile Christianity which would influence the formation, in time, of the Hebrew Christian-Messianic Jewish movement.

The Naturalization Bill - 1753

During this period the small Jewish community in Britain of about 8,000 was becoming embroiled in an important struggle – for formal status. Many of them were foreign-born and were not naturalized because one could only become a citizen if they would receive the Sacrament of the Church of England.[6]

In 1753 a bill was proposed for the Jewish people to be accepted as a distinct religious group owing allegiance to the oaths of Supremacy and Allegiance. This bill was also called the *Jew Bill*. There was, as there was in 1655, opposition from certain merchants, who feared competition. But the bill passed through Parliament by May 1753 and was endorsed by King George. Shortly afterwards, however, there was a huge clamour against it and the Government then repealed the bill in 1754.

Although much of the opposition was economic and political in essence, it was disguised in religious garb. The matter brought to the fore the varying

---

4 www.en.wikipedia.org/wiki/John_Wesley
5 This name came because of John Wesley's very methodical idiosyncrasies.
6 The law had been passed by King James I in order to exclude Roman Catholics from becoming citizens.

attitudes in Britain concerning the Jewish people, and it placed the future of Israel again on the agenda.

Opinions may have differed, but what mattered most was that the way was now open for Jewish people to become citizens of Britain, although this did not occur until the next century.

The Seven Years War (1756-63) and After

The *Jew Bill* brought the presence of the Jewish people in Britain to the public's attention. Many people, now alerted to the prophetic elements found in Daniel and Revelation and to Paul's treatise in Romans 9-11, were being attuned to the 'signs of the times.' They were looking for events happening in the world which could facilitate the fulfillment of the prophecies concerning Israel's restoration and national repentance and the end of the age.

The beginning of the Seven Years War (1756-1763) was one such event. Fought primarily between Britain and France this conflict spread throughout the known world, from India to the West Indies to Canada and even in Europe. Any such event was sure to stimulate interest. Just prior to the final outbreak of this war Thomas Newton wrote *Dissertations on the Prophecies which have remarkably been fulfilled and at this time are fulfilling in the World*. In this work Newton maintained that the conversion of Israel must occur before their physical restoration. The Bishop of London, Robert Lowth, conveyed similar ideas.[7]

These and other utterances on the subject did produce some sharp reactions. One notable reaction was from the eminent scholar Dr. Gregory Sharpe who clearly taught that 'Jerusalem and Jewish temporal power were destroyed for ever, never to arise again.'[8] He was followed some years later by the Archdeacon of Worcester, John Tottie, who delivered some scathing sermons on the subject which were then published in 1775. Although he did concede some ground concerning the state of the Millenium and Second Coming of Jesus, he nevertheless saw no place for national Israel in the end times. He wrote 'The Jews indeed had ... *universally* forfeited their national title to the temporal blessings of the Covenant.'[9]

But another Anglican minister, Joseph Eyre, had a completely different perspective on the subject of the covenant with Israel. In his *Observations upon the Prophecies, relating to the Restoration of the Jews*, Eyre showed how many writers had two basic attitudes relating to the prophecies about Israel's restoration, 1) to relate them to having been fulfilled in the restoration from Babylon, and 2) to allegorically transfer them to the Gentile Church.

---

7 Kobler, ibid, p. 41.
8 Gregory Sharpe, *The rise and fall of the Holy City and Temple of Jerusalem*, 1765. Quoted in Verete, ibid, p. 24.
9 John Tottie, *Sermons*, 1775 (Sermon XV: *Christ's Second Coming, the day of final judgment* - preached in 1774). Quoted in Verete, ibid, pp. 24-25.

Eyre pointed out, though, that the second restoration as prophesied in the Scriptures is synonymous to a time of absolute peace, tranquillity and bliss for mankind, and as this has never happened in the history of the Church, then those prophecies could not belong to the Church.[10] He then set out very clearly each prophecy and showed how each was never completely fulfilled or not at all, and therefore could not be applied to the Church, and must therefore relate to a future literal restoration of Israel.[11]

One of the many examples Eyre elaborates upon is from Acts 1:6, where he stated:

> This plainly shows that the Apostles themselves had an expectation that the Kingdom or Sovereignty of … Judea … should at some time or other be restored to the Israelites. [And] our Lord … does not deny the truth of that restoration they expected, but only says it was not for them to know the *times* and *seasons* when such a restoration was to take place. Nor can it be imagined that if the Apostles had been in an error of such consequence, our Lord would not have endeavoured to set them right.[12]

Time and again throughout his book Eyre stated the need to understand the terms 'Israel', 'seed of Abraham", Jerusalem' and 'Zion' in a literal sense, and also, where a physical restoration was spoken of, to understand it literally.[13] Joseph Eyre like almost all of the other restorationist writers was committed to a belief that Israel would come to believe in Jesus as Messiah – they weren't going back to the land of Israel for nothing. The big question, though, related to whether they would believe first and then return, or vice-versa, and to what extent Christians here and now had to be involved.

Eyre's thorough treatise was complemented the following year by the Anglican bishop, Richard Hurd. Bishop Hurd wrote in 1772 that the dispersion after the destruction of the Temple and Israel's ability not to be integrated into societies and their remaining as a single nation revealed there was a bigger purpose for them remaining as a nation distinct. He wrote:

> All this hath something prodigious in it which could be none other but what He had spoken through his prophets of their destiny in the Latter Days when He would gather them to their ancient land and to himself in true faith.[14]

While much interest in Israel's spiritual and physical restoration was taking place perhaps the first reference to a specific evangelistic outreach to the Jewish people was pronounced. On 10 October 1773 Selina, Dowager Countess of

---

10 Joseph Eyre, *Observations upon the Prophecies, relating to the Restoration of the Jews,* 1771. See Kobler, ibid, p. 41.
11 Verete, ibid, p. 23.
12 Verete, ibid, p. 23.
13 Verete, ibid, pp-24. 23.
14 Verete, ibid, p. 20.

Huntington, wrote in a letter, possibly to George Whitfield in relation to a work being done among the Cherokee Indians in Georgia, 'I am looking when some from among us shall be called to the Jews ...' The Countess later became instrumental in establishing the (London) Missionary Society.[15]

One other very significant contribution to an interest in the Jewish people was made by an Anglican minister, Edward Whitaker, who in 1784 wrote a work entitled *Dissertation on the Prophecies on the final restoration of the Jews*. Whitaker encouraged the study of Israel's restoration as a subject distinct from the millennium. He strongly maintained that the prophets when writing of a future restoration referred to God's covenant people or nation, and not to individuals. In this context he viewed Romans 11: 26, 'all Israel shall be saved.' He believed this ultimate spiritual restoration, the conversion of Israel, had to be a literal restoration as Abraham had been promised a specific piece of physical land. (Genesis 13:14)

Concerning this promise made to Abraham, Whitaker wrote that it 'is... absolute ... and part of the subject of this promise was the everlasting possession of that very country in which the patriarchs themselves sojourned.' Then, concerning the land of Israel, Whitaker concluded that it '... is assured unto the seed of Israel as long as any of that seed shall survive.'[16]

Whitaker then concluded that if the Jewish people would not be restored to the land that had been specifically promised to their forefathers, it would mean that that promise would fail. This would be a crisis of God's credibility, for it was promised and written in His word. This he predicted could not be, therefore it is obvious that the Jewish people have 'not forfeited their national title to the temporal blessings promised', and that they would surely 'be gathered together from the extensive dispersion in which they now exist, and restored to their ancient country.'[17]

Enter Wilberforce, Simeon and the Anglicans

The evangelical awakening until the 1780's had primarily affected the rank and file of British society. The Establishment was basically untouched, although there was the rare exception. John Newton was one such exception, being converted from being a slave trader into one of the Evangelical faith.

Britain at that time was ripe for social disorder. Poverty was widespread, with all of its resultant vices, including crime, thuggery and prostitution. Much of this was exacerbated by the Industrial Revolution and the desire of the wealthy to increase their wealth – often at the detriment of the less well off.

---

15 Letter of Countess of Huntington, 10 October 1773, G2/1/9, Chestbut College, Westminister. I am much indebted to Dr Stephen Orchard for providing me with this, and other relevant material on the subject matter.
16 Edward Whitaker, *Dissertation on the Prophecies on the final restoration of the Jews*, 1784. Quoted in Verete, ibid, p. 25.
17 Whitaker, ibid. See Verete, ibid, p. 26.

Reformation was sorely needed, not only of established religion, but also of society in general. But if it was to happen, and if the Evangelicals were to play a part in it, then they needed a leader.

In 1785 they received one: William Wilberforce, a Member of Parliament, and one highly esteemed by Prime Minister William Pitt. In that year Wilberforce was converted from 'mere nominal Christianity' to the 'vital Reformation Christianity' which those associated with Newton's group espoused.

Observing the terrible state of British society, Wilberforce wrote, '... the universal corruption and profligacy of the times, which, taking its rise amongst the rich and luxurious, has now extended its baneful influence and spread its destructive poison through the whole body of the people.'[18]

Wilberforce soon set about the task of reforming British society, and teamed up with a group of like-minded men, many of whom lived in Clapham village to the south of London.

This group of people, whom detractors thereafter named the Clapham Group,[19] in time involved the 'Who's Who of British Evangelicalism', although not all resided at Clapham (Rev. Charles Simeon occasionally joined them from Cambridge).[20]

They now set about earnestly to reform British society, but quickly realised that the implementation of their programme depended much upon a strong base of Evangelical clergy. Charles Simeon at Cambridge University was already making huge efforts to fulfill this requirement. Then in 1788 the *Society for the Relief of Poor, Pious Clergymen, Residing in the Country*, was established. Several years later there were some sixty clergymen on the list, and these, Brown wrote "were probably almost the entire roll of known Evangelicals to have 'happily emerged from their brethren.'"[21]

At this time the propertied classes and the Established Church more or less ruled society in Britain. Wilberforce and his Evangelicals indeed had a challenge before them, for in order to 'clean up Britain,' both of these parties, the aristocracy and the established Church, would need to be shaken out of their complacency.

In July 1789 that shake-up occurred.

The French Revolution

All of the expectations of the previous decades concerning events associated with the end of the age (which included the full restoration of Israel), came to

---

18 Robert Isaac Wilberforce and Samuel Wilberforce, *The Life of William Wilberforce*, (5 volumes, London, 1838), vol. 1, p. 84. Quoted in Ford. K. Brown, *The Fathers of the Victorians: The Age of Wilberforce*, (University Press, Cambridge, 1961), p. 2.
19 Also known as the 'Clapham Sect.'
20 Included were Henry and John Venn; Henry Thornton; Hanna More; Lord Teignmouth; James Stephen; William Smith; Granville Sharp; Charles Simeon; Zachary Macaulay; Thomas Gisborne; Thomas Grant; Edward James Eliot; Thomas Clarkson. See Stock, ibid, p. 42.
21 Brown, ibid, p. 9.

the fore immediately after July 1789 and the outbreak of the French Revolution. The late Professor Meir Verete stated:

> Several months after its outbreak Englishmen began to hear and to read that it was this great event that heralded the end of the generations and the impending advent of the kingdom of Christ.[22]

A Congregationalist stalwart, Joseph Hardcastle, saw events in France as clear signs pointing to the impending end of the age.[23] The Revolution in France and resultant atheism 'created' wrote Dr. Stephen Orchard, 'many a trauma amongst Evangelical minds.'[24] It had a definite effect upon the complacency of upper British society, who were afraid that the flames of the Revolution would cross the English Channel and affect them. Many now turned to God.

Thereafter numerous British Christians wrote concerning the Biblical significance of the events then occurring in France.[25] In 1790 Edward May (who had previously read Pierre Jurieu's book which predicted a future revolution in France) wrote *The Accomplishment of the Scripture Prophecies*. Amongst May's numerous statements were those connecting the fall of the French Monarchy and subsequent decline of the Pope to the countdown to the fulfillment of the biblical prophecies and would include the restoration of Israel.[26]

Also in 1790 Richard Beere wrote a treatise entitled *A Dissertation ... containing strong and cogent reasons to prove that the commencement of the final Restoration of the Jews to the Holy Land is to take place in the ensuing year, A.D. 1791*. Beere even went so far as to write a letter to Prime Minister William Pitt on 10 November 1790 encouraging him to sponsor a Jewish restoration to the land of Israel.[27]

A Baptist minister named James Bicheno then wrote *The Signs of the Times: or, The Overthrow of the Papal Tyranny in France, the Prelude of Destruction to Popery and Despotism; but of Peace to Mankind*, in 1793. Bicheno set out a basic belief that the French Revolution set in motion a series of events which would include the restoration of Israel and would culminate with the return of Jesus.[28]

Beginning of Modern Missions in Britain

The events from 1789 indeed increased Evangelical awareness within Britain of the seriousness of the times. One person affected was a young Baptist minister named William Carey. As a young man Carey had been impressed with the voyages of Captain Cook, and following further reading, he desired to share the

22 Verete, M. *The Restoration of the Jews*, p. 5.
23 See Orchard, ibid, chapter two, no page numbers.
24 Orchard, ibid, chapter two.
25 Richard Beere, in 1789, wrote *An Epistle to the Chief Priest and Elders of the Jews ... to which is added an investigation and computation of the exact time of their final Restoration*.
26 Verete, ibid, pp. 5-6.
27 Franz Kobler, *Napoleon and the Jews*, (Jerusalem, 1975), pp. 26-27.
28 James Bicheno, *The Signs of the Times: or, The Overthrow of the Papal Tyranny in France, the Prelude of Destruction to Popery and Despotism; but of Peace to Mankind*, (London, 1793).

message of Jesus among the 'heathen.' In 1792 he preached several messages on these very issues, and later in that year the Baptist Missionary Society was established. In 1793 Carey set sail for India.

This Baptist Missionary Society (BMS) was formed at a time of heightened interest in missions, stimulated, although not birthed, by the events of the French Revolution. Many evangelicals in Britain, believing they were entering into the last days, saw the need to obey the words of Jesus in Scriptures such as Matthew 24 and take the message of salvation to the ends of the world.[29]

One person who was very supportive of missions was Selina, Dowager Countess of Huntington, whose chaplain was Thomas Haweis. Haweis was also the leading spokesman for the mouthpiece of the Dissenting Church, the *Evangelical Magazine*. In October 1793 an article appeared in that magazine under the writer 'Horatio' entitled '*Remarks on the prophecies and promises relating to the Glory of the Latter Day*' which included a challenge for more mission work to be undertaken.[30]

The following year Melville Horne returned from an unsuccessful period as chaplain to the Sierra Leone Company, and published his *Letters on Missions*. Horne encouraged mission to every 'tribe, and kindred and tongue' and also connected the disturbing events in France to the urgency of taking the gospel message out to all nations.[31] Horne's challenge impressed Thomas Haweis.

The move towards a second and more expansive world-wide missionary move was furthered when in January 1795 a Scottish minister in London named John Love wrote an article, which appeared in the *Evangelical Magazine* and which also encouraged overseas mission.[32]

All of these challenges led to the coming together in September 1795 of a group of like-minded Christian men, and resulted in the formation of the Missionary Society (later known as the London Missionary Society, LMS). Six sermons were preached at the inauguration meeting, including one by Rev. David Bogue, most of which were millennial in context.[33] Thomas Haweis later concluded of this event:

> When was ever such an association of the ministers of Christ collected in this land? Every partition wall is broken down, and every heart big with expectation, that the time approaches, when the great Redeemer of lost souls will receive the heathen for his inheritance, and the uttermost parts of the

---

29 Verete, ibid, p. 5ff.
30 *Evangelical Magazine*, Vol. 1, 1793, pp. 175-6.
31 Melville Horne, *Letters on Missions, addressed to the Protestant ministers of the British churches*, (1794). See Stephen Orchard, *Evangelical Eschatology, 1790-1850*, unpublished thesis, (Cambridge, 1962).
32 *Evangelical Magazine,* 1795, Vol. III, p. 14. Quoted in Orchard, chapter two.
33 See Orchard, ibid, chapter two.

world for his possession.[34]

Shortly afterwards the first Missionary Society missionaries set sail for the south seas aboard the ship *Duff*. In the midst of the French Revolution and Revolutionary Wars, Evangelical Christians were embarking upon a new and exciting venture – to bring the message of Jesus 'to the ends of the earth.'

That this was an exciting adventure there is no doubt. Yet one matter seemed to be missing at that stage, and this was the commission to take the message of Jesus to ALL nations – which included the nation of Israel. Surely this was the very heart-beat of Jesus; and Paul expressed this sentiment clearly in Romans 1:16 where he stated that 'The gospel is the power of salvation to all men, to the Jew first and also to the non-Jew.' (Romans 1:16)

The implementation of this command of Jesus and heart-cry of Paul was soon to be taken up. In 1796 the *Evangelical Magazine* carried a profound article, entitled *The Conversion of the Jews*, which stated:

> The deplorable state in which the Jewish nation is now found, has a loud claim upon Christian philanthropy. In proportion to their former privileges and glory, it is to be lamented that they are now involved in gross ignorance, if not in real sensuality. The Israelites were formerly distinguished by such tokens of the divine favour, as no other nation ever enjoyed: But this was eventually the circumstance that increased their misery, as it had greatly aggravated their guilt. That those people, to whose custody the oracles and ordinances of God had been committed, and who ought neither to have been ignorant of the true character and interest; that they should crucify the Lord of Glory, was at one to fill up the measure of their iniquity, and to bring upon their devoted head the just vengeance of an insulted Deity.
>
> The Jews were, however, the natural branches of the spiritual vine; and notwithstanding, in consequence of their being broken off, the Gentiles were grafted in, yet there will arrive a time, in which *all Israel shall be saved*; in which there shall be one fold of Jew and gentile, and Christ, the great head of the Church, become the shepherd of the people. For this eventful period is the church now looking and longing; and as, previous to this, there must be a more full gathering of the Gentiles, efforts well adapted to this purpose are now making: And surely designs so consonant to prophecy, so harmonizing with Gospel promises and declarations, will not be frustrated, but be followed with a divine special blessing.
>
> The Christian world have felt it to be their duty to make exertions for the conversion of the heathen abroad, and the more complete spread of the Gospel at home. But, amongst all the benevolent plans which have been formed to secure the salvation of sinners, how little attention has been paid

---

34 *Sermons preached in London at the formation of the Missionary Society*, 1795, p. 161. Quoted in Orchard, ibid, chapter two.

to the state of the Jews! They have lived and traded with us, and we have scarcely reflected on their melancholy state, as the outcasts of God. But do not the promises and prophecies of the Scriptures lay us under equal obligation, and afford equal encouragement to attempt something for *their* good, as for the spiritual prosperity of the Pagan world? The object of this address is briefly to point out such methods, as are level to the circumstance of most; whereby Christians may be instrumental of real good to that people, whom God, in his providence, passed by to visit us.

It might be attended with very salutatory effects, if a select number of persons, possessed of a competent knowledge of the Hebrew tongue, would form a society for this very purpose, probably a few might answer the design of such an association, and carry into good effect the important object of their union ... The objects which present themselves to such societies are the following: To excite the attention of the Jews to the subject of religion in general: To gather from them some information of the state of their religious knowledge; which is an important measure, as it may guide and direct exertions for their conversion: To introduce amongst them Bibles, especially the New Testament.

The generosity of some opulent Christians might be well directed in distributing copies of the sacred book amongst these people in their vicinities. They should also be frequently and seriously conversed with, as opportunities might present themselves; and who can tell what a few minutes spent in prayer with them may do, if they can be prevailed upon (which may be tried) to unite with us in the exercise? They should also be invited to our public worship, and those, who from good motives frequent the house of God, would do well to urge this upon them, and accompany them. With such views no measure of obloquy can possibly attach itself to a professor. I have only to add that if *small* tracts were written by proper persons, and distributed amongst them, many beneficial effects might result from it.

These addresses might, first of all, be general, and then might afterwards be compiled more particular. Something of this kind will shortly be done by individuals; but in order that an extensive dissemination of this plan may take effect, it is thus publicly recommended to the Christian world at large. Above all, let this important object occupy a *constant* part in all our addresses to the throne of grace; especially let it never be forgotten in *public prayer*. Who can tell what God may do for his church in our days? What heart can express the joy resulting from a consciousness of having successfully aimed at the glory of God, and the salvation of sinners, both Jews, Gentiles, and Pagans?[35]

This article presented a clear challenge for the British Church now to reach

---

[35] *Evangelical Magazine*, 1796, pp. 403-5.

out to the lost sheep of the house of Israel, and it represents the convergence of two streams within British Christianity, the Puritan and Evangelical. The question now was: Would the British Church take up the challenge in the same way as Edzard, Spener, Zinzendorf and Callenberg had done in Germany?

It would, but it would first require a 'push' from a German – a German who had been richly influenced by those very same German streams.

Chapter 7

Joseph Levi and the New Covenant

Joseph Levi the young man

In 1789 while eighteen years of age Joseph Levi went to Hesse where he was a tutor for six children, teaching them Hebrew, writing and arithmetic. He remained in this position for three years, during which he also studied for the position of *chazzan* or cantor in the synagogue. Buoyed by this success, Joseph then began studying for the important and prestigious position of a *shochet* or ritual slaughterer, an undertaking, he stated, was taken because 'the pride of my heart was not satisfied.'[1] This was a very exacting training, but finally Levi received his 'honourable degree from the Rav, or Rabbi of Hesse Cassel.'[2]

Joseph Levi was about twenty-two years of age when his mother, who had taken on a business of supplying part of the Prussian army then encamped near Frankfort on the Maine, asked him to return home to assist her. Joseph complied with her wish, but shortly afterwards he realized that he had neither the skill nor pleasure to be involved in the trading business, and asked for his parents' permission to return to Hesse. They consented to his request, and upon departure his father blessed him with the words: 'The Angel of the Covenant be with thee.'[3]

Young Joseph then drifted around for about six months before finally returning to Hesse. Unfortunately he could find no satisfactory employment, so he then moved onto Hannover and from there to Hamburg and Altona. His life at this time was one of a restless mind and a restless body.

Levi introduced to the New Covenant

In 1793 while residing in Altona-Hamburg a fellow Jewish sojourner encouraged him to move onto Mecklenburg Schwerin[4], where, the sojourner informed him, there awaited a secure job as tutor for the children of a certain gentleman.[5]

While en-route to Schwerin Joseph travelled with a Jewish student and a young Christian, an agent for a tobacco factory in Hamburg. While on the journey the Christian man had observed how Joseph had punished himself by strictly observing *kashrut*[6] by eating only bread and drinking only water during

---

1 Frey, *Narrative of the Reverend Joseph Samuel C. F. Frey*, (London, 1809), p. 15.
2 Frey, *Judah and Israel*, p. 62.
3 Frey, *Judah and Israel*, pp. 62-3.
4 In the province of Mecklenburg-Schwerin in the north of Germany.
5 Frey, *Judah and Israel*, p. 63.
6 Jewish dietary laws.

the journey, while the other Jewish traveller 'made free with everything.'[7] The Christian man then said to Levi:

> "I am sorry to see you chastening yourself, and being troubled with the burdens which your fathers were never able to bear, and which you need not to observe; for ... the ceremonial law is fulfilled, and taken away by the Messiah Jesus, and a new covenant is made, as it was foretold by the prophet Jeremiah, (chapt. xxxi. 31-33): "Behold, the days come, saith the Lord, that I will make a new covenant with the house of Israel, and with the house of Judah: not according to the covenant that I made with their fathers in the day that I took them by the hand to bring them out of the land of Egypt; which my covenant they brake, although I was a husband to them, saith the Lord: but this shall be the covenant that I will make with the house of Israel: After those days, saith the Lord, I will write my law in their inward parts, and write it in their hearts; and I will be their God, and they shall be my people.""[8]

'These words,' Joseph later recalled, 'I had never heard before.'[9] Joseph then wrote how the observations of this man 'made a deep and lasting impression upon my mind, and for some time I was wretched and miserable, full of doubts and fears, and knew not what to do.'[10] Soon afterwards the thought of becoming a Christian first came into his mind. This thought somewhat astounded him, for until that time the very name 'Christian' was an abomination to him.[11]

The three travellers arrived later that day at Schwerin. Bidding the Christian farewell Levi then went in search of the Jewish family with whom he was to work as a tutor. Joseph was to receive quite a surprise, for when he introduced himself to the gentleman in question he was astounded to discover that the gentleman had made no such request – and didn't even have any children to be taught! This was an object lesson for young Joseph to learn, yet as he later wrote:

> But, blessed be the Lord my God, who has so overruled this circumstance that I can now adopt the words of *Joseph*, my namesake, "He thought evil against me, but God meant it unto good; to bring to pass, as it is this day, to save much people alive." [12]

Joseph, now in quite a predicament, decided to leave the following day (a Friday), for Gistraw. His Christian companion of the previous day was also on the stage coach, and Joseph informed him of his recent circumstances. The Christian

---

7 *Evangelical Magazine*, p. 4.
8 Frey, *Narrative*, pp. 22-3.
9 Frey, *Narrative*, pp. 22-3.
10 Frey, *Judah and Israel*, p. 66.
11 *Evangelical Magazine*, p. 4.
12 Frey, *Judah and Israel*, pp. 64-65.

man, Joseph recalled, showed some sympathy and stated, "put your trust in the God of Israel, and he will never suffer you to be moved."[13]

That evening in Gistraw Joseph attended the synagogue, but during the night he was very restless, being quite troubled by the events of the previous days. On the Shabbat, while the Christian man went about his business, Joseph wrote of his state:

> All that he had said to me came suddenly into my mind with great force, and his kind and affectionate behaviour, contrasted with the shameful conduct of my brother the jew [sic], had such an influence on my mind, that I immediately sat down and wrote a letter to him intimating that I would travel in his company to Berlin in order to inquire into the truth of Christianity.[14]

It never occurred to him that writing and sealing a letter were deemed violations of the *Torah*. At that point he went to synagogue, but upon his return to the inn he discovered that the Christian man had already left. Joseph was now in despair and later wrote, 'My conscience was now awakened, and it loudly told me that I was no longer a jew [sic], for that I had broken the sabbath.'[15] Joseph was so distraught for he believed that to sin on one point would be to break the entire *Torah*.

The life of this seemingly righteous man now began to unravel, and he thereupon shut himself away until the next morning. He then boarded a coach heading for Rostock, hoping to catch up with his Christian 'friend.'

With the words of Jeremiah's New Covenant ringing in his ears, his hopes were high, but alas upon arrival in Rostock he could not locate his new found 'friend.' Then, to add to his troubles, he was informed that no Jewish person could stay in Rostock without a special license.

As obtaining such a license would cost a considerable amount of money, Joseph informed the landlord at the local inn, that, 'I was a Jew by birth, but that I had come to that place to inquire into the truth of the Christian religion, and was resolved to embrace it if … I should become convinced of its veracity.'[16]

The following day his landlord took Levi to the home of a minister who, he later wrote, examined his 'knowledge of the Christian faith, and of the motives which I came to renounce Judaism.' As Levi could produce only one Scripture to show that Jesus was Messiah, from Genesis 49:10, the minister, Levi later wrote 'suspected my motives to be worldly; nevertheless he did not altogether discourage me, but went with me to some other ministers, and stated my request to the magistrate of Rostock.'[17]

---

13 Frey, *Narrative*, p. 23.
14 Frey, *Narrative*, p. 24.
15 Frey, *Narrative*, p. 25.
16 Frey, *Judah and Israel*, p. 67.
17 Frey, *Narrative*, p. 27.

Shortly afterwards Levi appeared before this same magistrate where he was 'strictly examined, and my testimonies were approved.' The magistrate informed Levi that many Jewish people had 'embraced Christianity only for secular advantages, who had lived afterwards as heathens, which had made them very careful of receiving any before they were thoroughly convinced of their sincerity.'[18]

Two weeks later Levi received their resolution: that he should go to three neighbouring towns and that if none of them would receive him, he should return to Rostock.

The birth of Joseph Wolff

While Joseph Levi was struggling with his conscience, another Joseph was born into a Jewish family at Weilersbach, near Bamberg in Bavaria.[19] Joseph Wolff was born in 1795.[20] Joseph's father David was rabbi for the small Jewish community there, but soon afterwards he moved to Kissingen, and then onto the larger city of Halle. It was while there, so Joseph wrote, that his father began 'to educate me strictly in Jew principles when I was four years old.'[21]

From a young age Joseph considered Christians to be 'worshippers of a cross of wood – idolators.'[22] But, like other Jewish children during this time of the Enlightenment, he attended a Christian school in order to learn German - but excused himself when religious subjects were broached.

Similar to most German Jewish boys, Joseph Wolff began reciting the *Siddur*, (the Jewish Prayer Book) at the age of six, although he later confessed that he never understood it. Then, quite surprisingly, at the age of seven while in his room Joseph had a fleeting thought of Jesus. This was an interesting experience considering that thereafter he endured some very deep struggles with sin in his life.

Thus while one very young Jewish boy named Joseph was just beginning to work through the matter of sin in his life, the other Joseph in our story was drawing a life changing conclusion about the matter of sin, and how to deal with it.

Levi accepts Jesus as Lord and Messiah

The first town visited by Joseph Levi was Wismar, a seaport on the Baltic Sea. Here he met Dr. Haupt, who found him an apprenticeship as a shoemaker. He resided here for eighteen months, and during that time met twice weekly with

---

18 Frey, *Narrative*, p. 27.
19 Wolff, J. Rev. *Sketch of the Life and Journal of the Rev. J. Wolff, Missionary to Palestine and Persia*, (Norwich, 1827), p. 5.
20 Wolff, J. *Travels and Adventures of the Rev. Joseph Wolff*, p. 2. In Wolff's book *Life and Journal*, he states the year as 1796.
21 Wolff, J. *Life and Journal*, p. 5.
22 Wolff, J. *Life and Journal*, p. 5.

Haupt, as well as comparing the German Old Testament with the Hebrew Bible (*Tenach*) and reading the New Testament, which he had never seen before.

Levi had quite a difficult period here, as the shoemaker himself was poverty stricken, and he was constantly teased by so-called Christians who would state to him, "You will certainly give up your new profession of faith as soon as you have made your fortune amongst us."[23] Then the shoemaker had to give up his business and Levi lost his apprenticeship. As the minister could not accept him into the Church until he had completed his apprenticeship, Joseph had to move on. His problem was further complicated by a law stating that no other master could receive him until he was baptized, as his name had to be registered in a book belonging to that trade. Levi stated 'as no jew [sic] can be bound apprentice in Germany, my name could not be registered till after I was baptized.'[24]

Shortly afterwards Levi met Matthias van Gilben who advised him to go to Mecklenburgh Strelitz in New Brandenburg where he knew the minister and Van Gilben supplied Levi with a letter of recommendation. Accordingly Levi followed this advice and became acquainted with Rev. R. Kortim, a Lutheran minister, who also recommended him to a shoemaker in order to complete his apprenticeship.

It was at Mecklenburg, on 8 May 1798, that Joseph Levi was publicly baptized. Although it was the custom in Germany for any Jewish person being baptized to receive both presents and several god-fathers, Levi refused both, so he would not be accused of being baptized for material benefit. It was also a custom to receive a new name, and this Levi did consent to, and Christian Frederick was added to his Joseph Samuel. Levi's family name was changed to Frey, based upon the scripture from John 8:32 and 36: "And ye shall know the truth, and the truth shall make you free" and "If the Son therefore make you free, ye shall be free indeed."[25]

Joseph Samuel Christian Frederick Frey

Joseph Frey thereafter went through various stages in his pilgrimage and in December 1798 he arrived at Prentzlow, in Prussia, where he found work as a shoeman's journeyman. Not knowing any other Christians, however, he succumbed to spending time in idle pursuits at the local inn where he was forced to reside during the weekends.

On one occasion Frey met Mr J. F. Thorman, a seller of aprons, who enquired upon his spiritual state. Frey explained that as he had to reside in the inn over the weekends, he had no choice but to join in the idle pursuits of his fellow journeymen. Thorman invited him to his home the following afternoon where,

23 Frey, *Narrative*, p. 29.
24 Frey, *Narrative*, p. 31.
25 Frey, *Narrative*, p. 33.

he informed Frey, 'several friends meet: you will become acquainted with them and be able to spend your time on Sabbath at their houses.'[26] Upon enquiry of his land-lady Frey was informed of Mr. Thorman's house that, 'it is a society of praying men'[27] – a term often used for the United Brethren or Moravians.

On the morning that he was supposed to attend this prayer-meeting, Frey wandered into a nearby Lutheran Church, where a Rev. Wolfe was ministering confirmation to a number of children. Wolfe, speaking from Job 27: 6 and Acts 24:16, challenged the children to keep near to the Lord Jesus and not return to the 'broad road which leadeth to destruction.' This message convicted Frey and he was led to a deeper repentance for his sins. He desperately needed fellow-believers at this point to help him to comprehend this deep conversion of the heart he had just experienced.

Frey himself wrote:

> I now firmly believed that I had not only broken the double covenant as a jew [sic], which was first made with God by my parents at my circumcision; and secondly, by myself, when I was thirteen years old; but also that covenant with God in Christ, which I had rashly made when I was baptized and joined the Christian church. It now pleased the Lord to teach me something of the spirituality of the law; I not only found myself guilty of very many sinful actions and words in my life past, but I was also convinced that "the thoughts and imaginations of my heart were only evil continually, Gen. vi.5."[28]

Joseph was now more convicted than ever of his sinful state and the need of a saviour. The remainder of that day seemed like an eternity to him, as he waited in expectation for the meeting with Mr. Thorman and his friends.

Finally the hour arrived when the brethren met. Of that first service he wrote:

> The service now began with singing, then followed a short prayer, and after that he read a sermon; Jesus Christ was the sum and substance of the discourse, from which I received much comfort; then he kneeled down, and he prayed. More than twenty minutes were spent in prayer for me, thanking God for calling me out of darkness, and more particularly that it would please the Lord to make me useful and faithful.[29]

So impressed was Joseph with this meeting of the Moravian brethren that he later asked his master if Mr. Thorman had studied, to which his master replied "No". Frey could not understand how anyone, not being acquainted with him,

---

26 Frey, *Narrative*, pp. 37-8.
27 Frey, *Narrative*, p. 38.
28 Frey, *Narrative*, pp. 40-1.
29 Frey, *Narrative*, p. 44.

could pray so long for him. "That is no wonder," said one of the family, "these people pray always."[30]

Joseph slept deeply that night. The following morning he awoke with a hunger for reading the Bible, and enjoyed his work as never before. His joy, however, especially when singing hymns, provoked some of his fellow journeymen who endeavoured thereafter to entice him back to his previous ways. When Frey refused their overtures, they ridiculed the 'society of Christians' he later wrote 'with whom I had just formed an acquaintance.'[31]

Thereafter Frey spent considerable time with Thorman who apart from expounding the Scriptures, also 'frequently read the periodical publications of the Basel society and other letters relative to the spread of the gospel among Christians, and especially the exertions of Christians in England to send the word of salvation to the heathen.'[32]

Frey's change of lifestyle also adversely affected the attitude of his employer towards him, and he was in time relinquished of his work as an apprentice. Not desiring to be idle, he informed Thorman of his intention to leave Prenzlow. Thorman informed him that a friend, Mr. Boettcher was departing soon for Berlin. Frey joined him, and Thorman gave Joseph a recommendation to a shoemaker in Berlin named Mr. Burgett.

Relating to his departure on 20 June 1799 for Berlin Frey stated, 'Never was anything more painful to me than my parting with this man. Nor have I scarcely ever met a man altogether like him.'[33]

Birth of Michael Solomon Alexander

While Joseph Frey was preparing himself to move to Berlin, and while Joseph Wolff was just beginning his life in southern Germany, another Jewish boy entered into the world. On 1 May 1799 Rabbi Alexander[34] in the small village of Schonlanke,[35] in the Grand Duchy of Posen[36] became the proud father of Michael Solomon.

Although quite close to Berlin, Posen was actually part of Greater Poland, but the region had been annexed by King Friedrich II of Prussia in 1772 during the first partition of Poland. Then, in 1793, during what is known as the Second Partition, the remainder of this region was annexed to Prussia and was known to them as 'Southern Prussia'.

---

30 Frey, *Narrative*, p. 45.
31 Frey, *Narrative*, p. 48.
32 Frey, *Narrative*, pp. 48-9.
33 Frey, *Narrative,* p. 51.
34 There is a bit of conjecture about his original name, that it was Pollack or even Wolff. For the purpose of this book however I will stick with Alexander.
35 Now Trzcianka in Poland.
36 A part of Greater Poland, known to the Poles as Wielopolska. After 1815 however it was referred to as Posen after the principal city.

Young Michael Solomon therefore grew up in a mixed German and Polish cultural milieu, although he would more than likely have been more orientated towards the German than the Polish culture. This factor would become evident as this young man's life progressed.

Joseph Frey arrives in Berlin

Joseph Frey's first day in the Prussian capital was life-changing. In the morning he met Rev. Woldersturff, a valiant soldier of the Messiah, through whom Joseph received instruction on 'how to put on the whole armour of God.' [37]

Then in the evening another companion took him 'to a chapel of the Moravians, or congregation of united brethren.'[38] This service deeply affected young Joseph, and he later wrote:

> The simplicity of the place of worship, the regularity and order of the congregation, the subject of discourse, and the manner in which it was delivered, made a lasting impression on my mind. Ever after I attended the public meetings of this christian [sic] society, and very soon obtained liberty to attend their private meetings on Wednesday and Friday evenings. I was just on the verge of being received as a member of this highly respected community, when I was prevented by joining the Missionary Seminary. But although I did not actually become a member, yet my attachment to these christians [sic] has never been diminished. My heart has ever rejoiced to meet with one of these plain and humble followers of the Lamb. It was among these christians [sic] I heard of the love of Jesus in every sermon, and saw him, as it were, crucified before my eyes ... A sermon without Christ, is like a body without a soul.[39]

After just a few days Frey gained employment in his trade and all seemed to be going well for him. Not long after though his health began to suffer. His employer (whom he calls his 'master') was sympathetic and procured a place for Joseph to study in a free school where he could train to become a schoolmaster. This seemed to be a perfect match considering his former role as a tutor. But alas this was not to be. One evening during his devotional hour Joseph was much impressed by these words from Matthew 16: 24-26:

> Then said Jesus unto his disciples, "If any will come after me, let him deny himself, and take up his cross, and follow me. For whosoever will lose his life for my sake shall find it. For what is a man profited, if he shall gain the whole world, and lose his own soul? Or what shall a man give in exchange

---

37 Frey, *Narrative*, p. 55.
38 Frey, *Narrative*, p. 55.
39 Frey, *Narrative*, pp. 55-56.

for his soul?"⁴⁰

Thus despite the attractiveness of this fresh opportunity, which would no doubt have been beneficial for his health, Joseph sensed that this new possibility could actually be potentially damaging for his spiritual life. He purposed then to continue in his present employment until God directed him otherwise.

Joseph didn't have to wait long, for during that very night he dreamt that he sensed the Redeemer was at his bed side and said these words, "Fear not, you shall be a physician to heal many of their diseases" to which Joseph then replied, "By what means shall I become a physician, who am a stranger in the land?" The reply as Joseph recalled was, "You have many friends in this place."⁴¹

At this point he awoke, and much disturbed by the dream, he fell upon his knees and prayed – obviously to the interest of his roommate! The following day his room-mate inquired of what had caused this disturbance, and Joseph finally informed him.

Unbeknown to Joseph, his erstwhile room-mate then informed others, and presuming it meant that Joseph would become a physician, he began to form a plan for the support of Joseph to study medicine. This same young man also introduced Frey to Rev. Johann Jaenicke the minister at the Bohemian chapel, also known as the Bethlehem Church.⁴²

Towards the end of 1799 while returning from a service at the chapel, several young men asked him, 'Well, brother Frey, should you like to go as a missionary?" To this question Joseph replied, "Yes ... I am willing to go anywhere whithersoever the Lord Jesus Christ should be pleased to send me."⁴³

These young men then advised Joseph to speak with Rev. Jaenicke and give his name, which was added to others who were likewise interested in enrolling in an institution which Jaenicke and others were desiring to establish in order 'to preach among the gentiles the unsearchable riches of Christ.'⁴⁴

The Berlin Seminary

Joseph Frey arrived in Berlin at a very opportune time. Momentum had increased in Germany during the previous years for the establishment of an institution similar to those recently established in Britain. In 1796 Baron von Schirnding of Dobrilugh (today Kirchkain) in Saxony had read an article in the *Hamburg Gazette* that the Missionary Society (LMS) had been formed, and he had promptly written an address entitled *Address to the British Nation* and sent it

---

40 Frey, *Narrative*, p. 58.
41 Frey, *Narrative*, p. 59.
42 Jaenicke (1748-1827) came from a community of Bohemian settlers in Berlin, but was an ordained Lutheran (Pietist) minister.
43 Frey, *Narrative*, p. 61.
44 Frey, *Narrative*, p. 61.

to Dr. Thomas Haweis, one of the Missionary Society (LMS) leaders.[45]

In his address Von Schirnding drew attention to the responsibility of taking the Gospel to the heathen.[46] Von Schirnding's *Address* appeared in the *Evangelical Magazine* in August 1796. Dr. Haweis' reply to Schirnding then found its way into the hands of Rev. Johan Straecke, a Lutheran pastor from Hatshusen. Rev. Straecke then appealed to his German countrymen in 1799 to establish a similar institution as the Missionary Society in Germany. Rev. Straecke's appeal was endorsed in a subsequent letter of Von Schirnding to the Missionary Society which was read on 11 March 1799 'offering to send missionaries to Nootka Sound and Africa, and to co-operate cordially with the Society …'[47]

While plans were being prepared for the establishment of this institution, Rev. Jaenicke gave Frey and another prospective candidate named Albrecht letters of recommendation and sent them to visit Baron von Schirnding, who would be the main benefactor of this would-be institution.

Several weeks after this meeting Frey received a message from Von Schirnding informing him that he and Albrecht were, as he wrote, to, 'quit our worldly occupations, and devote ourselves to study.'[48] The Berlin Seminary finally opened on 1 February 1800 'for training promising candidates for missionary employ.'[49]

Frey enters the Berlin Seminary

The Berlin Seminary commenced with seven students, 'for whose instruction a tutor was engaged.'[50] They would not receive any official credentials, for at that stage such credentials could only be attained through formal education at a university. The education these seven candidates received were in languages (Latin, Greek, Hebrew, Dutch, French, Arabic and Syriac) and related subjects such as theology, geography, music, medicine etc. From the outset Joseph applied himself rigorously to his studies.

Joseph, however, was not content just with studying the official subjects. He also translated three of Mr. Cooper's sermons, which he had preached among the Jewish people in London, from German into Yiddish[51] in anticipation, Frey wrote, that the Baron Van [sic] Schirnding would cause them to be translated

---

45 See Bridwell Library Manuscript and Documents Collection, British Manuscript Letters and Documents, Schirnding, August [Carl Friedrich] von, 1796, February 19, Dobrilugk in Saxony. "Oberforstmeister" MS folio ("first doctrines of evangelical Lutheranism"), (II/2:149). Thomas Haweis Collection, www.smu.edu/bidwell/html/Manuscript Collection.htm#Thaweis.
46 C. Hole, *Early History of the Church Missionary Society for Africa and the East to the end of AD 1814* (London, 1896), p. 82. Herrnhut was about 60 miles (100 kilometres) from Dobrilugh.
47 Lovett, R. *History of the London Missionary Society*, 1795-1895 (London, 1899), Vol. 1, p. 76.
48 Frey, *Narrative*, p. 62.
49 Hole, *ibid*, pp. 82-3.
50 Hole, *ibid*, pp. 82-3.
51 A high German language in origin, developed by the Ashkenazi Jews of Germany and used by them throughout Central Europe.

for the use of the jews [sic].'[52] In addition he also translated Luther's Shorter Catechism, as well as other materials, which he would then read out to Jewish people, even on Shabbat after the synagogue services.

From the outset the Berlin Seminary could only train and educate the missionaries for overseas work among the 'heathen', and refer them to other societies such as the Missionary Society and the recently established Church Missionary Society (CMS).[53] Ironically these British missionary societies were staffed primarily by Christians from central Europe, who were candidates either from the Berlin Seminary, or later from the Basel Bible College in Switzerland.[54]

The Berlin Seminary encapsulated much of the missionary zeal of the German Church, both Lutheran (Pietist) and Moravian, in much the same way as the Missionary Society and CMS encapsulated the Puritan and Evangelical streams of the English Church.

Unfortunately missionary zeal alone could not sustain the Berlin Seminary. Towards the end of 1800 Von Schirnding went bankrupt, and thereafter Rev. Jaenicke exerted much effort to raise funds from private subscriptions, and even at one point from his own private funds. Later the institution came under the patronage of the King of Prussia, Frederick William III. Thereafter the royal family became more aware of German evangelical initiatives overseas.

It was at this juncture, in early 1801 that the Danish Missionary Society requested that one of the German missionaries be sent to them for overseas ministry. All the students would need to undergo an examination, except Frey. Frey himself recorded that his exclusion was 'on account of his having been a jew [sic].'[55]

One could but imagine the pain and rejection Joseph experienced at this stage, when all the other students undertook the examination and he was excluded. Yet Providence prevailed, for Joseph was destined for other labours in the Lord's vineyard.

---

52 Frey, *Narrative*, p.83.
53 Established in 1799 by evangelical Anglicans, many of whom were from the Clapham group.
54 This Seminary was founded in 1816 by Christoph Gottlieb Blumhardt, as a training arm of the Basel Mission which he established in 1815.
55 Frey, *Narrative*, p. 64.

Chapter 8

Joseph Frey and the (London) Missionary Society

Joseph Frey goes to London

While Joseph was busily studying, and probably still deeply upset by this rejection, the Missionary Society sent a request to Rev. Jaenicke in June 1801 for three students who could be sent as missionaries to labour alongside Dr. Van der Kemp in the Cape Colony in Africa.[1] After prayer and consideration, Jaenicke chose Palm, Ulbricht – and Frey.

Joseph and his fellow German students left Berlin on 11 July 1801 for Hatzhausen in Friesland. Here they remained six weeks, under the tutelage of Rev. Straeke, who taught them the Dutch language in preparation for their future labours in the Cape Colony.

The three missionaries departed for England on separate ships in September, and Joseph arrived at Gravesend on 15 September 1801. While his companions had already proceeded on to London, Frey was delayed several days until his passport arrived. This was a lonely time for him, separated as he was from his friends, and not knowing a word of English.

Yet it was during this brief period that he had another dream which radically altered his future direction. He dreamt that he and his two German companions were to preach in London, and, he later wrote, 'that the Jews in particular were (in a most affectionate manner) invited to the discourse which I was to deliver. The appointed day approached; an immense crowd collected, and I was enabled to preach to them with great freedom, and to lift up my voice *like a trumpet*. I thought that the effect of this discourse was, that I was afterwards desired to stay in London, to preach both to Jews and Christians: to which I replied, that I could not possibly part with my dear brethren, Palm and Ulbricht, and let them go alone.; but that if the directors would send for another missionary, to accompany those brethren, I would consent; and with which, the directors having complied, I resolved to remain in England.'[2]

Frey recounted that after he awoke he prayed to God for wisdom and grace to prepare him for service, either among the Hottentots of Africa or amongst the Jews and Christians in London.

As soon as he received his passport Frey left Gravesend for London and went to the home of Joseph Hardcastle, treasurer for the Missionary Society. From

1 LMS Minutes for 21 September 1801, LMS Archive, SOAS, London.
2 Frey, *Narrative*, pp. 75-76.

here he was taken to the home of Mr and Mrs. Smith on Bishopsgate Street, where he was to lodge until a vessel arrived to take him and his companions to the Cape.[3]

Providence it would seem once again intervened. For five months no suitable vessel arrived for their onward journey to Africa. These were invaluable months for Frey. Apart from the help of the Smiths he also taught himself English by comparing the text of the German Bible with an English Bible, with a dictionary close at hand. He read the Gospel of John four times through comparing each verse between the two Bibles.

Frey also attended the German speaking service at the Savoy on the Strand, where he enjoyed listening to Rev. Ringeltaube and Rev. Charles Steinkopff preach, and regularly attended the Jewish synagogues, 'to converse with them [the Jewish people] in Hebrew, German, or Dutch.' This experience often left him sad, and he further stated, 'Very often I returned to my abode weeping and lamenting over the deplorable condition of these my dear brethren and kinsmen according to the flesh.'[4] Slowly but surely his attention was drawn away from the Hottentots in Africa towards the Jewish people in London's East End.

It was as a result of this turmoil that on one occasion he confessed to Mr. Smith, 'Could I stay but one year in London, I believe I should be able to preach to the Jews in English, so as to make myself understood by them. And oh, happy I should be to declare unto them the word of salvation, if ever so much exposed to their hatred and persecution.'[5]

And in time Frey's desire came to pass. Rev. Ringeltaube, minister of the German service at the Savoy, became aware of Frey's dream at Gravesend, and advised Frey to write to Hardcastle and the Missionary Society directors concerning this desire. Ringeltaube also offered to assist with the translation into English.[6]

Frey agreed to this suggestion and subsequently sent a letter to the Directors of the Missionary Society, on 1 December. In the letter Frey stated:

> The hope that perhaps I might be permitted to stay one year in London, in order to set forth Jesus Christ and him crucified to my brethren after the flesh, fills my heart with joy... It could be in vain to attempt a narrative of what conversations have taken place between myself and those of my nation in the course of the last three years. May Jesus Christ the Blessed of the Lord, cause a blessing to rest on them all.
>
> The grounds on which I build my hopes of having the favour to preach the Gospel to the Jews, at some period near or distant, are the following:

---

3 Frey, *Narrative*, pp. 76-77. See Minutes for 21 September 1801.
4 Frey, *Narrative*, p. 79.
5 Frey, *Narrative*, p. 79.
6 Frey, *Narrative*, p. 80.

1. Altho' baptized Jews in general, as is well known, meet with nothing but scorn, opposition and persecution from their own people, yet I never met with anything of that kind hitherto; but on the contrary received repeated tokens of their goodwill, esteem, and confidence, and yet did I never fail to point out unto them the preferable state of a believer in Christ before that of the best of Jews.
2. I possess an intimate acquaintance of their religious system, their unbelief and superstitions.
3. I am convinced from experience that they will believe me sooner, than another Christian, because I make it a point to address them constantly from the Old Testament. I know also, they will open their hearts sooner to me, than to a stranger.
4. I cannot but rank among the reasons for my calling to preach to the Jews the saving Gospel of a crucified redeemer, that invincible desire I feel for doing so, and which I never could get rid of.

I have sometimes been brought to reflect on the dangers of soul and body, that await a Missionary among the Jewish nation, but constrained by the love of Jesus, I felt myself always disposed to make a tender of my temporal life for the benefit of those unhappy sons of Abraham, who are not worse, than I myself have been, and consequently may be recovered from their lost estate. And with respect to the life of my soul, I mean to trust it into his hands, who is the beginner, and will be the finisher of my faith, and whom I intreat, that wherever I shall be, among Jews or Heathens, he may cause His spirit to exhort, reprove, and chastise me, so that I may be preferred for the day of redemption.

Nor could I but take my as yet imperfect knowledge of the Scriptures into consideration, a circumstance which, however, important, does not dishearten me since I know that the Lord Jesus in ancient and modern times Has been pleased to save by the foolishness of preaching [to] perishing sinners and children of the Wicked One. I am determined never to engage in longwinded disputes, but to preach Christ crucified according to my own experience.[7]

The directors took Frey's request seriously and on 13 December 1801 he was permitted to present his request in person to the directors. Several other meetings on the subject followed and finally the directors decided on 21 December 1801[8] to accept Frey's request.

---

7 Correspondence file, Box 81, LMS Archives, SOAS, Frey to LMS Directors, 1 December 1801. This letter is somewhat different to that which Frey has in his *Narratives*, which he dates as 24 November, 1801. See Frey, *Narrative*, pp. 81-87.
8 See Minutes for 13 & 21 December 1801, LMS Archives, SOAS.

This decision by the Missionary Society directors was bold, given that their stated goal was bringing the message of Jesus to the 'heathen.' Prior to this the Missionary Society had been involved in ministry to French prisoners-of-war, but work amongst the Jewish community was going to be a new area altogether, a work never before attempted in Britain as it was now to be.

Frey at Gosport

Frey's first task was to receive further theological studies, and to learn the English language, at the Missionary Society Seminary at Gosport which was under the direction of prominent Congregational minister and Missionary Society stalwart, Rev. David Bogue. Frey left London on 28 February 1802 for this new step in his life.

Bogue was to be another of those Gentile Christians destined to play a prominent part in shaping Joseph Frey's life of faith. Frey wrote of Bogue, 'Would to God I had words to express the high esteem which I feel for that man of God, and the great obligations under which I am to him for the inestimable benefits which I derived, and do daily receive, from his most excellent lectures on various subjects; from his wise, prudent, and most judicious advice, and from his exemplary conduct, both as a Christian, and as a minister.'[9]

Frey's life for the following three years was filled with studies, including English, Greek and Latin. He also provided Hebrew lessons to his fellow students, and seeing as there was an unsatisfactory grammar book available, he set about composing one himself.

Life for Frey, though, was more than just studying. One day he made an excursion to nearby Portsea to interact with some of the Jewish people who lived there. He had the misfortune, however, of being apprehended by a policeman who sought for his license as a foreigner. The policeman happened to be Jewish! Frey's excuse that he had left his license at Gosport but that he was known to some people at Portsea wasn't enough – and he ended up being a guest of His Majesty's Prisons for the night. The night turned out to be somewhat adventurous, and he actually found himself praying 'in a most affectionate manner, for the brother Jew, who had imprisoned me.'[10]

Despite the inconvenience of the situation he stated that he never enjoyed a more comfortable sleep. Then the following day he held an impromptu service, singing a hymn and reading a chapter of the Scriptures from Matthew 26 and 27, expounding upon the fact that himself as a Jew had believed that Christ 'did not only die for our offenses, but also rose again for our justification.'[11]

Bogue, meanwhile, having been informed of Frey's predicament, managed to obtain his release. But the experience was to bear long term benefits, for two

---

9 Frey, *Judah and Israel*, p. 72.
10 Frey, *Narrative*, p. 94.
11 Frey, *Narrative*, p. 96.

years thereafter he was permitted on the Lord's Day to cross over from Gosport to Portsea and preach at the prison.

At their annual meeting in May 1805, the Missionary Society stated the following which then appeared in their Annual Report, regarding Frey's request to minister the gospel amongst his own people:

> None can so well enter into the feelings, the principles, and the strong prejudices of a Jew, as one who has himself been educated in that religion, and has also been converted to the faith of the Gospel: - None can be expected to commiserate with such strong sympathy their moral state – or devote himself to their relief with more sincere and ardent solicitude, than one of their own nation, who has himself been melted into contrition by looking unto him whom their Fathers pierced. It will also be a source of satisfaction to the Society, that a ministry is thus to be opened, which is immediately and specifically addressed to the ancient people of God, and thus a commencement made towards the discharge of that immense debt of obligation and gratitude, which Christians are under to the Jews, as the medium through which they have received the inestimable gift of the Sacred oracles. The degree of success which may ultimately arise out of this endeavour to promote conversion, we cheerfully refer to him whose wise and sovereign purpose has connected the salvation of Israel, with the fullness of the gentiles; and thus held out the encouraging intimation that the extensive communication of the Gospel to the Heathen, is the signal which invites the exertions of Christians in favour of the Jews also …[12]

Shortly afterwards Frey moved to London and began speaking about Jesus, the mediator of the New Covenant, to the lost sheep of the house of Israel.

Joseph Wolff hears about Jesus

While Joseph Frey was preparing for the next stage of his journey, Joseph Wolff experienced another move in his young life. In 1802 his father was transferred to Ullfeld in Bavaria. Of this period it was recorded:

> Here young Wolff daily listened, with the highest interest, to the conversation of his father, when the Jews assembled in his house in the evening time and he spoke to them about the future glory of their nation at the coming of the Messiah, and of their restoration to their own land; and also about the zeal of many rabbis who had travelled to Jerusalem and to Babylon as preachers to the Jewish nation.[13]

---

12 LMS Report, 1805, pp. 23-4.
13 Wolff, *Travels and Adventures*, p. 2.

Rabbi David also on one occasion spoke of a story from the *Talmud* which mentioned the name of Jesus. Young Joseph was intrigued about who this Jesus was, and his father replied, 'That he had been a Jew of the greatest talent, but, as he pretended to be the Messiah, the Jewish tribunal sentenced him to death.' Young Wolff then asked his father, "Why was Jerusalem destroyed and why are we in captivity?" His father replied, "Alas, alas, because the Jews murdered the prophets." Joseph reflected in his mind for some time, and the thought struck him, 'perhaps Jesus was also a prophet, and the Jews killed him when he was innocent!' – an idea that took such possession of him, that whenever he passed a Christian church, he would stand outside and listen to the preaching, until his mind became filled with the thought of being a great preacher like 'Mymomides and Judah-Haseed…'[14]

Joseph often asked questions, and his questioning led to his first real encounter with Jesus at the age of seven. Joseph's mother purchased milk from a barber and his wife, but, in order to ensure that nothing impure was placed in the milk, Joseph was supposed to remain while the cow was being milked. On one occasion, however, young Joseph grew tired of waiting, so he went inside and conversed with the barber and his wife, 'about Messiah, whom I expected every day, and who would again build the temple at Jerusalem.'[15]

The barber and his wife, being true Christians, 'heard me' Joseph recounts 'with patience and compassion,' and then said to him, "my dear child! You do not know the true Messiah; Jesus whom your fathers did crucify was the true Messiah, but they expected an earthly not a heavenly kingdom, and killed him as they did the prophets; if you would read your own prophets without prejudice you would be convinced."[16]

They also suggested that Joseph go home and read Isaiah 53 – which he did in the Hebrew and German-Hebrew (Yiddish), and thereupon said to his father, "Dear Father, tell me of whom does the prophet speak here?" His father did not answer, and Joseph then went into his room and wept. He also heard his father then say to his mother, "God have mercy upon us, our son will not remain a Jew."[17]

Those words and impressions lit a light in young Joseph's soul which would not thereafter be extinguished. He now became confused and said to himself, "it is true Jews killed and persecuted the prophets because my father himself told me so. – Perhaps Jesus Christ was killed innocent." Indeed thereafter he did consider that Jesus had been 'unjustly put to death as the holy prophets had been, and that he was the true Messiah, and that Jews were rejected wanderers

---

14 Wolff, *Travels and Adventures*, p. 4. Mymomides = Maimonides.
15 Wolff, *Life and Journal*, p. 6.
16 Wolff, *Life and Journal*, p. 6.
17 Wolff, *Travels and Adventures*, p. 6.

driven from Jerusalem *because* they rejected him.'[18]

Joseph's curiosity was now piqued to such an extent that soon afterwards he went to the local Lutheran clergyman and told him, "I will become a X-n [Christian]." The minister upon ascertaining that Joseph was only eight years old, then informed him that, 'I was too young, and bade me return to him after a few years.'[19]

---

18 Wolff, *Life and Journal*, pp. 6-7.
19 Wolff, *Life and Journal*, p. 7.

CHAPTER 9

JEWISH MINISTRY WITHIN THE MISSIONARY SOCIETY

Frey's early endeavours in London

Shortly after moving to London in May 1805 Frey was introduced to two Jewish ladies who had become followers of Jesus and were attending different congregations in the city. Together with these and three Gentile-background Christians, he began a weekly prayer meeting in his own apartment. A year later he moved to the Zion Chapel.

As Frey had no designated place of worship he would preach and minister in various congregations around the city. But then from 6 July 1805 he also began a weekly lecture designated for Jewish people at Rev. Mr Ball's chapel on Jewry Street in Aldgate. The Missionary Society reported concerning this new initiative:

> These lectures ... consist principally of an explanation of the types and ceremonies of the Jewish dispensation; a statement of Christian doctrine, and an exposition of select portions of Scripture; and to this plan he has generally adhered: It has also been his custom on these occasions, to read a part of the Old Testament in the Hebrew language, and then pronounce the translation of it in English, sentence by sentence, accompanying the whole with suitable remarks. These lectures have been well attended, but principally by Christians. For a few weeks after their commencement, a considerable number of the house of Israel were present. This number afterwards decreased, as might have been expected, from various causes. Some of them had not courage enough to stand against the insults, mocking, and imprecations, to which they were exposed by their brethren who crowded the street; and many were prevented from attending by their superiors and relations.[1]

It wasn't long before the Jewish authorities prohibited attendance at synagogue of any individuals known to attend these lectures. In addition, any attendees were threatened, watched and occasionally punished. In the tightly knit Jewish community most people were unwilling to risk social ostracism, and stopped

---

1 Missionary Society Report, 1806, pp. 27-8. Frey, *Judah and Israel*, pp. 73-4.

any association with Frey's initiatives.²

Some individuals, though, were willing to run that risk, and in September 1806 three who had attended the lectures were publicly baptised, two in the Zion Chapel, and one in the Hoxton Chapel. One of these was Hannah Cohen, who later became Mrs. Frey.³ Three other Jewish people also attended 'and gave full evidence of their conversion to God.'⁴

Frey Seeks New Initiatives

Although many within the Missionary Society supported the object of introducing Jewish people to Jesus, the mediator of the New Covenant, some objected to funds being directed to this work. Others did not appreciate time in the Committee meetings being diverted away from the real calling of the Missionary Society - ministry to the 'heathen'.⁵

In accordance with these concerns the Missionary Society directors agreed on 13 August 1806 to form a Jewish Auxiliary Committee 'for the purpose of assisting Mr. Frey in the objects of the Jewish Mission.'⁶ This move amounted to the detachment of the Jewish work to be that of an adjunct of the ministry of the Missionary Society.

This sub-committee soon had its first challenge. It was apparent that the decrease in those attending Frey's lectures was caused by the opposition from the Jewish leadership. Several of those who wished to continue attending the lectures and having contact with Frey then applied to the Missionary Society for support and protection.

This was because if someone came to follow Jesus and were baptized they were sure to be cut off from contact with the Jewish community and even from their own families. Many of these prospective followers of Jesus had no profession by which they could earn a living, and would be left in a very untenable position as they would not be fully accepted in either community. They would be rejected by the Jewish community as being a *meshummad* (traitor), and not fully accepted by the Gentile Christian community, who would often be suspicious of them - especially if they wanted to retain their Jewish identity.

Most Christians or Gentiles would not employ a Jewish person unless they were of proven character, and in many instances it would require time and training before a new Jewish follower of Jesus had developed the skills necessary to be successful.

---

2 Frey was also frustrated at the lack of consistency in these lectures as he was often compelled by the directors to go on trips throughout Britain to preach and raise support for the Missionary Society. See Frey, *Judah and Israel*, p. 73.
3 As David Eichhorn points out, they must have married shortly after, as their first child, John Frey, was born on 6 September 1807. See Eichhorn, D. *Evangelizing the American Jew*, (New York, 1978) p. 21.
4 Frey, *Judah and Israel*, p. 74.
5 Frey, *Narrative*, pp. 104-5.
6 LMS Minutes, 13 August 1806.

Frey was now finding himself in a difficult predicament, not altogether that different from what he himself faced in Germany when he first became a follower of Jesus. He stated, 'Every application of the Jews produced opposite sensations in my mind: whilst, on the one hand, I rejoiced whenever one of my dear brethren called on me: on the other hand, my heart was overwhelmed with grief, on account of the above-mentioned difficulties.'[7] Frey therefore desired the Missionary Society to assist him in finding suitable employment for seekers or new followers of Jesus.

The *Free School* and further Jewish Opposition

In January 1807 a *Free School* for Jewish children was opened. In just a few months up to thirteen Jewish children were in attendance. *Free Schools* were common in London. Since the early 18th century such institutions were established by wealthy patrons to assist poverty stricken children. The object was to provide a basic Christian education, to teach the children to read and write, and even to provide them with an apprenticeship.

The socio-economic situation of the Jewish community in many ways reflected the wider community. Many Jewish emigrants had come to England and often the children ended up eking out an existence by begging in the streets, or worse still, becoming minor criminals. Many of these children had no education, and had no chance of ever receiving one.

This new initiative received considerable Jewish opposition, with the Chief Rabbi, Dr. Solomon Hirschel preaching against it in the Great Synagogue on 3 January 1807, and also by sending circular letters throughout Britain.[8] The Jewish community was so upset that they sent a delegation to meet Mr. Hardcastle, the Missionary Society treasurer, 'to declare their intention to obstruct this object.'[9]

Rabbi Hirschel then sent out a second edict on 10 January, stating very clearly the harsh consequences for any Jewish person who sent their child to the Missionary Society school.[10] The opposition from the Jewish leadership had the desired effect, and for two years thereafter no new children were added to the original number.

Frey's work encountered opposition and difficulty at every corner. Despite these obstacles the Missionary Society continued to give the Jewish work their support. In their 1807 Report the Missionary Society stated:

> The time will come when "the branches of the true olive," though broken off for a season, "shall be grafted in again;" and if their having been "cast away for a time," has been for "the reconciling of the world, what shall their reception be, but life from the dead?" The attempt is yet in its infancy;

---

7 Frey, *Narrative*, p. 104.
8 Frey, *Narrative*, pp. 114-5.
9 LMS Report, 1807, pp. 32-3.
10 Frey, *Narrative*, pp. 116-7.

great difficulties have occurred, and are likely to occur; yet the Directors trust that, acquiring knowledge by experience, and by patient continuance in well-doing, they shall reap a joyful harvest, if they faint not.[11]

Meanwhile, as Frey was endeavouring to establish a foundation, he came into contact with others who were interested in supporting his ministry and who were not associated with the Missionary Society.

Joseph Wolff continues his quest for truth

While the one Joseph was encountering such opposition in London, the other Joseph was continuing on his journey in Germany to discover the true Messiah of Israel. In 1806 Rabbi David became rabbi of Württemberg and Joseph thereupon was sent by him to study at the Protestant Lyceum at Stuttgart, where he learned Latin, Greek and Hebrew.[12]

Joseph did not remain there for long, as his father then sent him to Bamberg where he stayed for some time with a cousin, Moses Cohen, and his wife. Moses Cohen had been influenced by the Enlightenment, and indulged in reading the classics as well as Immanuel Kant, Goethe and Schiller. Cousin Moses appreciated Joseph's desire to read and seek understanding, so introduced him to a Roman Catholic Lyceum.

On one occasion Joseph spoke with several Deists who informed him, 'we are not obliged to observe Moses' law, he was an imposter, Jews and X-ns [Christians] have the same moral principles.' In response Joseph stated, he 'did not agree especially as to Moses' yet he did thereafter disregard Jewish ceremonies and began to doubt the necessity of revelation.[13]

At the Lyceum Joseph was deeply impressed one day by a lecture from Rev. Father Nepff about the conversion of Saul on the road to Damascus. In his lecture Nepff stated that 'the church of Christ contained people who trod in the footsteps of Paul: Francis Xavier and Ignatius Loyola, and the many missionaries who went forth to preach the gospel of Christ to the nations.'[14] Joseph returned home and informed cousin Moses and his wife, "My mind is made up. I will become a Christian and be a Jesuit; and I will preach the Gospel in foreign lands, like Francis Xavier."[15]

While his cousin Moses laughed at him and called him an enthusiast, Moses' wife became angry and evicted him from the house. Joseph, now penniless, set out towards Wurzberg. Before arriving at this destination, he was befriended by a Roman Catholic shepherd, who took him in for the night and although a poor man himself, still gave Joseph enough money to proceed on to Frankfurt.

11 LMS Report 1807, p. 33.
12 In Wolff, *Life and Journal*, ibid, p.7, he stated that he was sent to a wealthy Jewish lady in Germany 'who intended to have me taught latin and talmud, that I might be a rabbi and physician to Jews'.
13 Wolff, *Life and Journal*, p. 7.
14 Wolff, *Travels and Adventures*, p .7.
15 Wolff, *Travels and Adventures*, p. 7.

Formation of an *Auxiliary Committee*

Meanwhile in London, the Jewish Committee of the Missionary Society passed a resolution on 13 August 1807 permitting Frey to 'unite with some gentlemen' and also to follow-up contact with various Jewish applicants and, if necessary, find employment for them.[16] This resolution permitted Frey to attach himself and his task to others, not necessarily directly associated with the Missionary Society, who could support his ministry.

These would-be supporters met at Frey's home in September 1807, the first such meeting of what became known as the *Auxiliary Committee*. Those present were specifically burdened with the work amongst the Jewish people, as distinct from the Missionary Society directors and even the Jewish Committee of the Missionary Society, for whom this work was but an adjunct of the Missionary Society.

The present obstacles to Frey's work, due to the prohibition following Rabbi Hirschel's proclamation, and then a letter from an impoverished Jewish father of six children asking for assistance, encouraged members of the *Auxiliary Committee* to put together some plans for the future. Frey and his *Auxiliary Committee* were concerned that the children in the *Free School* would return each day to unsympathetic homes, where the good influences of the day at school would be quickly dissipated.[17] At a meeting of the *Auxiliary Committee* held in September 1807, it was resolved, 'That several of its members should deliver their judgement at the next meeting, on the following three questions, for the purpose of submitting a plan to the Jewish Committee.' These questions were:

1. The practicability of establishing a boarding school for Jewish children including a school of industry.
2. The best means of providing employment for the destitute, if a manufactory of any sort could be established.
3. The expediency of procuring a Place of Worship for Mr. Frey in order to raise a Church.[18]

In mid-October 1807 Frey on behalf of the *Auxiliary Committee* submitted a plan to the Jewish Committee. He began his submission by stating, 'It has pleased God in his infinite mercy and wise providence to choose you out of all other Societies in the world to send the glorious gospel of the Blessed God to the children of Abraham residing in this country.' But, he continued, 'can you be satisfied with 12 children in the school whilst at least 50 or 100 might share the same unspeakable blessings? God forbid! But however desirous the Society

16 Frey, *Narrative*, p. 118.
17 Frey, *Narrative*, p. 124.
18 See Meeting of Committee 30 Sept 1807 in Letters and Correspondence, Box 81. In Frey's *Narrative*, p. 122, it is dated 7 October 1807. This Church would be primarily for Jewish followers of Jesus and here we see an initial seed for the forthcoming Hebrew Christian-Messianic Jewish movement.

may be of obtaining this important desirable object it appears impracticable upon the present plan of the school for the following reasons.'

Frey then mentioned as reasons why the present plan for the school was impracticable: Firstly, that at present only the children of poor Jewish children could attend. This class of people, he stated 'set very little value upon education, whether religious, moral or civil.' Secondly, that the children by the age of eight or nine would be needed to help earn money for the welfare of the family, a benefit which the parents would lose if they were sent to school. Thirdly, that the repeated prohibitions by the 'Rabbi and rulers of the synagogue' are great hindrances. Fourthly, that many parents live a long way out and can't always get their children there. And fifthly, that some Jewish people in the country might desire to have their children educated at the Missionary Society school, but the present plan would be unsatisfactory for such a purpose.

In conclusion Frey wrote:

> To remove at once all these difficulties, and obtain the desirable object, nothing seems necessary but to establish a school upon a larger scale, to board, clothe, and educate the children till a certain age, and then bring them forward into suitable situations among Christians. The establishment of such a school is, therefore, submitted to the most serious consideration of the committee, and it is hoped will meet with the approbation of the society.[19]

Seven benefits of such an institution are then given by Frey.[20] He knew instinctively what one major concern of the directors would be with this grandiose scheme – finances. Hence he concludes with these amazing words, which point to how Frey saw this work and vision as a child of both the British and German Evangelical revivals:

> "Faith ... but as a grain of mustard seed will overcome Mountains of difficulties." By faith professor Franck laid the foundation of a most expensive orphan house in Halle, and was not confounded. By faith and exertions Mr Whitefield erected both Tabernacles and orphan houses in England and America. By faith a few individuals put a letter into the Magazine, which produced the Missionary Society, against which the gates of Hell shall not be able to prevail. And are the treasures of him who said, 'the Silver and the Gold is mine,' exhausted? Or will the known liberality of Britons be withheld from the Jews, to whom pertain the adoption; and the glory; and the covenants; and the giving of the Law; and the service of God; and the promises; whose are the fathers, and of whom as concerning the

---

19 Frey, *Narrative*, p. 140.
20 Seven according to a copy of his letter found in the Letters and Correspondence file of Box 81 at the LMS archives, but eight are listed by Frey in his *Narrative*, p. 140.

flesh Christ came, who is over all, God blessed forever. No God forbid. The joy and liberality manifested by Christians, of various denominations, when hearing but of 10 children in the school, assures [sic] us of the supplies [sic] of all our wants when hearing of an increase from 10 to 50 or 100... [21]

Frey's submission to the Missionary Society directors was followed soon afterwards by one on 16 October 1807 by the *Ladies Committee for Jewish Affairs*, the purpose of which was, 'For the purpose of considering of a plan for the future benefit of the Jewesses under their care.' One of the points raised by the ladies was, 'To propose to the gentlemen that a House be provided in some eligible situation for the females Institution.'[22] The ladies with a concern for the Jewish people saw the need for a house or school of industry where Jewish girls could learn a trade or industry.

The Jewish Committee of the Missionary Society met on 19 October 1807 to consider these two memoranda - Frey's plan and the request from the *Ladies Committee*. There was considerable discussion. In the minds of many, it seemed inconceivable that extra money would be released for these plans at a time when whatever meagre resources which were available should be prioritized for work amongst the 'heathen.'[23]

At this point, while the directors were considering this plan, Frey submitted a request for financial assistance. Although Frey acknowledged that since having come under the patronage of the Society they had supplied all his wants, yet he now found himself 90 pounds in debt.[24] Frey does not elaborate as to why he was in debt, but it may be that he utilized his own resources to supply the need lacking in the ministry.[25]

Disappointment sets in

The Jewish Committee of the Missionary Society met on 12 February 1808 and resolved that, 1) the lease of the chapel on Artillery Street should be bought for the use of the Jewish people, 2) that some rules or regulations regarding the school should be laid before the directors at their next meeting, and 3) that the request by the Jewish gentleman for his children to be received into a boarding school be declined.[26]

Although the decision on the third resolution upset Frey, he was relieved that according to the second resolution, the Society intended to do something about the school. Frey then wrote his plan for the *Free School*, coupled with

21 Memoir about Jewish School sent by Joseph Frey to the LJS Directors, 19 October 1807, in Letters and Correspondence, Box 81, LMS Archives, SOAS.
22 Letter from Ladies Committee for Jewish Affairs to the Directors, in 'Letters and Correspondence', dated 16 Oct 1807, and LMS Committee Minutes for 19 Oct 1807.
23 LMS Committee Minutes for 19 Oct 1807.
24 Frey to LMS directors, 23 October 1807. In Correspondence, LMS Archives.
25 Correspondence file, LMS archives, Box 81.
26 Frey, *Narrative*, p. 143.

suggestions as to how the extra funds for such an enterprise were to be raised.[27]

The representatives of the Jewish Committee met shortly after receiving this submission and appeared agreeable for Joseph and Mrs. Frey to take twelve children under their care and to lodge with them. Three of the Committee members and Frey then located a suitable apartment for this venture.

These recommendations from the Jewish Committee were, however, then overturned by the General Committee of the Missionary Society – in particular that there would be no charity school added to the *Free School*. According to Frey the chief reason was that no more money could be spared for the Jewish work.

This set-back prompted Frey to offer to raise the extra funds himself, to which several of the directors then charged Frey 'with threatening to establish a society in opposition.'[28] The Missionary Society directors finally concluded that Frey's plan was not feasible.[29]

The whole concept of a boarding school for Jewish children was very important for Frey, and from this point a deep disappointment beset him. As a result of his activities being curtailed due to the prohibition from Rabbi Hirschel, this initiative offered a step forward. Now this initiative was curtailed by his own General Committee.

Frey's annoyance in this attitude of the General Committee was due to his own understanding of just how difficult it was for Jewish people to overcome the obstacles and prejudices against Jesus and what they perceived as a Gentile Christian system, and how difficult it was for them after becoming followers of Jesus. He believed the Church and Christian society should do all they could to facilitate Jewish people hearing about Jesus. Frey later wrote in his book *Judah and Israel*, that 'the general conversion of the world will not take place till after the conversion of the Jewish nation.'[30]

Frey now resolved to leave the matter of the charity school behind him, and to concentrate upon his ministry at the chapel located at Artillery Street. On 15 April 1808 this chapel was opened for divine service and he preached his first sermon there. Frey also taught the children each Sunday, as well as giving evening lectures there on Fridays and holding a prayer-meeting on Tuesday evenings. It could be said that this was the very first 'Messianic' congregation in the modern period – albeit within a Gentile Church framework.

Several of the Missionary Society directors believed that merely by holding regular preaching at the chapel that Jewish people, like other people in London, would attend. But very few Jewish people actually attended such services. Once again Frey's ministry was seemingly impaired by a lack of understanding from

27 Frey, *Narrative*, pp. 145-6.
28 Frey, *Narrative*, p. 149.
29 Frey, *Narrative*, pp. 141 –150.
30 Frey, *Judah and Israel*, pp. 215-217.

some of the Missionary Society directors concerning the difficulties involved in ministry among Jewish people.

Initially a number of supportive Gentile Christians attended the services on a regular basis. But as there was no ordained minister there who could administer baptism and Communion, these too began to dissipate. So here was a chapel, now leased by the Missionary Society, in which little active outreach was taking place. The Jewish Committee therefore purposed to form a committee for supervising the affairs of the chapel, of which Frey was a member, and which met on 10 June 1808. This Chapel Committee soon realized they needed to ascertain from the parent body their real object for this institution. The General Committee had already resolved on 8 June 1808 that Frey 'should be ordained, generally, to the Christian ministry, but with an especial reference to its exercise to the Jewish people …'[31]

Just prior to these developments the fourteenth annual Report of the Missionary Society was released, in May 1808. In the Report the following was stated: 'Among the objects committed by the Society to the care of the Directors, the Mission to the Jews is not, in their estimation, the least important. It presents, indeed, peculiar difficulties, which experience shews [sic] to be no less formidable than in anticipation they were supposed to be…'[32]

The directors also expressed the difficulties facing new Jewish followers of Jesus 'whose attendance upon the Christian ministry deprives them of their ordinary means of subsistence among the members of their own nation. This' they continued, '… is an impediment which no attention, on the part of the Directors alone, can effectually remove.'[33]

The directors indeed may not be able to remove this impediment, but Frey thought he could. Herein lay Frey's frustration – he didn't think the directors wanted to assist him to remove this impediment.

---

31 Found in Frey, *Narrative,* p. 164.
32 Report of the Directors to the Fourteenth General Meeting of The Missionary Society, May 12, 1808, (London, 1808), p. 31.
33 Missionary Society Report 1808, ibid, p. 33.

Chapter 10

The Parting of the Way

Seeds of separation

Frey had much support and understanding from those in the *Auxiliary Committee*. These people, which included a Missionary Society stalwart Mr William Stevens, sympathized with his objective of reaching out to the poor Jewish people in tangible ways. Stevens wrote to Frey at this time and stated that it was unworkable to combine ministry to the Jewish people alongside ministry to the 'heathen.' The two, in his opinion, needed to be totally separated.[1]

The Jewish Committee of the Missionary Society meanwhile met on 14 July 1808 and passed a number of resolutions, which were not totally acceptable to Frey. Then at this juncture two issues arose which would have considerable bearing upon Frey's future direction.

First, he came into contact with Dr. Draper, who had supervised a society involved in charity, but who now was no longer able to do so. A number of the subscribers for this charity wished to consider supporting a similar charity to the poor. Stevens and another gentleman had both previously supported Dr Draper's charity, so now they suggested that Frey form 'a society for visiting and relieving the sick and distressed, and instructing the ignorant, especially such as were of the Jewish nation.'[2]

The second issue was a request made by the congregation at Artillery Street Chapel to Frey, signed by sixty-two congregants, for him to become their pastor.[3] It seemed that Joseph Frey was now being set up for effective ministry.

Challenges for young Joseph Wolff

While Frey was contemplating these new options, Joseph Wolff, while studying in Frankfurt, informed a Protestant professor that 'my only wish was to be instructed in the Gospel and baptized and enabled by studying latin (sic) and greek (sic) to preach it.' The Professor replied to this heart-felt request, "it is not necessary to become a X-n! (sic – Christian) because Christ was only a great man like Luther, and you can be a moral man without being a X-n, and that is all that is necessary!"[4] Young Joseph was stunned.

This answer seemed to contradict what he had previously heard from Christians, but was somewhat in accordance with what he heard from non-Christians. It

---

1 Stevens to Frey, *Narrative*, pp. 155-6.
2 Frey, *Narrative*, p. 160.
3 Frey, *Narrative*, p. 162.
4 Wolff, *Life and Journey*, p. 8.

was no surprise that for the following three months Wolff learnt Hebrew, Greek and Latin without any great enthusiasm and at the end of that period became quite seriously ill.

It was while in hospital that young Joseph then 'began to reflect about eternity' and resolved thereupon to be different. The first stage of this resolve was to visit his father, but he then learnt that his father had died. Next was to visit Halle and seek out Professor Knapp at the university. Knapp immediately asked Joseph, "Do you know Christ? He is God over all. If you do not believe this you commit a great sin by becoming a X-n."[5]

Wolff then began to earnestly study among Protestant students, and although he heard many contrary opinions about the person of Jesus, the teaching of Professor Knapp satisfied him. The professor challenged Joseph, "Young man, if you would become a Christian, merely because you believe that Jesus Christ was a great philosopher, remain what you are. But if you believe that Jesus Christ is the Son of God, and God above all, blessed for ever – then pray to God that this belief may penetrate into your heart and soul."[6]

Despite having now found a place in which to learn and study, life in Halle was not without its trials – from secularist 'Christians', from some of his Jewish brethren who often persecuted him, and from his own very active mind. Joseph was on a journey, and this journey was traversing both the Jewish and Christian worlds. He was yet to determine to which world he truly belonged.

Initial formation of the London (Jews) Society[7]

Joseph Frey was also continuing his journey at this time. On 4 August 1808 Frey, Stevens as well as Messrs Cooper, Fearn, Pearce, Smith and Wood met at the Artillery Street Chapel and resolved, 'That a society be immediately formed which shall be called "The London Society for visiting and relieving the Sick and distressed and instructing the ignorant especially such as are of the Jewish Nation."'[8]

It was also resolved that Frey would be President and Samuel Fearn would be the treasurer, and a managing committee would be formed.[9] A short address put together by this committee of the London (Jews) Society stated:

> The Conversion of the Jews to Christianity ... is a most desirable object.

---

5 Wolff, *Life and Journal*, pp. 8-9.
6 Wolff, *Travels and Adventures*, p. 9.
7 Although the name London (Jews) Society is not used as such in the original sources, I have employed it at this point in order to minimize confusion between the two entities.
8 LJS Minute Book A, 4 August 1808, Bodleian Library.
9 LJS Minute Book A, 4 August 1808, Bodleian Library. The Committee was comprised of Frey, Mr Thomas Ackland, Mr Chambers, Mr Cooper, Mr Fearn, Mr S. Parkinson, Mr J. Pearce, Mr Smith, Mr William Stevens and Mr S Wood. A second meeting was held on 11 August, to which Mr. Joseph Fox was added to the committee.

The certainty of its accomplishment, and that such effects will flow there from, no one who believes in the Bible can doubt for a single moment ... It is true, we cannot point out the exact time when ALL ISRAEL shall be saved, yet it is certain that a remnant is to be called in our day ...

By the preaching of the Gospel, we hope the Missionary Society has laid a foundation for the conversion of the Jews, against which the gates of Hell will never be able to prevail. To assist in raising the superstructure, by joining the other means before-mentioned, and also to be useful to distressed Christians, is the design of the London Society, on behalf of which the Committee now solicit the aid of a liberal Public.

The obligations of Christians of all denominations to promote the conversion of the Jews are more than could be mentioned in this short Address ... [10]

Shortly afterwards Frey and Stevens met with Mr Alers of the Missionary Society to inform him of the formation of the London (Jews) Society and to assure him of their intention of it being 'carried on in *union* and *harmony* with the Missionary Society.'[11] Frey also stated to the Missionary Society leaders that if they restrained him from uniting with others and *"limit my exertions for the benefit of the Jews, I shall then be under the painful necessity of leaving the Missionary Society, and accept of the call above-mentioned, and be ordained as an Independent minister."*[12]

Frey was now gradually moving away from the Missionary Society. This inference, alongside the formation of the London (Jews) Society, indicated that some crucial plan had now to be developed in order for the Missionary Society to establish its authority over Frey. The Missionary Society directors were also undecided how to proceed with Frey's request for ordination until it became clear what Frey's connection would be with them.[13]

The wording of Frey's letter seems to indicate the influence of others. It would be very doubtful that Frey, after having been so devoted to the Missionary Society for seven years, despite some problems, would have made such a bold statement on his own accord. He would surely have had considerable assurance from others that he would be taken care of if in fact he did sever his relationship with the Missionary Society.

There is a strong hint of this in a communication he sent to Mr Townsend soon afterwards in which he stated that he had 'been much encouraged by finding several most respectable persons, both in the established Church as well as out of it', who had supported his plan and who were 'willing to exert

---

10 An Address from the Committee of the London Society to the Friends of the Jews with A Plan of the Institution, Missionary Society Archives, Box 81.
11 Frey, *Narrative*, p. 163.
12 Frey to Rev. G Burder, 18 August, 1808, in *Narrative*, ibid, pp. 164-5. This letter was read at the LMS meeting on 22 August 1808. See Missionary Society Minutes for 22 August 1808.
13 See *Circular Paper*, in Frey, *Narrative*, p. 223.

themselves in raising a Fund for that purpose.'

Frey also then drew attention to a very important factor in this developing situation, adding, 'But ... none of them would unite with the Mission to the Jews except it be wholly separated from the mission to the Heathen; and a Society formed from among the Directors of the Missionary Society, and others, whom they may think proper to associate with themselves; having for its object the Conversion of the Jews.'[14]

Bogue's challenging letter

On 26 August 1808 Frey received a letter from his mentor, Rev David Bogue. Bogue was clearly upset with Frey and began by stating that he trembled for Frey's future, and that he was 'standing on the brink of a precipice; a few steps more, and you are undone.' Bogue reminded Frey of the investment of the Missionary Society in him for the last six years, and that this investment was so that Frey "*should be their missionary to the jews* [sic]; *and under their direction, preach the gospel to them in England, or abroad, as God may open a door.*" Bogue reminded Frey that the Missionary Society had recently established him in a place of his own in which to preach.[15]

If Frey left the Missionary Society, Bogue wrote, his character would be ruined, as the Christian public would consider that he had used the Missionary Society as a tool 'while you needed their help; and when you thought you could do without them, you cast them off, and looked for more liberal patrons.' Further, Bogue continues, Frey would be cast off by most of his friends, and pulpits everywhere would be closed to him and even in those still open to him 'you will be looked upon with suspicion and distrust.'[16]

Bogue revealed his complete opposition to Frey's plan 'of setting up a *boarding-school* for Jewish children, and supporting everyone who professed to have a regard to Christianity,' which he felt was 'bribing people to be Christians.'[17] For Bogue the main goal of missionary work was, 'The preaching of the gospel' which was 'the grand means of conversion; and where that prevails not, nothing is done.'

Bogue believed that Frey was too attached to his own way.[18] Indeed Frey clung to his idea of a charity or boarding school for Jewish children with a passion, even though it was clear there was considerable opposition to such a plan.

But did Frey's plan really involve bribing people to become Christians? Frey

---

14 Frey to Mr. J. Townsend, 28 November 1808, Missionary Society Archives, Box 81. A meeting then took place on 26 August 1808 between representatives of the two Societies. See Frey, *Narrative*, pp. 167-68.
15 Bogue to Frey, 26 August, 1808, in Frey, *Narrative*, p. 169.
16 Bogue to Frey, ibid, p. 171.
17 Bogue to Frey, ibid, p. 172.
18 Bogue to Frey, ibid, pp. 172-3.

himself does not think so, and clearly stated that it was his intention that Jewish people who believed in Jesus 'ought to be assisted in one way or other, to obtain a livelihood amongst Christians by *labour and industry alone*.'[19]

There is little doubt that Bogue's letter summed up the feelings of many of the Missionary Society directors, especially his concluding comment, 'Remember, there is no stability in any of your plans and views, however flattering they may be: *the work will have stability and duration under the Missionary Society alone*.'[20]

Towards a Final Split

During the last months of 1808 there were numerous meetings of both Societies, communicating fresh plans and proposals, all with the purpose of trying to work out a satisfactory solution whereby the objects of both Societies could be achieved.

The climax occurred on 19 December 1808 when Frey again submitted his Plan – and the Missionary Society directors again refused to endorse it completely, especially the proposal for a boarding school. This was the final blow for him, and he requested a meeting with the directors.

Frey was summoned to appear before the Missionary Society directors on 9 January 1809, whereupon he requested some explanation concerning their resolution of 19 December 1808. Frey stated that he felt only part of his letter had been noticed "and wished to know if the Directors intended making any alteration in their proceedings respecting the Jews – if not," he continued "he had got his resignation in his pocket, which he should give in." At that point the chairman informed him "that the Directors had considered the whole of his Letter – but out of kindness and tenderness to him, they did not put a direct negative upon those proposals which they disapproved of – and affectionately intreated him to consider the matter seriously before he determined on sending in his resignation."[21]

Now there was honesty. Frey asked for a direct answer and he received one. The Missionary Society directors had finally and conclusively stated their opposition to his 'Plan'. Frey now knew he had only one course of action left. On 16 January 1809 he sent his letter of resignation to Rev. Burder.[22]

Now there was no turning back. The Missionary Society was entrenched in its opinion that *their* plan for the Jewish ministry was the only viable plan, that they could not back the plan of Frey and the London (Jews) Society. Conversely Frey and his supporters were entrenched in their way and they could not see how the Jewish work could proceed within the narrow confines imposed upon

---

19 Frey, *Narrative*, p. 181.
20 Bogue to Frey, ibid, pp. 174-5. It is unclear if the italics were in the original or are Frey's own insertion.
21 Missionary Society Minutes 9 January 1809.
22 Missionary Society Minutes for 23 January 1809.

the work by the Missionary Society directors.

As sad as this situation was, it was probably the inevitable conclusion, as ministry amongst Jewish people and among Gentile people required separate principles. The London (Jews) Society actually stated this was a far better arrangement, as their 'attention is undividedly directed to one end.' That one end was the Jewish people, and the Jewish people alone.[23]

The London (Jews) Society held its fifth meeting on 15 February 1809, whereupon the Committee resolved that in view of Frey intimating that his service with the Missionary Society would terminate shortly, then 'in future this Society shall be denominated The London Society for the Promotion of Christianity amongst the Jews.' Frey, Stevens and Fox were then 'requested to prepare a prospectus which shall embrace the particular objects of this Society …'[24]

One of the last official acts of the relationship between Joseph Frey and the Missionary Society took place at the Missionary Society committee meeting on 27 February 1809, when the 'Jewish Committee reported that Mr Frey having requested to know whether he should preach at Artillery Street Chapel on the Sabbath Day after the Quarter Day next, they have agreed to inform him that the Committee would provide preachers.'[25] Rev. Burder then formally wrote to Frey on 28 February 1809 informing him that his services with the Missionary Society would cease as of Lady Day next. Frey accordingly preached his last sermon at Artillery Street Chapel under the patronage of the Missionary Society, on Friday 24 March. Frey wrote of this final meeting:

> This concluding service was honoured with the presence of no less than six directors of the Missionary Society, although during my ministry, for the two preceding years, I do not recollect that two ever attended, and not even *one* more than twice or three times.[26]

The parting of the way between Frey and the Missionary Society was not completely satisfactory. Yet one is reminded of a situation many centuries before involving Paul and Barnabas, who parted following a difference of opinion, and went their own way. Thereafter there were four men taking the good news of Jesus out into the Mediterranean world whereas previously there had been just the two.

Now there were two ministries working amongst the Jewish people in London, one being supported by people from the Dissenting Church, and the other

23 LJS Archives, Bodleian Library, c.5, No 7.
24 London Society Minutes for 15 February 1809, Minute Book A. Henceforth LJS Minutes.
25 Missionary Society Minutes 27 February 1809. The committee also resolved that 'Mr Burder and Mr Buck be requested to draw up a Statement of the Case between Mr Frey and the Society for general circulation amongst the friends of the Society.'
26 Frey, *Narrative*, p. 219.

being supported by people from both the Dissenting and Established Churches.

It remained now to be seen if Bogue's assessment about Frey and the London (Jews) Society would prove correct, or if it would actually survive and perhaps even prosper.

Chapter 11

The London (Jews) Society

Official beginning of the London Jews Society

At the meeting of the London Jews Society Committee on 1 March 1809 the rules were drawn up and office bearers established. Samuel Fearn was the treasurer, Joseph Fox the secretary, and Joseph Frey the president.[1]

Frey resigned from the presidency shortly afterwards, preferring, he stated 'to be a member of the Committee and in the hope that some Gentlemen of Piety, rank and influence may hereafter be induced to become the President, vice-Presidents of this Society.'[2]

Letters were then written to bishops and known Evangelical Christians in senior high positions.[3] Only several months had passed before the name of Evangelical Britain's favourite son, William Wilberforce, appeared in the Minutes[4] and an invitation given for him to become a vice-President of the new Society.

Although Frey stepped down from the prestigious position of presidency, he was not neglected, and the General Committee resolved that he would receive £100 a year for lecturing and £100 a year for other services rendered. This was an indication that Frey and his family would be well looked after financially.[5]

Official theological position

There is little doubt that the formation of the London Jews Society was due greatly to the millennial anticipation of the times, on all manner of subjects related to Israel's restoration and the last days. Yet there was a collective agreement that they were involved in a work related to the words of Paul in Romans 11, that there was to be a large turning of the Jewish people to the Messiah. In the first written report of the London Jews Society, written on 23 May 1809, the Society stated:

> At this awful and momentous crisis, when the hand of God is evidently stretched out, and his arm uplifted, to strike some great, perhaps, decisive blow, tending to the accomplishment of his mysterious and vast designs in the kingdoms of the world; and whilst Christians are looking with a dim, but attentive eye, for the fulfillment of that glorious promise, *that all*

---

1 See Missionary Society Archives, Box 81 & LJS Minute Book A, for 1 March 1809.
2 LJS Minutes, 17 March 1809, Minute Book A.
3 LJS Minutes 9 June 1809, Minute Book A.
4 LJS Minutes, 28 July 1809. Ibid.
5 LJS Minutes 17 March, 1809, ibid.

shall know God, from the least unto the greatest; to be constant in prayer, that his kingdom may indeed be set up in the hearts of all mankind; and more especially in the hearts of his once chosen and highly favoured people, the Jews. It is well known that many Christians have entertained this feeling already; and the London Society are justified, in appealing to the wisdom and judgment of the Missionary Society (amongst others) as a sufficient authority for the propriety of the general principle, THAT THE TIME IS COME, WHEN CHRISTIANS OUGHT TO MAKE SOME EXERTION FOR PROMOTING THE KNOWLEDGE OF THE TRUTH, AS IT IS IN JESUS, AMONG GOD'S ANCIENT PEOPLE.[6]

This statement also referred to the scorn and derision that Jewish people were then undergoing in many parts of the world as being evidence of the fulfillment of biblical prophecy relating to the Jewish people becoming 'the scorn and reproach of all people.' It continued:

The exact and literal fulfillment of these pointed prophecies is the surest and safest evidence, that those which relate to the restoration of the Jews will not be less faithfully accomplished; various circumstances, too, conspire to induce us to believe, that the time cannot be far off when this great event is to take place.[7]

After mentioning cases of individual Jewish people coming to faith in Jesus they continue:

When we take a view of the prophetic page of Scripture, and cast our eyes upon the present dispersion of this once highly favoured people, and look toward the end, we cannot help heaving a sigh that they have been so long left unassailed by exhortation from those who have been blessed by divine light; and express an astonishment at the delay, especially when we consider what great efforts have been made to carry on the Redeemer's kingdom amongst mankind in general ... and why should not similar efforts be made that all Israel may be saved?

We therefore have thought it proper, and suitable to the glory of God, to establish a Society for the SOLE purpose of exciting the attention of the Jews to the words of eternal salvation ...[8]

The Society further stated, '... all denominations of Christians, however different their Creed may be in other respects, unite in the belief that an important period is fast approaching, when there will be some remarkable manifestation of Jehovah's will concerning his people Israel, and the Gentile nations.'[9]

6 LJS First Report, 1809, pp. 5-6.
7 LJS First Report, pp. 9-10.
8 LJS First Report, p. 11.
9 LJS Second Report, 1810, p. 21.

Non-denominational structure

Joseph Frey's association with Pietist Lutherans, the Bohemian-Moravian congregation in Berlin, Congregationalists and now Anglicans, gave him an awareness of the diversity of the confessing Church, and his sentiments are represented in the first Report of the London Jews Society, which stated '... it is our earnest desire, that the word *denomination*, may be lost in that of *Christianity*, in support of an institution of such great importance.'[10]

In its second Report, of 27 December 1809, the LJS stated:

> Your Committee, anxious to avoid all appearance of party spirit, have from the first invited the co-operation of Christians of every denomination. They conceived that no jealousy or suspicion of each other could possibly exist in the minds of good men, when the views of the Society should be distinctly stated, and its objects be properly understood; and that Christianity would be best recommended to the consideration of the Jews by a cordiality and union amongst Christians themselves; who, although differing on minor points of doctrine or discipline, were all equally agreed in one sentiment – that Jesus Christ was the true Messiah.[11]

The Committee appreciated the structure of the Bible Society, stating that it was 'a Society in which the Dignitaries of the National Church have taken a prominent part, aided and supported by all classes of Protestant dissenters.'[12] They then adopted the Bible Society as its model.

Establishment of the Jews' Chapel

There was one immediate practical problem to solve though: ministers of the Established Church could not preach in a place that had not been consecrated for divine Anglican services, and Non-Conformist ministers could not preach in Anglican Churches. This problem was quickly solved.

Towards the end of April 1809 the LJS had discovered that the former French Huguenot church in Brick Lane Spitalfields, together with the adjoining house, were available for lease. It was the ideal location, in the midst of a Jewish area of London. The Committee endorsed the idea and the lease was pursued and signed for three years.[13]

On 12 May it was decided that henceforth the French church would be known as the 'Jewish (or Jews')Chapel', and 'that this title be written in large Letters on a conspicuous part of the building with the addition in Hebrew of "I

---

10 LJS First Report, p. 11.
11 LJS Second Report, pp. 2-3.
12 LJS Second Report, p. 5.
13 LJS Minutes, 29 April 1809 and 5 May 1809, Minute Book A.

will raise up the tabernacle of David that is fallen" Amos Chapter 9:11.'[14] The tablets of the Decalogue were soon altered to Hebrew and English lettering, thereby furthering the Hebrew character of the property.

Thereafter Frey preached and lectured regularly at this location, to a congregation comprised of Jewish followers of Jesus and some Gentile followers, while he and others gave lectures there on Sunday, Wednesday and Friday. At this point no communion was administered as the Committee was, they stated 'anxious to conduct the Institution on the principles of strict impartiality, and to avoid giving occasion of offense to the conscientious members of the Established Church who were subscribers to the Institution, did not think it advisable that the Jews' Chapel should be permitted to assume any form of a Dissenting church; and the sacrament of the Lord's Supper has consequently never been administered there.'[15]

Later though when Jewish people did enter into covenant with Jesus the question concerning baptism became an issue. Some accordingly received baptism in the Established Church, while others were baptised at the Jews' Chapel by a minister of the Presbyterian and National Church of Scotland.[16]

Frey also gave lectures each Sunday evening at Mr Becks Meeting House in Bury Street, while numerous presentations were held in both Anglican and Dissenter churches. While Frey conducted Non-Conformist services at the Jews Chapel, numerous Anglican ministers periodically offered services on behalf of the Society, at their churches.[17]

In 1810 the Committee secured the lease of a five acre property in Bethnal Green whereupon they would construct an Episcopal Chapel for services according to the Anglican Church, as well as other buildings for the use of the LJS.[18]

Strained Relationship with the Missionary Society

While matters seemed to be progressing on many fronts, Frey and the Committee still had a problem to work out with the Missionary Society. The Missionary Society had written up a Circular Paper to their supporters explaining, as objectively as they felt possible, the reason for Frey's departure.[19] This Circular was sent to Frey on 24 March 1809 for his perusal, with these words added to an attached letter, 'I hope you will find that it is *accurately* done, and that it *candidly*

---

14 LJS Minutes, 12 May 1809, ibid.
15 *JE* 1815, p. 150.
16 *JE* 1815, p. 150.
17 LJS Second Report, p. 3.
18 The Committee discussed the manner of having Frey ordained on 28 November 1809. In January 1810 he was ordained to be a minister to the Jewish people, but not with any particular denomination. LJS Minutes, 28 November 1809, Minute Book A.
19 Written by Rev. Burder on 20 March 1809.

represents the whole affair.'[20]

The Missionary Society emphasized that Frey's departure was entirely of his own voluntary accord 'merely because the directors could not, consistently with their views of propriety and economy, concur with him in the measures which he proposed.'[21]

The *Circular* then stated that Frey 'associated himself with a *few persons*, who styled themselves 'The London Society,' of which Mr. Frey was constituted *president*; and who professed, among other objects, to have in view the conversion of the jews. [sic]' Frey, they claimed, accepted this office without consulting with their directors, although he was employed by the Missionary Society. The gentlemen who comprised the London Society 'considered the Missionary Society *inadequate* to the task they had undertaken; and judged that their own measures would be more effectual.'[22]

The remainder of the *circular Letter* comprised of a chronological outline of the developing situation. Frey was upset by this Circular, stating in a letter to Burder on 25 March 1809, that some of the statements were 'absolutely false'[23] and also '*garbled* and *mutilated*'[24] and that if the Missionary Society did circulate this letter Frey would need to respond with his version.

The situation then became somewhat unsatisfactory, with letters and meetings between representatives of the two Societies and paragraphs in the *Evangelical Magazine*. Ultimately Frey felt compelled to write his version of the entire situation, in what then became known as Frey's *Narrative*.

When his *Narrative* was completed a copy was sent to the Missionary Society secretary, Rev. Burder for perusal – and it was thus desired that the Missionary Society would finally give their blessing upon Frey's departure. When this did not appear likely to happen, then the *Narrative* was released into the public domain for all and sundry to read. The matter was not satisfactorily resolved between the two Societies.

Expanding the vision

One of the objects of the LJS was to expand their vision from a London-based ministry to being a national and even internationally based work. The first

20 Rev. G. Burder to Frey, 24 March, 1809. Frey, *Narrative*, pp. 219-20. Italics probably placed there by Frey.
21 *ircular Paper of the Missionary Society*, 20 March 1809, located in Frey, *Narrative*, p. 221.
22 *Circular Paper*, ibid, pp. 222-3. As I have taken this source from Frey's *Narrative*, I am unsure if the italics are Frey's or in the original.
23 Later in the *Narrative* Frey stated, 'The reader will observe, that this letter was written immediately after I had read the preceding paper, at the moment when my mind was a good deal hurt, and before I had sufficient time fully to consider and compare its contents with the various circumstances to which it referred. Had I to write it now, I should say, "not strictly true," instead of "absolutely false.' See Frey, *Narrative*, ibid, p. 232.
24 Frey to Rev. Burder, LMS Archives, Box 81.

move in this vision occurred at the 19 May 1809 Committee meeting when it was agreed to enlist corresponding members from both the Established Church and amongst the Dissenters who would further the work in their areas.[25] Within a short period of time corresponding members were enlisted and numerous auxiliaries were established throughout the country.

One of the most significant country members was Rev. Charles Simeon, possibly the leading Evangelical minister and lecturer in Britain.[26] Any cause supported by Simeon would be noticed, so his active involvement with the LJS enhanced the Society's credibility.

One very important auxiliary was established in Ireland. The Irish Evangelicals firmly supported the vision of the London Jews Society and in 1810 established the Dublin Auxiliary, known also as the Irish Jews Society.

By 1813 there were auxiliary societies in Glasgow and Edinburgh in Scotland as well as in Bath, Bedfordshire, Cambridge, Chester, Colchester, Frome, Greenock, Haddington, Halifax, Hull, Kendal, Leicester, Leith, Liverpool, Manchester, Melton Mowbray, Newton, Shrewsbury, Stafford, Stourbridge and York - and the number increased yearly.

The auxiliaries enabled the LJS to become known throughout Britain and Ireland. British Christians during this period were enthusiastically supporting the goals and objectives of the LJS. Those supporters included some very influential people.

Wilberforce, Way and the Duke of Kent

An important component was to enlist the support of the Anglican hierarchy. On 1 April 1809 Stevens reported that he had already met with the Archbishop of Canterbury 'requesting his countenance of this Society.'[27] By 8 December 1809 the committee could report they had received a favourable response from the Bishop of Salisbury and provided he received a list of objects and aims, he would then present these to the Bishop of London.[28]

In a very short time the London Jews Society's membership became like a *Who's Who* of British society. William Wilberforce became a vice-President in 1810 and was joined by his fellow Parliamentary colleague Thomas Babbington. Their involvement provided the LJS with great credibility. Amongst the other vice-Presidents were such names as the Duke of Devonshire, the Earls of Bessborough, Crawford and Lindsay; Lords Calthorpe, Dundas and Erskine;

---

25 LJS Minutes, 19 May 1809, Minute Book A.
26 Simeon had in 1783 become minister of Holy Trinity Church in Cambridge. He played a major role in spiritually guiding the Clapham group and was a close associate of Wilberforce. As a leading evangelical in the Anglican Church Simeon was also one of the founders of the Church Missionary Society in 1799. He also in time set up the 'Simeon Trust; whereby he influenced the placing of evangelical clergy in many parishes.
27 LJS Minutes 1 April 1809, Minute Book A.
28 LJS Minutes, 8 December 1809, Minute Book A.

three Irish bishops, Cloyne, Killaloe and Meath, and many more.

Another new recruit was a wealthy land owner named Lewis Way, who was a relative by marriage of Wilberforce. Way had inherited a fortune in 1804 which was to be used for 'the glory of God' and he was constantly thereafter on the look-out for a worthy cause in which to invest his inheritance. In 1811 he was quite amazingly introduced to the concept of the restoration of Israel, and joined the ranks of the LJS in 1812. He felt he now had found his worthy cause.

Evidence of the growing popularity of the fledgling London Society was gained when the Duke of Kent, son of King George III, and father of the future Queen Victoria, agreed to become the patron in 1812. Alongside the presence of William Wilberforce and Charles Simeon, the Duke's presence now gave the LJS a triumvirate of prestigious figureheads.

It would be hard to believe that just eleven years previously a young Jewish follower of Jesus arrived in England from Germany and had a dream about helping the Jewish people in London to hear about Jesus the Messiah. That dream was now in the process of being fulfilled.

The Free School
The London Jews Society and Frey in particular were very committed to the concept of ministry through education. The background for this was Frey's own personal experience. As a child he was sheltered from Jesus by his family and the Jewish educational system. Therefore he wanted to provide opportunities for Jewish children to be exposed to the teachings of Jesus.

The London Jews Society began running a Free School almost immediately after its inception, and it very quickly outgrew its present location at the Jews Chapel. The General Committee was divided into four sub-committees in April 1809, and one of the sub-committees was then dedicated to the issue of education. On 29 September 1809 the Committee stated that it required new and larger premises.[29] Within a year of its opening, there were some four hundred children in the Free School.

But Frey in particular was more committed to a Charity School, as he believed that only in this way would children be able to overcome prejudices, experience love and care and become so well established that they could later take care of their families. It was, to be recalled, these very issues which precipitated his departure from the Missionary Society.[30]

---

29 LJS Minutes, 29 September 1809, Minute Book A.
30 The London Society also learned that due to an edict from the reign of Queen Anne [1Ann. c. 30.] a Jewish child, if 'converted' could apply to the Lord Chancellor for protection. In July 1810 a Jewish man, Israel Isaacs had his attorney submit a writ against the London Society. Isaacs had been incarcerated in prison some years before and his son Hyam had ultimately been admitted to the London Society charity school.

Houses of Industry

Another of Frey's major confrontations with the Missionary Society concerned the matter of securing employment for Jewish followers of Jesus. He himself had experienced the prejudices against new Jewish disciples when he lived in Germany. But he had also experienced the care and consideration of sincere Christians, and in particular the influence of the Moravian community.

Needless to say that one of the first issues raised by the London Jews Society concerned finding places of employment where Jewish followers of Jesus could be trained in an apprenticeship.

However there were some deeply ingrained negative attitudes towards the employment of Jewish apprentices by the populace at large. The Committee wrote:

> Your Committee have repeatedly experienced disappointment upon the subject of employment; and they have no difficulty in admitting that they cannot and do not expect great success with the lower classes of the adult Jews, until they are enabled to establish a manufactory.[31]

If a Jewish person became a follower of Jesus through their ministry, then the London Jews Society had a responsibility towards that person. If he or she could procure no employment, then the London Jews Society had to financially support them. But if they could assist this new disciple to gain meaningful work they would be free of this financial encumbrance.

In the event that no work could be procured for the new disciple, the Committee proposed the establishment of a manufactory for spinning cotton and a printing office wherein that new disciple could work. By 1811 such a manufactory had been established and the first work of the printing press was a new edition of Van der Hoogt's Hebrew Bible which Frey himself had edited.[32] In time this aspect of the Society's work continued to grow and expand.

The other aspect, the cotton spinning, and candle-wick making, provided employment for those with few work skills, and was really intended for those who could not find an apprenticeship. However this aspect of the work failed to meet expectations, and was disbanded in 1814. It was replaced by a basket making manufactory, but this too closed after a year, leaving a considerable financial debt.

Despite these glitches, however, this experiment was seen to be beneficial, and provided a template for such institutions elsewhere where the London Jews Society established itself.

---

31 LJS, Second Report, p. 14.
32 LJS, Third Report, p. 6.

Publications

From the very outset the LJS was dedicated to publishing materials associated with the cause. As early as 1809 copies of its first Reports were printed for distribution. Then in 1813 *The Jewish Repository* was first published which was complete with reports of the LJS's work, as well as articles from numerous people on matters related to the Jewish people. Over the following decades this journal adopted different names, but the general trend remained virtually the same.

The first *Report* of the London Jews Society dedicated thirteen pages to the *Institutum Judaicum* in Halle. Here was a clear indication how this British-based institution understood that its own ministry among the Jewish people was indebted to the vision and work previously undertaken by the pious Christians in Germany.

Chapter 12

The Movements of Joseph Wolff

The journey to Vienna and southern Germany

While Frey and the London Jews Society began to consolidate in London, Joseph Wolff continued to languish in a spiritual quagmire in Germany. Despite some positive advancement in Halle, it would seem the persecution there from the Jewish community propelled him to again uproot.

In the year 1810 at the age of fourteen and a half, Joseph found his way to Vienna. He recorded of this time of despondency:

> I was walking sorrowful in the suburbs of Vienna, without a penny, sighing and praying to the Lord, when an Austrian officer followed and enquired the reason. I mentioned my wish to be instructed in the X-n faith, and assisted in my studies, but no one helping me my money was gone. Having seen my testimonials he offered to take me as his servant till I could find an instructor.[1]

Shortly afterwards the officer sensed that Joseph had been 'chosen by the Lord' to be his servant, and offered for Joseph to remain with him until a Christian sponsor could be found. Being a poor soldier himself, Joseph could not remain indefinitely with him and when a suitable sponsor did not appear, Joseph had to leave and thereupon continued his journey in the direction of nearby Bavaria.

While travelling he passed a Catholic convent and decided to go in 'because he had read that in a cloister good X-ns assemble to sing hymns to Jesus.' Upon entering though, Joseph asked the abbot if he could be admitted, baptized and taught to become a clergyman![2] Although obviously impressed by Joseph's enthusiasm, the abbot was constrained by Austrian law, which forbade a Jewish person under the age of eighteen from being baptized without their parent's consent.

In view of this constraint, and in view of Joseph's enthusiasm, the abbot desired him to remain there until he came of age and 'to study the gospel and be more comforted with the light of Xty' But in a way similar to Joseph Frey's rejection from Denmark, 'the monks soon objected to a Jew remaining there.'[3]

So once again young Joseph Wolff hit the road, and en-route to Munich he stopped in Molk, where he remained for some time, learning Latin, and also

---

1 Wolff, *Life and Journal*, p. 9; *Travels*, pp. 9-10.
2 Wolff, *Life and Journal*, p. 9.
3 Wolff, *Life and Journal*, p. 9.

teaching Hebrew. His sojourn here however was terminated when he once was taunted with an anti-Semitic lyric by the female cook, whereupon he slapped her in the face - and was duly asked to leave.[4]

In Munich he met a Catholic priest and then studied at the Catholic Gymnasium for six months. The priest showed him the difference between Judaism and Christianity and also gave him numerous other books to read, some Christian and some secular. The conclusion he later made concerning this experience was that 'my soul was not then prepared to receive the grace of X-ty, I entered not yet into the recesses of my heart to speak with Christ as my friend.' Wolff testified that at that point the Lord prevented his baptism.[5]

It is unclear how long Joseph remained in Munich and under the influence of the priest, but it does seem he was somewhat disgusted with the idolatry of the Roman Catholics in some places. Once again he was sent on his way, and his search thereafter took him to Anspack where he became acquainted with some quite liberal Protestant professors.

By 1811 Joseph Wolff was studying at the Lyceum in Saxe Weimar, where he became acquainted with the poet Johann Falk. When Joseph informed Falk of his desire to become a Christian and become like Francis Xavier, Falk retorted, "Wolff, let me give you a piece of advice. Remain what you are; for if you remain a Jew, you will become a celebrated Jew, but as a Christian you will never be celebrated, for there are plenty of other celebrated Christians in the world."[6]

Despite this advice though one day Falk introduced him to the famous philosopher Goethe, who told him, "Young fellow, follow the bent of your own mind and don't listen to what Falk says."[7]

Although Wolff liked Weimar he found it confusing with so many philosophers and others holding to a mixture of eastern, Greek and Christian beliefs. And so his journey continued, first to Heidelberg, and from there to the Santa Maria Einseidlen Monastery. Here he was informed not to let anyone know that he was Jewish. Yet on one occasion he mentioned this fact to his room-mate, who was so shocked that he yelled in unbelief – and thereupon the entire village became aware of Wolff's national identity. In time he was also asked to move on from this location.[8]

Ultimately Wolff returned to Prague whereupon, while passing by a church, he entered in and heard a sermon. Following the service he introduced himself to the preacher, a Franciscan friar, and explained to him of his seemingly endless quest for finding the truth, and of being baptised.

The friar took him seriously and introduced Wolff to the bishop and the

---

4 Wolff, *Travels*, p. 10.
5 Wolff, *Life and Journal*, p.10.
6 Wolff, *Travels*, p. 11.
7 Wolff, *Travels*, p. 11.
8 Wolff, *Travels*, p. 13.

monastery hierarchy. Bishop Haim stated to Wolff after hearing of his story, "Thou art not a common Jew…"[9]

Wolff is baptised

While at the monastery in Prague, Wolff came under the supervision of a monk and read the 'prophets, gospel, and spiritual authors.'[10] Then finally, on 13 September 1812, at the age of seventeen, Wolff was baptised at the Benedictine Monastery of Emaus, by the abbot, Leopold Zaldo.

For all intents and purposes, Wolff had now arrived at 'home' – albeit a Roman Catholic home. The fears of his parents had been realised, and from their perspective Joseph had now left the faith of his fathers.

From Prague Joseph then returned to Vienna where he remained for some time studying. He now felt somewhat settled: he was now a baptised follower of Jesus, and was finally permitted to study unhindered in a learned environment.

To his family Joseph may have been regarded as a *Meshumad*, but to Joseph he was a Jew who had found his spiritual home – in Jesus. It may be that his new home had the outward trappings of the Roman Catholic Church, but it was clear to Joseph that he had not forsaken his Jewish heritage.

It may be that at this point Joseph had merely come to a major turning on the road of his journey. He was still deeply restless and desired to continue on to conclude the destiny he felt he was destined to fulfill – to be a modern day version of Francis Xavier.

Wolff's stay in Vienna was very full, taken up by translating the Hebrew Bible into German, and meeting all kinds of prominent people. Word about this rather interesting young Jewish follower of Jesus filtered through to another convert to Roman Catholicism, Frederick Leopold, the Count of Stolberg, who was located near Bielefeld in Westphalia. This austere Count invited Joseph to stay with him and his large family in 1814.

Wolff complied and while he only remained there for three months, he created quite a sensation. Among the Count's visitors was General Blucher, who would soon gain fame at the Battle of Waterloo. Although a devout Roman Catholic, Stolberg nevertheless did not fully adhere to many of the dogmas of the Church, especially the adoration of Mary.

The Count had a special affection for Wolff, whom he considered not as a Christian but as a Jew. On one occasion he said to Joseph, "I feel great concern and love for you, and for your brethren, the children of Abraham."[11] Indeed the two men did form a special bond, a bond which was prematurely broken in 1814 with the news of Napoleon's escape from captivity in Elbe.

At least two of the Count's sons joined the Prussian Army to fight Napoleon.

9 Wolff, *Travels*, p. 14.
10 Wolff, *Life and Journal*, p. 10.
11 Wolff, *Travels*, p, 29.

The aged Count himself realised that it was expedient for him and his family to leave and move further inland, as he had been a strong opponent of Napoleon. At the subsequent battle of Waterloo in 1815, the young future Count died in battle.

Alas Joseph could not go with the Count, and left the Count's home on 3 April 1815, moving on to Tubingen where he attended the Protestant University.

Joseph Wolff in Tubingen

The University of Tubingen was the enclave of the Lutheran Church, which Joseph very quickly discovered each time he endeavoured to defend the Roman Catholic Church. Yet when he did defend the Roman Catholic Church, it was pointed out to him that his views were more of those of Count Stolberg than of the Church in Rome.

Joseph was never one to accept ridicule. When on one occasion he was denied a privilege which was given only to Lutherans and not to Roman Catholics, he wrote to the King of Wurttemberg, a close associate of the Count of Stolberg – and soon afterwards the University lifted its ban against Wolff the Roman Catholic and he received equal privileges.[12] Such was the *hutzpah* of Joseph Wolff. From another notable Wolff received a yearly allowance to the equivalent of 25 pounds, enabling him to enjoy comfortable lodgings in Tubingen.[13]

All was not well at Tubingen though. Joseph had anticipated teaching Hebrew to the students in order to receive support, but he found that the professors and many of the students were even more thorough in their knowledge of Hebrew and the ancient languages than he was.

As much as Tubingen was an academic challenge for Wolff, he still desperately desired to follow in the footsteps of Francis Xavier. To do so he would need to go to Rome and to study in the missionary training college, the *Propaganda Fide*. He bided his time, but his sights were now firmly focussed upon Rome.

12 Wolff, ibid, p. 33.
13 Wolff, ibid, p. 34.

Chapter 13

Palestine Place and the *Benei Abraham*

Palestine Place

The level of interest shown by London and indeed British society in the London Jews Society is very evident in an event which took place on 7 April 1813 – the laying of the foundation stone for a new church, which would become known as the Episcopal Jews Chapel (where Anglican services would be held).

The Episcopal Jews Chapel would be the central building in a large complex, which in its entirety would be known as Palestine Place. This large complex in Bethnal Green was acquired on a 99 year lease and would, when completed, have the Episcopal Jews Chapel as well as schools for boys and girls, housing and more.

The foundation stone was unveiled by the Patron, the Duke of Kent in front of an attendance estimated as 20,000. Also in attendance that day were the Lord Mayor and Sheriffs of London, the Earls of Bessborough, Crawford and Lindsay, Lord Dundas and Lord Erskine, William Wilberforce, Thomas Babington and Lewis Way, who all later gave brief speeches at the celebratory meal at the London Tavern.

The order of service that day saw the various dignitaries pass through a line formed of the militia with presented arms, while the band played 'God Save the King.' The delegation began with the Committee followed by the Stewards, Clergy, the Rev. J.S.C.F. Frey (schoolmaster), Jewish boys, Jewish girls, Vice-Presidents, Master builder – and then His Royal Highness the Duke of Kent.[1]

The only person personally named in the entourage in the *Jewish Repository*, the magazine of the LJS, was Rev. J.S.C.F. Frey – the German-born Jewish disciple of Jesus. This must have been an absolute high point in his life. Indeed had it not been for Joseph Frey's presence and perseverance over the previous twelve years, the London Jews Society may never have even come to this point.

The Episcopal Jews Chapel opened for Anglican services in 1814.

The formation of the *Benei Abraham*

From the time of the inception of the London Jews Society the number of Jewish people committing their lives to follow Jesus, and then being baptised, grew. These Jewish followers thereafter met in different congregations where they were greatly outnumbered by Gentile followers of Jesus. Frey and others

---

1 *Jewish Repository*, 1813, p. 69.

saw the increasing need for these Jewish followers to be able to spend time together, whereupon they could relate to, and empathise with the struggles of each other.

In accordance with this heart-felt need, and with Frey's encouragement, some forty-one Jewish followers of Jesus met in the Jews Chapel on 9 September 1813. There they formed the association known as the *Benei Abraham* (Sons or Children of Abraham). Moses Marcus chaired this initial meeting but Frey was then elected as the chairman of the *Benei Abraham*.

The *Benei Abraham* may not have been comprised of many people, and may not have been that well-known to the wider community, but its formation was an historic turning point in the history of the world-wide Church.

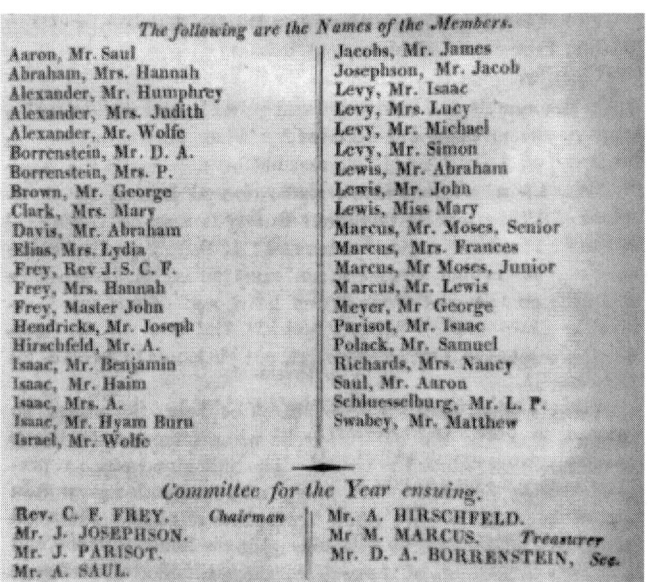

In his book, *Hebrew Christianity: The Thirteenth Tribe*, B.Z. Sobel stated: 'Hebrew Christianity was born in England at the beginning of the nineteenth century through the efforts of a group of converts calling themselves the Benei Abraham, or sons of Abraham.'[2] W.T. Gidney, the official historian of the London Jews Society at the time of its centennial in 1909, claimed that the *Benei Abraham* was 'The first exclusively Hebrew Christian Association.'[3]

Indeed it may have been, for there cannot have been too many occasions in the previous centuries when some forty-one Jewish followers of Jesus came together of one accord to worship their Messiah and the God of their

---

2 Sobel, B.Z. *Hebrew Christianity: The Thirteenth Tribe*, (New York, 1974), p. 177.
3 Gidney, W. *The History of the London Society for Promoting Christianity among the Jews*, p. 43.

forefathers. The LJS wrote:

> Do the annals of History present us with such an interesting scene as this meeting has afforded? What may we expect as the result of FORTY JEWS assembling together in the name of Jesus Christ, and offering supplication to heaven for themselves and their Jewish brethren? Surely it may be considered as the first fruits of a glorious harvest! If there is joy in heaven over one sinner that repenteth, how must the angels above rejoice at a little company of Jews of one heart and one mind, returning again to their father's house. And how readily does he who wept over Jerusalem stretch out his hands to receive his *long lost sheep*.
>
> Nothing is too hard for Jehovah. The holy Scriptures assure us, that "in the latter days he will circumcise the hearts of the Israelites to love the Lord." The little cloud which at present appears but as a man's hand, may portend a great rain which may moisten the whole hemisphere of Israel. Hath not Jehovah declared that he will pour out upon the house of David, and upon the inhabitants of Jerusalem, the spirit of grace and supplication, and they shall look upon him whom they have pierced, and mourn?[4]

These were indeed prophetic words. For, as history later would reveal, that little cloud which was no more than the size of a man's hand, has indeed grown and is moistening the spiritual atmosphere of Israel.

The members of the *Benei Abraham* were all Jewish, and were required to pay a subscription fee and were strongly encouraged to meet together for prayer and edification on Friday evening at the Committee Room of the London (Jews) Society in Spitalfields. They would, in addition, join together at the service at the Jews Chapel on Sunday morning, and where necessary to visit daily, in twos, any fellow member who had become ill.

Numerous rules for how this new Society would operate were adopted, but some of these were later dropped or modified. Rules aside, the heart of all the members is echoed in a statement recorded in the first Report of the *Benei Abraham*, which stated:

> ... that those who for years lived crucifying the adorable Saviour, now stately assemble to praise him, and through him as their Mediator to pray to that God who will gather the outcasts of Israel, that he may be pleased to turn their hearts, and the hearts of the many thousands of the seed of Abraham, who are still in ignorance and impenitence; and that they thus unite their efforts in using such means as may, under the influence of the Spirit of Grace, promote their conversion and salvation; - this indeed is their highest wish,

4 *JR*, 1814, p. 506.

and its accomplishment, its consummation, and its crown. What has already been done, is sufficient to confound the sceptic, and lead us to exclaim, What has God wrought! God has predicted all Israel shall eventually be saved, and nothing is too hard for him to perform.[5]

Indeed this was the heart-cry of these Jewish followers of Jesus, that the miracle God had wrought in their lives, would be manifested time and again – until such time as 'all Israel' would be saved.

There had been Jewish followers of Jesus scattered through the lands over the course of the previous 1800 years, yet now they were uniting their voice, and later their efforts, in earnestly praying that more Jewish people would come to know their Messiah.

The *Benei Abraham* was not an institution such as the *Institutum Judaicum* or the London Jews Society. It was more-so a movement, and it was into this movement that more Jewish followers of Jesus became involved in the future years, Jewish followers who were involved in numerous denominations and institutions and from many countries.

This was the very small beginning of a movement which would in time come knocking loudly at the doors of Gentile Christendom saying, "Here we are as followers of Jesus, and here we are to stay - as Jews. We are here to remind you Gentiles not to be arrogant and boast … "

הנה מה טוב ומה נעים שבת אחים גם יחד

On Thursday Evening, Sept. 9, 1813, a Meeting was held at the Committee Room, Jews' Chapel, by the Jews under the Patronage of the London Society, for the purpose of forming themselves into a Society, to be called

בני אברהם:

THE
CHILDREN OF ABRAHAM.

Mr. MOSES MARCUS, Sen. in the Chair.
(In consequence of the absence of the Rev. Mr. Frey.)

The Meeting was opened by reading the Rules and Regulations, to which every Member readily subscribed his name.—After which a suitable Address was given on the important objects of the Institution; appropriate parts of the Holy Scriptures were read; and one of our Christian friends prayed.

The following Rules were unanimously adopted for the government of this Society.

I. This חברה (or Society,) shall have a Committee, consisting of five Members, a Treasurer, and a Secretary.

II. The Members of this Society are expected to meet for prayer, at the Jews' Chapel, every Sunday Morning at half past 10 o'Clock, and Friday Evening at 7 o'Clock.

III. On Friday evening, after prayers are over, the Members forming the Committee are to meet, for the purpose of admitting new Members, and to transact such other matters as regard the views and intentions of this Society.

---

5 *JR*, 1815, p. 503.

CHAPTER 14

THE ANGLICAN SOCIETY

Financial and ecclesiastical difficulties
Despite the good intentions of the founders of the London Jews Society, reality finally caught up. There were definite benefits in having a Society representing both the Established and Dissenting Church, but ultimately this arrangement became unwieldy. Although the Society had been recognized to a degree by the Established Church leadership, yet nevertheless many 'conscientious men' in that Church declined to support it 'upon the alleged ground of its connection with the Dissenters in matter of discipline; and especially because the Jews' Chapel was considered as a place of worship.'[1] It was in accordance with this concern that the Society set out to build the Episcopal Jews Chapel at Palestine Place.

This large project, coupled with other projects undertaken during the Society's first years had accumulated a large financial debt. Those debts by 1814 had accrued to the sum of about 14,000 pounds.

At a General Committee meeting held on 14 December 1814 two separate committees were established and were entrusted with the responsibility of raising the funds to cover this large debt. The Anglican or Established Church committee was to raise 4,000 pounds, while the non-Anglican (or Dissenter) committee was to raise 2,000 pounds.[2]

The Dissenter sub-committee found the task beyond their ability, and accordingly met on 6 February 1815 and decided that this matter needed to be presented to all of the Dissenter subscribers of the Society. These subscribers then met on 14 February 1815.

The Dissenter subscribers thereupon agreed, concerning the need to raise extra funding, that they would not be able 'to contribute more support to the Society than they have done hitherto.'[3] The third resolution they passed that evening is very revealing:

> III. That as it appears that many zealous members of the Established Church have expressed their conscientious objections to unite with this Society, whilst its affairs are managed by a Committee consisting of persons of different religious denominations, and have intimated their willingness to support

---
1 *JE* 1815, p. 152.
2 *JE* 1815, pp. 153-55.
3 Resolution No II, meeting 14 February 1815, quoted in *JE,* 1815, p. 156.

it if carried on exclusively by Churchmen: - this Meeting embraces this opportunity of proving that they never, as Dissenters, had any other design but the conversion of the Jews to Christianity: - and, as it is probable that the Assets are nearly sufficient to cover the debts, - they therefore cannot feel the smallest objection to withdraw, in favour of such of their brethren of the Established Church who testify a lively zeal in this grand cause, possessing also sufficient means for promoting it.[4]

This really is an extraordinary statement. One of the contributing factors for the initial separation from the Missionary Society was that some from the Established Church who wished to support the vision, would not do so while the Missionary Society 'controlled' the work. Thus in 1809 the London Jews Society was established as a Society to be run along the lines of the Bible Society whereby both Established and Dissenter Churches could work together.

But now that the Established Church had taken a stronger hold of the Society, the argument was given that there were other supporters from the Established Church who wanted to be involved, but who would not do so while the Society was jointly run with the Dissenters. The London Jews Society had once been run entirely by the Dissenters, who had the vision to launch into work among the Jewish people, and now it had been taken over completely by those of the Established Church.

Regardless of how the Dissenter constituency were feeling at this point, they made a very commendable decision. But where would this decision leave Joseph Frey? He most certainly could not now return to the Non-Conformist operated Missionary Society, nor could he now branch out and establish another Non-Conformist work to the Jewish people.

The following resolution from the Dissenter committee was then dedicated to the future of Joseph Frey. It stated:

IV – That this Meeting feels itself called upon to express the high sense they entertain of the faithful and zealous exertions of the Rev. Mr. Frey during the continuance of this Society, not only in publishing to his brethren of the house of Israel the truth as it is in Jesus, but also for his unwearied labours in travelling through all parts of England, Scotland, and Ireland, to make known to Christians in general the design and objects of the Society, whereby those funds have been procured which were constantly found to be so necessary to its existence.[5]

There was genuine concern for the welfare of Frey in this new situation, and the

---

4 Resolution No III, meeting 14 February 1815, quoted in *JE*, 1815, p. 156.
5 Resolution IV, meeting 14 February 1815, *JE*, 1815, pp. 156-57.

Dissenters wanted to ensure that the Established Church understood the vast experience of Frey and the great debt of gratitude the Society owed him for its very existence. The question would be though, how would Frey adapt to being under the tutelage of the Establishment, and how would the Establishment cope with someone of Frey's character and theological background.

The London Jews Society becomes an Anglican Society

Following on from the suggestion of the Dissenting members, the General Committee held a meeting on 17 February 1815 and agreed to accept the Resolutions. They then had to draw up a new set of Rules and Regulations, and planned to meet with the members of the Society at a meeting set for 28 February 1815.

At that meeting which was chaired by Thomas Babington MP, the recent history was explained and a Resolution was proposed, that the Established Church accept the offer of the Dissenting Church to withdraw and hand over the running to the Established Church. This Motion was accepted.

Several men from both sections of the Church then addressed the crowd. The London Jews Society recorded: 'The Dissenting Gentlemen expressed their determination, though they had withdrawn from the management, still to continue their aid to the Institution, both by their influence and example, and they thus evinced themselves to be actuated by principles of the most exalted Christian philanthropy and liberality, which we trust will be both felt and imitated in every part of the kingdom.'[6]

At that point numerous resolutions were passed which affected the Rules and Regulations of the Society, namely that henceforth the children under the charge of the London Jews Society would be instructed according to the principles and formularities of the United Church of England and Ireland; that public worship in the future would be conducted in strict conformity to the Liturgy and formularities of the Church of England as the law determined; that should any Jewish follower of Jesus 'entertain conscientious scruples in respect of conformity to the rites of the Church of England' then they could receive temporal aid from the Society.[7]

Sir Thomas Baring and Lewis Way

A prominent banker and Member of Parliament Sir Thomas Baring then became the President of the Society. Baring also had an interesting challenge at the beginning of the Society's new life. Shortly after accepting the position as President, Baring was made aware of the dire financial state of the Society by Lewis Way. Baring stated of this situation:

---

6 *JE*, 1815, p. 159.
7 Resolutions of meeting 28 February 1815, in *JE*, 1815, pp. 159-60.

What was my surprise when, at our first meeting, I found the outstanding debts and liabilities exceeded 14,000 pounds! I told him [Mr. Way] on this discovery I must withdraw myself from it, that I never could consent to connect myself with a Society in debt, and that I saw no remote probability of its relieving itself from its difficulties.

Now mark what this great and good man did. *He put a draft of 10,000 pounds into my hand.* The other 4,000 pounds was soon raised, and the debts of the Society were at once discharged.[8]

Now set upon a firmer financial footing, the London Society was determined to act more prudently concerning all future projects.

Frey's future and the Jews Chapel

At a meeting of the new Committee held on 1 March 1815 it was decided that a deputation including Wilberforce and Babington would meet with the Bishop of London to acquaint him with the changes to the Constitution of the Society; to pave the way for Frey's ordination into the Church of England; and concerning the licensing of the Jews Chapel for Anglican worship.[9]

The intention at this point was for Frey to be ordained by the Bishop of London so as to continue his work within the new Anglican Society, and to officiate at services held in the Jews Chapel Spitalfields, where many Jewish people attended.

At the Society's next meeting, held on 14 March, the new rules associated with the adapted Constitution were passed, and it was declared 'exclusively a Church of England Institution.'[10] Sir Thomas Baring was also voted in as the new president of the London Jews Society.

The Bishop of London procrastinated over the matter of Frey's ordination.[11] The result of this was that public service could no longer continue at the Jews Chapel, and it was decided that 'a notice had to be placed on the door of the Jews Chapel notifying that as the character of the LJS had recently changed, public worship would henceforth be in the strict conformity to the Liturgy and formularies' of the Church of England, and that 'Notice is hereby given that the above place of Worship will be shut up for the present till arrangements shall be made accordingly.'

The notice concluded with these 'comforting' words:

---

8 Stirling, A. *The Ways of Yesterday*, p. 134.
9 LJS General Committee, 1 March 1815, Minute 4. At the meeting of 14 March others including Baring were to be added to the deputation (LJS Minutes 14 March, Minute 16).
10 LJS General Committee, 14 March 1815, and Gidney, ibid, p. 47.
11 LJS General Committee, Minute No 26, 23 March 1815.

> Those of the Jewish nation and others who have been in the habit of attending the above Chapel will be accommodated in the interval at the London Society's Episcopal Jews Chapel Bethnal Green.[12]

At that point there were some fifty Jewish followers of Jesus worshipping at the Jews Chapel, and they now moved to the Episcopal Jews Chapel at Palestine Place. It would be interesting to know their feelings at this time, especially for those who were more comfortable worshipping God in a Non-Conformist environment.

An off-shoot of the closing of the Jews Chapel was that Frey's ministry there was effectively suspended. The Committee now seriously deliberated about his future role, a matter which they felt was 'highly expedient'. What is interesting to note is that at this point there is a change in Frey's title: prior to February 1815 he was invariably known as Rev. Frey, but now as Mr. Frey![13]

Frey's role was thereafter adapted to meet the circumstances. He would remain as the LJS missionary and would speak on behalf of the work of the Society around the country, and would be the Superintendent of the schools (especially the Boys' School) and the printing office.

Throughout the remainder of the year and into 1816 no progress was made concerning Frey being ordained into the Church of England. Accordingly he could not continue with the ministry he had previously done, and so was entrusted with numerous other tasks, one of which was with the Boys' School.

At the LJS AGM held on 5 May 1815 Rev. Mr. Grimshaw spoke very strongly in favour of Frey, the Minutes recording that 'he considered the character of Mr. Frey so identified with that of the Institution, that the one could not be assailed without injury to the other. It had been generally asked' he continued 'What is to become of Mr. Frey, under the present circumstances of the Institution?'

Grimshaw then answered the question himself: 'What? When a voice from heaven bids the children of Israel to go on, to enter in, and possess the land, shall the prophet be left behind? No! – The cloud moves on and he must follow it ...'[14] In the view of Grimshaw and perhaps many others besides, Joseph Frey was the prophetic voice of the London Jews Society.

At the LJS General Committee meeting on 25 July 1815 mention was made of three young Jewish men who were seeking assistance. It was agreed that Lewis Way, who was then establishing a College at Stanstead Park, be approached

---

12 LJS General Committee, Minute No. 27, 23 March 1815.
13 LJS Report, 1815, p. 12.
14 LJS AGM 5 May 1815, *JE*, 1815, p. 239. One issue that did arise then which would have been very close to Frey's heart involved Rev. Luther Leo of the Callenberg Institute. At the LJS AGM it was resolved: 'That the thanks of this meeting be presented to the Rev Luther Leo for his very handsome present of the Books of the Callenberg Society which near One Hundred Years ago set the example of making exertions for the Conversion of the Jews.'

'to permit them to reside near him for the benefit of their participating in the instruction & education afforded by him to the other young men of the Jewish nation at present under his patronage.' The Committee also stated that it would be 'desirable that Mr Frey (who is still restricted from the performance of his ministerial functions) should reside with them at or near Stanstead in order to further ... assist them in their theological studies.'[15]

In the meantime, though, Frey was agreeable to take these three young men under his roof for the cost of 15 shillings per week,[16] and as Frey's home was too small, another location was sought in order to accommodate these three young men.[17] All this was temporary, as the Committee desired that these men shall ' be placed under the tuition of Mr Frey & others in the neighbourhood of Stanstead.'[18]

Prior to the move to Stanstead Frey continued to provide private religious tuition and instruction to young Jewish disciples of Jesus, including Coshman Jacob.[19] It would seem that he was still holding on to the hope that he would be quickly ordained and then could continue his ministry at the Jews Chapel. Such hopes were soon crushed.

On 12 December 1815 the Committee resolved to sell the lease on the Jews Chapel in Spitalfields.[20] This decision effectively ended any chance for Frey ministering in London under the auspices of the LJS. The other decision was that 'in consequence of actual state of the finances of the Society it has become expedient at present not to admit any more Adult Jews under its protection...'[21]

The decision to sell the lease for the Jews Chapel was very painful for Frey, as it and he were closely identified one with the other. It was in the Jews Chapel that he had preached, taught and discipled many of the Jewish followers of Jesus. It was almost as if to lose it would be to cut him off from his own heritage in the work. It was a reminder to him of the Society's pre-Anglican roots.

Frey accordingly communicated his sentiments to the Committee, in conjunction with Mr Thomas Stevens of Zion Gardens, 'that he, as a Trustee for the property of the Society, will not consent that the lease of that Chapel should be sold, & that it is his determination that this Chapel, & the Episcopal

---

15 LJS General Committee Minute 219, 25 July 1815.
16 LJS General Committee Minutes 241, 242, 243, 4 August 1815.
17 LJS General Committee Minute 256, 29 August 1815.
18 LJS General Committee Minute 271, 29 August 1815. There is an interesting Minute from the meeting of 26 September 1815 whereby Frey applied for money owed to him. The Committee agreed to pay the amount requested, but stated that they 'highly disapprove the practise of bringing accounts for payment which have not been passed by the competent Subcommittee.' Minute 291.
19 LJS General Committee Minute 228, 28 November 1815.
20 LJS General Committee Minute 347, 12 December 1815.
21 LJS General Committee Minute 348, 12 December 1815.

Jews Chapel, shall not be separated but shall stand, or fall, together.'[22] But alas it was a lost cause. The finances of the newly constructed Society could not handle two separate places of ministry.

Frey's plight seemed to only get worse, as he communicated to the General Committee on 26 December 1815, which they recorded:

> Mr Frey stated that from a conversation he had with the bishop of London, last week, he finds it will be absolutely necessary for him to become a graduate of a University, before he can expect ordination from his lordship; he hopes therefore, that this Committee will decide this question without delay, & that till the Subject be decided, he thinks it would be improper that he should remove with his family to Stanstead.[23]

This decision by the Bishop of London would mean that Frey would not be able to effectively remain involved with the work of the LJS in London as he could not effectively combine university studies and involvement in London.

Undoubtedly saddened by these two decisions, Frey had no choice but to make the move with his family to Stanstead Park, which they did in early 1816.[24] In the wake of the traumatic events of 1815, this move to Hampshire provided an opportunity for a new beginning to his life and ministry.

Michael Solomon Alexander

While Frey was about to make this move, and while Wolff was continuing with his journey of discovery, Michael Solomon Alexander was the more settled of the three sons of Abraham at this stage. He stated of his early life in Posen, 'that until that time I had not the slightest knowledge of Christianity, not did I even know of the existence of the New Testament.'[25]

That he had no intention of pursuing belief in Jesus is evident, as he stated:

> Strong impressions of prejudice against the very name of Christ was all the knowledge I possessed of him, and in blindness, and ignorance, I never felt curious to inquire the reason of that prejudice. I looked upon all other sects besides Jews, as the Gentile idolators mentioned by Moses and the Prophets, from whom I found sufficient reasons and commands to abhor their practices.[26]

22 LJS General Committee Minute 349, 13 December 1815. In a subsequent meeting on 26 December, Minute 361, Frey expressed the view that the wording of Minute 349 was incorrect, as should have read, ; 'Mr Stevens authorized Mr Frey to inform the Committee that it is not in their power to sell the Jews Chapel, & if they do, he as a Trustee will nullify it.' Frey's contention, however, was opposed by Mr. Barker, who believed the original wording was correct.
23 LJS General Committee Minute 359, 26 December 1815.
24 LJS General Committee Minute 375, 2 January 1816.
25 Hatchard, J. *The Predictions and Promises of God Respecting Israel, (Appendix),* (London 1825), p. 37.
26 Hatchard, ibid, p. 37.

These impressions of prejudice against Christianity were furthered by what he witnessed in the Roman Catholic traditions he observed in Catholic dominated Posen. Rev. James. Cartwright wrote later of Alexander's boyhood observations:

> Of Christianity he had no other idea than that which he had derived from the slanderous traditions of the Talmud, occasionally illustrated by a passing view of a Romish procession in honour of some saint in his native town; and he regarded it accordingly as idolatry, to be abhorred by every faithful Israelite.[27]

Although geographically near to Prussia and Berlin, which were experiencing the Enlightenment and accompanying emancipation, Schonlanke was much more conservative. The Jewish community there was not so influenced by these trends. Michael Solomon at this time was educated as he stated, 'principally in the Talmud and in the strictest principles of Judaism'.[28] At the age of sixteen (in 1815) he was already a teacher of the Talmud[29] and the German language.[30]

It would appear that a bright future was in store for this young man within mainstream Jewish life.

---

27 Sermon of Rev. James Cartwright, Episcopal Jews Chapel London, 28 December 1845, in *JI*, 1846, p. 58.
28 Hatchard, ibid, p. 38.
29 *Talmud* was comprised of two parts, the *Mishna* (the whole code of Jewish law) and *Gemara* (a commentary of the *Mishna*).
30 See Sermon of Rev. James Cartwight, Episcopal Jews Chapel London, 28 December 1845, in *JI*, 1846, p. 58; and Hatchard, ibid.

Chapter 15

Frey to America and Wolff in Rome

Frey moves to Stanstead

The new year saw Joseph Frey and his family settling into Stanstead Park. The three young Jewish men moved with him and continued to live under his roof and to receive his instruction.

Lewis Way had at this time other Jewish disciples under his tutelage, and he was investing heavily in building up his library. Stanstead Park was in many ways becoming a Hebrew College. Way's home and estate were continuously visited by people of note, as Way by this stage was being regarded as the spokesperson for the Society – a position previously held by Joseph Frey!

It was not long, though, before comments were already returning to London concerning the three young men under Frey's tutelage. At the General Committee on 27 February 1816 it was stated of these three young men that they 'exhibit a very great fondness for dress, & manifest a constant solicitude to wear an appearance far above & altogether unsuited to their circumstances & seeming vocation ... They had used the allowance given to them in an inappropriate way.'[1]

The Committee then called them to account.[2] The behaviour of these young men undoubtedly reflected badly upon Frey. This financial situation was soon followed by another, this time directly relating to Frey. He owed the Society 150 pounds for printing his Bible and the LJS was inclined to regain this sum by retaining his salary. Frey then stated to the Committee 'that it would be very inconvenient to him to have his salary retained at the present time towards the payment of this sum'.[3] The Committee accepted his request, but resolved that parts of his salary would be withheld during the following year in order to regain the outstanding sum.

Frey undoubtedly would have felt humbled by the treatment he received in this situation.

Frey dismissed

While based at Stanstead Frey continued speaking on behalf of the Society and raising funds for its operations. Hopes for him being ordained had not completely dissipated. Then in May a very serious situation arose. At a special meeting which convened on 28 May 1816, the Select Committee mentioned,

1 LJS General Committee Minute 425, 27 February 1816.
2 LJS General Committee Minute 425, 27 February 1816.
3 LJS General Committee Minute 434, 26 March 1816.

'the disclosure of certain gross improprieties in the conduct of Mr Frey …'[4] They then resolved that:

> … having taken into consideration some facts recently disclosed respecting the conduct of Mr Frey feel themselves under the painful necessity of recommending;
>
> 1st. That Mr Frey should no longer be permitted to hold his present situation or to continue to be a member of the Society & that his salary do cease in three months from this time.
>
> 2nd. That in the event of Mr Frey's being disposed to retire to the Continent, he shall be allowed (as soon as he shall have made a faithful disclosure of his circumstances, & settled with his creditors) the sum of £50, to convey him to such place as he may choose to withdraw to, & £50 more to settle him there.[5]

The Society leaders would not disclose to the general public just what the 'gross improprieties' were. Their silence thereafter elicited considerable speculation. Most it would seem thought it related to misuse of finances, although the London Jews Society always clearly refuted such an allegation.

The 'gross improprieties' involved serious misconduct against the wife of a Jewish follower of Jesus, who accused Frey of seducing her.[6] Subsequent inquiry determined that other women too levelled similar charges against Frey.[7] The LJS leadership did their utmost to protect both Frey and their own reputation in the matter.

While the London Jews Society was embroiled in this great crisis, across the Atlantic something of great significance was taking place. Following on from the initiative taken in July 1815 by Hannah Adams and the ladies of Boston when they sent a contribution of fifty dollars to London, on 5 June 1816 these same ladies established an American branch of the London Jews Society named the *Female Society of Boston and Vicinity for Promoting Christianity amongst the Jews*.[8]

This new Society was an Auxiliary of the London Jews Society, and marked the foundation in America of Christian work among the Jewish people.

Frey leaves for America

Initially the London Jews Society was willing to cover Frey's expenses back to Germany. But by mid-June Frey had decided his future lay not in his former

---

4 LJS General Committee Minute 507, 28 May 1816.
5 LJS General Committee Minute 508, 28 May 1816.
6 Jonathon D. Sarna writing for the *Journal of American History* stated that 'according to one source Frey seduced a convert named Mrs Josephson'. Jonathon Sarna, 'The American Jewish Response to Nineteenth Century Christian Missions', in *Journal of American History*, Vol. 68, No. 1, p. 37.
7 Frey was also known to have had extra-marital relations with ladies of ill-repute from Ipswich. See Eichhorn, ibid, p. 26, and G.J. Miller, *Bibliographical Society of America*, Vol. XXX, 1936, pp. 1-56.
8 Eichhorn, D. *Evangelizing the American Jew*, (New York, 1978), p. 30.

homeland, but across the Atlantic. The LJS stated on 25 June 1816 that Frey was determined 'to proceed to America.'[9] Numerous financial arrangements were now required, as Frey owed the LJS money, so he offered them copies of his Hebrew Bibles in exchange.

Joseph and Mrs Frey and their four children left England aboard the brig *Factor*, on 23 July 1816, destined for America.[10]

Several months later, on 22 October 1816, the LJS recorded they had received £100 from Mrs. H. Adams[11] of Boston as the first remittance from an Auxiliary formed in Boston. It could be presumed that this remittance was due in part to Frey's ministry, as the LJS Minute states, 'the secretary be requested to state confidentially the particulars of the circumstances concerning Mr Frey's separation from the Society.'[12]

Adams, an Episcopalian, had first become aware of the existence of the London Jews Society through reading Frey's *Narrative*. When the Society became an Anglican institution in early 1815, Adams then became a supporter of the work, and sent her first contribution in July – arriving in London in October.

Not only was this the first American branch of the London Jews Society, but this was one of the first organised works in the United States for ministry among the people of Israel. Ministry to Jewish people in all of America in time became the most significant in the world – and it could point to the influence of Joseph Frey as being part of its very foundations.

Ironically as this first American work was beginning, Frey was en-route to America – but he would not become part of the LJS operations there.

Wolff in Rome

The year 1816 witnessed Joseph Wolff finally moving to Rome. As always he had numerous adventures en-route. At Aarau in Switzerland he lodged with a Roman Catholic priest named Volk, and it was here that he became acquainted with Baroness de Krudener. Wolff relates that the Baroness had received a vision and had come to know Jesus, and then while in Paris in the period after the Battle of Leipzig,[13] she had met with Czar Alexander who seemingly came to personal faith in Jesus.[14]

The Baroness convinced Wolff to visit the infant Basel Seminary, established by the Reformed Church, and where prominent men such as Dr. Blumhardt and

---

9 LJS General Committee Minute 533, 25 June 1816.
10 Frey, *Judah and Israel*, p. 83.
11 Hannah Adams was a direct descendant of President John Adams, and had, since the age of 49 been imbued with a desire to present Jesus as Messiah to the Jewish people. Adams became aware of the work of the London Jews Society through Frey's book *Narrative*.
12 LJS General Committee Minute 609, 22 October 1816.
13 Known also as the Battle of the Nations, where Napoleon was defeated in 1813.
14 Wolff, *Travels*, p. 35.

Christian Spittler were involved. Wolff was unimpressed with the Seminary due to its strong dislike of the Roman Catholic Church.[15] On one occasion while there he was involved in a heated discussion about the Roman Catholic Church in which he confessed that he did not believe in the infallibility of the Pope, to which Blumhardt stated, "With your sentiments you will be banished from Rome." In response Wolff replied, "This is still to be ascertained."[16]

Following stop-overs in Milan, Turin, Genoa and Leghorn, Wolff arrived in Rome in May 1816. News of the 'young man of the Jewish nation' who desired to 'enter the Propaganda'[17] spread quickly and that very day his arrival was impressed upon Pope Pius VII.[18]

Several days after his arrival young Joseph Wolff personally met the Pope himself, who stated to him, "The Propaganda is not yet restored from its confusion during my exile, but you shall go to my own Seminary, and hear the lectures at the *Collegio Romano*, until order is re-established. I shall give instructions for your reception."[19] Wolff then received the blessing of the Pope – and then employing a touch of Jewish *hutzpah*, Wolff gave him a slight pat of thanks on the shoulder.

Wolff's presence in Rome also became known among the foreign community, and he became acquainted with many of them, as well as other visitors to Rome. Among these were Barthold Niebuhr, a renowned historian and the Prussian diplomatic envoy to Rome, and his assistant Dr. Christian Bunsen.

By September 1816 Joseph Wolff was in the *Collegio Romano*, which was dedicated to training priests for the diocese of Rome. His admission there was by direct intervention of the Pope himself. Yet this did not hinder Wolff at the very beginning of his tenure from openly stating his opposition to the infallibility of the Pope. Not surprisingly his sentiments caused more than a mild stir at the College.[20]

Further disputes followed. On one occasion a student alluded to Wolff having placed his hands upon the Pope's shoulders. This student stated that Wolff should not have done this as the Pope was God. Wolff 'became as red as a turkey cock' and responded, "How can you dare to say such a thing! The Pope is dust of the earth … If he was God I could not have touched him." Wolff's bold statement drew all the College leaders out of their seats in defence of their Pope. But Joseph Wolff did not back down.[21]

The theological objections, however, were secondary to what Wolff found was

---

15 Wolff, ibid, p. 36.
16 Wolff, ibid, p. 37.
17 The Propaganda College (or Fide) was the training centre of the Pope to spread the Roman Catholic faith.
18 Wolff, ibid, p. 45.
19 Wolff, ibid, p. 46.
20 Wolff, ibid, p. 48.
21 Wolff, ibid, pp. 58-59.

a spiritual indifference among the professors and lecturers. It was more than apparent that what Wolff sought above all else was to know his Saviour Jesus in a deeper and more personal way. In his zeal to reach this goal he would often times exhibit, as he himself stated, an un-Jesus like behaviour to his superiors.[22]

Joseph deeply desired to learn and understand the ancient Biblical languages, so that he could understand the original meaning of a text. This attitude also put him at variance with the leaders, who preferred that he read and study the works of the Church divines.

It would be reasonable to say that without Papal support it was a miracle that Wolff was able to remain at this prestigious college as long as he did. His time there however would soon end, as restoration work on the Propaganda College was soon to be completed.

---

22 Wolff, ibid, p. 51.

Chapter 16

New Pastures

Joseph Frey reaches America

Despite being ousted from his field of labours in England, Frey took hold of every opportunity of ministering on board ship, meeting for family worship twice a day and preaching on deck on Sundays, weather permitting.[1]

When he arrived in New York on 15 September 1816 Frey was met with immediate disappointment, as the Rev. Dr. Mason, whom he expected to meet, had gone to England. This disappointment though was quickly compensated for. On 18 September 1816 a special committee of the Dutch Reformed Church in New York, which was reviewing a need for a specific ministry among Jewish people, held a meeting in New York. Eichhorn presents the Minutes, which stated:

> Mr. Joseph S. C. F. Frey, who had lately been connected with the Society for the Conversion of the Jews in London and had recently … arrived in this country, was providentially present at the meeting.[2]

After submitting his various letters of recommendation from Bogue, Lewis Way and others, Frey was able to preach in different churches, including the vacant pulpit at Mason's congregation.[3] His first sermon though was at Cedar Street Presbyterian Church on 22 September 1816, of which the *Christian Herald* newspaper recorded:

> To hear the unsearchable riches of Christ proclaimed by a converted Jew was too interesting a circumstance not to excite a very extensive desire in Christians of all denominations among us to attend the worship. It accordingly drew many more than the Church could contain … It was a subject of much regret that very few Jews were present that evening, owing to its being the commencement of a great feast day among them …[4]

Further invitations followed for Frey to speak in different churches throughout New York. His popularity also elicited opposition, from both Christians and Jews. Such opposition merely furthered his popularity.

1 Frey, *Judah and Israel*, p. 83.
2 Eichhorn, ibid, p. 33, referencing Lee M Friedman, *Early American Jews*, p. 101.
3 Frey, *Judah and Israel*, p. 82.
4 *Christian Herald*, 28 September 1816. Quoted in Eichhorn, ibid, p. 34.

While Frey was increasing his exposure in his new adopted homeland, the Dutch Reformed Church committee held a meeting in New York on 6 November 1816 in which numerous denominations participated, to determine if a specific work among the Jewish people was warranted on a non-denominational basis.

The Committee agreed that it was necessary, and on 30 December 1816 the *American Society for Evangelizing the Jews* was established. Joseph Frey was appointed as the first missionary of this Society.[5] Professor Yaacov Ariel, an acknowledged authority on Christian work among the Jewish people in America, stated in his seminal book *Evangelising the Chosen People: Missions to the Jews in American, 1880-2000*, that 'American Protestants first began to evangelize Jews in 1816.'[6]

It seemed like Frey was about to embark on a successful new ministry in his second adopted homeland. He began his ministry by conducting a series of lectures at the North Dutch Church in New York in January 1817. Unfortunately very few Jewish people attended these lectures. Undeterred Frey then set out on a speaking tour to the New England region,[7] including Boston - but he did not speak on behalf of Hannah Adams and her American branch of the London Jews Society.

Although this tour met with a certain degree of success, the failure of the New York lectures to impact the one thousand strong Jewish community adversely affected the interest of the supporters in this venture. By mid-1817 it closed down.

Following a suggestion by several people Frey then established a congregation in a school-house in Mulberry Street in June 1817. This small congregation then out-grew its location.[8] When the congregants wanted him to become their minister he demurred, 'as rumours unfavourable to my character, had been whispered about, I refused to accept of a call until the return of Dr. Mason from Europe, to testify respecting my character.'[9]

When such testimonials arrived, the congregation voted in favour of appointing Frey as their minister. Frey then approached the Presbyterian Church of the United States to become an ordained minister. His application was received and he was ordained on 15 April 1818 by New Jersey's Morris County and New York's Westchester County Presbytery.[10]

This was a turning point for Frey, and a key date in American Christian history, as he became the first Jewish follower of Jesus to be ordained in

---

5 Eichhorn, ibid, p. 34.
6 Ariel, Y. *Evangelising the Chosen People: Missions to the Jews in American, 1880-2000*, (University of North Carolina, 2000).
7 Eichhorn, ibid, p. 36.
8 Frey, *Judah and Israel*, p. 85.
9 Frey, *Judah and Israel*, p, 86.
10 Frey, *Judah and Israel*, p. 87. Eichhorn, ibid, p. 37.

America.¹¹ Several years later, in 1820, circumstances arose whereby Frey left that congregation, and he then applied for a position with the New York Presbytery, and was accepted there in October 1821.¹²

Joseph Wolff in the *Propaganda Fide*

The restoration of the *Propaganda Fide* (College) was completed in December 1817, providing Joseph Wolff the opportunity to now finally fulfill his desire to be trained in order to become a modern day Francis Xavier. He entered the College on the day of Epiphany, an event of much pomp and celebration. Dignitaries including ambassadors and ecclesiastical leaders were all present, and Wolff gave his presentation in five languages, much to the acclaim of all present.¹³

It may have been a new College, but it was the same Wolff. Wherever he felt an issue was contrary to the clear wording of Scripture, it was challenged by Wolff. On one occasion he refuted the teaching of the instructor that the Pope had the right to burn heretics. While the debate continued two men stood at the doorway and observed. One was an Englishman named Henry Drummond.

Afterwards Drummond said, "Wolff, go with me to England," to which Wolff responded, "No; I shall not stir until I am turned out." Wolff was not turned out immediately; the controversies continued thereafter; and his popularity with the hierarchy deteriorated.

Wolff's confidant and friend Barthold Niebuhr, the Prussian ambassador to Rome, once warned him, "Wolff, your life is in danger"¹⁴ and Drummond wrote to him and said, 'Wolff come out of Babylon.' This particular letter was intercepted and read by the Roman Church authorities before it reached him.¹⁵

More controversies followed, and on one occasion he wrote to the head of the College, Cardinal Liotta, 'The Protestants of Germany were right, the Propaganda teaches errors.'¹⁶ Such open comments could be tolerated for a while, but ultimately Wolff's constant challenges were too much. Finally the inevitable occurred, and on 15 April 1818 he was summoned to the office of Cardinal Liotta, who informed him:

> Your sentiments my dear Wolff are clearly known; your correspondence is known; and we know by that correspondence your opinions and manner of thinking. I therefore have to tell you the sentence of Pope Pius VII, who is acquainted with all the circumstances.... you must leave us, for if you remain longer, you will spoil all the rest... You are not for the Propaganda; your

---

11 Eichhorn, ibid, p. 37.
12 Frey, *Judah and Israel*, p. 87.
13 Wolff, *Travels*, p. 60.
14 Wolff, *Travels*, p. 61.
15 Wolff, *Travels*, p. 63.
16 Wolff, ibid, p. 63.

views differ from ours; you must return to Vienna.[17]

At that point Wolff was escorted to an adjacent room where he received new clothes and shoes, two letters of introduction, and was then escorted out of the building by a 'member of the Holy Order', meaning the Inquisition. Outside he bumped into Bunsen, and informed him, "Dr … Bunsen, I am taken to the Inquisition." Bunsen then quickly found and informed Ambassador Niebuhr.[18]

Wolff was then put under house arrest for fifteen hours and finally he was placed in a carriage under guard and escorted out of Rome. Joseph Wolff had entered the very bastion of institutional Christianity and dared to challenge the religious *status quo*. Rome was not interested in heeding his challenge.

Two decades later another Jewish follower of Jesus would again challenge this *status quo*. That challenge though would not be in Rome – but in Jerusalem.

Michael Solomon Alexander

Michael Solomon Alexander's father, Rabbi Alexander, died in 1817. His eldest son now become the rabbi of Schonlanke. According to Deborah Ransom (the daughter of Michael Solomon) her father's brother was 'a terrible bigot.'[19]

The loss of his father and change in the family situation affected Michael Solomon and he thereafter immersed himself in the *Talmud*. Michael Solomon was now on a journey, a journey to discover his true identity. He henceforth spent many hours in the synagogue reading through the many books of rabbinic Judaism and trying to grasp the tenets of the faith of his forefathers. Instead of drawing sustenance from these writings, however, he became progressively less satisfied with the teachings they eschewed.

Michael Solomon's restlessness and inquisitiveness was noticed by his eldest brother, who questioned him. The now Rabbi Alexander was abhorred to hear that Michael Solomon dared question the authority of the *Talmud*, and gave his younger brother an ultimatum - desist from this trend and questioning, or leave home. Michael Solomon chose the latter.

Leaving Schonlanke Alexander chose to head to his father's homeland – England, where he hoped also to teach German and, rather ironically considering his present ambivalence, the *Talmud*. Not for the first time in his adventurous life Michael Solomon had thrown down the gauntlet to the establishment and dared to challenge the *status quo*.

Prior to his departure Michael Solomon prepared himself for an uncertain future, and trained for the position of *shochet* or ritual slaughterer, which according to his own words was, 'given to persons peculiarly qualified, and who

---

17 Wolff, ibid, pp. 64-65.
18 Wolff, ibid, p. 65.
19 D.R.M Ransom, *Life of Mrs. Ransom,* Unpublished manuscript, (London, 1913) p. 5.

must go through the strictest examination by the High Priest.'[20]

Wolff returns to Vienna and then Val-sainte

While Alexander was en-route to England, Wolff was en-route back to Vienna. When he returned there Wolff was quite distraught as the impact of being banished from Rome came home to him. He stayed for a short time there, before moving to join a Redemptorist monastic order at Val-sainte in Switzerland.

Wolff's time at Val-sainte was not pleasant, due mostly to the severe physical abuses administered by the leader of the community and because he could not see how this institution was preparing him for his destiny, to be a missionary. At one point the leader of the community had students spy on Wolff to see if he had any Protestant leanings.[21]

He ultimately left the order, and being in Switzerland, he visited Lausanne. One day while walking he met an English woman, and asked her, "Do you know Henry Drummond."[22] It so happened that she did and that she had even heard of Joseph Wolff! The lady, Miss Greaves then took him to the home of Professor Lavande, where he was informed that expenses for Wolff to travel to England and meet with Henry Drummond would be met.

Wolff arrives in England

Together with Rev. Thomas Jones, Wolff set out in July 1819 on a circuitous journey to England that took in numerous locations including Paris. It was here that he became acquainted with the Scotsman Robert Haldane.[23] Haldane was so enamoured with Wolff that they travelled together to London. On the journey Haldane made Wolff more familiar with the doctrine of justification by faith.

Upon arrival in London, Wolff lived with Henry Drummond, the esteemed banker. While there Drummond took him to several Baptist services. When asked by Drummond if he liked the first service, Wolff responded, "Not at all." Wolff did not believe there to be any reverence in the service.[24] Unperturbed Drummond thereafter took him to a Quaker service, which Wolff likewise did not appreciate.

A meeting and discussion with a Methodist minister somewhat satisfied him, and then Drummond suddenly realised, "I see what you want Wolff!" Drummond then took him to the Episcopal Jews Chapel where the service was performed according to the rites of the Church of England, by the Rev. Charles

20 Hatchard, ibid, *(Appendix)*, p. 37. High Priest refers to senior or chief Rabbi.
21 Wolff, ibid, p, 74.
22 Wolff, ibid, p. 76.
23 Robert Haldane (1764-1842) although a Scotsman, was trained by Rev David Bogue. Alongside his brother John he was involved in an Evangelical awakening in Scotland.
24 Wolff, ibid, p. 79.

Hawtrey.[25]

Wolff felt quite comfortable at this service, 'enchanted with the devotion and beauty of the ritual ... and at once expressed himself satisfied.' Drummond then said to him. "I see you will belong to the Church of England; nevertheless you will find a great deal of pride and annoyance in that Church, as well as in the Church of Rome."[26]

Wolff becomes attached to the London Jews Society
From that point forward Wolff felt himself a member of the Church of England, although he had no problem also attending and taking communion from Dr. Steinkopf of the Lutheran Church. He had no problem with this, as his view was basically 'that members of the living Church of Christ, i.e, those who in the last days shall compose the Church which is to be the Bride of the Lamb, are to be found among the baptized members of all denominations ...'[27]

Wolff had now found a spiritual home: a Church stream which suited his ecclesiastical bent, and was dedicated to introducing Jesus as Messiah to his own people. Hawtrey and Drummond then introduced him to Lewis Way in 1819. Way had not long before returned from his epic journey to Russia and the Crimea, during which he met with Czar Alexander and also spoke on behalf of the Jewish people at the peace conference in Aix-le-Chapelle.

Way then had Wolff introduced to Charles Simeon at King's College in Cambridge. Simeon, together with Dr Marsh of Colchester and Hawtrey agreed that Wolff should attend Cambridge, at the expense of the LJS, and study theology under Simeon and the ancient languages under the tutorship of Dr. Samuel Lee.

Simeon was more than just an academic mentor for the young Wolff, he also found himself playing the role of a father. Wolff had never learned to properly shave himself. Of this necessary hygienic act, it was written, 'Mr Simeon actually appointed an hour (12 o'clock) to instruct him, in the first place, how to sharpen a razor; but the moment Wolff tried, although Simeon had told him to keep the blade flat, he did just the contrary and cut the razor- strop in two. Simeon gave him a slap, laughed, and gave up the shaving lesson.'[28]

Wolff excelled in all his studies, learning amongst other subjects, Arabic, Persian, Chaldean and Syriac, and then on Sunday also spending personal tutorial time with the esteemed Rev. Simeon in his home. He continued in his studies for two years, and if the LJS and Simeon had their way it would have been for longer. But Henry Drummond perceived even before Wolff himself did, that the time had come for him to be released into the world – as a Jewish

---
25 Wolff, ibid, p. 79.
26 Wolff, ibid, p. 79.
27 Wolff, ibid, pp. 79-80.
28 Wolff, ibid, p. 85.

missionary in the mould of Francis Xavier.

Alexander arrives in England – Colchester and Norwich

While Wolff was half way through his studies, Michael Solomon Alexander arrived in England in 1820.[29] Unfortunately the employment he had anticipated as a teacher of German and the *Talmud* never eventuated, so he applied to Solomon Hirschel, Chief Rabbi of the Polish and German Jewish communities in England for work. Rabbi Hirschel appointed him as a private tutor to the children of a Jewish family in Colchester, Essex. Concerning his future employer, Michael Solomon stated, 'My employer was a man of strict integrity, and strongly attached to the principles and ceremonies of Judaism.'

Alexander's move to Colchester would radically change his life. While there he became acquainted with Rev. William Marsh, who was rector of St. Peter's Church.[30] Marsh, unbeknown to the young Alexander, was a prominent and active member of the London Jews Society, and on one occasion he spoke to Alexander about the New Testament. Alexander, however, claimed ignorance of both it and the English language.

Soon after, Michael Solomon saw an advertisement concerning the London Jews Society on a billboard, and enquired of his employer what it meant. Alexander wrote that he:

> … was the first who acquainted me with the exertions which are making in England for the conversion of the Jews, but treated them with derision, and said that every Jew ought to read the New Testament, in order to be more convinced in his own religion.[31]

Alexander wrote of his response to this challenge:

> This roused my curiosity, and not able then to read and understand English, I procured a German Bible. I was greatly struck with the first chapter of St. Matthew, and had no idea that Christians knew anything of our patriarchs; - I was still more struck with the character of Christ, and the excellent morals which he taught; but having gone no further than merely to admire them, it produced no particular effect upon my mind, though it considerably lessened my prejudices.[32]

---

29 According to Alexander himself [Hatchard, ibid, *Appendix*, p. 37] although according to Brian Taylor, *Alexander's Apostasy: First Steps to Jerusalem*, in *Christianity and Judaism*, Ecclesiastical Historical Society, (Blackwell Publishers, Oxford, 1992) it was 1819.
30 Marsh had been influenced by Simeon about the Jewish people. Later, while rector of St. Thomas's in Birmingham, Marsh was affectionately known as 'Millenial Marsh.' Taylor, ibid, p. 365.
31 Hatchard, ibid, p. 38.
32 Hatchard, ibid, p. 38.

Alexander read the New Testament with the same inquisitive mind as he had read the *Talmud* while in Schonlanke. Although inwardly intrigued, he tried to squash these feelings of interest, and thereafter devoted himself more to the study of English and to his teaching.

The Chief Rabbi soon afterwards appointed him to be Rabbi of Norwich,[33] although Malcolm Brown, stated that he was more likely to have acted as no more than a *hazan* and a *shochet* in the early 1820's.[34] While in Norwich Alexander had both the opportunity and time to give Hebrew and German lessons, and to develop his English, a matter which the *Norwich Chronicle* of 1822 also attested to.[35] Alexander wrote that as his English continued to improve it 'afforded me the means of access to many pious Christians.'[36] It would be hard not to, due to the location of the synagogue! The small synagogue was located in the churchyard of St. George's Church, and opposite the local Anglican Cathedral.[37]

After becoming more familiar with the faith and teaching of Christians and the New Testament, Alexander wrote, 'I was in an especial manner led to read the New Testament, and found many of the references there given to the Old Testament prophecies, incontrovertibly fulfilled.'[38]

In all likelihood one of those *pious* Christians he met was a Miss Hancock. In later years Miss Hancock (who seemingly was an invalid, as was her mother) communicated consistently with Alexander, and by all accounts, she was very well versed in the prophecies concerning Israel's restoration. [39]

The familiarity these Christians had with certain Old Testament prophecies that Michael Solomon knew well, and which the Christians saw as being fulfilled in Jesus, greatly perplexed him. More than perplexing him, he was actually becoming quite confused and disorientated by these new interpretations. Relating to this challenging period he stated that he 'endeavoured to shrink and turn away from the divine light which had thus begun to dawn upon me.'[40] More than merely shrinking from this challenge, Michael Solomon needed escape from it.

---

33 Patrick Irwin, *Bishop Alexander and the Jews of Jerusalem,* in Studies in Church History, Vol. 21: Persecution and Toleration, ed. W.J.Shields, (Oxford 1984), p. 317 & Taylor, ibid, p. 366. Brown, see below, though, likened him to an itinerant or peripatetic.
34 Malcolm Brown, *The Jews of Norfolk and Suffolk before 1840* in Jewish Historical Society, Transactions of The Jewish Historical Society of England, Vol. 32, 1990-92 p. 231. He is refuting the reference in the *Jewish Repository,* 1840, p. 240.
35 *Norwich Chronicle,* 6 July and 28 December 1822, See Malcolm Brown, ibid, p. 233.
36 Hatchard, ibid, *Appendix),* p. 38.
37 The Synagogue was also located in the rather ungainly sounding area known as Tombland. It was disused after 1849. Today, 2006, it is the offices of Saunders & Senior Solicitors.
38 Hatchard, ibid, p. 38.
39 See Hancock to Alexander, 1 October 1830, MSS 3397, 136-7, Alexander Papers. Lambeth Palace Archives. [Henceforth 'Lambeth']
40 Hatchard, ibid, p. 38.

Joseph Wolff leaves England

Joseph Wolff now also needed to 'escape' the intellectual confines of Cambridge. After two years of studies Wolff received a letter from Drummond asking why he needed to continue his studies any further. Wolff responded that they wanted him to remain a bit longer so that he could get a bit more 'knowledge of the world' and also to spend some time with Lewis Way at Stanstead Park, again so that he could gain 'more knowledge of the world.'[41]

Drummond was not amused and told Wolff that he was 'as great an ass as my friends Lewis Way and Charles Simeon are … Knowledge of the world can only be gained in the world.'[42] Despite Drummond's reproof, Wolff nevertheless moved down to Stanstead Park. He had not been there long before he realised that Drummond was right. It was time to move out into ministry. The world beckoned, and now Wolff was ready – being sent out by the London Jews Society and financially assisted by Henry Drummond.

Prior to his departure in March 1821 Wolff visited the Jewish synagogue in Duke Street, London. Revealing about as much tact as he had in Rome, Wolff began to hand out pamphlets from the LJS. He was duly cast out of the synagogue and roughed up in the process.[43] This was a foretaste of some of the adventures which lay before him.

A new venture for Frey

Being a minister of a congregation was something quite new for Frey, but for the present he was able to slow down his pace of life. But then in early 1819 he received a very lengthy letter from a Jewish follower of Jesus named John Marc, who was originally from Silesia and was then working for the London Jews Society in Frankfurt, Germany. John Marc requested Frey's assistance in setting up a settlement in America for Jewish followers of Jesus.

Frey initially was not so interested in what Marc wrote. But the final words of Marc's proposal deeply challenged him, 'The blood of the Jews will be found in the skirt of your garment if you do not make the attempt'.[44]

Marc's proposal was then read by Frey to a New York group entitled the Morris County Society for Promoting Learning and Religion, in April 1819. They endorsed the concept, and ultimately requested that Frey and Rev. Stephen Grover take the matter in hand. Together they re-established the defunct Prayer Union for Israel in New York City, and then in November 1819 Frey presented the proposal to four leading Christian ministers from eminent institutions. They were in basic agreement at the soundness of the proposal.[45]

---

41 Wolff, ibid, p. 88.
42 Wolff, ibid, p. 88.
43 Wolff, ibid, pp. 90-91.
44 Eichhorn, ibid, p. 40.
45 Eichhorn, ibid, p. 41.

Frey then presented the proposal to a well renowned former statesman and Christian named Elias Boudinet, on 25 November 1819. Boudinet also endorsed the proposal. Armed with these endorsements the New York Prayer Union decided on 25 January 1820 to officially establish a society in order to establish a settlement in America for Jewish followers of Jesus.

The name of this society, the *American Society for Colonizing and Evangelizing the Jews*, drew immediate opposition from the Jewish community of New York. They stated that the name violated the American Constitution and ultimately succeeded in having the name dropped.

Frey and his colleagues then changed the name to the *American Society for Meliorating the Condition of the Jews*. This time they were successful and were permitted by the New York State Legislature to incorporate their society under that name, on 14 April 1820.[46]

Due to his commitments to his congregation, Frey could not invest much time in this new work for several years, although he did attend the Board meetings when he could. John Marc meanwhile was very active in Germany, and enlisted the support of Count von der Recke who owned an estate at Duesselthal in the Rhine Valley. In early 1821 this estate then became a training ground for these would-be colonisers, Jewish followers of Jesus, before they left for America.[47]

---

46 Eichhorn, ibid, pp. 43-44.
47 Eichhorn, ibid, pp. 48-49.

Chapter 17

Wolff goes to Jerusalem

Wolff departs

On 17 April 1821 Joseph Wolff finally set out on a journey that would place him in a league not akin to Francis Xavier, but in one all of his own. Joseph Wolff was beginning a journey which would make him the great pioneer missionary to the Jewish people in the modern period.

Calling first at Gibraltar Wolff was immediately pressed into service at the Wesleyan Mission. Shortly later he was introduced to Rabbi Gabbay, a well-known Jewish resident. These two learned men then held lengthy discussions in a number of languages. The Rabbi was aware of Lewis Way's great work on behalf of the Jewish people at Aix-le-Chapelle, to which Wolff responded that 'true Christians in all ages have loved the Jews.'[1]

Through Rabbi Gabbay Wolff also met other notable Jewish people. With one, a great Hebrew scholar named Joseph Hassan, Wolff asked what he thought of Jesus' words, "Think not that I have come to destroy the law or the prophets: I am not come to destroy but to fulfil." Hassan replied that he never before read the New Testament, but offered his view about Jesus being the Messiah, stating:

> The design of the Messiah was, according to the prophets, to restore Israel into their own land, and to make them kings and priests; to redeem them from captivity, and to make them a righteous people. And He, the Messiah, must be their king, and mighty to save. But Jesus was sacrificed, it might have been for a good purpose, but this very circumstance shows he was not the Messiah.[2]

To this Wolff responded, "I am entirely of the same opinion that the Messiah will come one day, and restore Israel to their own land: and every true Christian believes it; but they first look on Him whom they have pierced and mourn."[3]

After two months Wolff needed to continue his journey onward – Jerusalem was his goal. The London Jews Society desired a foundation to be laid in the City of the Great King.

---

1 Wolff, *Travels*, p. 93.
2 Wolff, ibid, p. 94.
3 Wolff, ibid, p. 94.

Malta

In mid-June Wolff arrived in Malta and after being released from quarantine he was invited to stay in the home of Dr Cleardo Naudi. Naudi was the local representative for the British and Foreign Bible Society, the Church Missionary Society and the London Jews Society.[4]

As was to become the norm, Wolff's presence caused a stir. When he and several British companions entered the synagogue, the *shamash*[5] said to him, "Thy memory and thy name be blotted out from the book of life! Instantly you leave."[6] Wolff and his companions decided to leave peacefully. He was, however, invited by Sheridan Wilson of the Church Missionary Society to preach, which he did, in Dr Naudi's home.

Egypt

Despite the outbreak of war between Turkey and Greece (part of Greece's fight for independence), Wolff nevertheless continued on to Alexandria. Upon arrival he was met and hosted by the British Consul, Mr Lee. Wolff also met the Consul-General, Mr Salt, who resided in Cairo.

Salt complained to Wolff concerning Melchior Tschoudy, who the London Jews Society had commissioned to go to Palestine in 1820.[7] Tschoudy had been one of the very first Protestants to visit the region.[8] He was followed by Levi Parsons of the American Board of Commissioners for Foreign Missions, who visited there in February 1821.

Parsons and his colleague Pliny Fisk had been sent out from Boston in November 1819 and had made their initial base at Smyrna. They had been instructed by the Board to establish a base in Jerusalem, but, so the instructions stated, 'If the time is not come for a mission to be established at Jerusalem, you will direct your attention to Bethlehem.'[9]

Although the American Board of Commissioners had a vision to introduce all peoples to Jesus as Messiah, both of these pioneer American missionaries had a special feeling for Israel and the Jewish people, as revealed in their farewell sermons, preached in Boston on 31 October 1819. Parsons' sermon on *'The Dereliction and Restoration of the Jews'* using Hosea 3: 4-5 as his text, was an excellent summation of the future restoration of the Jewish people to their spiritual heritage.[10]

---

4 Cleardo Naudi was a Roman Catholic who espoused the Evangelical faith.
5 The 'servant' of the synagogue, basically similar to the deacon or warden in the church.
6 Wolff, ibid, p. 103.
7 Wolff, ibid, p. 108. Salt informed Wolff that Tschoudy was a fake. Wolff accordingly informed the LJS of Salt's observations, and Tschoudy was dismissed.
8 He was preceded by Christian Burckhardt of the British and Foreign Bible Society, who had visited briefly there in 1818-1819.
9 Instructions, as reported in *LJS Report*, 1820, p. 434.
10 Mizrachi, E. *Two Americans Within the Gates*, (Hagerstown, 1995), pp. 111-118.

Another pioneer evangelical Christian to visit Jerusalem was James Connor of the Church Missionary Society (CMS), who although staying briefly in Jerusalem, nevertheless managed to hand out numerous pamphlets.

Wolff, meanwhile, did not take long before he was engaged in conversation, argument and discussion. On one occasion he discussed with a number of Jewish people about Jesus for several hours in Hebrew. His first public meeting was at the British Consulate, the congregation being the numerous British subjects who lived in Alexandria. Numerous were the meetings with various residents of Alexandria, but the one Jewish man who impressed him most was a Russian Jew, en-route to Jerusalem to await the coming of the Messiah. This man, Yehiel, had heard of a man going to Jerusalem in order to convince the Jewish people that Jesus was Messiah. Wolff confessed, "I am going to Jerusalem." Yehiel then proceeded to inform Wolff that if the Jewish people, dispersed among the Gentiles for 1700 years, had not accepted Jesus, then they would not do so now.[11]

From Alexandria Wolff travelled to Cairo, and upon arrival there was a guest at the British Consulate, courtesy of Mr. Salt. While in the Egyptian capital he conversed with whom ever wanted to sit with him. His presence in Cairo quickly became general knowledge, and even Muhammed (Mehmet) Ali, the viceroy of Egypt, became aware of him.

An opportunity then arose while he was in Cairo for him to travel to Mount Sinai in the company of two gentlemen. Wolff hired several camels and took with him pamphlets in various languages, including Hebrew, and they set out in October 1821. Visiting Mount Sinai was an emotional experience for Wolff, but his trip was probably just as memorable for him due to being caught up in the centre of local politics.

The relationship between the monks at St Catherine's Monastery and the local Bedouins was not good, and at the end of his trip he was left destitute and had to be assisted by Consul Salt.[12]

The journey to Jerusalem

After returning to Cairo, somewhat the worse for the wear after several tiring incidents in the Sinai, Wolff then set out for Jerusalem in December 1821 accompanied by twenty camels laden with literature and he joined a caravan comprised of numerous types of people. When he finally arrived at Jaffa Wolff decided not to journey on to Jerusalem, but to head north first, and spend extra time learning the local Arabic dialect. His travels then took him to Mount Carmel and Acre, where he stayed with the British Consul Mr Abbot.

While continuing northwards to Beirut he travelled with two Jewish men who

11 Wolff, ibid, p. 114.
12 Wolff, ibid, p. 128.

were followers of Jesus – due to having received pamphlets from Melchior Tschoudy! At Sidon he spoke to a group of Jewish people about Jesus, and then spent considerable time in a Maronite monastery on Mount Lebanon. His time in Lebanon was full of interesting discussions and debates with Maronite leaders, often about the rightness of Protestantism over against Catholicism.

His circuitous journey to Jerusalem now led south again, but before arriving at Jaffa he was robbed by Bedouins who took all his personal belongings – including his clothes. After receiving replacement clothes in Jaffa, Wolff was ready to head up to Jerusalem.

Jerusalem

Joseph Wolff arrived at the gates of Jerusalem on 8 March 1822. Due to fears of attacks by roaming Bedouin the gates were closed - but were opened for him. He spent the first day with the Franciscans and then moved to the Armenian Convent. There his room very quickly became a meeting place for all kinds of different people. He also discovered that the Greek Bishop Procopius had tracts in various languages which had been distributed by Connor of the CMS, and Levi Parsons of the American Mission.

While appreciating the opportunity to speak with the various types of people he met, the focus of Wolff's visit was to present Jesus to the Jewish people. It was a high honour therefore when he was called for by the much respected Rabbi Mendel. Mendel had one main intention in mind – to bring Wolff back to the faith of his forefathers. As the two men met, the room quickly filled up with many observers. This was just the first of many such meetings while Wolff remained in Jerusalem.

Finally after much time and effort Mendel asked Wolff, "What do you think now of the Talmud?" Wolff replied, "The Talmud is a lie from the beginning to the end."[13] Mendel had tried his best, but on this occasion had not succeeded in his quest to bring Wolff back into the fold.

Apart from spending time in theological debate with Rabbi Mendel and other Jewish people, Wolff also spent time studying languages, and either selling or handing out some of the large amount of material he had with him. Often Christians from many of the different groups called on him for material in their language. As could be expected the Jewish authorities did not want any materials taken which included the New Testament, and soon some of the Roman Catholic leaders forbade their flock from taking the Protestant Bibles.

After a stay of some three months Wolff was obliged to depart primarily due to a conflict between the rival pashas of Acre and Damascus.[14] Despite this somewhat hasty departure, he was able to report to the LJS: '... even the Jews

---

13 Wolff, ibid, p. 130.
14 Wolff, *Life and Journal*, p. 71.

of Jerusalem were ready to listen to what I had to say.'[15]

Wolff travels north

Departing from Jerusalem Wolff travelled north to Tripoli, then to Latakia and arrived in Antioch by May 1822. Wolff then continued on to Aleppo where he resided with the Dutch Consul, Monsieur Mayseek. There he circulated materials to the local inhabitants in Hebrew, Arabic and Persian, and had a meeting with some respected Jewish people concerning the identity of Jesus. When Wolff proclaimed that He was the Son of God, they all departed. One, however, later confessed that Wolff was right –and then was found dead the day after.[16]

It was while in Aleppo that the region suffered a major earthquake and many cities were partly destroyed.[17] Concerning this time Wolff stated, 'It did not cost me much trouble to induce Romanists, Greeks, Maronites to kneel with me a Jew, and pray to our Lord Jesus Christ. In such an hour the difference of sects was forgotten ... But earthquakes interrupted our prayers.'[18]

Leaving the mainland Wolff then sailed to Cyprus. It was an inopportune time as the Turks were in the process of massacring Greek civilians in Nicosia. Wolff managed to save the lives of six Greeks 'by his earnest intercession.' He also managed to save some children and sent them to England where Drummond and others provided for them.[19]

Leaving Cyprus Wolff returned to Egypt and shortly later Consul Salt introduced him to the Egyptian leader, Mehmet Ali, who, Wolff wrote, 'was certainly one of the greatest tyrants who ever lived.'[20] He then returned to Malta for a two week respite, whereupon he met Pliny Fisk and Jonas King associated with the 'American Board of Commissioners for Foreign Missions'. Fisk later wrote to Hannah Adams in Boston:

> We have been cheered and encouraged lately by the arrival in this part of the world of a fellow labourer, from whose exertions we hope for great good, especially among the Jews. I refer to the Rev. Joseph Wolff, a Polish Jew, who embraced Christianity ... and has lately come to this country to preach the Gospel to his brethren according to the flesh ...[21]

The three ambassadors for Jesus then left Malta in January 1823 destined first for Egypt. Consul Lee was absent from Alexandria when they arrived, so they

---

15 *JE* 1823, p. 159.
16 Wolff, *Travels*, p, 169.
17 Wolff, *Travels*, p. 170.
18 Wolff, *Life and Journal*, p. 75.
19 Wolff, *Travels*, p. 172.
20 Wolff, *Travels*, p. 173.
21 Fisk to Adams, quoted in Mizrachi, ibid, p. 268.

were advised to spend the night at the home of a Jewish lady named Stella. Although later informed that she was a 'Rahab', King in particular stated that they would stay in the same place and be a witness for Jesus. A service was then held in 'Stella's place', with Wolff preaching in Arabic, Hebrew, German and Italian, Fisk in English and modern Greek and King in French. Among the congregation were the French and Italian consuls as well as a number of Jewish people.[22]

Fisk was eager to discuss the claims of Jesus with Jewish people as well as Gentiles. On one occasion he was involved in a conversation and did not seem to be proceeding far. Then he asked Wolff to pray in Hebrew, which he did, whereupon, Fisk recorded, 'After this they were more attentive and serious than before.'[23]

Return to Jerusalem
After spending some time in Cairo the three followers of Jesus set out for Jerusalem, arriving there in mid-April 1823. Wolff wrote of their arrival: 'Fisk and King took their lodging in the Greek Convent and I took mine among the Jews of Mount Zion. They went to the uncircumcision and I to the circumcision.'[24]

Initially Wolff was warmly welcomed, even by Rabbi Mendel, who obviously believed he could still woo Wolff back into the rabbinic fold. One other who welcomed him back was A. Ben David, who Wolff had introduced to Jesus during his first sojourn in Jerusalem.

While King and Fisk then continued on to Lebanon, Wolff remained for several more months. Following their departure Wolff became quite ill with fever, and it was opportune that a British officer, Colonel Craddock arrived in Jerusalem at that time and nursed him back to health.[25]

Despite this impediment Wolff made the most of every opportunity presented to him. When he finally left Jerusalem in July 1823 he wrote to the LJS:

> ... there is now at Jerusalem, by God's grace, a feeling and a spirit of enquiry, excited among the Jews, even according to the confession of the Rabbis, which never existed before.[26]

His positive (albeit over-positive) reports encouraged the LJS to consider establishing a permanent base in Jerusalem. Such optimism was furthered when Dr Cleardo Naudi wrote to the LJS: 'Jerusalem was thought impracticable for missionary undertakings; the Jews there peculiarly inaccessible from pride,

---

22 Wolff, *Travels*, p, 175.
23 Mizrachi, ibid, p. 271.
24 Wolff, *Life and Journal*, p. 90.
25 Wolff, *Travels*, p. 178.
26 *JE* 1824, p. 64.

bigotry, &c. But Wolff has cleared the way, and himself in great measure succeeded with them.'[27]

The LJS decide to open a base in Jerusalem

Impressed with the positive reports of Wolff, the LJS decided in 1823 to establish a permanent base in Jerusalem. They accordingly sent out their most trusted ambassador, Lewis Way. Lewis Way was accompanied by Rev. William Lewis, an Irishman, who would then remain in Jerusalem once the foundation had been laid. Prior to their departure a special fund was established in Britain, entitled the 'Palestine Fund' for the erection of various institutions 'within the precincts of the Holy Land.'[28]

These men travelled first to Beirut and thence to the Mountain of Lebanon. From Jerusalem Wolff had continued north to Sidon, and then into the mountains to meet with Way, Lewis, and the American missionaries at the monastery of Antoura. The purpose of this meeting was to develop a common strategy for the establishment of an evangelical witness in southern Syria (which was also known as Palestine).

Wolff wrote that it was Way's desire for him, 'to remain in the mission house he has hired here to assist Mr. Lewis in hebrew, [sic] and then to proceed with him on the mission.'[29] It was not, however, part of Wolff's mandate to remain stationary. Way later wrote of Wolff:

> As a pioneer I deem him matchless … but, if order is to be established, or arrangements made, trouble not Wolff. He knows of no church except his own heart; no calling but that of zeal; no dispensation but that of preaching. He is devoid of enmity towards man, and full of the love of God. By such an instrument – who no school hath taught – whom no college could hold, is the way of the Judean wilderness preparing…[30]

While Wolff then departed and made his way on to Damascus and further East, Way and his colleagues continued with their planning. Unfortunately all did not work out well for Way and he was forced to return to Britain before he could make his journey to Jerusalem. The task of laying the permanent foundation in that venerable city would now be entrusted to Rev William Lewis, who later in the year ventured there accompanied by the Americans Fisk, King and Bird, and Rev William Jowett of the CMS.

These men failed in their efforts, and in the following years the LJS also sent Dr. George Dalton and Rev. John Nicolayson to Jerusalem. Despite their faith and perseverance though, the established Islamic *status quo* held firm – and no

---

27 *Jewish Expositor*, 1824, quoted in *Life and Journal*, p. 71. Naudi also mentioned how the American missionaries were also now desirous of having a permanent resident in Syria instead of Smyrna.
28 LJS Report, 1823, p. 224.
29 Wolff, *Life and Journal*, p. 112.
30 Wolff, *Travels*, p, 179.

permanent Protestant work was permitted there.[31]

Lewis and Dalton well understood this dynamic and wrote to the LJS in London that any Protestant work in the city and indeed the land were fruitless unless there would be a change of government there, and that a British consulate was established in Jerusalem.[32] Wolff might have opened the door, but it was going to require a miracle if any Evangelical foundation was going to be permanently established in Jerusalem.

Frey's work in America
Elias Boudinet died in October 1821, and in his will he left the American Society the choice of either a cash sum, or a large acreage in Pennsylvania for them to use to settle Jewish followers of Jesus from Europe.

Count von der Recke then sent an emissary named Bernhard Jadownicky to America. His arrival in January 1822 made the American Society, and particularly Joseph Frey, realise that indeed this was a serious venture. Frey then resigned his pastorate in September 1822 and went full time into working for the American Society.

Frey embarked on a long speaking tour throughout eastern America in December 1822, which was only completed in June 1823. This tour was so successful that the American Society held a public meeting, on 9 May 1823. In that meeting they agreed not to accept Boudinet's offer of land, but instead to accept the $1000 in cash and purchase land closer to New York for the settlement of Jewish followers of Jesus.

Interest in this vision now grew and the American Society Board was soon comprised of numerous very well respected American citizens. Interest may have mounted, but so too did opposition. A Jewish magazine known as *The Jew* then began, and spent considerable space attacking both the aims of the American Society, and Frey personally.

Meanwhile in 1823 several Jewish followers of Jesus left Duessenthal and made their way to America where they anticipated being supported by the American Society. After their arrival Frey and four other Hebrew Christians formed themselves into a 'Jewish Converts Society'.[33]

One of those who arrived from Europe was Erasmus Simon. Thereafter

---

31 Dr. Dalton from Ireland died in Jerusalem in 1825. Nicolayson, was a Pietest Lutheran from Denmark, who was challenged to enter into missions by Moravian missionaries. He trained at the Berlin Seminary – following in the footsteps of Joseph Frey.
32 *JE*, 1824, p. 380 & 382; *JE* 1825, p.16-17. Lewis wrote on 21 June 1825 'I hope the Committee and the friends to the general welfare and peace of Jerusalem, have determined before this to effect something, with the view of obtaining a resident consul or protector, in behalf of visitors and European settlers at Jerusalem, Jews as well as Gentiles.' *JE*, 1825, p. 427; *JE*, 1826, p. 76.
33 Eichhorn, ibid, pp. 53-4. Some more Jewish followers later joined, but this, the 'Jewish Converts Society', ended in 1826.

he and Frey travelled extensively promoting the aims of the American Society. Frey was so esteemed by the supporting constituency that in 1824 he was elected a Director for Life.[34]

The American Society finally leased land for the proposed settlement in 1825 about eighty kilometres from New York City, which was known as Harrison Farm. At the time of their annual meeting on 13 May 1825 the Society had some 2,750 subscribers.[35]

Unfortunately the venture did not succeed.[36] With the collapse of the Harrison Farm venture, the American Society lost all of the Jewish followers (or as they preferred to refer to themselves, 'Hebrew Christians') except Frey. A crisis now enveloped the American Society. After six years of operations they had very little to show for the huge investment in it. The question was now asked: where to now?

The American Society Board decided to change one clause of the Constitution and to now embark not upon colonisation but evangelism. But it was then revealed that legally they could not do this, while in addition many of the contributors also objected. Eichhorn wrote: 'Jewish settlement or missionary society? A mood of confusion and helplessness settled over the Board. It knew not what to do. No activities were being carried on, no money collected.'[37] Even their organ, *Israel's Advocate*, stopped publication in 1826.

Frey was deeply affected by all these happenings. The American Society Board encouraged him to return to ministry as a minister. Then matters suddenly changed during 1827 during which property was leased at Yorkville, and Frey moved there with his family. He then made an effort to establish a Presbyterian church at Yorkville. When this venture also failed Joseph Frey was thrust into yet another personal crisis.

---

34 Eichhorn, ibid, p. 56.
35 Eichhorn, ibid, p. 58.
36 See Eichhorn, ibid, pp. 59-60 for more details.
37 Eichhorn, ibid, p. 61.

Chapter 18

Alexander in Plymouth

A Move to Plymouth

Providence was soon to once again play a role in the life of Michael Solomon Alexander. In 1823 the Chief Rabbi recommended him for the position of *Schochet* and Prayer-reader in Plymouth.[1] Alexander wrote of this change, 'I felt to become reconciled to my former views, and regain my peace of mind, with a full determination to have no intercourse with Christians.'[2]

On arrival shortly afterwards at Plymouth, the *parnos,* or head of the synagogue, took him to the home of his mother-in-law, Mrs. Levy (also spelt Levi). There Michael Solomon met a young Deborah, Mrs. Levy's daughter. It was, he later recalled, love at first sight. Only three months later Alexander gave her an official letter of proposal, and three days after that, they were officially engaged.

Re-introduction to Messiah Jesus

For the first three months of his residence in Plymouth Alexander had no contact with Christians. Then he was asked to give Hebrew lessons to Rev. Benjamin Golding, curate of St George's chapel in Stonehouse.[3] Together they studied the Old Testament and looked at prophecies relating to the person and coming of the Messiah. It was during this time that Alexander came 'almost to the conviction that Jesus was the Messiah.'[4] Alexander now entered into a deep internal conflict. He would secretly go down to Stonehouse Church on Sunday evenings 'and under the shadow of its walls listen to the psalms and hymns'.[5]

Another who befriended the young rabbi was Captain Thicknesse of the Royal Navy (Stonehouse chapel was located close to the naval docks). On one occasion Thicknesse loaned him an account of a rabbi who believed in Jesus as Messiah named Rabbi Solomon Druitch. Alexander wrote 'I derived much benefit by it, as it is very much according with my history.'[6]

Alexander now entered into a troubled period as he wrestled with the

---

1 There was no official rabbi in Plymouth between 1815-1829. A *shochet* was appointed in 1822, perhaps Alexander's predecessor. His task was not only to slaughter animals but also to assist the *hazzan* or reader, to teach the children for two hours on Sunday, Monday, Tuesday and Wednesday mornings. B Taylor, ibid, p. 367.
2 Hatchard, ibid, p. 38.
3 St. George's Church in Chapel Street, Stonehouse, erected in 1789, no longer exists. It was partly destroyed in the blitz and its remaining stones were used in the repair of St. Andrews.
4 Hatchard, ibid, p. 39.
5 Corey, ibid, p. 13.
6 Alexander to Golding, 23 July 1824, MSS 3393 [1-2], Lambeth.

conviction of Jesus as Messiah. Finally, while walking with Deborah at Stoke, he took out and gave her a pamphlet explaining the coming to faith in Jesus as Messiah. More than likely this was the pamphlet about Rabbi Solomon Druitch, although Muriel Corey states it was about a certain Joseph Wolff.[7] Deborah was horrified, and told her mother about this unexpected development. Mrs. Levi was even more distraught than her daughter. Deborah wrote a letter to break off the engagement. Yet Michael Solomon's love for her had not changed. In speaking to her mother Michael said: "Did I believe the Christian religion to be the true one, I would embrace it at all costs."[8]

When news got out of Michael Solomon's interest in Jesus, the family became very negative towards him. Deborah's brother-in-law declared that the marriage must not take place. Michael Solomon and Deborah did however write to each other. In these letters he asked her to read certain passages in Isaiah, which she did in secret. Deborah was slowly coming to the same realization as Michael Solomon. Her mother detected such changes, and gave her a very difficult time. Mrs. Deborah Ransom, daughter of Alexander, later wrote of this period:

> Papa and Mama both suffered persecution for their faith. Mama was shut up a whole winter's night in the drawing-room with no covering but the hearth rug, as her mother vainly hoped that by that course Mama would give up her fiancé (Papa), who had been for many months unsettled in his belief.[9]

Deborah's brother and sister also tried to get her to renounce Michael Solomon, which in turn caused Deborah to inform them that they were going the right way to cause her to follow in Michael Solomon's footsteps. This apparently caused her relatives to change tactics and permitted her to see him again, and, over the following thirteen months, consent to marry was given and withdrawn some five times.

This was indeed a trying time for Alexander. He wrote in July 1824 to Golding, then having removed to Kingston-upon-Thames, in response to a letter he had received from Golding:

> I can assure you my dear friend, that it was as a healing medicine to me, as it met me in the midst of affliction and trouble in body and soul, at the same time it did not less affect me, as it brought to my mind the happy and instructive intercourses which I enjoyed, while you were here, and of which

---

7 Corey, ibid, p. 13. Alexander stated that Captain Thicknesse presented him with an account of how Rabbi Solomon Druitch came to faith in Jesus. See: Alexander to Golding, 23 July 1824, MSS 3393 [3-4], Lambeth.
8 Corey, ibid, p. 15.
9 Ransom, ibid, p. 6.

I am now deprived of. I can impossibly express how much I did and do still feel your absence, for though I am happy and grateful to say, that the Lord is dealing graciously with me, in enlightening my understanding more & more ; still at the same time, satan is not backward in using his instruments & Power to raise difficulties & Doubts in my mind, in order to destroy my happiness and peace, which I am so far convinced is only to be found in true conviction and dependence on Him, who is gracious to all his followers.'[10]

Marriage

Mrs. Levy's harsh attitude forced Michael Solomon and Deborah to marry sooner than they would have desired. The marriage finally took place according to Jewish tradition under the *huppa* on 3 November 1824,[11] at the Crown Hotel in Devonport, a village across the waterway from Stonehouse and Plymouth.

The Alexanders lived in Plymouth for several months, during which time Captain Thicknesse often visited Michael Solomon. During this period Alexander once again went through a difficult period as his unhappiness often returned.

Finally Alexander confided about his struggles with an old learned Jewish man. It was a mistake, as the old man exploded with rage. Before long the whole matter was blown out of control and the Chief Rabbi was consulted. Rabbi Hirschel, 'treated it as a temptation of the devil, and wrote to Alexander begging him to go before the Ark in the synagogue and curse the God of the Christians.'[12]

Much pressure was now brought to bear upon Michael Solomon. His dilemma was well addressed by one Jewish man, Mr. Altmann, who asked him 'if he believed Jesus of Nazareth was the messiah'. Alexander replied: 'That is the difficulty, and on this I cannot make up my mind.'[13]

This sentiment sums up Alexander's predicament. Yet he was not without encouragement. During this difficult period he received letters not only from Golding, but also from Marsh, and Miss Hancock, to whom he wrote on 7 September 1824:

> I am only happy to say, that we are both growing stronger in the truths of Xnty & in seeing our former Blindness, but I am sorry to say that I have not at present strength enough to open my mind publicly, our principal feast & the day Atonement will be in a fortnight and I shall have more opportunity then to declare my sentiments, whereas if I should do it now I should be too much persecuted, and I do not know how I should bear it myself.'

10 Alexander to Golding, 23 July 1824, MS 3393, 1-2, Lambeth.
11 Taylor, ibid, p.367. It was reported in the *Plymouth and Devonport Journal* on 11 November 1824.
12 Corey, ibid, p. 18.
13 Corey, ibid, p. 18.

Alexander also said that there were two or three people who knew of his sentiments, but they did not say anything publicly about them. 'I trust, in respect of that' he wrote to Miss Hancock, 'the Lord will soon give me strength & Spirit that I may declare his name among my Brethren & unto kings and not be ashamed.'[14]

Entering into covenant with Jesus
The Jewish community was loath to lose Alexander. The Synagogue elders consulted the Chief Rabbi Solomon Hirschel again, and this time Hirschel temporarily suspended Alexander from office. Michael Solomon wrote of this period:

> This was one of the most painful periods of my life; Satan stirred up every possible means to present fears and doubts to me.
>
> Those who are acquainted with human nature, and with the influence of early education, will easily be able to judge in what a painful situation I was then placed – by following the dictates of my conscience, I had nothing else to expect than to lose all that was valuable to me in this world, a comfortable and sufficient livelihood, together with the affections and friendship of all who were dear to me – but by yielding to the entreaties of my friends I should have inflicted a wound upon my conscience – in short, many painful ideas presented themselves to me ...[15]

Alexander added as a footnote to the above struggle, 'that so great was the struggle and so earnest the entreaties of my friends at that time, that I was even induced to appeal personally, and also by letter, to the leader of the congregation to say, that I should be happy to retrace my steps, if any means could be found to remove the difficulties by which I was encompassed.'[16]

To compound Michael Solomon's situation, Deborah's relatives now pressured her to leave him. On one occasion her mother came to Plymouth from Devonport to visit Deborah, and upon hearing that she would not leave her husband, the exasperated mother began wailing as if for the dead. Mrs Levy left the house threatening to drown herself, but Michael Solomon followed her from a discrete distance and ensured she arrived home safely.[17]

Michael Solomon's quest for truth led him more and more into the open. This quest was in a sense determined for him by his suspension from office. He then regularly attended St. Andrews Church (located adjacent to the Synagogue) and heard 'a dear friend', undoubtedly Rev John. Hatchard,[18] preach. Concerning the

---

14 Alexander to Miss Hancock, 7 September 1824, MSS 3393 [3-4],Lambeth.
15 Hatchard, ibid, p. 40.
16 Hatchard, ibid, p. 40.
17 Corey, ibid, p. 19.
18 John Hatchard had only recently arrived at St. Andrews in August 1824.

'spiritual instruction' he received from this man, Alexander said he was 'greatly indebted.'[19] Then on Good Friday 1825 he walked with a friend to nearby Plympton and heard a sermon on the text, 'As Moses lifted up the serpent in the wilderness, even so must the Son of Man be lifted up.'[20]

Shaken by the rebuffs, and challenged by his quest for truth, Michael Solomon continued to read through the *Tenach*[21] and New Testament, aided by Golding, Hatchard, Thicknesse and Mr John Synge from Ireland.[22] By mid-1825 Michael Solomon came to the ultimate realization that indeed, Jesus did fulfill the Messianic prophecies.

The baptism was set for 22 June 1825. As could be expected tensions were high, especially considering that St. Andrews was adjacent to the Plymouth Synagogue where Alexander had officiated. On the night before the baptism there was a failed attempt to kidnap Deborah. That same night the maid overheard two Jewish people say, 'If that apostate will be baptized, I will set fire to his house if I die for it. He shall not disgrace our holy religion.'[23] The Alexanders spent the night at the Hatchard's house. Several Jewish people came asking the maid if the Alexanders were home, and when told they were not, they left.

Baptism

The service at St. Andrews was very well attended. Rev Robert Lampen read the prayers, while Captain Thicknesse and Rev John Golding were his sponsors. Deborah attended the service, but she was in a state of semi shock throughout.

Hatchard preached a powerful and challenging sermon, from Hosea 3:4-5, entitled 'The Children of Israel shall abide many days...' and provided a profound historical analysis of the Jewish nation, of their receiving God's promises and mercies, and then turning away and provoking God to anger, culminating in the rejection of Jesus the Messiah, 'the man who was Jehovah's fellow.'[24]

But it was his in-depth description of the future restoration of Israel that was most stirring. Concerning the second part of Hosea's prophecy, 'they shall return in the latter days' Hatchard proclaimed:

> It has been considered by some that the predictions and promises respecting the restoration of the house of Israel, received their full accomplishment in their return from captivity in Babylon, therefore, no further manifestation of mercy shall be made on behalf of those, who for so long a series of years,

19 Hatchard, ibid, p. 40.
20 Corey, ibid, p. 19. There are two churches he could have visited, St Mary's or St. Maurice.
21 *Tanach* =the Old Testament. *Tanach* (also spelt *Tenach*) is an acronym for T = Torah, N = the Prophets, and CH = the Writings.
22 John Synge was from Glomore Castle in Ireland and was in Plymouth for the benefit of his wife's health. Synge had been a member of the Church of Ireland Jews Society Committee since 1822.
23 Corey, ibid, p. 20.
24 Hatchard, ibid, p. 12.

were the unthankful and rebellious recipients of the favours of the Lord of Hosts.

The testimony of both the Old and New Testament scriptures expressly shows, that 'God hath *not* cast away his people which he foreknew' [Romans 11:2] for although 'as concerning the gospel they are enemies for your sakes; but as touching the election, they are beloved for the father's sake.'

What saith the Holy Ghost by the prophet Jeremiah? 'I will gather them out of all countries whither I have driven them in mine anger, and in my fury, and in great wrath; and I will bring them again unto this place and I will cause them to dwell safely; and they shall be my people, and I will be their God: and I will give them one heart, and one way, that they may fear me *forever* ... so will I bring upon them all the good that I have promised them.'* [chapt 32:42,47]

This most gracious promise assuredly has not yet been fulfilled respecting our elder brethren, the Jews – for they *have* departed from the Lord – the *everlasting* covenant here promised to be made unto them, has *not* been entered into; and therefore we confidently anticipate the arrival of the period when the Jew and the Gentile shall be found one fold under one shepherd, even Jesus Christ the mediator of this new, this better, this everlasting covenant.'

Leaving Jeremiah, Hatchard then turned to Ezekiel and addressed the issue of the dry bones of Israel, as well as explaining certain restorationist promises in Micah and Zechariah.[25] Hatchard then proclaimed:

Thus too the apostle Paul, in the 9th, 10th and 11th chapters of his epistle to the Romans, most clearly demonstrates that he looked forward with delight and gratification to the period when his brethren should be saved – when the receiving of them should be, as life from the dead.[26]

Hatchard then progressed from the theoretical to the practical, and addressed the issue of why they were gathered together in St. Andrews on that day. He continued:

If the conversion of a soul from the ways of sin to the ways of righteousness is a matter upon which there is joy among the angels in heaven, surely when the vail which remaineth upon the children of Israel is done away in Christ, it is a cause for *peculiar* thankfulness unto him ... Such an event, my Christian brethren, I have this day the delight to announce to you – A member of the house of Israel, will at this time 'Subscribe with his hand unto the Lord, and surname himself by the name of Israel [Isaiah 45.5].

---

25 Ezekiel 37; Micah 4:42; Zechariah 8:10; 12:10
26 Hatchard, ibid, pp. 24-25.

Hatchard then challenged any Jewish people then present to be like the Bereans of old and search the Scriptures – as Alexander himself had so painstakingly done over a period of years. He also challenged the Christians present to 'pray for the long neglected and widely scattered nation of Israel', stating, 'be assured, our Zion cannot become the praise of the whole earth, until the remnant of Israel and Judah be brought in – the language of prophecy, the signs of the times, the event of this memorable day, all conspire to animate the Christian heart, and ought to encourage us in the use of every means for the consummation of that era, when both to the Jew and the gentile, Christ shall be all and in all.'[27]

His final challenge was to Alexander himself, commissioning him to walk steadfastly before the Lord, and to 'give no rest day or night unto God until he make Jerusalem the joy of the whole earth.' This challenge was then followed by an admonition:

> Be assured your friends, your enemies, the world at large, angels in heaven, and the condemned spirits in hell, will be carefully marking the line of conduct you pursue, many I trust will follow you with their prayers, whilst others will not be deficient in zeal to draw you aside from the path into which you are now entering; but fear not, greater is he who is for you than all who are against you.[28]

Alexander was also encouraged to pray for his brethren according to the flesh.[29] Concerning this most extraordinary service, the local newspaper *The Plymouth and Devonport Weekly Journal*, wrote:

> Mr Alexander, late Reader to the Jewish congregation in this town, and who has held other offices of character and respectability among the Jews, was baptized in the Christian Faith, by the Rev. Mr. Hatchard, in the presence of an immense congregation who appeared to take great interest in the ceremony.[30]

Although the Christian community was pleased and even intrigued by the event, the local Jewish community, and even the wider Jewish community, was shocked by the event.[31]

Exeter & Deborah's Baptism

That night the Alexanders stayed at the vicarage at Stonehouse with Golding. The following day they proceeded to stay with a Mr. and Mrs. Groves in Exeter.[32] Shortly afterwards, Alexander sold his books and furniture and gave up

---

27 Hatchard, ibid, pp. 30-31.
28 Hatchard, ibid, p. 35.
29 Hatchard, ibid, p. 34.
30 Hatchard, ibid, p. 40.
31 Taylor, ibid, p. 363.
32 So states Corey, ibid, p. 24. Alexander himself wrote on one occasion that he was much in despair 'especially on account of Mrs Alicarz [sic].' (Alexander to Golding, 5 July 1825, MS 3393 [5-6]), Lambeth. On another occasion he stated how he was very fond of Mr and Mrs Graves [sic Groves] (Alexander to Golding, 30 September 1825, MSS 3393 [7], Lambeth.

his house in Plymouth and they moved into lodgings near St. Sidewell's parish church in Exeter.[33]

Unsurprisingly at this juncture Alexander became unwell. The stress and pressure of the preceding months must have been almost unbearable upon the young former rabbi. He wrote to Golding on 5 July 1825 that since coming to Exeter he had experienced much despair, 'my struggles of mind have been great since I came to Exeter. I do not find that spiritual comfort here,' and mentioned just how much he needed the Spirit and how much he missed the communications and instructions from Golding and Hatchard, and also made special mention of 'our dear friends Mr and Mrs Synge.[34]

Alexander's situation was not unique as most adults, both Jewish and Gentile, encounter tough spiritual struggles when renouncing their former life and entering into covenant with Jesus. In Alexander's situation, though, he was now cut off from the support apparatus which had helped him through the difficult situation at Plymouth. It was indeed a testing time for his faith. Thankfully, there were sympathetic people who could support the couple and a Miss Paget lent him her pony and he went riding each day for three months which assisted him in recuperating his health. It would not be the first occasion that Alexander would endure health problems.

Meanwhile Deborah, obviously deeply touched by the tremendous changes in her husband's life, continued her reading of the Scriptures. Michael Solomon wrote to Golding on 30 September 1825, 'I have much less earthly care and I find myself nearer to the Lord.' He wrote how appreciative he was of his wife's advancement, and that she was:

> Much advanced in spiritual knowledge & comfort, I can truly say now, she is a great help for me, she is fully determined by the blessing of the Lord to dedicate herself to him by baptism, which I hope will take place a day or two before we leave Exeter, at the next Jewish meeting which will be on the 27th of October, when Mr. Hawtrey and Mr. Marsh will be here, and after that we expect to go to Dublin.[35]

Unfortunately this happy occasion had to be postponed for several months. Deborah's pilgrimage of faith was interrupted on 11 October 1825 when she prematurely gave birth to twin girls. The stress of life and child birth then seriously affected her health, and she herself became perilously ill, almost to the point of death. Unfortunately the babies died and Miss Paget obtained a nurse who brought Deborah back to health.

Once fully recovered, Deborah became convinced that Jesus indeed was

---

33 The original St. Sidewells, on Sidewell Street in the centre of Exeter is no longer standing.
34 Alexander to Golding, 5 July 1825, MS 3393 [5-6], Lambeth.
35 Alexander to Golding, 30 September 1825, MSS 3393 [7], Lambeth.

the promised Messiah of Israel. She was baptized at All Hallows Church[36] in Exeter, on 9 November 1825. Golding and Synge were present, and Hatchard assisted with conducting the service.[37]

In many ways this was the perfect setting for Deborah's baptism after all their ordeals. She was away from the scrutiny of family in Plymouth and in the presence of so many of their new friends and supporters.

---

36 This church was bombed out during World War Two, but was located very close to the Cathedral.
37 In the register she has the name Deborah Mary – probably taken at her baptism.

Chapter 19

Wolff goes East

Damascus
From Antoura Wolff proceeded to Damascus which he entered on 24 October 1823 and stayed at the Capuchian Monastery. The monks there cared for him when he was struck with fever. Shortly before his arrival the leading Jewish man in the city, Raphael Farkhi, had been dragged by force out of the synagogue by Turkish soldiers, causing the Jewish community considerable angst.[1] When Wolff ventured onto the streets he 'saw weeping women and children, old men trembling and praying; the men not daring to complain lest it should cost their heads, yet visibly mourning trough silently.' Wolff was able to encourage them during this traumatic time, and stated to them all, "Behold your King cometh!"[2]

The plight of the Jewish community in Damascus could have been played out anywhere in the region under the control of Islam. According to Islamic understanding any non-Muslim was classified as a *dhimmi* – a second class citizen. The non-Muslims were required to pay a special tax known as the *jizre*, but on numerous occasions the local rulers for one reason or another could enact further taxes upon the unsuspecting and unprotected *dhimmi* population. In most instances the *dhimmis* had no-one they could turn to for assistance and protection.

Although the Jewish people living under the dominion of Islam (the region known as *dar al Islam*) often fared better than they did under the control of Christendom, nevertheless their position at the bottom of the social ladder meant they were constantly on edge.

Ironically it was the presence, and involvement, of British missionaries who often provided local Jewish communities with some respite from such occurrences as the one the community in Damascus was now facing, as the local authorities did not want to upset Britain in any way.

While in Damascus, Wolff tried to encourage as many of the 4,000 Jewish people as he could, never neglecting to share with them about the one who offers more comfort than anyone else – Jesus. As was by now his custom Wolff either sought out, or was sought out, to enter into any manner of theological discussion concerning the merits of Jesus.

---

1 One year later Farkhi was released from prison.
2 Wolff, *Life and Journal*, p. 115.

Aleppo

Wolff departed from Damascus in December 1824, accompanied by a Jewish follower of Jesus named Reuben Costa (who had previously accompanied Lewis Way, but then joined Wolff) and returned to Aleppo, which was still in a dilapidated state following the earthquake of 1822.

During his two months in Aleppo, Wolff spent much time debating, chiefly with Roman Catholics, and also preaching each Sunday in the parlour of Mr Barker's home (the British Consul) to which some of the seven Jewish consuls[3] in the city came.[4]

Wolff then joined a large caravan and continued further east, crossing the Euphrates River near to where his illustrious forefather Abraham once crossed – but going in the opposite direction. This was quite an emotional experience for Wolff.

Along the route he stayed some time in the town of Orpha which was inhabited by all manner of different nationalities. Several leading Jewish men approached Wolff, and informed him that they knew of him, and wanted to lock horns with him in debate. Wolff only too gladly agreed.[5] Wolff not only enjoyed discourse with the Jewish people there, but also appreciated contact with the Jacobites (followers of Jesus who claim their traditions go back to the preaching of James in Jerusalem.)

Towards Baghdad and Basra

Jewish biblical sites abounded in this region, including the traditional grave of Terah, and Haran, which he visited, and also Paddam-haran, where Jacob met Rachel. Thereafter the route that he was following became progressively more difficult, and at one point the group he was with was taken captive by the Kurds of that region. When he began to debate with his captors about faith the chief became angry and said, "Do you come here to upset our religion?" Wolff merely replied, "I come here to show you the way of truth." He was duly tied down and the bottom of his feet lashed 200 times.[6]

His recovery time from the painful injury was spent with the local Jacobite Christians, to whose Patriarch Wolff informed that he was 'travelling about for the purpose of making the Jewish nation believe that Jesus was the Messiah.' The Patriarch replied that he was 130 years old and had never heard of such an undertaking until that day.[7]

Indeed until Joseph Wolff no attempt had been made in those regions in the modern period to introduce Jewish people to the claims of Jesus as Messiah.

---

3 Wolff, *Travels*, p. 184. The seven Jewish consuls were all from the Picciotto family.
4 Wolff, *Life and Journal*, p. 116.
5 Wolff, *Travels*, p. 188.
6 Wolff, ibid, p. 190.
7 Wolff, ibid, p, 192.

Once his feet were healed Wolff then visited with other Jacobite leaders in the region, as well as meeting with leaders of other Christian traditions - and then he left for Mosul.

In Mosul Wolff stayed with the Jacobite bishop for two weeks and during that time discussed Jesus with the Jewish people. He was amazed to hear that one hundred years before a Jewish man had translated the New Testament into Hebrew from Arabic. When he then gave copies of the New Testament to the Jewish people he was scolded by the local Christians, who said, "Why dost thou throw pearls before swine?"[8] They obviously held out little hope of Jewish people coming to know Jesus as their Messiah.

Wolff's aim was to get to Baghdad as quickly as possible, but he was delayed due to numerous troubles. Finally 'exhausted and depressed by his many fatigues; poor, despoiled of all he had, with wounds still in his feet, did Wolff arrive in Baghdad, after his wanderings…'[9] It was fortunate that a company of British personnel was there at the time en-route to Britain from India. They replaced Wolff's clothing while Dr. Lamb of the East India Company, cured his feet.

Once he was cured and rested, Wolff then set about presenting the claims of Jesus as Messiah to the Jewish people. There was a large and well respected Jewish community in Baghdad, of whom Wolff wrote, 'all the Pacha's commerce is in their hands.'[10] Wolff made an interesting observation while there, 'I found among Jews at Bagdat [sic] bibles, testaments and tracts with my name in them, given to Jews at Jerusalem! My mission also was known to them.'[11]

After a month in Baghdad he then set off down the river on 17 May 1824 towards Bossurah (Basrah), where he was hosted by Captain Taylor of the East India Company. Here too there was a sizeable Jewish population, and Wolff 'had whole days' conversing about Jesus.[12] The Syrian priests also allowed Wolff to preach to the Roman Catholics there in Persian and Arabic.

Into Persia
Wolff remained in Basra for several months, before proceeding on to Bushire in Persia (Bushere in Iran today) where he was hosted by the resident agent for the East India Company, Col. Stanners.[13] Some 200 Jewish families resided in Bushire, but Wolff was too unwell to spend his time walking the streets and conversing with them. Instead he invited them to come to the British residency, and many did, intrigued by this strange phenomena – a Jew who followed Jesus!

---

8 Wolff, ibid, p, 197.
9 Wolff, ibid, p, 201.
10 Wolff, *Life and Journal*, p. 126.
11 Wolff, *Life and Journal*, p. 126.
12 Wolff, ibid, p. 203.
13 Although at this time shipping went from India to Britain via the Cape of Africa, the East India Company often sent messages home via the Red Sea and Persian Gulf.

He also preached to the English and Armenian residents on 'the sabbath.'[14] At both Basra and Bushire Wolff established small schools with funds supplied by Drummond and Mr Bayford.[15]

Wolff departed from Bushire on 1 December 1824, venturing first to Kasseroon and then on to Shiraz. The state of the Jewish people here was explained to him by a Persian Muslim, "Every house at Shiraz with a low narrow entrance is a Jew's. Every man with a dirty woollen or camel's hair turban is a Jew. Every coat much torn and mended on the back with worn sleeves, is a Jew's. Everyone picking up old broken glass, dirty robes and old shoes and sandals is a Jew. That house into which no quadruped but a goat will enter, is a Jew's."[16]

When entering into the Jewish quarter he saw the accuracy of that description, and wrote, 'I went home saying to myself, "what a sight I have seen!" and repeating with tears the words of my poor brethren. They are here pale, yellow and of little stature, indeed a poor Israele, and from their daughters all beauty is gone, they too are a poor Israele! I wonder not their harp is silent, and their only song now is, "only one pool[17], I am a poor Israele."'[18]

Within Persia itself Wolff visited numerous locations, particularly those with sizeable Jewish populations. By 21 January 1825 he was in Isfahan, where he lodged with the Armenian archbishop.

The highlight of this time was his visit to the local synagogue. Wolff wrote, 'Crowds of Mussulmen [Muslims] accompanied me to the synagogue, whither I carried the hebrew (sic) prophets and N.T. Jews lived here in the time of Solomon who is said to have built Ispahan … During the four years of my mission I have never been received with such cordiality in any synagogue as in that at Ispahan, "Shalum!" (peace!) was the exclamation of Jews and Jewesses when I entered. There were about 250 ancient copies of the law on skins …'[19]

On 13 March 1825 Wolff finally arrived in Teheran, where he was met by the British agent. In quick time he was handing out materials to the Jewish residents. Then, he stated, within a few days the Jewish people began to hand the books back again. It seems that one Sephardi rabbi had been in Jerusalem when Wolff was there, and knew, he wrote, 'I excited sentiments among Jews there which had never existed before; and on this account advised these Jews to return the books.'[20]

From Teheran he travelled onto Tabreez where he lodged at the home of the British ambassador. Here he also received official permission from Prince

14 Wolff, *Life and Journal*, p. 134.
15 Wolff, *Life and Journal*, pp. 152-3.
16 Wolff, *Life and Journal*, p. 140.
17 The coinage of the time.
18 Wolff, *Life and Journal*, p. 141.
19 Wolff, *Life and Journal*, p. 153.
20 Wolff, *Life and Journal*, p. 155.

Abbas Mirza, heir of the Persian throne, to establish a school, as he had done already in numerous other locations.[21]

Back to Europe

Following a considerable period in Tabreez, Wolff then began his journey back home, travelling north first to Odessa, which he reached in December 1825, then south to Adrianople (Edirne) where quite a large Jewish population lived. This city had been the capital of the Turkish Empire before Constantinople became the capital in 1453.

Finally in January 1826 Wolff arrived in Constantinople. Shortly after arriving he dined with Sir Stratford Canning, the British ambassador, who warned him not to venture amongst the Muslims at this time - an instruction which he obeyed.[22] This was a time of increasing tension between the Turks and the Greeks, who were agitating for their independence.

While in the Turkish capital he stayed with the Armenians, and learnt the Turkish language. Quite interestingly he found much great openness among the Jewish population to hear about Jesus. Although a number professed to be interested in being baptized and becoming Christians, Wolff was advised against proceeding with this by Ambassador Canning.[23] Such an action at that time was sure to stir up opposition as it would seriously upset the established *status quo* then operating in the Ottoman Turkish Empire.

After almost two months residence in Constantinople Wolff made his way to Smyrna (Izmir) where he introduced Jewish people to the message of Jesus and gave lectures to the resident British and Italian subjects. His time here marked the end of his first major missionary journey.

In March 1826 Wolff embarked upon the ship *Eblana* and set sail for Dublin. Never one to be idle, he made the most of the journey which lasted two months, preaching to the sailors, and taking a collection from them for the 'London Society for Promoting Christianity among the Jews.' [24] Wolff, the Irish Jews Society recorded, 'collected 2 pounds and two shillings from the crew 'in behalf of the Jews.'[25]

His next port of call was Dublin.

---

21 Wolff, *Life and Journal*, pp. 156-7.
22 Wolff, *Travels*, p. 230.
23 Wolff, *Life and Journal*, p. 159.
24 Wolff, *Travels*, p. 231.
25 IJS Minutes 15 August 1826, Minute Book 318 1.2, RCB.

Chapter 20

Alexander and Wolff meet in Ireland

Dublin

Despite the improved conditions for the Alexanders in Exeter, Michael Solomon accepted a job as a Hebrew teacher in Dublin, as well as work in the 'German' Church[1] there.[2] They departed from England in the early months of 1826.[3]

The day after their arrival they attended the Bethesda Chapel in Dublin, where they also met a Catholic man during the service – and soon afterwards led him to a personal relationship with Jesus.[4]

Alexander later became acquainted with a notable banker named Robert Newenham,[5] who invited the Alexanders to be his personal guests. While there Michael Solomon had a relapse of poor health again. When he had recovered he also became acquainted with the Archbishop of Dublin, Dr William Magee. The Archbishop's second son took advantage of Michael Solomon's linguistic skills in order to learn Hebrew.

The Alexanders also met and befriended Sir Richard and Lady Steele, people of some renown in Dublin, as well as Mr Arthur Guinness – of the famous brewery family. Therein lies the hint of why a young Bishop in Jerusalem many years later was thankful of a certain liquid gift!

Michael Solomon's Jewish identity assisted him in many ways during his stay in Ireland. One of these was with a new job with the Church of Ireland Jews Society.[6] Alexander began initially as an errand boy, working three hours in the afternoon as assistant to the secretary.

Shortly after entering upon his new responsibility, Alexander teamed up with Rev William Lewis – one of the pioneer LJS and Protestant missionaries in Palestine[7]. Lewis spoke at the Annual Meeting of the Irish Jews Society on 11 April 1826, and enlightened everyone concerning establishing a Protestant work in Jerusalem.[8]

---

1 The German Church began circa 1779, for the German speaking community of the City. Oddly, in the *Dublin Register* of 1826 it is named the 'Danish & German-Lutheran Church' and in 1841 it is named as the Dutch Church. See *Dublin Register*, National Library of Ireland, Dublin.
2 Alexander to Miss Hancock, 30 June 1826, Alexander papers, DS 125.3.A5, St. Anthony's College, Oxford,[henceforth St. Anthony's].
3 *Autobiography*, p. 32.
4 *Autobiography*, pp. 33-34.
5 *Autobiography*, p, 35.
6 'Irish Auxiliary to the London Society for Promoting Christianity among the Jews' founded in 1810.
7 Rev William Bucknor Lewis, from Ireland. After leaving Jerusalem he established a work in Smyrna, Turkey.
8 Irish Jews Society [IJS] Minute Book, No 318 1.2, 11 April 1826, Representative Church Body [RCB] Library, Dublin. [henceforth RCB].

Alexander thereafter became more active in his job with the Irish Jews Society. In May he accompanied Lewis on a speaking tour to Cork in the south east of Ireland, and then organized another tour to the north. This tour was to be in conjunction with a fellow Jewish believer who was then due in the country – one Joseph Wolff! When it became apparent that Wolff's arrival would be delayed, this tour was deferred until his arrival.[9]

Wolff in Ireland

Wolff finally arrived in mid-August 1826,[10] and was ordered into quarantine for three weeks. Through the efforts of Alexander and a colleague, the time was shortened to three days. Of this time Wolff stated in a letter to Sir Thomas Baring:

> We were not allowed to land for three days, as we were quite starved out, I sent on shore for a pleasant dinner for myself, as well as for the captain and his wife, - ordering salmon, turkey, turtle soup, pudding, apple pie, jelly and a handsome dessert, so that the hotel-keeper, when reading over the list, said, 'This reverend gentleman knows also about the good things of the world.'[11]

When he was finally released from quarantine Wolff stayed with the Alexanders. This proved to be an unforgettable experience as Michael Solomon and Deborah had to keep their bedroom door locked as Wolff was in the habit of intruding upon their privacy early in the morning informing his hosts that he wanted to read to them accounts from his journal.[12]

Now that he was 'set free' Wolff and Alexander set out upon their speaking tour to the north, taking in Newry, Lisburne, Belfast, Ballymena, Coleraine, Derry, Strabane, Moneymore, Tallymore, Park [sic], Dundalk and Drogheda. This was surely an exhausting, as well as exhilarating, journey. It is not stated how Alexander fared – but no doubt he heard every one of Wolff's many adventures from the land of their forefathers, and indeed from wherever Wolff had travelled. Shortly later Alexander accompanied Wolff and Rev Thomas Kingston on another tour, this time to the south of the country.

Alexander wrote of their time together:

> I cannot describe the interest excited, many had never seen a Jew and were little aware of his miserable state. That two of these "dry bones," having received flesh and spirit, yes, having been washed in the precious blood of the atoning Saviour, should bear united testimony that God in his faithfulness

---

9 See IJS Minutes for 24 & 31 July 1826, Minute Book 318 1.2, RCB.
10 Interestingly Wolff's account renders the date as May. See Wolff, ibid, p. 231.
11 Wolff, *Travels*, p. 231.
12 *Autobiography*, p. 33.

has not cast away his people; is encouraging! ... Dear Wolff is the most powerful instance what the strength of the Lord can do. Strong in spirit, in godly zeal as a lion, but harmless and calm as a dove.[13]

During his time in Ireland Wolff also stayed with Lord Rodem and the Archbishop of Tuam, where 'he was shaved by an old woman, who made him pay 2s. 6d. for the job.'[14] His time with the Archbishop might have been pleasant, but in many places his reception among the Roman Catholic leadership was less than pleasant, and his public addresses were often disturbed. The Roman Catholic leadership was only too aware of Wolff's activities at Rome and former life as a Roman Catholic.

Wolff and Alexander venture to England
After returning from the second speaking tour, Wolff and Alexander travelled together to Liverpool to meet Hawtrey (the LJS Secretary) and Marsh.[15] Wolff then, at the invitation of his great benefactor Henry Drummond, continued on to London where he lodged with a friend of Drummond named Edward Irving.

Irving actually was not at home when Wolff arrived, but left instructions for him to go to the home of Lady Olivier Sparrow. It was there that Wolff was introduced to a certain Lady Georgiana Walpole, daughter of Sir Horatio Walpole, the late Earl of Orford. Of this lady Wolff said to himself, "that Lady Georgiana Walpole will become my wife."[16]

The lady in question made such a lasting impression upon Wolff, that before retiring that evening, he said to his host that he would like to have a barber come in the next morning to shave him. The next morning there was a knock on Wolff's door, and Irving himself entered, all suitably attired as a barber and proceeded to remove Wolff whiskers. This was merely the first such shave administered on Wolff by Irving.

News of this interesting event leaked out, and soon there were caricatures showing Irving shaving 'a wolf.'[17]

Drummond and the Albury Park Conference
Drummond then invited Wolff to join him, and others in a conference at his country manor named Albury Park in Surrey. Those present included Lady Theodosia Powerscourt, Edward Irving, Rev Hugh McNeile, William Cuninghame and Lewis Way.

The purpose of this Conference, Wolff wrote, was to discuss 'the personal

---

13 Wolf, *Life and Journal*, pp. 169-170.
14 Wolff, *Travels*, p. 232.
15 IJS Minutes 22 September 1826, Minute Book 318 1.2, RCB.
16 Wolff, ibid, p. 233.
17 Wolff, ibid. p. 234.

reign of Christ, and future renovation of the world; the restoration and conversion of the Jews; and judgments on the Christian Church for their infidelity and unfaithfulness; each person speaking out his peculiar views.' On matters relating to the Hebrew text they referred to Wolff's expertise.[18]

The result of this, and subsequent such meetings, so Wolff wrote, was, 'that all became of [the] opinion that the system of interpreting fulfilled prophecy, in a grammatical, historical, or, as it is commonly, but not quite correctly, called literal sense; and unfulfilled prophecy in a phantomizing, or, what is commonly called, spiritual manner, is a miserably rotten system, and one leading to infidelity.'[19]

In other words those in attendance agreed that it was necessary to be consistent, and use the same principles of interpretation for all prophecies, those which had been fulfilled in the past, and those which had as yet to be fulfilled.

At the conclusion of the Conference, Wolff then travelled all over England, Scotland and Wales speaking on behalf of the London Jews Society. Here was a man who never tired of travelling and speaking for the sake of the extension of the Kingdom of God. The response was more than expected: 'The report of his speeches in newspapers induced persons to subscribe who previously would not hear of the society. Whilst in some fashionable circles he was enabled by divine grace to awaken a more important concern for personal salvation, as well as an enquiry into the prophecies respecting literal Israel.'[20]

Alexander in Dublin

Alexander, meanwhile, was travelling the length and breadth of Ireland.[21] Then, later in the year, he was given more hours of work with the Irish Jews Society.

In November 1826 the IJS Committee agreed to a request from Alexander for himself and his colleague, Mr. Michael John Mayers, also a Jewish follower of Jesus, to visit their Jewish brethren in 'Prague, Breslau & Berlin.'[22] There were two sponsors for this trip, one of whom was William Marsh of Colchester. It is unclear, though, if this tour actually happened.

During this period Alexander had an interesting encounter with Archbishop Magee. Michael Solomon was preparing himself for entrance into Trinity College, when the Archbishop wanted to fast-track him through the ordination

18 Wolff, ibid, p. 234.
19 Wolff, ibid, pp. 234-235. Further Conferences were held at Albury Park, and then from 1831 at Powerscourt in County Wicklow in Ireland. Outgrowths of these Conferences were the Catholic Apostolic Church associated with Irving and Drummond and the Plymouth Brethren associated with John Nelson Darby. A certain theological hermeneutic developed out of these Conferences. For further details about the theological consequences of these Conferences there are other sources, including *For Zion's Sake* by Paul Wilkinson, (Paternoster, 2010).
20 Wolff, *Life and Journal*, p. 170.
21 *Autobiography*, p. 38.
22 IJS Minutes, 13 November 1826, Minute Book 318 1.2, RCB.

process, presumably so that he could take over the 'German' Church. [23]

Alexander initially declined, but when the two men finally met Alexander stated his desire first to study, and pleaded his lack of reading and preparation. To this Magee replied, "I will give you six months to study deeply. If I knew Hebrew and German as you do, I should be very well satisfied." [24] If only the Bishop had bestowed such favour upon Joseph Frey!

Ordination

Alexander passed an examination at Archbishop's Palace, St. Stephens Green, Dublin. He then soon afterwards went to London 'whither I went' he wrote to Miss Hancock, 'for the purpose of many things connected with the German service I am to have.' While in London he also had occasion to meet Mrs. Levy – Deborah's mother, a visit which seemed to have been relatively calm.

Michael Solomon was then ordained deacon on Trinity Sunday, 10 June, 1827 in St. Anne's Church, and preached his first sermon in Sandford Church in the evening, taking as his text Psalm 51:15, 'Oh Lord, open Thou my lips.' His wife wrote: 'My beloved husband was much affected, and so was I, and felt deeply the responsibility and the honour conferred upon us.'[25] Of this occasion the LJS wrote:

> We have much satisfaction in stating, that Mr. Michael Solomon Alexander, formerly reader of the Jewish Synagogue at Plymouth, of whose conversion we have given an account, and who has since resided in Dublin, was admitted into Holy Orders on Trinity Sunday last, by his Grace the Archbishop of Dublin.
>
> Mr Michael John Mayers, also a converted Jew, was ordained on the same occasion.[26]

Some probably questioned the propriety of ordaining a man only two years a follower of Jesus. In response to this, a later acquaintance, Rev James Cartwright, wrote of Alexander:

> His views of the great fundamental truths of Christianity were remarkably deep and clear, and often touchingly experimental. He had evidently learned much during his first years of sharp mental conflict. I believe that at that time he was eminently taught of God; and that if he was clear on the important subjects of a sinner's acceptance with God, of justification by the blood of Christ through faith alone, and of sanctification by the renewing influences

23 *Autobiography*, p. 41
24 Corey, ibid, p. 28
25 Alexander to Miss Hancock, 30 June 1827, MSS 3393 [14], Lambeth.
26 *Jewish Expositor*, 1827, p. 319-20. According to the IJS Minutes of 4 June 1827, Alexander was to be 'Minister of the German Church' and Mayers 'Curate to St. Lukes parish in Dublin.' IJS Minute Book 1827-1844, 318 1.3, RCB.

of the Holy Ghost; it was because he had fought out, as it were, these great questions in secret conflict and prayer; under deep conviction of sin, he had learned his need of the free mercy of the Gospel ... Thus experience, temptation and prayer, had been his first commentaries on the doctrines of the Gospel; and, therefore, when in little more than two years from his baptism, Ordination was offered to him, entirely unsolicited and unexpected, by a prelate who was esteemed strict in his requirements from candidates for Holy Orders, he was found to possess suitable qualifications for the Christian ministry.[27]

Set-backs
Shortly after his ordination Michael Solomon experienced a set-back, stating in a letter to Miss Hancock on 30 June 1827 that there were '... difficulties in the way of my getting the German Chapel appointed for me...' Despite this set-back, he concluded, 'I shall likewise view the Hand of God in it, if it should come to naught. It is wonderful that the Archbishop should grant me ordination on that idea. Of course I shall be more free. However I can and must say nothing about it. I must only wait for the opening of the Lord's ways. I desire to be resigned entirely to his Holy will.'[28]

The closure of one door – the German Church – meant the opening of another. In early July 1827, he travelled to London with Deborah to meet Mrs. Levy. While there he was invited to speak at Palestine Place on 8 July 1827, on the text, very appropriately, from Romans 1:16; 'The gospel is the power of God for the salvation for everyone, for the Jew first and also for the non-Jew.'[29]

Soon after returning to Ireland, Alexander (and Mayers) set out, on 1 August 1827, on a speaking tour. Their first stop was Cork, whereupon Alexander became very unwell and had to return to Dublin, where he was taken care of by Dr. Cheyne. Alexander quoted Cheyne as saying to some common friends 'I (humanly speaking) could not be alive by next Spring if I remain in this Country.'[30]

Despairing to lose such a valuable part of their work, the Irish Committee at their meeting on 10 September 1827 stated that because of Alexander's 'very delicate state of health ... his Physician has declared that change of air is absolutely necessary for his re-establishment'.[31] Dr Singer, representing Alexander, enquired if the London Committee would consider employing

---

27 Sermon by Rev. J. Cartwright at Episcopal Jews Chapel London, on 28 December 1845, in *JI*, 1846, pp. 60-61.
28 Alexander to Hancock, 30 June 1827, DS 125.3.A5, Alexander Papers, St. Anthony's; and Corey, ibid, p. 30.
29 Corey, ibid, p. 29
30 Alexander to Golding [now in Edinburgh], 11 September 1827, MSS 3393 [16] Lambeth.
31 IJS Minutes, 10 September 1827, IJS Minute Book 318 1.3, RCB.

Michael Solomon temporarily for service on the Continent.[32]

At this point the LJS was about to expand its operations in Germany, and Rev. W. Ayerst was being prepared to embark upon this venture. It was possible, they conceded, that Alexander could accompany him. The LJS Committee summoned an *ad hoc* meeting of all London Committee members willing and able to meet Alexander in late September 1827. So for the third time in just a few months Michael Solomon crossed the Irish Sea to London.

Michael Solomon was accepted to work alongside Ayerst on a twelve month probation period.[33] It seems that at this point he returned to Dublin, where he was ordained priest by Dr Lyndsay, the Bishop of Kildare, by letters emissary from Archbishop Magee.[34] Picking up Deborah and his young family, Alexander then departed on the next portion of his pilgrimage of faith.[35]

Wolff marries Lady Georgiana Walpole

While the Alexanders were about to embark on a new adventure, Joseph Wolff was about to have an adventure of a completely different nature. In accordance with his words spoken when he first met Lady Georgiana Walpole, Wolff then proposed to the one he called his 'darling angel in earthly shape'.[36] It could not have been a more unusual match, she a woman of the upper class, and he a German Jewish follower of Jesus who could not even shave himself!

Such a match indeed caused quite a stir within British society, and within her own family. Wolff resolved to minimise the tension by signing a declaration with her brother, the Earl of Orford, and witnessed by Henry Drummond and several other men, renouncing all claims to her estate if she died prior to Wolff without bearing children.[37]

The wedding ceremony took place on 6 February 1827 and was conducted by Charles Simeon. The wolf, one could say could now lie down with the lamb.

Mr and Mrs Wolff travel to Europe

Joseph Wolff now had a devoted travelling partner, and they began their new life together in April 1827 by going to Amsterdam. They were joined there by the LJS worker, Rev. J. C. Reichardt. Here, as had been his norm, Joseph presented the claims of Jesus to the Jewish people, and also spoke in Leiden, Zeist, and Utrecht. Other opportunities for ministry were also found, although

---

32 See Minute 563, 13 February 1827 and Minute 1044, 25 September 1827, in CMJ Minute Book c. 12, Bodleian Library, Oxford. [henceforth Bodleian].
33 Minute 1077, 16 October 1827, CMJ Minute Book c. 12, Bodleian.
34 Corey, ibid. p. 29. Corey states he was ordained in December. There are no dates in the official records of the RCB Library in Dublin. Alexander was already on the Continent in December, so presumably he was ordained priest earlier or in absentia.
35 Prior to departure however he spent some time on deputation work with Wolff in Lancashire.
36 Wolff, *Travels*, p. 237.
37 Wolff, ibid, pp. 237-238.

one leading Jewish lawyer blandly refused Wolff's invitation to speak to him about the claims of Jesus.[38] While in the Netherlands the Wolffs met two very prominent Jewish followers of Jesus, Isaac da Costa and Dr. Cappadose.

Reichardt then accompanied the newlyweds to Germany. One location where Wolff spoke was at Count von der Recke's settlement at Duesselthal. Some of the Jewish followers of Jesus there were awaiting departure to the United States to join the venture that Joseph Frey was developing.

While at Duesselthal Wolff was reconciled to his mother and sister, who had travelled there to meet him. Wolff preached in the Lutheran Church there in which both his sister and mother participated. Joseph's mother 'wept the whole time he preached.'[39] Afterwards mother and son debated the merits of Jesus, and one observer, Lady Engels, stated of this special occasion of being able 'to hear a mother argue with her son with all the tenderness of a mother and a son declare to his mother the way of salvation.'[40]

Although Joseph was not able to see his beloved mother openly confess belief in Jesus as Lord and Messiah, his sister Jetta did later confess faith in Jesus and was baptised.[41] There could have been no better outcome for Joseph Wolff as he departed the land of his birth.

---

38 Wolff, ibid, p. 241.
39 Wolff, ibid, p. 242.
40 Wolff, *Life and Journal*, p. 189.
41 Wolff, *Travels*, p. 242.

Chapter 21

The Mediterranean and Germany

The Wolffs begin their Mediterranean trip

Following their return to London Joseph was commissioned by the London Jews Society to take the message of Jesus to the Jewish people in the East. Joseph and Georgiana set sail on 26 July 1827.

While at Malta a major geo-political event occurred not that far away at Navarino on the Peloponnese Peninsula of Greece. For some years the Greeks had been fighting for their independence from the Ottoman Turks. The Egyptians then joined with the Turks and on 20 October 1827 opposed a combined British, French and Russian armada at Navarino. The Egyptian-Turkish fleet was destroyed.

When news of the victory reached Malta there was great celebration and a victory ball was planned. The Wolffs were invited, but declined. Joseph stated that it was not right to celebrate when so many lives had just been lost.[1]

At this time the Wolffs made another major decision, declining henceforth to receive financial support from the London Jews Society. Joseph informed Sir Thomas Baring of this, stating that they would live off Lady Georgiana's annual allowance, and that, besides this, it would strip his opponents of an argument that he was preaching the Gospel for a salary.[2]

Joseph then made another difficult decision – to leave Georgiana and their unborn child in Malta while he continued with his work. The first port of call was Smyrna, where he was advised by Mr Leeves of the British and Foreign Bible Society not to be too obvious as the Turks were still very upset by the defeat at Navarino.[3]

Wolff's next task was to search the Greek Isles for Jewish communities, and to speak with as many Greek people as he could about entering into a personal relationship with Jesus. He had numerous adventures along the way, one of which included being pursued by pirates and then ending up shipwrecked. He lost everything he had. Later Wolff and the crew were taken into the care of the Governor of Cephalonia, Colonel Charles Napier.[4]

Napier knew of Wolff, particularly his known bent at that time for fixing dates 'for the end.' Seemingly Wolff at one time had predicted that the end was not 'the destruction of the world' but 'its renovation and the restoration of the

1 Hopkins, H. *Sublime Vagabond*, p. 124.
2 Hopkins, ibid, p.126.
3 Wolff, *Travels*, p. 247.
4 Later General Sir Charles Napier.

Jews, at the coming of the Messiah in glory.'5 Thankfully Wolff later dispensed with the idea of trying to fix dates.

Despite his own lack of interest in Wolff's message, Napier nevertheless brought both Jews and Greeks to hear Wolff when he was quarantined at Cephalonia, and then after his release, Napier took Wolff into his own home and brought visitors to see Wolff there.

After departing he travelled through the Greek Islands for several months, and spoke on numerous occasions to all who were willing to listen. Wolff returned to Malta, and thence to Alexandria where he was reunited with 'his little angel' Lady Georgiana.

Alexander returns to Germany

While Wolff was making his way to Alexandria, Michael Solomon Alexander, accompanied by Ayerst, travelled via Holland to Germany, arriving there in early November 1827. During the next weeks they travelled to both Berlin and Posen before arriving at Danzig on 22 December 1827.[6] Alexander later visited Posen again, and wrote on the impact of this visit:

> I cannot describe my feelings on finding myself now in Posen my native country, when I reflect on the wonderful dealings of the Lord with me since I left this place nine years ago. I was then a wandering sheep from my Saviour's fold, walking in darkness, and in the shades of death, ignorant of the Lord that bought me. How did he lead me? The blind by a way I knew not. My soul doth magnify the Lord, because my spirit rejoiceth in my God, as my saviour, especially when I consider I am now engaged as a humble, but unworthy, instrument to preach the glad tidings of salvation, and to declare to my brethren, what the Lord hath done for my soul. When my prospects of usefulness are dark, I look to my Lord and say, "Thy grace is sufficient for me; thy strength is made perfect in my weakness."[7]

Alexander also recorded that he had sent a letter to his brother, who 'is rabbi to the large Jewish congregation twelve miles from Posen' informing him of his arrival, 'and requesting that we might have a meeting'. The brother agreed and according to Michael the meeting was rather cordial. Michael was able to state to him 'the Gospel, and declared also to him an account of the hope that was in me.' Following this meeting Michael Solomon received a letter from his brother, which, Michael Solomon wrote 'encourages me to hope that our meeting was not in vain.'[8]

It was not long before Alexander and Ayerst began their work in earnest in

---

5 Wolff, *Travels*, p. 250.
6 *JE*, 1828, p. 259. Danzig is present day Gdansk in Poland.
7 *JE*, 1828, p. 260.
8 *JE*, 1828, p. 260.

Danzig. Ayerst wrote on 29 January 1828 that they had 'commenced a regular service in the English church every Sunday' and that he hoped Alexander would soon begin a service in German on Saturday afternoon to accommodate the German Jewish people.[9] In the same letter Ayerst asked permission to set up a small school. Permission was granted, and although expectations were high, Ayerst stated in July 1828 that it 'was still unvisited by any Jewish children.' Jewish children did later attend the school, where instruction included needlework which was taught to the girls by Mrs. Alexander and Mrs. Ayerst.[10]

Alexander and Ayerst carried out numerous journeys, sometimes together, sometimes individually. They undertook one such journey during June 1828 where they visited Stargand, Mewe, Nuremberg, Grandanz, Rehden, Lessen, Freistadt, Nydick, Rosenberg, Reisenberg, Stuhm and Marienburg. In all these locations Alexander and Ayerst made every attempt to meet with the Jewish people, and particularly with the local rabbi. On some occasions they were given a positive welcome, while on other occasions they were met with derision.[11]

During their speaking tour in August 1828 Alexander and Ayerst visited Chrisburg, Osterode (in present Lower Saxony, Germany), Saalbeld (in present Thuringen, Germany), and Altmark (in north eastern Germany). Of Chrisburg, Ayerst wrote that they met the liberal minded rabbi and several others, who 'seemed to think that the writings of Mendelsohn are most likely to benefit the Jews. He strongly condemned the absurdity of the Jews praying in an ancient, and now dead language ... which it is impossible for those who have not leisure to study, to understand in any tolerable degree.'[12] This comment indicates the struggle for internal emancipation then within the Jewish community, as many were desiring to follow the example of Moses Mendelsohn, and throw off the vestiges of Orthodox Judaism.[13]   Ayerst also wrote, concerning Alexander's contribution:

> It is a great advantage to Mr. Alexander, in speaking with these better informed Jews, that he has been brought up in their own way; and it has generally been a rule with us, when entering a strange place, to visit first the rabbi, who is often engaged as teacher, and thus we sometimes learn at once much about the state of religious instruction amongst them.[14]

It seems that Ayerst and Alexander never tired of these exhausting missionary

---

9 *JE,* 1828, p. 260.
10 *JE,* 1830, p. 67.
11 *JE,* 1828, pp. 458-459.
12 *JE,* 1828, p. 459.
13 Mendelsohn, 1729-1786, was a former Talmudic scholar who became a philosopher of religion and greatly influenced Jewish thinking in central Europe against *Talmudic* Judaism. Ayerst later wrote of what he termed the 'new temple Jews' –'the friends and followers of the celebrated philosopher Mendelsohn, have introduced into their service, not only the custom of preaching in German, but also singing with an organ, and many other things like those which we have.' *Jewish Expositor,* 1830, p. 5.
14 *JE,* 1828. p. 459.

tours. In October 1828, during the period of the Feast of Tabernacles, they set out again. Their first stop was at Meve, where they were invited to speak at the opening of a new church. The next location however would possibly be Alexander's most challenging so far – Schonlanke.

They decided it best to stop at a Christian inn (most of the best ones were owned by Jewish people) in order to minimize exposure as much as possible. They then sought a meeting with Michael Solomon's sister, a widow, who agreed to come to the inn, not knowing initially the matter in hand. Ayerst describes what followed:

> When she came, as it was uncertain how she would feel towards him, I spoke to her first alone, and when I asked her, whether she had not a brother, who some years since went to England, and whether she knew that he was now returned to Germany, she inquired after him mostly kindly; and when I asked whether she wished to see him and speak with him, I shall not soon forget the affectionate warmth with which she said, "If it be possible." This Mr. A. overheard in the adjoining room, where he had been waiting during this short but interesting interview, and you may easily imagine the grateful feeling with which he came forward to receive to his arms a beloved sister, from whom he had in the leadings of God's providence been so long separated.[15]

The following day Alexander and Ayerst visited the local Christian minister in the town, and Alexander also managed to briefly explain the message of Jesus as Messiah to his former *Talmud* teacher. At this juncture however several other Jewish people, when acquainted with whom this visitor was, became uncivil. This attitude upset Michael Solomon's relatives, and they took leave of him. Despite this small incident however, Alexander was more than pleased with the outcome of his visit. He later wrote of it:

> ... this journey has left a deep impression on my mind, that a wonderful change has taken place amongst my brethren of that part of the country, since the time I left it ten years ago. There is a general anxiety to converse about the truth of Christianity, which, when I left, was considered an abomination: and surely it may be considered no small proof of better feeling on the subject, that they now receive one of their brethren, who has gone over to the Christian religion and comes to declare the truth of it to them, and treat him generally with affection and kindness. This I have found, far beyond my expectation. I have found numbers of my former acquaintances and friends, who listened with great feelings of interest and sympathy, to my statement of how the Lord has led me and brought me to the knowledge of that Saviour ... I have read letters regretting that I did not spend longer among them, and that we might visit them soon again. Anyone that is well acquainted

15 *JE*, 1829, p. 183.

with the strong prejudices and hatred which the Jews have always manifested, especially towards one whom they consider an apostate, will look upon the fact, as decidedly favourable for the Gospel truth amongst them.[16]

Back in Danzig Alexander and Ayerst continued with their efforts to consolidate the school, as well as general mission work, in the port city itself and in the surrounding villages. Then in April and May 1829 Alexander visited deep into Poland, spending eight days in Warsaw. Although his letter abounds with some of the normal optimistic observations (perhaps assisted by the editor's pen!), he was very impressed by the work of Alexander McCaul of whom Alexander wrote:

> I have been astonished at the acquirements of dear brother McCaul, in Jewish and Hebrew learning, which can only be accounted for, besides his natural talents, by the zeal and love which he has for the Jews. His heart and soul seem engaged in the matter, and where this is the case, the Lord will not leave such endeavours unblessed. I was almost overwhelmed, when I heard him on Saturday address a considerable number of Jews in their own language, and place the Lord Jesus Christ powerfully before their understandings, in the Hebrew tongue.[17]

Upon return to Danzig, Alexander and Ayerst then embarked upon an exciting form of ministry. During the summer period Polish Jewish traders would come down the Vistula River to the port of Danzig to sell their grain. Many of these would live in temporary huts near the river. Alexander and Ayerst hired a room in this neighbourhood, and distributed Scriptures and other materials to these Jewish merchants.

Beginning in September 1829 Alexander set out again on a tour that included Marienburg (now Malbork in Poland), Stargard (now Szczecinski in Poland), Czersk (near Warsaw), Conitz (now Chojnice, south of Gdansk), Zempleburg (in the province of Pomerania in northern Poland), and other towns and villages. His reception was mixed, but of one incident with a young Talmudic student he wrote:

> I found a young Jew sitting reading the Talmud aloud, at the same time smoking tobacco! Such darkness I have not found for a long time! This young man, though indeed, on the whole intelligent, was full of Talmudic stuff, and seemed to know no other source of bliss. I was very much reminded of my own days of ignorance, and could, therefore, feel for this poor young

16 *JE*, 1829, p. 184.
17 *JE*, 1829, p. 424.

man. This was the fast of Gedaliah[18], and in this manner the poor Jewish Talmudists spend the fast-day, and think of doing God service. I spoke to this young man with earnest and affectionate entreaties, but he seemed rather dissatisfied that anyone should tell him that this was not the way to heaven.[19]

Alexander's last journey in Germany

One of Michael Solomon's last journeys took place in early 1830, again accompanied by Ayerst. They visited numerous locations, including Lessen, where upon entering the inn he 'found the room full of drinking and drunken Poles, who had just come from their church, (that day being Epiphany).' Later on that day, after conversing with the local rabbi, they felt inclined to pass out tracts to the locals, as 'This was a good opportunity to show the Jews that we are also endeavouring to promote true religion among those who are called Christians; several of them seemed greatly astonished at seeing us do this, and we became more deeply impressed with the importance of a Missionary to the Jews having an eye also upon those among whom they dwell, on that account.'[20]

This journey was Alexander's final sojourn in the land of his birth. Soon afterwards he was summoned to return to London. It seemed that the Society had a financial problem, and required the workers to come to England and speak around the country and raise funds.[21]

Alexander adhered to the directives of the London Jews Society Committee and was London bound, retracing the steps almost of one of his predecessors some thirty years previous.

Tragedy for Joseph Wolff

The Wolffs remained in Alexandria until May 1828 and then departed for Beirut, where the plague was then present. Although they desired to travel to Jerusalem, permission was not granted, so they went to Cyprus.

Here all three members of the Wolff family became ill, and unfortunately Wolff's little daughter died there aged ten months. Afterwards they returned to Damiat in Egypt where they resided with the British consul, Signor Surer. Here Wolff again became unwell, which forced a move to Cairo where they stayed with the CMS missionaries, John Lieder and William Kruse. Yet even here his health continued to deteriorate.

Wolff survived this latest ordeal. Once he was healthy enough he accepted

---

18 Gedaliah was the leader for the remaining Jewish people in Judah appointed by Nebuchadnezzar. However he himself was then assassinated. Fearing a Babylonian reprisal for this act the remaining Jewish people then fled to Egypt. The *Gemara* teaches that the death of a righteous person is almost on a par to the destruction of the Temple. In this context it was the consequences of the death of righteous Gedaliah – the exile of the remaining Jewish people in Judah. This fast is called after *Rosh HaShanah* – the Jewish New Year.
19 *JE,* 1830, p. 69.
20 *JE,* 1830, p. 84.
21 Minute 805 & 806, 17 March 1830, LJS Minute Book c.13, Bodleian.

visitors to his home, including Jewish people, some of whom he had debated in Jerusalem many years before.

The return to Jerusalem

Wolff desired very much to introduce his wife to Jerusalem. At last his desire was fulfilled and they set off from Cairo in July 1828, boarding a 'ship of the desert' for the long crossing of the Sinai Desert.

While camping near Gaza one night they were woken by a terrible noise, a mixture of laughing and crying. Upon inquiry their servant Ahmad told them, 'it proceeded from one of the Bedouin Arabs, who was called *Haj-Ali,* i.e a Pilgrim Ali, for he had been in Mecca, and who was possessed with a devil. This dreadful misfortune some people have imagined to be only lunacy, but it is far otherwise. After listening a few minutes longer, Wolff called out in a loud voice in Arabic, "In the name of Jesus be silent!" And immediately all was hushed.'[22] Later the same procedure happened again. Wolff the next day prayed with the man to believe in Jesus and gave him a New Testament before departing.

Thereafter the caravan continued its way to Gaza, then Ramle, Abu Ghosh, and finally, into Jerusalem. Wolff's third visit would be so different from his previous visits. The three leading rabbis whom he had previously known had all died, and the new rabbis 'knew not Joseph.' A new generation had come, despite an absence of only five years.

Joseph was distressed by the lack of recognition and appreciation for what he had done for them on his previous visits. Then he experienced more grief. On one occasion in a coffee shop he was offered coffee, and soon after drinking it he began to convulse all over. Joseph had been poisoned, and only the quick intervention of a passing Greek saved his life. This Greek man managed to get him to the Armenian convent and then a Latin (Roman Catholic) doctor came and gave him medical help.

Wolff was seriously ill, and yet managed to get well enough after three weeks. He lived the remainder of his life with the effects of the poison in his body.[23] The effects of the poisoning also caused them to stay seven months in total in Jerusalem, during which there were more incidents that can be recounted. But at the end of that period he and Georgiana moved on, and made their way to Jaffa.

They left Jaffa for Cyprus on 7 July 1829, where, upon arrival, Georgiana again became unwell. Upon her recovery they continued on to Alexandria. Once here he took up preaching to the resident foreigners who lived there, as well as to any Jewish people willing to come to him.[24] In Alexandria Wolff did something which Joseph Wolff would do: he wrote out a challenge to the Muslim leaders

---

22 Wolff, *Travels,* p. 259.
23 Wolff, *Travels,* p. 262.
24 Wolff, *Travels,* p. 266.

'to repent and turn to Christ: and he predicted to them the speedy downfall of the Muhammedan power....'

Wolff then 'sent out one of these written calls, made out in Arabic, by a donkey driver, to the Governor of Alexandria. The poor fellow was flogged for being the bearer of such a message, and came back in a violent rage and almost knocked Wolff down ...' His wrath was appeased, though, when Wolff offered him $2.[25] Wolff's impetuosity earned him a severe note from Mehmet Ali through the British Consul - 'that he must leave Alexandria.'[26]

Leaving Georgiana behind (as she was heavily pregnant) he departed and thereafter visited numerous locations, and on one occasion had to flee destitute when attacked by pirates. He and his companion managed to survive for several days before finally reaching Saloniki (Thessalonika).

While in this most important city Wolff met with some of the adherents of the false messiah Shabbtai Zvi, who initially thought Wolff was one of them. When they discovered that he wasn't, they quickly disappeared.[27] But there were still many more Jewish people who lived there who were not adherents of the false messiah, and Joseph wasted no opportunity in furnishing them with pamphlets and New Testaments.[28]

Return to Malta and fresh vision
From Saloniki Wolff returned to Smyrna and from thence to Malta where he was soon afterwards reunited with Georgiana and their new born infant son, Henry Drummond Wolff. It was there that he was informed by his host Mr. Hookham Frere that there were many Jewish communities in the region of Bokhara and Afghanistan, and even remnants there of the ten lost tribes.[29]

Wolff accordingly informed the London Jews Society of the possibility of visiting these scattered Jewish communities. The LJS Committee though first wanted him to return to London. They were somewhat apprehensive about matters associated with Wolff's over-indulgence in date speculating, and some other potential problems, including his belief in modern day miracles (as evidenced by his published account of having cast an evil spirit out from the Bedouin). Wolff informed the Committee that he would indeed return, but via Bokhara, Afghanistan and Calcutta! Mr. Frere had committed 500 pounds to defray his costs for this trip, and Wolff now began planning for what became his greatest expedition thus far.

Frey becomes a Baptist
While Alexander and Wolff were embarking on their respective journeys,

25 Wolff, *Travels*, p. 266.
26 Wolff, *Travels*, p. 266.
27 Wolff, *Travels*, p. 271.
28 In 1941 there were about 56,000 Jewish people in Thessalonica, and some 96% of this community was murdered in Auschwitz-Birkenau Death Camp.
29 Wolff, *Travels*, p. 272.

Joseph Frey too was embarking on a new journey – an ecclesiastical one. Frey's unfortunate departure from the American Society and inability to form a Presbyterian congregation in Yorkville, prompted him to seek acceptance into the Baptist Church.

Frey himself wrote that the stimulus for this move was the birth of his fifth child in 1827, although there were more than likely other factors involved. Whatever the reason, Joseph Frey was baptized at New York's Mulberry Street Baptist Church on 28 August 1827.[30] Hereafter would begin another step in his most illustrious journey.

Shortly after his introduction into the Baptist Church, Frey became minister at the Baptist Church in Newark in New Jersey, where he remained for two years.[31] Yet despite this new beginning, his past continued to follow him, and he was obliged to receive a statement from the secretary of the American Society stating that he did not leave that Society due to any financial impropriety.[32]

Frey remained at Newark until April 1830 when he moved to the Baptist Church at Sing-Sing, New York, in April 1830.[33]

---

30 Frey, *Judah and Israel*, p. 88.
31 Eichhorn, ibid, p. 64.
32 Eichhorn, ibid, pp. 68-9.
33 Frey, *Judah and Israel*, pp. 88-89.

Chapter 22

Consolidation in London

Alexander returns to London

Alexander and his family returned to London in April 1830. Michael Solomon was to temporarily fill the position of the home missionary, Rev J.C Reichardt, who would be absent for some months on a tour of duty to the LJS's scattered stations.

He began his work quietly, but soon saw the need for a more regular plan for interacting with the Jewish people. He asked for, and received, permission to live in one of the houses at Palestine Place, one room of which he could use 'for the purpose of meeting & conversing with the Jews.'[1] Part of his work also involved delivering a lecture every Saturday afternoon.

Michael Solomon made numerous initiatives to reach the Jewish people. He circulated a *Notice* among the Jewish people informing them about this room and his availability to meet with them. During that period he also co-operated with the tutor of the Seminary at Palestine Place[2] and was involved in outreach to the Jewish people in sundry ways.

In addition he made numerous speaking tours, including visits to both Plymouth and Bristol. One interesting tour included Norwich, where his old friend and supporter Miss Hancock set up a meeting, and insisted that Alexander present 'a fundamental lecture on the prophecies.'[3]

It soon became apparent that Michael Solomon was fulfilling an important task in England, and he was ultimately asked to remain in England permanently. He would fulfil the role of a second worker, thereby releasing Reichardt to take charge of the newly opened Jewish Operative Institution.[4]

Michael Solomon then returned to Danzig to pack and ship his belongings to England. He also took the opportunity to visit centres along the way, including Berlin, where, it seems, he again asked for a position. The Committee had to impress upon him that London was to be his 'general residence and principal scene of operation.'[5] It would appear that his two years sojourn in Posen had envisioned Michael Solomon to again be actively involved amongst his own people in his native homeland.

1 Minute 958, 19 June 1830, LJS Minute Book c.13, Bodleian.
2 The Seminary had originally been at Stanstead Park, but in 1827 it moved to Palestine Place.
3 Hancock to Alexander, 1 October 1830, MSS 3397 [136-7], Lambeth.
4 Minute 1424, 11 May 1831, LJS Minute Book c. 13, Bodleian and Minute 94, 8 November 1836, LJS Minute Book L, Bodleian.
5 Minute 1506m 13 July 1831, LJS Minute Book c. 13, Bodleian.

At a special meeting of the LJS Committee on 5 November 1831, Alexander and other workers entering into new duties, were prayed for and commissioned. One other Jewish follower of Jesus present on that occasion was Frederick Christian Ewald, who was then entering into the Hebrew seminary at Palestine Place.

The Alexander family moved into a house at No 7 Palestine Place close to the Episcopal Jews Chapel. Shortly later another daughter, Deborah, was born. She wrote later of her impressions of Palestine Place:

> It was a peaceful, secluded spot, an oasis in the desert. Iron gates enclosed it, which were shut at night. A Chapel, a School for 50 Jewish girls, and one for 50 Jewish boys, a College, the Operative Jewish Converts Institution, the Chaplain's House, several good houses, two lodges, and a lovely double avenue of Lime trees, were the result of much effort on the part of the Society, and every May, for very many years, from far and near, came many visitors – friends to Jewish Missions – to hear what was being done.[6]

Professor of Hebrew & Rabbinic Literature

A new institution named King's College was founded in London in 1831.[7] Shortly afterwards they offered Alexander the title and position of Professor of Hebrew and Rabbinic Literature. Alexander submitted this proposal to the LJS Committee, who responded negatively, stating it 'would be incompatible with the performance of the duties of a Missionary of this Society.'[8]

The LJS, however, was forced to modify its opposition in light of Alexander's desire to fulfill this position, and agreed to his request at their meeting of 12 July 1832. It was a wise decision. Not only did this position provide Alexander with wonderful teaching opportunities, it also permitted him exposure to a broader section of British ecclesiastical society than he would encounter if he worked only with the LJS, as well as the honour associated with holding a position with such a potentially prestigious institution. Richard Erlich wrote of this appointment:

> At that time he must already have been exceptionally learned, for a Chair of Rabbinical and Talmudic Law was specially created for him. His inaugural lecture, which appeared in print, had as its subject the importance of Hebrew and Rabbinical literature. He was granted the title of Doctor of Divinity.'[9]

---

6 Ransom, ibid, p. 1.
7 The College was opened on 8 October 1831.
8 Minute No 153, 27 June 1832.LJS Minute Book c. 14, Bodleian. According to Hearnshaw F.J.C, *The Centenary History of King's College London*, London, 1929, p. 110, Alexander was appointed to this position on 8 June 1832.
9 Ehrlich, Richard A. *Michael Solomon Alexander, The First Evangelical Bishop in Jerusalem*, in AJR Information, April 1963, London, p. 13.

There was, though, a strain in the relationship between Alexander's two employers over the following years, but both managed to work through these minor problems. The inaugural address of Alexander was finally delivered on 7 November 1832. It was a lecture of much depth and insight, in which he stated, '…The object of my present introductory address is, simply to point out the importance of Hebrew and Rabbinic Literature;…' [10] Concerning Hebrew he stated:

> …The Jews…universally believe that it was the language in which Jehovah made known his divine will to man…
> … it is acknowledged by all that Hebrew is the most ancient of all known languages… Instead of its being, as some would have it, a mere dialect of the Semitic languages, we have every reason to view it as the mother of all the others, which easily accounts for the great similarity that exists between them.[11]

Alexander then explained, in brief, the importance of understanding rabbinical literature:

> The advantage of being able to read the rabbinical writings, on account of the light which they throw on the Scriptures. These are generally decried as worse than useless; but it can only arise from the ignorance of them. It is true, they contain much that is absurd and erroneous, and in many instances they even most awfully pervert the sense of the Scriptures; but nevertheless, they contain much that is most useful, and calculated to throw light upon them.[12]

Alexander was delivering a direct challenge for the Gentile dominated Church to understand the mind-set of the Jewish people, as well as gain a valuable understanding of their own Scriptures.[13]

Shortly after beginning his labours in London Alexander was joined by Alexander McCaul who had returned from Warsaw on sick leave in 1831. The LJS Committee decided in July 1833 that 'his residence in England is very important to the progress of the work amongst the Jews of this country and requested him to occupy a house in Palestine Place.'[14] Thereafter Alexander laboured alongside McCaul and Reichardt.

These three talented men were involved in numerous projects, one being involvement in shared lectures. They were also directly involved in quite an

---

10 Introductory Lecture delivered on 17 November 1832, in *King's College Calendar*, 1832, p. 4.
11 Introductory Lecture, in *King's College Calendar, 1832* pp. 5 & 7.
12 Introductory Lecture, ibid, p. 25.
13 Some 180 years afterwards, these sentiments of Michael Solomon Alexander are being explored and taught through Alexander College and Shoresh Study Tours in Jerusalem!
14 Minute 94, 8 November 1836, LJS Minute Book L, Bodleian.

innovative form of outreach, Saturday evening lectures at No 18 Aldermanbury Street, commonly known as the Aldermanbury Conferences. These began in November 1832 and were intended as a forum for debate and discussion between Jewish and Christian leaders on matters concerning the Messiah, Judaism and similar subjects.

The Eastern Question
The beginning of Alexander's labours in London coincided with another great turning in world affairs, revolving around the Levant or the Eastern Mediterranean. The geo-political dynamics associated with this period are often referred to 'the Eastern Question.'

Napoleon's incursion into the East in 1798-99 had radically altered European, and especially British, foreign policy towards that region. Thereafter Britain was determined to ensure that no rival European power ever gained a toehold there again, and thereby potentially sever Britain's link to India and the Eastern Empire. Britain was particularly concerned lest the French again encroach near the area of Egypt (and in particular the region where the Suez Canal would later be built); and that the Russians would not come down from the Black Sea through the Bosphorus and Dardanelles and enter the Mediterranean. All of Britain's political decisions from 1800 until 1915 were based upon this dictum. In addition Britain was wary of any potential Russian move overland towards India.

During this very same time the Egyptians under Mehmet Ali (or Muhammed Ali) had imperial ambitions of their own. Egyptian forces under Ibrahim Pasha invaded the region of Syria in late 1831, seriously harming the political *status quo* of the region. In no time at all he was threatening Constantinople itself.

In desperation Turkey sought European assistance. The British Foreign Secretary, Lord Palmerston, was determined to offer assistance. Unfortunately for him a political imbalance in Britain weighed against him and he was forced to remain neutral. In desperation the Turks turned to their arch-rivals Russia for assistance. Russia was all too keen to accept the invitation, and shortly afterwards a strong Russian military presence was evident in Constantinople. In return for assistance, the Russians secured the Treaty of *Unkiar Skelessi* from Turkey, gaining for Russia important political and military benefits. Palmerston in particular was furious that such an alliance had been allowed to happen – right under Britain's nose the Russians were gaining easy access into the Eastern Mediterranean.

Such political happenings in the region of the land of Israel (Palestine) stirred the Evangelical Christian world, especially those disposed towards seeing Israel's restoration. And it was not only these Christians who were interested in

Israel's restoration. The LJS worker John Nicolayson[15] wrote from the Eastern Mediterranean region in August 1831:

> The disposition of Jews in Europe to return to this land of their fathers, seems to grow stronger as the period fixed for the appearance of their great Deliverer is approaching. They here still stick to their calculation of the term, which is now reduced to the short space of eight years…We are told again and again that eight short years will decide the great question between us, to their triumph and our confusion.[16]

Many Jewish people both in Europe and Turkish *Palestine* were of the opinion that the period of the Jewish year coinciding with 1839-1840 would witness the coming of the Jewish redeemer. The question alluded to by Nicolayson would be – had this redeemer appeared before!

It was also during this very same period, thanks to the somewhat tolerant Egyptian regime, that the LJS and indeed evangelical Protestant Christianity were finally able to secure a permanent presence in Jerusalem and the land of Israel. Although Islamic and Turkish law forbade foreigners the right to reside in Palestine, the Egyptians however, in their endeavours to placate the Europeans, provided Protestant Christianity the opportunity to settle in the region. The invitation was there, if anyone wanted it. This offer was taken up by John Nicolayson of the LJS in October 1833, becoming thereby the first permanent Protestant resident in Jerusalem.

The foundation laid by Joseph Frey in London in 1805 and Joseph Wolff in Jerusalem in 1821 was finally going to be built upon in Jerusalem itself, first by Nicolayson, and then later by another Jewish follower of Jesus named Michael Solomon Alexander.

---

15 Nicolayson, from Logumkloster in Denmark, had been sent to Palestine by the LJS in 1825 to sojourn alongside Dr George Dalton, who himself had only recently arrived there. Nicolayson found it near impossible to settle in Jerusalem, but remained in the region awaiting the opportunity to reside in Jerusalem.
16 *Jewish Missionary Intelligence*, (*JMI*), 1832, p. 124.

CHAPTER 23

WOLFF'S EPIC JOURNEY

Wolff departs from Malta

Armed with a passport from the Duke of Wellington, Joseph Wolff left Malta on 31 December 1830. Leaving behind his beloved wife and new-born son, Wolff was destined to take the message of Jesus as Lord and Messiah to Jewish people – all the way from Constantinople to Calcutta, following in the footsteps for much of the way of one of Britain's most well-known Evangelicals, Henry Martyn![1]

Wolff made his way slowly to Constantinople. There in the Turkish capital he received a letter from Sir Robert Gordon, the British envoy extraordinary as well as a *firman* from the Sultan and letters from other ecclesiastical leaders to aid him with his onward journey.[2]

Mounting a horse, and with a companion Wolff set out to travel eastwards, a journey of many hundreds of miles over rough and mountainous country. At Tokat he visited the grave of Henry Martyn. While there he also became quite unwell. Undeterred though, he continued on with his journey towards Trebizond where he stayed with the British consul, Mr Brant, and preached to the Greeks who were there.

While heading towards Erzerum the capital of Armenia, Wolff traversed Mount Ararat. Following his visit to Erzerum he continued on to Khoy, and from there on to Astaraa in the north of Persia, where he met the British Ambassador in Persia, Colonel Campbell. While at Astaraa, Wolff preached in the presence of the Russian ambassador on the text in Revelation 12, and 'showed that the woman mentioned in the first verse was the Jewish nation; and the child which was born was Christ; and the time of the spiritual conception of the Christ in the Jews, will produce a war in heaven between Michael the Archangel and the dragon. And he showed that in that conflict Michael will be victorious and will expel the dragon ... This fall of the dragon will fill him with wrath, and then he will persecute the Jewish nation, when those mighty wonders shall be performed, which are alluded to in Micah vii. 15 ... '[3]

---

1 Henry Martyn (1781-1812) was encouraged by Charles Simeon to be a missionary. He worked as a chaplain for the East India Company in Cawnpore in India from 1806 and translated the New Testament into both Urdu and Persian. He died at Tokat en-route back to England.
2 Due to Britain's support of Greece, there was no British ambassador in Turkey between 1827-32, but Sir Robert Gordon looked after British interests. Sir Stratford Canning did return for a period in 1831-32 to determine the borders between Greece and Turkey.
3 Wolff, *Travels,* p. 281.

Wolff's sermon so impacted those present that the Russian secretaries wrote it down and sent it to their foreign minister Count Karl Nesselrode.

The British ambassador also gave a letter to Wolff for the Persian king, asking him to give Wolff letters of recommendation to enter into the region of Bokhara. Armed with this letter Wolff then headed towards Tehran, the Persian capital. Despite warnings of the dangers of venturing on to Bokhara, Wolff was determined to visit this intriguing city, and upon receiving several cases of literature from India, he set out on his most dangerous journey thus far. Prior to departure Wolff spoke to a 'learned man' (or *Hadshee*) and said to him, "I go about in the world to proclaim that Jesus Christ came the first time to suffer for our sins; and that he will come the second time to reign on earth in glory and majesty; and I am now going to Bokhara to find out about the ten tribes of Israel."[4]

The two agreed to travel together as part of a large caravan. All went well until on the fourth day when they neared Khorassan[5] they were surrounded by a group of tribesmen - the Al-Ammaan. Surprisingly they did not attack nor take anyone captive. When they asked where the group came from and Wolff replied from Persia, they fled – as they had heard the plague was then in Persia.[6]

The caravan continued its journey and finally arrived at Boostan (Garden). There Wolff heard that the Al-Ammaan were by now aware that they did not carry the plague and were waiting for them. Wolff then met with Prince Ismael Mirza, and said, 'that his object in getting safely to Bokhara was, that he might be able to converse with the Jews about Jesus, and inquire into the truth of the idea, that they were the descendants of the ten lost tribes.'[7]

Fearing an attack by the Al-Ammaan, Wolff took an alternative route, and joined another caravan. They had travelled for several days before Wolff was apprehended by a local chieftain Ameer (Amir) Assad on suspicion of being a spy sent by Prince Abbas Mirza of Persia. He was taken to Burchund and interrogated there by the local spiritual leader and the Amir himself. After satisfying them he was not a spy, Wolff was even able to distribute the Christian materials he brought with him.[8]

The Amir then released Wolff and provided two escorts for him so that he could continue onwards. War was brewing at that time between Abbas Mirza and the Persians against some of the local Amirs, so Wolff found himself in quite a delicate position as Abbas was accompanied by some British officers.

Then trouble came upon Wolff from another direction. The caravan he was travelling with was surrounded by a group of local bandits and everyone was

---

4 Wolff, *Travels,* p. 287.
5 Province in north-east Persia.
6 Wolff, *Travels,* p. 288.
7 Wolff, *Travels,* p. 290.
8 Wolff, *Travels,* p. 296.

captured. All were robbed, stripped naked, tied to their horse's tails and then flogged. Wolff prayed, and confessed – 'in such hours one learns to pray.'[9] When the leader of the gang asked him who he was, and Wolff replied that he was a follower of Jesus he was released and allowed to ride on a horse.

Shortly afterwards, however, Wolff was in grave danger of being murdered by this gang, but he managed to extricate himself. He was then released and allowed to continue to the next town of Trobad-Hydaree where he arrived in November 1831. Relieved to have survived, Wolff exclaimed to the local Jewish people upon arrival, in Hebrew, "Hear O Israel the Lord our God the Lord is One."[10] The Jewish community then took him into shelter, and he was permitted to share with them about Jesus.

His troubles though were not yet over. Once again the local chieftain had Wolff imprisoned and chained, but thankfully this only lasted a short time for another warlord allied to the Persian army then captured that location. Wolff was released for the second time, and after witnessing terrible ordeals of local justice, he proceeded on his way – more than relieved to get away from that location.

By December 1831 Wolff finally arrived at Meshed, the main city in Khorassan, a place of great importance for the Turkomen people. Several weeks later he met Prince Abbas Mirza who had several British officers with him. It was from these British officers that Wolff was able to procure some clothes to replace those previously taken from him.

In Meshed Wolff continued to do that which he was best at, introducing Jesus, 'to the Jew first and also to the non-Jew.' He remained in Meshed until late January 1832, 'conversing … with both Jews and Muhammadans, preaching to them Jesus Christ crucified, and Jesus Christ glorified; and dwelt much on his second coming, when he shall reign personally on earth.'[11]

To Bokhara (Bukhara)

Joseph Wolff's goal was to get to Bokhara. His journey there was fortuitous. At that time numerous of the local Turkomen chieftains were afraid of Prince Abbas Mirza, so they came to meet him at Meshed. Abbas was determined to stamp out hostage taking and slavery in that region, and thereupon entered into an agreement with the locals. One of the conditions was that two of their men would become hostages to ensure that Joseph Wolff arrived safely in Bokhara![12]

With this assurance, Wolff set out, and despite more adventures en-route in early March 1832 he finally arrived in Bokhara, the city of Genghis Khan. One of Wolff's first acts was to present his credentials to the local leader or Amir - King Nasrallah Khan - via his prime minister, Hakim Beyk. Beyk asked

9 Wolff, *Travels*, p. 302.
10 Wolff, *Travels*, p. 305.
11 Wolff, *Travels*, p. 314.
12 Wolff, *Travels*, p. 316.

Wolff which nation he was from, to which Wolff replied that 'he was of the Jewish nation; but had embraced the religion of Jesus Christ, and was now a naturalized subject of the King of England, also that he was travelling in order to preach Jesus Christ to the Jewish nation, and to find out about the ten tribes of Israel ...'[13]

All seemed to be going well in his interview, until one Jewish man who overheard the proceedings, claimed that Wolff was a Russian spy. Wolff once again was called upon to use all of his intellect and experience to prove this accusation to be false. His story was ultimately believed and he was released and commanded to move only among the Jewish people and not to discuss his beliefs with the local Muslims.[14]

Wolff spoke to many of the Jewish people, not only about Jesus, but also about the other reason for his trip, to ascertain if these were descendants of the ten lost tribes of Israel. This latter concern was actually one of the reasons for this trip and the reason for the generous gift of Mr Frere in Malta. He concluded:

> There cannot be the slightest doubt that the Jews in Khorasan, Bokhara, Samarkand and Balkh; as well as the descendants of Tshingis Khan, and the Nogay Tatars, and those called of the tribe of Naphthali, are all remnants of the ten tribes. This is not a hypothesis but a relation of their own assertions.[15]

On to Afghanistan

After three months, Wolff departed for Cabul (Kabul). His first stop of consequence was the town of Balkh which was reached after crossing the Oxus River and eluding another band which was out to take slaves. He conversed with the Jewish people in this town who then introduced him to the local ruler, who strongly advised him to continue in the guise of a Muslim. This Wolff refused to do and he somehow managed to get through that region unscathed. Later, however, when he reached Doab he was once again taken captive, robbed and stripped naked. He would have died had he not stated that he was an Englishman.[16]

Wolff was quite relieved to reach Kabul, the capital of Afghanistan, on 1 May 1832, whereupon he was welcomed by several Britons. One of these was Lieutenant Alexander Burnes, who had been informed by Governor-General Bentinck in India to keep an eye out for Wolff. Together with Burnes, Wolff enjoyed some interesting official meetings, although he spent much of his time in discussion and debate with the Jewish leaders.

13 Wolff, *Travels*, p. 330.
14 Wolff, *Travels*, p. 333.
15 Wolff, *Travels*, p. 369. This issue of the ten lost tribes of Israel is not the purpose of this book, but if anyone is interested in the subject they can read more from Wolff's various publications, as well as other sources.
16 Wolff, *Travels*, p. 358.

To India

After about a month in Kabul Wolff then continued his journey eastwards and several weeks later arrived at Peshawar, adjacent to the Khyber Pass. Here he was hosted by the local Muslim leader Sultan Muhammed Khan, who requested Wolff to speak on his behalf to the British Governor-General Lord William Bentinck in India. Wolff did not comply, stipulating that his task was to be a preacher of the word of God.

From Peshawar he continued on through to Attock, where he was cordially received by the local ruler and presented with various letters, including one from Governor-General Bentinck. His Majesty Rundjud Singh then sent congratulations to Wolff for having accomplished such an arduous journey.[17]

The Governor-General, once he became fully aware of Wolff's missionary fervor, requested that Wolff come to Simla as quick as possible, so as not to stir up any religious controversy.[18] But Wolff was not to be rushed, and following a visit to Gujerat he finally arrived at Lahore, the capital of the Punjab region, where he stayed at the home of General Allard of the East India Company.

The Maharajah, Ranjit Singh wanted to see Wolff and on the appointed day he sent an elephant to bring the intrepid traveller to meet him at Amritzar. There the Maharajah, himself of a small stature, attempted to entertain Wolff in sundry ways, all of which were not appreciated by Wolff.

The Maharajah was aware of Wolff's propensity to preach about salvation in Jesus, yet challenged him, "You say that you travel around for the sake of religion; why, then do you not preach to the English in Hindoostan, who have no religion at all?"[19] Wolff later discovered that this was the attitude of Indians all over the country. Following this the two men entered into a long discussion, with Wolff holding back nothing from belief in the all sufficiency of Jesus.

Wolff departed on 22 June 1832 and came to Ludhiana where he was welcomed into the home of Captain Claude Wade and his wife – and thereupon exclaimed thanks for this privilege of being with a British family again. It was from here that he was invited to the home of Sir Jeremiah and Lady Bryant, who was a relative of Georgiana, at Subathu. There he preached and lectured to the British subjects.[20]

From there he went to Simla, the summer residence of the British Raj, arriving on 5 July 1832, and stayed as a guest of Governor-General Bentinck and his wife for almost two months. Both these people were strong Evangelical Christians, as too was the chaplain, Rev Henry Fisher, a former disciple of Charles Simeon and who knew Wolff at Cambridge. Despite Wolff not being an ordained Anglican, he was invited to preach the following Sunday, and, other

17 Wolff, *Travels*, p. 367.
18 Wolff, *Travels*, p. 368.
19 Wolff, *Travels*, p. 375.
20 Wolff, *Travels*, p. 383.

Sundays as well, to a congregation comprised of many of the leading British entities of India![21]

Kashmir beckoned Wolff, so he then set out and visited various places beforehand, until he arrived at Srinagar on 11 October 1832. On the return trip he visited various locations again before arriving at Meerut, where he stayed with Mr Whiting the chaplain of the East India Company, in whose chapel he preached. Thereafter he continued on to Delhi, the seat of the Great Moghul, whom he met shortly after arrival there.

Like many before and after him, Wolff visited the Taj Mahal in Agra, and was struck by the majesty of the building. Then he moved on to Cawnpore (Kanpur), where, as was now becoming the custom, he preached to the Protestant community present. While here he was hosted by a resident officer of the East India Company, one Major Arthur Conolly.

At nearby Lucknow he was invited by the local ruler to present a lecture to all of the Muslim mullahs and British residents. So pleased was the King of Lucknow with Wolff's presentation that he presented him with a gift, the equivalent of 1000 pounds –which enabled Wolff to repay some of his debts.[22]

By this time Wolff was setting his sights on returning home, albeit firstly in an easterly direction. Thereafter he visited Allahabad, Benares, Buxor, Dinapore, Patna, Bancoorah, Burdwan, and while en-route he received a letter from the Bishop of Calcutta, Daniel Wilson. Wilson wrote, '… Of course you do not expect such an old fellow as me, to enter into your particular views as to unfulfilled prophecies. But on the grand vital truths of Christianity, applicable to Jew and Gentile, in all ages and at all times, and in all countries, you will find me exactly as I was thirty years since…'[23]

Wilson invited Wolff to be his guest while in Calcutta, where he arrived on 22 March 1833. The Bentincks at Government House then invited Wolff to stay with them, which he did. While in Calcutta he preached and lectured on numerous occasions and met with many chaplains of Cambridge training as well as a young Scottish minister named Alexander Duff.[24] There were also Jewish people residing in Calcutta, and he 'conversed with both the white and the black Jews.'[25]

The trip home begins

Finally on 27 April 1833 Wolff boarded the ship *Fifeshire* and began the journey westwards. But at Masulipatam he disembarked, and thereupon made his way first to Hyderabad, then to Madras. On this journey he was hit by a sudden storm and subsequently fell ill to cholera. Sensing that his life was coming to

21 Wolff, *Travels*, p. 384.
22 Wolff, *Travels*, p. 412.
23 Wolff, *Travels*, p. 424.
24 Duff (1806-1878), was the first Scottish missionary in India.
25 Wolff, *Travels*, p. 429.

an end he wrote a notification for his journals to be sent to Georgiana.[26] He was then rescued by a saintly woman, and then tended to by a Dr. Tom Cooper, a Scotsman. Then shortly later while he was deep in sleep the hut in which he was staying burnt to the ground - but not before Wolff had been extricated![27]

When he was sufficiently recovered Wolff continued on to Madras, albeit in a weakened state. There some of the clergy permitted him to preach in the pulpits, but others did not on account of him not being ordained in the Church of England![28]

Once recovered in health he continued onwards, first to Cochin, then arriving on a palanquin at Pondicherry, which was a French settlement, on 1 September 1833. Thereafter he visited Cuddalore, Trichinopoly, Mellore, Madura, Travancore and Kotiam (Kottayam) which was on the Malabar coast.

Wolff finally arrived at Cochin on 4 October 1833 whereupon he 'assembled there the white and black Jews, and spoke to them, saying, "I am one of your brethren, a child of Abraham, Isaac and Jacob" and proceeded thereupon to reveal Jesus as the promised seed of Abraham "by whom all the nations of the earth were to be blessed" and who "was brought as a lamb to the slaughter for the iniquities of his people."'[29]

On a later occasion he went to the Jewish section of the city during the Feast of Tabernacles, and found many of the Jewish people 'drunk' – but he still shared Jesus with them even in their celebratory mood!

Wolff then continued on to Calicut, Connomore and arrived at Goa on 31 October 1833. Upon arrival and witnessing the numerous crosses and sound of church bells, he was overjoyed that here the Gospel had witnessed 'the triumph of the cross over idolatry.'[30] This triumph he knew, and the same was told to him by many in the city and surroundings, was due primarily to the work of his great hero, Francis Xavier.

Wolff spend close to a month in and around Goa and visited with many of the Christian communities spread through the city and surrounds. He enjoyed numerous lengthy discussions with priests, monks and clergy, as well as with the Portuguese rulers of the city.

Leaving Goa on 4 November he travelled north via Belgaum, Satura and Poona (where the British commander refused to see Wolff as he classified all the Jews of Germany as 'rascals.'[31]) Poona was also home to the *Benei Israel*, whose origins go back to the dispersion after the destruction of the first Temple. In the modern period Scottish missionaries had worked among them at Poona.[32]

26 Wolff, *Travels*, p. 448.
27 Wolff, *Travels*, p. 449.
28 Wolff, *Travels*, p. 450.
29 Wolff, *Travels*, p. 458.
30 Wolff, *Travels*, p. 464.
31 Wolff, *Travels*, p. 468.
32 Wolff, *Travels*, p. 468.

Wolff met with some of their leaders and enjoyed a healthy discussion including one on the lineage of Jesus.

Whereas the British commander refused to see Wolff in Poona, when he arrived in Bombay (Mumbai) on 29 November 1833 he was invited by the British Governor, Lord Clare, to join him for dinner. Clare also invited all the members of the government of Bombay to join them.

Wolff's reputation had once again gone before him and he was invited on numerous occasions to give lectures and presentations, to a wide variety of groups. One group though, the *Benei Israel*, closed ranks against Wolff as they had heard that he made people Christians through witchcraft. Never one to be put off, Wolff insisted on visiting the leader of the community, named Captain David, and ultimately convinced him that he was not a magician. David then opened the synagogue and Wolff was able to visit with the Jewish people.[33]

Wolff departs from India

On 11 December 1833 Wolff boarded the ship *Coot* in Bombay harbor and began his homeward journey. They stopped briefly at Macullah on the Arabian coast on 23 December, and there Wolff preached to a group of indifferent Bedouins.[34]

The ship continued its westward journey and on 28 December came to Mocha, where some Jewish people lived. Wolff also visited Saana. On 16 January 1834 the ship landed at Massowah on the Abyssinian coast, where Wolff was able to meet with numerous Abyssinian Christians. Thereafter the smaller boat on which they now travelled made its way up the Red Sea, stopping at several locations including Jeddah. At one point while in Jeddah (Jiddah) Wolff sat by the road leading to Mecca and chanted portions of the Psalms and from Isaiah 34 to the pilgrims heading towards the holiest place in Islam. Needless to say Wolff received a stern warning for his actions from a Muslim leader![35]

On 25 February 1834 Wolff boarded another steamer, the *Hugh Lindsay*, and headed towards Suez. From Suez he made his way overland to Alexandria, arriving there on 15 March. After a short time in Alexandria he made the final leg back 'home' to Malta.

Return to Malta

Joseph Wolff's epic journey ended on 4 April 1834 when he landed again at Malta, after an absence of over three years. There to meet him was his amazing wife Georgiana and young son Henry Drummond Wolff, who had been graciously hosted by Hookham Frere during Joseph's absence.

Wolff had accomplished what few others until that time had done - he had

---

33 Wolff, *Travels*, p. 472.
34 Wolff, *Travels*, pp. 472-3.
35 Wolff, *Travels*, p. 476.

travelled the distance from Constantinople to India over land. He also achieved what no-one in the modern period had done – he had presented Jesus all the way, to the Jew first and also to the non-Jew.

Later when he summarized his journey, Wolff wrote down numerous points of interest, the most significant probably being his eighth point:

> All the Jews, everywhere, were astonished and amazed to see one of their nation going around preaching Jesus as the Messiah and Son of God.[36]

---

36 Wolff, *Travels*, p. 480.

Chapter 24

Frey, Alexander and Wolff's varied ministries

Frey in America

Joseph Frey resigned his position at Sing-Sing in 1832,[1] and thereupon left pastoral work and devoted his time to lecturing throughout the United States. For nearly three years he spoke in hundreds of churches and travelled thousands of miles.

Such a lifestyle could not be sustained long term. In December 1835 he commenced preaching near Jamaica on Long Island 'to a people scattered along the Atlantic coast, most of whom seldom, if ever, went to a place of worship.'[2] This group then grew, and Frey established a Baptist Church to minister to the needs of this group.

At this time Frey began to sense the desire to be more actively involved in presenting Jesus as Messiah to the Jewish people in the United States. As there were so few Jewish residents in the United States then, and those few were widely scattered, he resolved to write to them, through his 1836 publication *Joseph and Benjamin*.

In 1836 he proposed that the American Society publish this book and distribute it among Jewish people in America and Europe. The American Society agreed, but as no funds to do so could be raised in America, it was decided on 22 November 1836 to send Frey to Britain to raise funds for its publication and translation into German.[3]

Then at a meeting of Conference of Baptist Ministers of the City of New York and Vicinity on 5 December 1836, a testimonial was written, endorsing Frey to the Baptist ministers of Great Britain.[4] A similar testimonial was also written, signed by ministers from Episcopalian, Reformed Dutch and Presbyterian Churches, endorsing Frey's upcoming trip to Britain and Germany.[5]

Frey gave up his pastoral work in January 1837. 'I have been enabled' he wrote of his time in the United States, 'to travel more than 50,000 miles, and preached five thousand one hundred and forty-seven times, and I have abundant reason to believe that my labours have not been in vain in the Lord.'[6]

1 Frey, *Judah and Israel*, pp. 88-89.
2 Frey, *Judah and Israel*, p. 90.
3 Frey, *Judah and Israel*, pp. 97-98.
4 Frey, *Judah and Israel*, p. 98.
5 Frey, *Judah and Israel*, pp. 99-100.
6 Frey, *Judah and Israel*, p. 90.

New Testament and Book of Common Prayer translated into Hebrew

Back in London the LJS was about to take on two very serious academic projects: the translation into Hebrew of both the New Testament and the Book of Common Prayer. They stated to their supporters in 1834, 'Your Committee have felt it their bounden duty to do all in their power to give to the Jews an accurate edition of their own Scriptures...'[7] The revision of the Society's Hebrew Bible was entrusted to Alexander, McCaul and Reichardt and was completed in July 1836.[8]

Concerning the translation of the Liturgy of the Church of England into a Hebrew Prayer Book the Society stated, in its 1834 *Report*, that the Rabbinical Jews in particular accused the Christians of being without God. The LJS concluded:

> What better proof can be given to them of their mistake than a copy of the authorized daily prayers of our Church, in which they must discover a spirit of deep and devoted piety, and moreover a striking similarity, both in the contents and the ceremonies, to the prayers and usages of the synagogue. The very circumstance that a certain portion of the Psalms, to which all pious Jews attach such importance, is appointed for every morning and evening, must give the Jew a very different idea of Christianity...There is a large body of Jews scattered through the world, and amongst them the most learned and the most devout who will read nothing but Hebrew, and if they are to see our Liturgy at all, it must be in a Hebrew dress ...
>
> Rabbinical Jews, who have all their lives been accustomed to a form of prayer, and that in Hebrew, feel a great want of something to supply their place when they become Christians ...
>
> ... There can be no doubt that divine service conducted in Hebrew, according to the forms of our Church, would be highly useful at Jerusalem, and other places where Hebrew is much studied. The number of Jews who understand the Hebrew prayers is much larger than is supposed by some; and it is hardly necessary to observe, that all who understand the language esteem it above all others. The very circumstance of Christian worship in Hebrew would go far to remove the prejudices against Christianity. Everyone who knows anything of the Jews, knows that a good knowledge of Hebrew is the key to a Jew's heart.[9]

This translation work was originally undertaken by Mr M Czerskier at Warsaw, but was then entrusted to Alexander, McCaul and Reichart for revision.[10] By 1835 the first portions were available, and in November 1836 the full version

---

7 LJS Report, 1834, p. 59.
8 See Minutes 1839, 1840 & 1842, 23 February 1836, LJS Minute Book c.14, Bodleian.
9 LJS Report, 1834, pp. 61-2.
10 According to Elizabeth Finn (McCaul) they were assisted in this task by Mr. Stanislaus Hoga, 'an accomplished Hebraist, who was a Roman Catholic converted from Judaism in Poland and who came to London.' See E. Finn, *Reminiscences*, p. 25.

of the Hebrew Liturgy of the Book of Common Prayer was complete. All members of the Committee received copies and copies were also sent to all the Bishops in England and Ireland, as well as the Professors of Hebrew in the various Universities.[11]

The complete version was first used at the Episcopal Jews Chapel on 5 February 1837. The LJS wrote of this occasion:

> It is with great pleasure that your Committee are now able to report to you, that a *regular Hebrew Service* has been established in your Episcopal Chapel. After the lapse of centuries, Christian worship has again commenced in the holy language of the Hebrew nation. On Sunday, the 5th of February, at three o'clock in the afternoon, the Hebrew translation of the Liturgy of the Church of England was used, for the first time, in public. The prayers were read by Rev. A. McCaul, and a sermon was then preached in English by the Rev. M.S. Alexander, upon the appropriate words, "If by any means I may provoke to emulation them which are my flesh, and might save some of them." (Rom xi. 14). A little band of Hebrew Christians joined with Gentiles in worshipping the Redeemer of Israel, in the language and words of their forefathers. It is to be hoped that this remarkable restoration of Christian Hebrew worship may be viewed as a gracious pledge of the approaching revival of the Hebrew Church. It is, at all events, a visible sign of the union of Jew and Gentile, and a striking illustration of the apostolic declaration, that Christ "is our peace, who hath made both one, and that He hath abolished in his flesh the enmity, even the law of commandments contained in ordinances; for to make in himself of two one new man, so making peace."[12]

In the following years Alexander regularly presided at the Hebrew service, often assisting McCaul.[13] He also attended regular mission duties, as well as travelling and speaking at the LJS Auxiliary stations around the country.

Alexander was quite settled during these years, although in 1835 he received an invitation to become British chaplain at Constanz (on the border of Germany and Switzerland) for a twelve month period. Both King's College and the LJS agreed to him accepting this position, if he so desired, and LJS offered for him to return afterwards to the same task and salary as he enjoyed previously.[14]

It seems, however, that Alexander did not accept the position, but remained at his post in London, and continued his work as before. In the middle of 1835 he was to be joined again, albeit for only a brief season, by Joseph Wolff.[15]

---

11 Minute 116, 22 November 1836, LJS Minute Book c.14, Bodleian.
12 LJS Report, 1837, p. 38.
13 Minute 255, 28 February 1837, LJS Minute Book L 15, Bodleian. There it was stated that McCaul was to conduct the Hebrew services and Alexander was to assist.
14 Alexander to H Smith, 11 May 1835, A9 1835; King's College Archive. Minute 1163, 24 March 1835, LJS Minute Book, c.14, Bodleian.
15 Minute 116, 22 November 1836, LJS Minute Book c.14, Bodleian.

Wolff's trip to Britain …

While Alexander was enjoying a settled life in London, Wolff was in Malta recovering and being reunited with his family. He then received a request from Sir Thomas Baring, Henry Drummond and Charles Simeon to come to Britain to speak on behalf of the LJS.

The timing of his visit was so that he could speak at the Annual General Meeting of the LJS, which was held in Exeter Hall on the Strand on 8 May 1835. It was standing room only as so many wanted to hear Wolff's amazing episodes. He did not disappoint them.

Wolff shared the platform that day with one of his mentors, Charles Simeon. Simeon in many ways was to Wolff what Bogue had been to Frey. Simeon, like the others present that day listened to how the providence of God had sustained this 'wandering meteor' (which is how Rev. Hugh Stowell described him) through those many years of travelling.

Wolff, though, was not just interested in tickling the ears of his audience about the wild and exotic. He desired to stir in their hearts a passion to do similar things to those he had done, and he did this by issuing a clear challenge, "The caution of a Christian is to pray to God and then go forward, doing His will wheresoever he may lead us."[16]

The following two months were filled with speaking engagements all over the country, and in Ireland. Although in most places doors and pulpits were open, there were some doors which were closed to him, as some thought his views on the restoration of Israel and the personal reign of Jesus as well as his rather wild nature, were somewhat off-putting.[17]

It seems it was not just clergy who found Wolff somewhat off-putting. Another was Michael Solomon Alexander's daughter, Deborah, who wrote of a visit from Wolff to their home at this time:

> He was very wild, untidy and had dirty finger nails. His black hair hung in curls and he talked very loudly. Everything he did and said was noisy. He bounced about our house, thundered at our knocker at all hours, and one very early morning I heard him in our garden, loudly calling out "Alexander, Alexander, I cannot find a barber, I want my hair cut." This was quite early.
>
> He preached at the Chapel one Sunday morning. Our pew was just under the pulpit, and I was afraid the cushions would come down on our heads, he was so excited. Two ladies in front of us got more fidgety than usual, after he had preached for an hour, so he leant down and said to them, "Ladies, you disturb me, please sit still and don't go. Your dinners will not run away". When we got home after his 1-½ hours sermon, we were at dinner, when we

---

16 *JMI* 1835, quoted in Hopkins, ibid, p. 244.
17 Wolff, *Travels*, pp. 484-85.

heard his thundering knock, and in he came. He said, "Robert[18], my dear, I have left my spectacles in the pulpit. Just run and fetch them." Robert put down his plate of cherry tart, and the Dr. sat him down and ate it up!

One day he and Mr Stoddart ... came to dinner. I remember the dessert was laid out in the drawing room, and Bessie and Minnie were sitting one on each side of the chimney piece ... The doctor walked in, and went straight up to the table, and put his dirty hand into a dish of Normandy pippins, spilling the juice on Mama's cherished table, and gulped it down. I couldn't bear him, especially because one day he put me up on a table. I was only 6 years old, and made me show him how he finished his sermon, as he had been told I made fun of him.[19]

Once having fulfilled his duties for the London Jews Society, Wolff returned to Malta in October 1835. Prior to departure, however, he ordered more supplies of materials from the British and Foreign Bible Society, including on this occasion some in Amharic.

... then to Abyssinia

Wolff really was the 'wandering meteor' and he was soon planning his next great adventure. He sent Georgiana and young Henry Drummond Wolff to Geneva to live and then in January 1836 he left for Abyssinia, travelling via Alexandria and Suez. From Suez he again visited the traditional site of Mount Sinai. Here he received evidence that one of the New Testaments he left there in 1821 had been read by a Jewish man from Smyrna. This man seemingly had come to be a follower of Jesus as a result.[20]

Upon his return to Suez Wolff boarded the *Hugh Lindsay* which took him to Jedda. He then met two men associated with the CMS, Hadara and Andreas Muller, whom Samuel Gobat, the head of the CMS work in Abyssinia,[21] had sent there to get money.

While sailing from Jedda to Abyssinia Wolff began to learn the Amharic language, and upon arrival in Abyssinia he headed inland towards Adwah where Gobat was residing with his family.

Wolff was constantly reminded of the story that the Queen of Sheba had married King Solomon and their child had introduced Judaism into Abyssinia. At Asmara he went into a church and was much struck by the similarity to how the ancient Temple in Jerusalem was arranged.[22] He handed out material in the Amharic language to the Christian people there.

18 The second eldest child, Robert.
19 Ransom, ibid, pp. 2-3.
20 Wolff, *Travels*, p. 486.
21 Samuel Gobat was born in Switzerland in 1799 and although being a Lutheran, had proceeded to London to learn Arabic. While there the Church Missionary Society asked him to go to Abyssinia which he did in 1829.
22 Wolff, *Travels*, p. 491.

At the time of his arrival the people were expecting a new *Aboona* (Abuna = leader) to be sent from the Coptic Church in Egypt. They had a belief that the *Aboona* would come in disguise – and thus they came to believe that Wolff was their new *Aboona*. Despite his protestations they persisted, and did not stop until Wolff arrived at Adwah and met Gobat, whom they knew was trying to convert them.

Arriving at Adwah, the capital of the district of Tigre on 26 June 1836, Wolff found Gobat very unwell. Gobat's young wife had a small child and was pregnant again and was also very sick. Wolff realized that Gobat needed to leave and get back to Europe, so he offered to go with him to Jedda. This he could not do though until September as the rainy season was soon upon them.

He used this waiting time to learn the Abyssinian language and the customs of the people. While there he also visited the holy city of Axum. Wolff also ascertained that a large number of Jews lived in Abyssinia, called "Falashas". As much as he wanted to visit them he could not, due to Gobat's illness and his commitment to help him get to Europe.[23]

On 1 September 1836 Wolff left Adwah with Gobat and his family, Gobat being 'carried on a kind of bedstead over the mountain, by the faithful Hadara and Andreas Muller.'[24] The party arrived at Jeddah finally at the end of September, and Wolff was able to place Gobat and his family safely upon a ship headed north to Suez.

Wolff in Arabia and Yemen

With this mission accomplished Wolff now spent considerable time wandering around the Red Sea. At Al Hodeydah (in Yemen) he was privileged to have an interview with the local Egyptian ruler, Ibrahim Pasha (a nephew of Muhammed Ali), who questioned Wolff about all manner of theological and political matters. One of those present was a Greek, who upon seeing Wolff, said, "Is this *Yosef Wolff Ebraios*? 'i.e. Joseph Wolff the Hebrew' who was taken by the pirates near Salonika ....?"[25]

From Al Hodeydah Wolff slowly made his way inland to Saana as he heard that Jewish people lived there. Upon arrival he met with the local ruler, or Imam, whom he found in a total state of drunkenness. Wolff had a more profitable time with Chief Rabbi More Joseph Alkaree, with whom he discussed Isaiah 53.[26]

When Wolff left Saana on account of his health, he travelled back towards the coast. While en-route he was accosted first by a group of a fanatical Wahhabis, who horse-whipped poor Joseph, and then later by a swarm of Bedouin who

---

23 Wolff, *Travels*, p. 498.
24 Wolff, *Travels*, p. 499.
25 Wolff, *Travels*, p. 504.
26 Wolff stated, on page 510 of *Travels*, that several Jewish men and their families came to faith and were baptised.

demanded money. Joseph was forced to surrender all that he had – and was once again left destitute.[27]

India and America

Wolff's health was now so poor that he had to forego returning to Abyssinia, and instead boarded the *Hugh Lindsay* which was en-route for Bombay. One of those who welcomed him upon arrival was a Jewish man named Mr. Goldsmid, who said to him: "Wolff I love you for one thing, and that is, because you make yourself known everywhere as a descendant of the Jews, and show yourself at the same time to be a living epistle of Christ."[28]

Wolff was not long in India before he realized his health was in such a poor state that he could not remain or return to Africa. He then took up the offer of proceeding on to America, stopping en-route at St Helena Island, where he was hosted by the Governor and where he gave a lecture to the British residents.[29] Wolff finally arrived in New York in August 1837, some twenty years after Joseph Frey had first arrived there. Frey, though, was not there to meet him, as he was in Britain.

Within days of his arrival Wolff was hosted by numerous church dignitaries, both Episcopal and non-Episcopal, and he was even invited to stay in the home of a certain Mr. Stuyvesant! It was also suggested that he should be ordained as a deacon into the Episcopal Church. There were some, though, who opposed this move, and there were numerous protests, one of which was that he was a follower of Edward Irving and believed in the speaking in different tongues. Wolff did not deny that he had a close relationship with Irving, Drummond and John Bayford, but would not actually say that he was an Irvingite, and that he was not associated with the speaking in tongues.[30]

Joseph Wolff was accordingly ordained as a deacon in New Jersey, and remained in Salem for a brief period before preaching on numerous occasions on the eastern sea-board. Then at the request of the ex-president of the United States, John Quincy Adams, he also spoke to the House of Congress.[31] Now that was indeed a long way from those humble beginnings in a remote German village!

Ordained a priest in Ireland and move to Yorkshire

Following an intense period in the United States, Wolff left for Southampton on 2 January 1838, and on 3 February he was re-united with his wife and young son. Wolff then began a lecture tour on both the mainland and in Ireland, and had numerous meetings within aristocratic and ecclesiastical circles.

---

27 Wolff, *Travels*, p. 511.
28 Wolff, *Travels*, p. 513.
29 Wolff, *Travels*, p. 513.
30 Wolff, *Travels*, p. 516.
31 Wolff, *Travels*, p. 517.

One such meeting was at Trinity College in Dublin where an honorary doctorate was bestowed upon him. Then on 25 June 1838 he was ordained a priest in the Church of Ireland by the Bishop of Dromore. Wolff and Alexander both now had the common heritage of being German Jews, and being ordained as priests in Ireland!

At the conclusion of his speaking tour Wolff accepted an invitation to be a curate in Linthwaite, in Yorkshire. His decision was not welcomed by Henry Drummond, who wrote to him, 'Your call is to be an evangelist for all the nations of the earth, and for this you are fit; but, to use your own simile, "you are as fit for a parish priest as I am for a dancing-master."'[32] Wolff did not immediately heed Drummond's words, although he did move from Linthwaite to High Hoyland in Yorkshire in 1840 and thereafter enjoyed the life of a parish priest for the following three years.

Frey returns to Britain

Joseph Frey departed New York in February 1837, and accompanied by his wife and youngest child, returned to Britain after an absence of twenty years.

Upon arrival he was met by considerable opposition, by people who opposed the colonization scheme, and by those who had been informed that Frey had a poor reputation in America and that he had previously absconded from Britain taking 3,000 pounds of LJS's money. On 24 April 1837 a meeting took place at Devonshire Place whereby it was resolved that the charges against Frey 'are utterly unworthy of credit.' A Committee was then formed, headed by Sir Thomas Baring as treasurer, to represent the American Society in their efforts in Britain.[33]

A large public meeting was then held at the Congregational Library on 28 April 1837, at which a letter was read from Sir Thomas Baring, bearing testimony to Frey's 'entire honesty in every transaction connected with the pecuniary affairs of the Society for promoting Christianity amongst the Jews.' Baring then added, 'Had Mr. Frey been guilty of embezzling or of improperly appropriating to himself any part of the funds of the Society, I must have been cognizant of the fact; and you are perfectly at liberty to make use of my name in answer to any charge of dishonesty that may be preferred against Mr. Frey, to give to it the most decided contradiction.'[34]

With this endorsement, Frey then proceeded to visit churches in various parts of Britain and have his small book *Joseph and Benjamin* published.

---

32 Wolff, *Travels*, p. 520.
33 Frey, *Judah and Israel*, pp. 102-3.
34 Frey, *Judah and Israel*, pp. 101-2.

To Germany and back

In May 1838 Frey sailed to Germany. One of the more important places he visited was Berlin, where he met with the leaders of the Berlin Society for Promoting Christianity among the Jews.'

Frey met with success in this meeting, as Eichhorn records, 'the Berlin Society for Promoting Christianity among the Jews endorsed the settlement proposition and offered to distribute five thousand copies of "Joseph and Benjamin" among German Jewry if Frey would make a German translation and raise the funds for the printing and binding. This Frey promised to do.'[35]

Upon his return to Britain Frey then travelled over the land, including Ireland, and raised the necessary funds. But when an accounting was made of his expenses as against the money raised, there was a shortfall. Frey had no finances to pay this short-fall, nor did he have money now to pay for his return fare to the United States. Sir Thomas Baring now assisted to a degree, while Frey was also forced to sell his library to the New York Conference of Baptist Ministers.

Frey returns to the United States

Upon his return to America in in October Frey was met with news that his finances were in a deplorable state, and he discovered that he was owing to various entities some $1000.[36] Frey turned to the American Society for assistance, and was distraught when the Board decided against assisting him with this financial burden. He was deeply hurt by this, and requested their assistance a second time, during which he also asked if they would employ him as their missionary in New York City.

The American Society Board pondered these requests, and for the second time they decided not to refurbish Frey for his out of pocket expenses. This decision effectively ended Frey's involvement with the American Society. Joseph Frey was once again rejected from a work in which he had invested much of his time and energy.

Frey thereupon began a ministry to the Jewish people from the South Baptist Church on Nassau Street in New York in December 1839. When this venture failed, he accepted a position as minister at the Bethel Baptist Church in Williamsburgh on Long Island, New York.[37]

At the age of sixty-seven it seemed that Frey's journey on earth would now possibly end in New York.

Tragedy for the Alexanders

At that same time Michael Solomon Alexander, twenty eight years his junior, was being prepared for the next step of his journey - to Jerusalem. Before this

---

35 Eichhorn, ibid, p. 71.
36 Eichhorn, ibid, pp. 71-72.
37 Eichhorn, ibid, p. 73.

new season began though, tragedy struck the Alexander household. In the middle of 1840[38] the Alexanders eldest daughter, Sarah, died of inflammation of the lungs. Deborah, the younger, wrote:

> Mama was a very long time getting over her death. Papa wrote a little memoir of her life called The Flower Fadeth.
>
> She died in June – the month of roses. To this day, scent of faded roses reminds me of her, surrounded by a profusion of those dear flowers.[39]

The little Memoir that Michael Solomon wrote about his daughter was entitled *Memoir of Sarah J.W. Alexander, daughter of Rev M.S. Alexander. Written by her father.* This untimely death was heard of far away, and the *Dublin Record* wrote on 16 June 1840: 'His name and exertions will long be remembered in the city of Dublin, by those who take an interest in the welfare of the ancient people of God.'[40]

---

38 Ransom states it was 1838.
39 Ransom, ibid p. 4.
40 MSS 3393 [25], Alexander Papers, Lambeth.

Chapter 25

Is this the Time for Israel's Restoration?

Rome and Jerusalem

The 1830's were a period of intense Evangelical activity. Conversely there were also efforts being made within the Anglican Church for a rapprochement with the Roman Catholic Church. This activity was being carried out by the Tractarians (also known as the Oxford Movement, or the Puseyites, after its leader, Philip Pusey). One of its prominent members was John Henry Newman.

Newman resided for some time in Rome, and while there in 1833 he met Christian Charles Bunsen (one of Joseph Wolff's former acquaintances) whom he described as 'most hospitable and kind'. Newman wrote:

> I think I am right in saying that it had been long a desire with the Prussian Court to introduce Episcopacy into the new Evangelical Religion, which was intended in that country to embrace both the Lutheran and Calvinistic bodies. I almost think I heard of the project, when I was at Rome in 1833, at the Hotel of the Prussian Minister, M. Bunsen.[1]

Another in Rome during this time was Anthony Ashley Cooper, later the 7th Earl of Shaftesbury, or commonly known as Lord Shaftesbury. In January 1834 Shaftesbury dined with his cousin, Philip Pusey, and sat next to Bunsen (now in a senior position in the Prussian delegation in Rome), whom Shaftesbury described as 'a most simple, unaffected, learned man.' Several days later Shaftesbury dined with Bunsen again and their relationship thereafter further developed.[2]

In 1835 while back in England Shaftesbury met a prominent English evangelical named Edward Bickersteth.[3] Bickersteth who was a leader in the CMS, held a strong belief that the Jewish people would return to Palestine and that following this Jesus would return.[4] Thereafter Shaftesbury adhered to the basic belief that the Jewish people would return to Palestine, hear of Jesus as Messiah, and Jesus would return around that time to Jerusalem.[5]

---

1 Newman, J, *Apologia Pro Vita Sua*, (London, 1890), p. 141.
2 Hodder, E. *The Life and Work of the Seventh Earl of Shaftesbury* (London, 1887), p. 100.
3 Bickersteth was a prominent evangelical and staunch opponent of the Tractarian movement and was one of the secretaries of the CMS.
4 Battiscombe, G. *Shaftesbury, A Biography of the Seventh Earl 1801-1885.* (London, 1974), pp. 100-101.
5 Shaftesbury became a LJS vice-President in 1835, and then President in 1848, and held this position until his death in 1885 – a total of fifty years official involvement.

Shaftesbury then joined the LJS as a vice-President in 1835. What made Shaftesbury's involvement important was his strong Evangelical stance, and his family connections: he soon became the step-son-in-law of the Foreign Secretary, Lord Palmerston. Both of these men would greatly influence the future movements of Michael Solomon Alexander.

Progress in Jerusalem

The European and Jewish communities benefitted from the Egyptian rule over Syria during the 1830's, although they did upset some local Muslim Arabs by their more efficient form of government. John Nicolayson settled permanently in Jerusalem in 1833 and was soon afterwards joined by workers from the American Board of Commissioners for Foreign Missions.

The LJS then decided in 1835 to establish a more permanent presence in Jerusalem by purchasing property and building a Protestant Church in Jerusalem. After much trial and error Nicolayson, finally, in 1838 was able to purchase property inside the walls of Jerusalem for the LJS centre. The property was located immediately opposite the Citadel or fortress of Jerusalem and adjoining the Jewish, Christian and Armenian sections of Jerusalem.

Nicolayson obtained his objectives through the direct intervention of Shaftsbury and Sir Thomas Baring, as well as the British Consulate in Egypt, as directed by Lord Palmerston. Ever since the Treaty of *Unkiar Skelessi* Palmerston was determined to abort Russian (and French) initiatives in the region by encouraging any British-led initiative in the region.

Shaftesbury in particular was excited by this development in Jerusalem. He wrote in the *Quarterly Review Magazine:*

> ... a more important undertaking has already been begun by the zeal and piety of those who entertain an interest for the Jewish nation. They have designed the establishment of a church at Jerusalem, if possible on Mount Zion itself, where the order of our service and the prayers of our Liturgy shall daily be set before the faithful in the Hebrew language ...
>
> To anyone who reflects upon this event, it must appear one of the most striking that have occurred in modern days, perhaps in any days since the corruptions began in the Church of Christ. It is well known that for centuries the Greek, the Romanist, the Armenian, and the Turk have had their places of worship in the city of Jerusalem, and the latitudinariansim of Ibrahim Pasha has lately accorded that privilege to the Jews. The pure doctrines of the reformation, as embodied and professed in the Church of England, have alone been unrepresented amidst all these corruptions; and Christianity has been contemplated both by Mussulman and Jew, as a system most hateful to the creed of each, a compound of mummery and image-worship.[6]

6 Hodder, ibid, pp. 239-241.

By establishing a Protestant presence in Jerusalem a clear challenge was being thrown out to the ecclesiastical *status quo* in Jerusalem. Although the Egyptians were governing Jerusalem, and wished as much as possible to placate the British, Mehmet Ali nevertheless realized that building a new church in Jerusalem (a Hebrew-Protestant one at that!) could easily inflame Muslim sensitivities in Jerusalem, as it violated a high principle of Islamic jurisprudence – no churches could be built in the region under the control of Islam. He referred the matter to Turkey, even to the Sultan, the custodian, or *Caliph,* of Islam.

A British Consulate in Jerusalem

Due to the more tolerant Egyptian occupation of Syria, Palmerston decided to establish a British vice-consulate in Jerusalem in 1838. The British Consulate would enable the British to monitor Russian and French initiatives in the region – the Russians were the official protectors of the Orthodox Christians, while the French were the official protectors of Catholics.[7]

This move by Britain was of tremendous significance, both geo-politically and concerning the status and welfare of the Jewish people. Amongst the initial instructions given to the British vice-consul, William Tanner Young, were those, 'to afford protection to the Jews generally.'[8] Young wrote to Palmerston shortly after his arrival:

> There are two parties here, who will doubtless have some voice in the future disposition of affairs – 'The one is the Jew – unto whom God originally gave this land for a possession, and the other, the Protestant Christian, his legitimate offspring. Of both these Great Britain seems the natural guardian.[9]

By stating that there was a position and future for the Jewish people and the Protestants, Young gave a direct challenge to the established *status quo,* according to which the Muslims were at the top of the social ladder, followed by the Christian communities while the Jewish people were on the bottom rung. The Protestants were not even on the ladder. The stage was being set for the biggest challenge to the *status quo* in Jerusalem for centuries.

Eastern Question flares up again

Tensions meanwhile between Turkey and Egypt remained high. In 1838 Mehmet Ali announced plans to unite Egypt and Syria into a hereditary kingdom. This threat concerned Palmerston as he feared French encroachment due to her involvement with Egypt.[10]

---

7 The legal provision for this was the *Capitulations,* laws enacted by the Ottoman Turks regulating foreign involvement in the Turkish Empire. France had entered into a *Capitulation* with Turkey in 1535, and Russia, following the defeat of Turkey in war, received concessions to provide protection to Orthodox Christians within the Turkish Empire, in 1774.
8 Bidwell to Young, 31 January 1839, FO 78/368 No 2.
9 Young to Palmerston 14 March 1839, FO 78/368, No 8.
10 Ridley, J. *Lord Palmerston* , p. 222. Quoting Palmerston to Granville, 27 May 1839.

The situation deteriorated when in June 1839 a Turkish army was heavily defeated in Syria by Ibrahim Pasha's Egyptian forces.[11] Shortly afterwards the Sultan died in Constantinople, and the Turkish Viziers (ministers) agreed to bestow upon Mehmet Ali permanent sovereignty over Syria, which included Palestine.

Palmerston, Prince Metternich of Austria, and other foreign ministers asked the Turkish government not to agree to these Egyptian demands. Palmerston maintained that Britain's interests would not be served if Egypt (with French support) occupied Syria, especially while Russia was still bound by her treaty with Turkey.

The European Powers wished to solve the situation politically and have Egypt leave Syria. Russia, Austria and Prussia supported Palmerston in this initiative. The French, however, procrastinated, and made it clear to Palmerston that they would not force Mehmet Ali to leave Syria if he failed to do so willingly. Palmerston responded by stating that the other Powers (including Russia, Austria and Prussia) would remove him - if necessary without the French.

At this juncture of political manoeuvering the new Turkish Sultan, Abd-ul-Mezid, issued a reform aimed at satisfying European desires for more leniency for non-Muslims in the Turkish Empire. Although quite ineffective, the *Hatti Sherif of Gulhane*, when issued in November 1839, was nevertheless a progressive move by the Turkish regime.

The Damascus Blood Libel

During this unsettled time a Capuchin friar, Padre Thomas (who was under French protection) was murdered in Damascus in February 1840. A rumour quickly spread that the monk had been murdered by the Jewish people, who used his blood for the Passover meal, and persecution then erupted against the Jewish community.[12]

The French Consul also condemned the Jewish people and the French government supported his verdict. Palmerston was determined to assist the Jewish people and provided a high level Jewish delegation utmost support while they travelled to Damascus and the Isle of Rhodes (where a similar *Blood Libel* had occurred). This delegation was led by Sir Moses Montefiore, the scion of British Jewry.

Although political factors influenced Palmerston in this decision, namely his desire to thwart all French ambitions in the East, nevertheless he also felt great sorrow for the welfare of the defenceless Jewish people.[13] Sometime later Palmerston dispatched a Memo to his representatives in the Turkish Empire

---

11 See, Ridley, ibid, p. 220.
12 Albert Hyamson, *A British Consulate in Jerusalem in relation to the Jews of Palestine 1838-1914*, (London, 1939), Vol. 1, p. xxxvii.
13 Mordechai Eliav, M. *Britain and the Holy Land, 1838-1914: Selected Documents from the British Consulate of Jerusalem*, (Jerusalem, 1997), pp. 130-131.

and other areas where Jewish people resided, informing them to look out for the interests of Jewish people residing there.[14]

People everywhere were abhorred that such a case reminiscent of the Dark Ages could occur in this age of enlightenment. The Jewish people in Jerusalem were extremely perturbed by this event and by the possible ramifications. The rabbis sent a delegation to George Pieritz, one of the Jewish followers of Jesus, and asked him to 'do what he could to rid them of this calumny; and, in fact, requested him to go with one of their rabbis to Damascus for this purpose'.[15] Nicolayson dispatched Pieritz to Damascus to plead on behalf of the Jewish people. This was such a profound move that even the rabbis offered prayers for success of the venture.[16]

In Britain Alexander McCaul and Michael Solomon Alexander called for the Jewish followers of Jesus to come together over this terrible incident and fifty-seven of them added their names to the following declaration:

> We, the undersigned, by nation Jews, and having lived to the years of maturity in the faith and practice of modern Judaism, but now by the grace of God members of the Church of Christ, do solemnly protest that we have never directly nor indirectly heard of, much less known among the Jews, of the practice of killing Christians, or using Christian blood, and that we believe this charge, so often brought against them formerly, and now lately revived, to be a foul and satanic falsehood.

The Memo was signed by 'M.S Alexander, Professor of Hebrew and Rabbinical Literature in King's College, London; Formerly officiating Rabbi in the Jewish Congregations at Norwich and Plymouth', and also the names of the fifty-seven Jewish followers of Jesus.[17]

1840 – War & calls for Israel's Restoration

The embers of the Damascus and Rhodes *Blood Libel* cases had barely simmered when on 15 July 1840 the ambassadors of Prussia, Austria and Russia signed an agreement with Britain, represented by Palmerston, calling upon Egypt to withdraw from Syria.

The European Powers now began formulating strategies for the future of southern Syria (Palestine) once the Egyptians were ousted. The LJS in particular was aware of the proclaimed belief amongst Jewish people that the year of their redemption was drawing near, and great things were anticipated in the Jewish year 5600 between September 1839 and September 1840. Shaftesbury wrote in his diary on 25 July 1840:

14 Palmerston to Ambassador Ponsonby, 21 April 1841, FO 195/181 (No 95).
15 Nicolayson Diary 16 March, 1840, Conrad Schick Library & Archive, Alexander College, Christ Church, Jerusalem. [Henceforth Schick Library]
16 Nicolayson Diary, 18 March 1840, Schick Library.
17 *JI,* 1840, pp.240-41.

Anxious about the hopes and prospects of the Jewish people. Everything seems ripe for their return to Palestine...Could the five Powers of the West be induced to guarantee the security of life and possessions of the Hebrew race, they would now flock back in rapidly augmenting numbers. Then by the blessing of God I will prepare a document, fortify it by all the evidence I can accumulate, and, confining to the wisdom and mercy of the Almighty, lay it before the Secretary of State for Foreign Affairs.[18]

Shaftesbury's desire was for a clause to be inserted into the final Treaty allowing for the restoration of the Jewish people to Palestine, hopefully under British protection.[19] Several days later, on 1 August 1840, he presented his scheme to Palmerston, who, he wrote, was impressed by the proposal.[20]

Lord Shaftesbury's efforts were greatly aided by Erasmus Scott Calman, a Jewish follower of Jesus and member of the LJS mission in Jerusalem, then in London.[21] Calman, at Shaftesbury's encouragement, wrote a Memorandum on 3 August 1840, in which he stated that his sojourn in Palestine had convinced him that Jewish people would return and till the land so long as there was security of life and possession. He wrote:

A Proclamation like that of Cyrus would be echoed by hundreds of thousands of Jews in Poland, Russia and elsewhere, and by the rich as well as by the poor who would gladly exchange their present harassed and uncertain mode of life for the quiet and more certain one that would result from the cultivation of the soil ... They would be enabled to sit under their vine and fig-tree and none should make them afraid.[22]

Shaftesbury's proposal impressed Palmerston, who in turn then sent the following dispatch, on 11 August 1840, to his ambassador, Ponsonby, in Constantinople:

There exists at present among the Jews dispersed over Europe a strong notion that the time is approaching when their nation is to return to Palestine; and consequently their wish to go thither has become more keen, and their thoughts have been bent more intently than before upon the means of realizing that wish. It is well known that the Jews of Europe possess great wealth; and it is manifest that any country in which a considerable number of

---

18 Hodder, ibid, p, 166.
19 Ashley to Palmerston, 25 September 1840, quoted in Hodder, ibid, pp. 168-169. This situation is not all that different from that confronting Cyrus, King of Persia. Faced with a potential rival in Egypt and a vacant buffer zone between Persia and Egypt, perhaps strategic, economic factors may have induced him to permit the return of the Jewish people to the land of Israel.
20 Hodder, ibid, p. 167.
21 Friedmann, I. *The Question of Palestine*, (New Brunswick, 1992), p. xviii.
22 Memorandum by E.S. Calman, 3 August 1840, encl in Ashley to Palmerston, 25 September 1840, encl No 1 in Palmerston to Ponsonby, 25 November 1840, FO 195/165, No 261.

them might choose to settle, would derive great benefit from the riches which they would bring into it.²³

Palmerston needed to arouse the interest of the Sultan in the positive aspect of Israel's restoration, and therefore exaggerated the condition of the Jewish people, as further evidenced in the same Memo:

> ... it would be of manifest importance to the Sultan to encourage the Jews to return to, and settle in, Palestine; because the wealth which they would bring with them would increase the resources of the Sultan's dominions; and the Jewish people, if returning under the sanction and protection and at the invitation of the Sultan, would be a check upon any future evil designs of Mehmet Ali or his successor.²⁴

What Palmerston was proposing was the establishment of a buffer zone between Turkey and Egypt, in the land of Israel, and for this buffer zone to be occupied by the Jewish people. That this idea was common is revealed by an editorial in the prestigious *Times* newspaper on 17 August, which also endorsed the concept of the restoration of Israel.²⁵ Shaftesbury and many Evangelicals were excited by these events, seeing in them a modern day Cyrus decree which would permit the restoration of Israel. ²⁶

Calman's Memo was added to Shaftesbury's letter and both were sent to Palmerston on 25 September 1840, and then forwarded to Ambassador Ponsonby on 25 November 1840.

Outbreak of War

Meanwhile French opposition to the Allied ultimatum increased, and by October 1840 they began increasing their Mediterranean fleet. The French King notified Queen Victoria of the negative mood in France towards the Allied position. There was, he stated, a strong group in France desiring a united Syria and Egypt, under French patronage (as Palmerston was looking to a Jewish presence in Palestine somehow under British patronage). The King assured Queen Victoria that he doubted France would go to war against the Allies.²⁷

Yet war was imminent, especially when Mehmet Ali adamantly refused to comply with the Allied request. The campaign to oust him began in late October, and climaxed on 3 November 1840 when an Allied, mostly British, fleet bombed and captured Acre, the primary seaport along the Mediterranean coast. The British commander, Admiral Sir Charles Napier, then induced Mehmet Ali to surrender, and in return to accept the offer of a hereditary monarchy in Egypt.

23 Palmerston to Ponsonby, 11 August 1840, FO 78/390, No 134.
24 Palmerston to Ponsonby, 11 August 1840, FO 78/390, No 134.
25 Lieber, S. *Mystics and Missionaries,* The Jews in Palestine, 1799-1840, (Salt Lake City, 1992), p. 374.
26 Hodder, ibid, p. 168.
27 Lord Palmerston to Queen Victoria, 11 November 1840. Connell , *Regina v Palmerston* , pp 25-27, quoted in Ridley, ibid, p. 239.

Although temporary Turkish control was re-established over Palestine and, indeed Syria, a final decision on the future status of the region would now need to be determined by the European powers and Turkey. It would be at least six months until this final decision would be reached, in London, in July 1841, with the *Treaty for the Pacification of the Levant*.

British Reactions to Victory

The conflict in the 'Holy Land' engendered considerable interest in Britain. The Commission of the General Assembly of the Church of Scotland sent a Memo to the Foreign Office on 23 October 1840 in which they appealed for Israel's restoration.[28] Palmerston also forwarded this to Ambassador Ponsonby on 24 November, strengthening his case as previously presented by Shaftesbury. In his letter to Ponsonby, Palmerston added:

> ... that the matters to which it relates excite a very deep interest in the minds of a large number of Persons in the United Kingdom, and the Sultan would enlist in his favour the good opinion of numerous and powerful classes in this country if he were immediately to issue some formal edict or declaration granting and assuring to such Jews as may choose to fix themselves in any part of the Turkish Dominions, but more especially in Syria, full security for their Persons and Property, and free liberty to go and come and ... probably contribute much to give confidence to such Jews as might determine to settle in Palestine, in consequence of such an Edict ...[29]

The LJS wrote in an editorial of its mouthpiece the *Jewish Intelligence*:

> The course of events, of late, in Syria, has been attentively watched by all those who are anxiously looking for the restoration of Israel, and awaiting the fulfillment of the sure word of prophecy ... It is true, that the Jewish nation were in no degree involved in the cause of contention, and formed no part of the elements in collision; but who shall say what is the hidden meaning and intention of the array of emphatic events which has lately passed before our eyes in the East?...
>
> The way ... seems to be opening remarkably for the restoration of the Jews...[30]

As if to encourage Palmerston in his thinking about making serious proposals for the future of the 'Holy Land', Consul Young who had temporarily vacated Jerusalem during the War, wrote to the Foreign Secretary soon after returning:

---

28 Acting Committee of the General Assembly of the Church of Scotland for Promoting Christianity among the Jews' to Viscount Palmerston, 23 October 1840. Quoted in *JI*, 1840, p. 35.
29 Palmerston to Ponsonby, 24 November 1840, FO 78/391 (no 248).
30 *JI*, 1841, p. 34.

It is perfectly clear my Lord that without the aid of the British Forces the Turks could not have regained possession of Syria – and I would respectfully submit to Your Lordship my humble opinion, that without the continued aid of the British Government to advise, and assist in enforcing measures for the general good and tranquility of the Country – the Turks cannot govern Syria.[31]

The LJS strengthens its base in Jerusalem
Meanwhile, in January 1841 the LJS recalled Nicolayson from Jerusalem in order to determine future operations there in view of the expected influx of Jewish people. The LJS Committee made numerous Resolutions, and recorded the following:

> That the strong feeling known to exist amongst the Jews now scattered and dispersed over the habitable Globe to their beloved City Jerusalem, and their expectations so prominently entertained by them at this time of a speedy return to their promised land, together with the equally anxious desire manifested on the part of the Christian community to do good to Zion, constitute the objects contemplated in the foregoing Resolutions …[32]

Those Resolutions were in anticipation of the expected influx of Jewish people, and thus of greater increase in ministry opportunities amongst them.

European Plans for Jerusalem and the land of Israel
The anticipated restoration of the Jewish people also affected the secular press. The correspondent of the *Times* wrote:

> Let the four Allied Powers now publish to the four quarters of the world their determination to restore the Jews from all nations to the Holy Land, and to assist them in rebuilding the walls and temple of Jerusalem; and assuredly, the multitudinous descendants of Abraham, already restless with the anxiety of desire, and excited by the anticipated fulfillment of this regeneration, would arise to the summons as one man. The extremest time fixed by their rabbies [sic] for the coming of Christ is passed – the close of last month quenched their expectations of the advent, and they are, in consequence, just now unusually shaken. Let, I repeat, the Quadruple Alliance take advantage of this conjuncture, and issue a manifesto for the restoration and independence of the Hebrew tribes, and by next spring the banks of the Euphrates would be once more thronged, and the long line of the European and African coasts be crowded by the gathering hosts of Israel. From the different ports on these shores they could be readily shipped, and, convoyed by the fleets that now cruise in the Mediterranean, be triumphantly landed on the strand of

---
31 Young to Palmerston, 25 January 1841, p. 160, FO 78/444.
32 LJS Minute Book M, Minute 1334, 10 April 1841, Bodleian.

their long-lost Palestine – a more befitting occupation this, than the waging of a petty war to the hazard of all Europe's peace.³³

While the British were pushing the Jewish cause, the other Powers during this period also submitted their agendas for the future of the 'Holy Land'. The French proposed the *internationalisation* of Jerusalem with them and Russia taking the pre-eminent position. This plan, proposed by the French foreign minister Francois Guizot, was also called the 'Jerusalem Plan.'³⁴ Guizot also contacted Prince Metternich about this plan, in order to strengthen the Roman Catholic position. Metternich, though, realized, as did Palmerston, that the object at this stage was to stabilize and not destabilize the Ottoman Empire. Metternich was aware of Muslim sensitivities on this issue, as the Sultan was the Caliph of Islam, and would never release one of the holy Islamic cities. The Turks, he believed, would never consent to Jerusalem becoming a free and Christian city, and certainly not a Jewish dominated one!

Metternich thought of setting up a Turkish Commissioner in the Holy Land for the protection of Christian pilgrims and travelers. But the Russians opposed this idea, as the Russian foreign minister Nesselrode stated that the proposal 'did not appear to him a necessary or desirable measure, and that the Consuls in Syria were adequate to protect the Europeans whom commerce, piety, or curiosity might attract to that country.'³⁵

It seems that the Russians never agreed to any of the other plans, as they had their own. At this point they seemed desirous of fostering good relations with Britain, and thereby weren't eager to endorse any purely French (or Roman Catholic) Plan. But Nesselrode did propose that the area of Palestine be made a separate *pashalik*, with independence for Jerusalem, which would be governed separately directly from Constantinople.

The new king in Prussia, Frederick William IV, who came to the throne in 1840, was also keen to enhance Prussian interests in the East. The Prussians envisaged a treaty between Turkey and the Europeans, guaranteeing control and direction by the Christians over the predominately Christian areas of Jerusalem, Bethlehem and Nazareth. Under this arrangement, Russia would appoint the Orthodox representative, the French and Austrians would appoint the Roman Catholic representative, and the British and Prussians would appoint the Protestant representative.³⁶

Later, in early 1841, Lieut. Helmuth von Moltke, the Prussian military attaché

---

33 Quoted in *JI*, 1841, p. 35.
34 Brugiere de Barante, *Souvenirs*, Vol 6, pp. 558-60. Quoted in Verete, ibid, pp. 142-3.
35 Verete, M. *Internationalization*, p. 151.
36 Wolf, L. *Notes on the Diplomatic History of the Jewish Question*. (London, 1919), p. 105. In a covering letter to this proposal which was addressed to the British Government, it was stated the need for (the Prussians) gaining property near to the Church of the Holy Sepulchre. See R. W. Greaves, 'The Jerusalem Bishopric 1841' in *English Historical Review*, 64, 1948, p. 336.

in Constantinople, proposed creating Palestine as a buffer zone between Turkey and Egypt, and placing it under Prussian protection.[37]

On 30 March 1841 the Prussian king dictated to his close associate Joseph Radowitz[38] the address he wanted delivered to the Heads of State at the forthcoming Peace Conference. These revealed the King's intentions of taking advantage of the unprecedented opportunity offered by this present situation. William Hechler[39] recorded that the king himself stated that his idea 'was capable of general extension, not merely as a Prussian, but a German question; and again, not merely as a German, but a general Protestant question, when viewed in its connection with the entire Protestant Church.'[40]

There were so few Protestants and even fewer Germans in the Holy Land, that the King's ideas of establishing a purely German entity there were negligible. Hechler wrote of the King's predicament:

A starting and central point now had to be found.

What spot on earth, in this respect, would be so suitable for his purpose as Jerusalem, the historical centre of Judaism and Christianity? Here was the place to exhibit the true Unity and catholicity of the Church of Christ, varying no doubt in form, but of one common pure origin.[41]

Many also saw this as an ideal opportunity of enforcing the stipulations of the *Hatti Sherif* and confirming protection for Christians in the East. The Earl of Chichester, the President of CMS, wrote to Foreign Secretary Palmerston on 25 March 1841 expressing the view 'that British Christians should have the same protection and religious liberty in the Ottoman Empire as other Christian Churches.' He proposed there be 'ecclesiastical authority' directing 'the Clergy of the Church of England in those parts.'[42]

Meanwhile Consul Young in Jerusalem sent an alarming dispatch to Palmerston on 4 June 1841, stating that the Greeks were constructing two new buildings 'to be at the disposal of Russia' and for use by Russians.[43] Similar observations were made concerning French aspirations and activities through the Catholics.

All of these proposals for the future status of Jerusalem and the land of Israel

---

37 Eliav, M. *Eretz Israel and its Yishuv in the Nineteenth Century (1777-1917)* (Jerusalem, 1978) [Hebrew], p. 48.
38 Joseph Maria von Radowitz (1797-1853) was a Prussian general and statesman.
39 William Hechler, 1845-1931 whose father was a LJS staff member, researched in the 1880's the history of the Bishopric concept. Hechler who at one stage was tutor for the Grand Duke of Baden's children and therefore knew members of the German royal family was later chaplain of the British Embassy in Vienna, and was instrumental in introducing Theodore Herzl's Zionist programme to the German Kaiser.
40 Hechler, W. *The Jerusalem Bishopric*, (London, 1883), pp.26-27. F. Bunsen, ibid, volume 1, quoted in Skinner, J. *The Three Anglican Bishops in Jerusalem*, in Church Quarterly review, July 1884, p. 328.
41 Hechler, ibid, p. 27.
42 Orchard, ibid, p. 205, quoting CMS letter book G/AC1, p. 405 letter of 20 March 1841.
43 Young to Palmerston, 4 June 1841, FO 78/444.

would need to be submitted at the upcoming Peace Conference scheduled to be held in London in July 1841. Some of those plans and proposals however had been compromised by Admiral Napier, who had concluded an agreement with Mehmet Ali at the close of 1840, whereby in exchange for surrendering the Turkish fleet and accepting the terms of the 1840 Treaty of London, Napier would ship out the remaining Egyptian soldiers before they were massacred by the locals. Napier also promised that the Sultan would confer a hereditary *pashalik* upon Mehmet Ali in Egypt. Napier's superiors were furious for this move without their agreement. Nevertheless this was finally agreed to on 13 February 1841, although the Egyptians had still to accept the sovereignty of the Sultan over Egypt.

Despite whatever the final status of the 'Holy Land' would be, the conflict of 1839-40 had seriously changed the geo-political and spiritual dynamics in the Eastern Mediterranean. Nothing would be the same again.

Chapter 26

The Jerusalem Bishopric

The New Prussian Proposal

In April 1841 the Prussian King summoned Christian Bunsen,[1] his envoy and confidant, to the Sans Souci Palace at Potsdam near Berlin. Bunsen wrote to his wife on 24 April 1841:

> Early in the morning, the thought was clear and living before my soul, that the King had called me with a view to do something in the Holy Land; and that it might be the will of the Lord, and probably would be that of the King, that in Jerusalem the two principal Protestant Churches of Europe should, across the grave of the Redeemer, reach to each other the right hand of fellowship.[2]

Bunsen was no stranger to the affairs in Jerusalem and of the LJS, as he knew Shaftesbury, and had been acquainted with Wolff in Rome. According to a letter Bunsen wrote to his wife, both he and Shaftesbury had together worked on a plan, stated as 'the Jerusalem Plan' as early as 10 December 1838.[3] It was this Plan that the King was about to discuss. Bunsen had a desire to strengthen Protestantism at the expense of Rome.[4]

Following his departure from Rome, Bunsen spent time in England, where he was acquainted with Shaftesbury, McCaul, and perhaps Michael Solomon Alexander. Bunsen also was acquainted with other leading personalities such as C. J. Blomfield, the Bishop of London, Samuel Wilberforce and William Gladstone.[5]

Through the following weeks the King and Bunsen laboured at Sans Souci Palace over the 'Plan' for establishing German Protestantism in Jerusalem in partnership with the British.[6] King Frederick William IV realized that the only possibility of establishing a Prussian presence in the 'Holy Land' was to be attached to the British concerns in Jerusalem. P.J. Welch stated it nicely:

---

1 Bunsen had just received a commission as Prussian minister at Berne when he received a call by the King of Prussia in 1841. Later he was the Prussian representative in London from 1841-1853.
2 Bunsen to his wife, 26 April 1841 in Bunsen, F. *Memoirs,* I,(London, 1868), p. 594. Greaves, W, ibid, p. 335. Bunsen to his wife, 26 April, 1841, quoted in Hechler, W. *The Jerusalem Bishopric,* (London, 1883) p. 26.
3 Bunsen to his wife, no date, in Bishop Wilberforce, *Life,* Vol. I, p. 608, quoted in James Skinner, ibid, p. 329.
4 Parry, Y. *British Mission to the Jews in Nineteenth Century Palestine,* (London, 2003), p. 53.
5 Welch, P.J. *Anglican Churchmen and the establishment of the Jerusalem Bishopric,* in Journal of Ecclesiastical History, Vol 8, No 2, 1957, p. 193.
6 Message given at LJS AGM, May 1842, in *JI,* 1842, p. 191.

Frederick William was intelligent enough to see that political and economic facts ruled out an exclusively Prussian episcopate in the Holy Land: it was a shrewd move to attach German congregations to a bishopric closely associated with the Church of England.[7]

Yet the King also had local ambitions for the Jerusalem Plan, as Robert Blake reveals:

> He was also anxious to bring about a union between the Protestant churches. Episcopacy was a serious difficulty ... But, although no Lutheran bishops actually existed, bishops were not incompatible with Lutheranism. The king and Bunsen hoped – and their opponents feared – that the Jerusalem Bishopric would lead to episcopacy in Prussia. Protestant unity, alleviation of the Christian condition in Jerusalem, and an increased diplomatic leverage in Turkey combined to encourage the project baron Bunsen put forward to the British Government in June 1841.[8]

Two reasons made it imperative that the King of Prussia move quickly to present his *Plan* to the British. Firstly, in June 1841 the British Government passed the *Colonial Bishoprics Act*, whereby it was decided to establish overseas bishoprics, the first to be in New Zealand, the second in the Mediterranean, either at Malta or Gibraltar. If the King wanted to 'use' Britain as a stepping stone to the East, that is, Jerusalem, he had better move before any decision was firmly made concerning either of these other Mediterranean locations.

The second reason was that on 5 June 1841, the Whig Government of Lord Melbourne and Palmerston was defeated in the House of Commons. It would be some time before the Tories could establish a new Government, so the Prussians needed to move quickly while they had a sympathetic hearing in England.

Bunsen would go to England with three proposals, two of which were to be attached to the Memorandum for the 15 July Conference, the *Treaty for the Pacification of the Levant*. One of these was for the Turks to issue a new land settlement law, permitting Protestant Christians the right to own land in Palestine. The second proposal called for the setting up of a Protestant corporation so that 'members of the two national churches of England and Prussia' could capitalize upon the benefits of the *Hatti Sherif* reform. The third Prussian proposal, separate from the two attached to the Peace Conference, and for direct discussion with the British Government and Church, pertained to the establishment of a *Protestant Bishopric* in Jerusalem. The King's instructions were for Bunsen to ascertain and propose:

---

7 Welch, ibid, p. 193.
8 Blake, R. *The Origins of the Jerusalem Bishopric*, in Church State and Society in the 19th Century, (Munchen, 1984), p. 90.

In how far the English National Church, already in possession of a parsonage on the Mount Zion, and having commenced there the building of a church, would be inclined to accord to the Evangelical National Church of Prussia a sisterly position in the Holy Land.

This proposal then suggested that 'THE ENGLISH CHURCH ERECT A BISHOPRIC OF IT'S OWN at Jerusalem' which would 'connect itself with the foundation and buildings already begun on the Mount Zion, and comprehend all evangelical Christians willing to take part in it...' The King would then 'allow one or more clergy and missionaries of his subjects, for the sake of the Jewish converts who speak German, and for the benefit of the evangelical Christians of the German language, to join this Episcopal arrangement.' To reveal his seriousness about this proposal, the King would 'allow such persons to obtain ordination from the English Church.' The Prussian King then concluded that he 'specially desires to see this place in Jerusalem itself.'[9]

The King obviously wanted some political advantage for Prussia. But it appears he also entertained some ecclesiastical changes in the structure of the German Church, and thought Jerusalem would be a good place to experiment. Samuel Wilberforce wrote, that 'The king of Prussia's hope is, by degrees, to get ... his future bishops ordained in Palestine, in order to co-operate with us. Of course, a stubborn old-grown Lutheran would kick.'[10]

Bunsen in England
Bunsen arrived in London on 18 June 1840. On 24 June, he met with Shaftesbury, who wrote, 'My friend Bunsen has just called, and has brought me a most honourable and gratifying message from the King of Prussia...The mission of Bunsen is a wonder; God grant that its issue may be a wonder.'[11] Of this meeting Bunsen wrote to his wife, 'It is to me an indescribable delight to be enabled to-day to read to that excellent Lord Ashley the "Instruction" and my further statements; for he was the man who took up our plan for both in the night of December 10, 1838 ...'[12]

Thereafter Bunsen met with Palmerston on 4 July and several days later with Queen Victoria, as well as with Howley, the Archbishop of Canterbury; with Blomfield, the bishop of London; with Kaye the bishop of Lincoln; and with Dr. Vernon Harcourt, the Archbishop of York. Further meetings with Shaftesbury followed, about whom Bunsen wrote to his wife on 13 July, '... he

---

9 *The Jerusalem Bishopric*, (London, Hatchard & Son, 1856), p. 4.
10 Bishop Samuel Wilberforce, *Life*, Vol , p. 201, quoted in James Skinner, ibid, p. 331. In 1817 King Frederick William III had united the Lutheran and Reformed Churches into the Evangelical Church of Prussia. Later, pressure was brought upon Lutherans who opposed this unification, and some were imprisoned, while other 'old Lutherans' emigrated to America and Australia.
11 Hodder, ibid, p. 199.
12 Bunsen to his wife, no date, Bishop Wilberforce *Life*, Vol. I, p. 608, quoted in James Skinner, p. 329.

was the man who took up our cause, and set the Jerusalem bishopric a-going.'[13]

While discussions for the Bishopric were proceeding the *Treaty for the Pacification of the Levant*[14] was ratified in London on 15 July 1841. None of the Allied proposals for the future status of the 'Holy Land' were accepted. Palestine (southern Syria, the land of Israel) would return to Turkish control.

Palmerston did have one triumph though – the 1833 *Treaty of Unkiar Skelessi* was revoked. Henceforth the Boshporus, Sea of Marmara and Dardanelles would be closed to foreign warships as long as Turkey was at peace.

The Protestant Bishopric – The British Position

The issue of a Protestant Bishopric in the Mediterranean was part of a larger issue confronting the Anglican Church. Following the American War of Independence, the Anglican Church was forced to legislate to provide Episcopal supervision for the Anglicans remaining in America. Evangelical Anglicans later took advantage of this legislation in promoting the establishment of a bishopric in Calcutta, India, in 1812.[15]

As the British Empire continued to expand, especially eastward, the need was seen for the establishment of further bishoprics. So in 1840 the *Colonial Bishopric Fund* was established, in order to fund bishoprics in the British Colonies, including New Zealand. The Bishop of London had responsibility for such entities. These cases were quite clear cut, the United States of America was once a British colony, and New Zealand a present one.

A new situation, however, began arising from 1815 onwards as the Church Missionary Society (CMS) in particular, and the LJS, began entering into the Mediterranean region, an area not part of the British Empire. Some suggested placing these men under the Episcopal authority of the Roman Catholic Church or the Greek Orthodox Church.

Most evangelical Christians, however, were not inclined towards either of these ancient Churches. Many, and in particular the CMS, favoured the establishment of their own Anglican Bishopric, on the British held territory of Malta.[16] From 1837 the CMS was involved in establishing a chapel on Malta, so this seemed the logical location. Even the American missionary Eli Smith urged the appointment of an Anglican bishop perhaps at Malta to protect the Protestants of the East.[17]

This last stated suggestion was endorsed by the Earl of Chichester, the President of CMS, who wrote to Foreign Secretary Palmerston on 25 March 1841 expressing the view 'that British Christians should have the same protection

---

13 Bunsen, ibid, I, 608, 13 July 1841.
14 Also known as the *Straits Convention*.
15 Orchard, ibid, p. 202.
16 Orchard, ibid, pp. 203-4 and footnotes 4 and 5.
17 Meeting of 22 December 1840 considering a letter of Eli Smith dated 4 July 1840, CMS Minutes Vol XIX, G/CI, p. 295. Quoted in Orchard, ibid, p. 204, footnote 8.

and religious liberty in the Ottoman Empire as other Christian Churches.' He proposed there be 'ecclesiastical authority' directing 'the Clergy of the Church of England in those parts.'[18]

Shaftesbury, had also proposed the establishment of a Bishopric. In October 1838 he had written of the possibility of establishing a Protestant Bishopric in Jerusalem – not Malta:

> Could we not erect a Protestant Bishopric at Jerusalem, and give him jurisdiction over all the Levant, Malta, and whatever chaplaincies there might be on the coast of Africa.[19]

By the middle of 1841 there was momentum for an Anglican bishop somewhere in the Eastern Mediterranean, with the CMS bidding for a Bishopric at Valetta in Malta. Simultaneously the LJS was seeking to further its operations in Jerusalem in preparation for an expected large scale Jewish restoration. Despite Shaftesbury's diary entry of 1838 it does not seem that the LJS was strongly agitating for the Bishopric to be established in Jerusalem. All that changed, however, with Bunsen's arrival in London.

The Bishopric Proposal Accepted in Principle

Shaftesbury and the LJS were totally enthusiastic about the Jerusalem Bishopric proposal. The major problem at this time was timing. The sympathetic Whig Government of Melbourne and Palmerston was on its way out, soon to be replaced by the less enthusiastic (as far as the Jewish question was concerned) government of Peel and Aberdeen. It was imperative that Shaftesbury do all he could to get the *Plan* accepted in principle as quickly as possible.

By 19 July 1841 it seemed that Palmerston was in agreement. Now they needed the right person for the position. The obvious choice was the renowned Gentile 'rabbi' – Dr Alexander McCaul. McCaul's daughter Elizabeth Ann, recalls that 'on a July afternoon' she noticed a distinguished carriage outside her father's door. It was none other than Bunsen, come to convey the King's wish for him to become the first bishop. 'My father's reply to the King, after thanking him,' wrote Elizabeth, 'was that he considered that the Bishop of Jerusalem ought to be of Hebrew descent, and as he had not this honour, he asked leave to recommend his friend, the Rev. Mr. Alexander.'[20]

There is good reason to believe that Shaftesbury also proposed Alexander to be the new bishop. Perhaps Shaftesbury had proposed two candidates, McCaul and Alexander, indicating that if McCaul refused then Bunsen would merely

---

18 Chichester to Palmerston, 20 March 1841, CMS Letter book G/ACI, p. 405. Quoted in Orchard, ibid, p. 205.
19 Hodder, ibid, p. 125.
20 Finn, E.A. *Reminiscence of Mrs. Finn*, (London & Edinburgh, 1930), pp. 33-34. See also Gidney,W. T. *The History of the London Society for Promoting Christianity Amongst the Jews*, (London, 1908), p. 207 and Corey, ibid, p. 52.

go next door and ask Alexander. Alexander accepted the invitation, prompting Bunsen to record in his diary on 19 July 1841: 'So the beginning is made, please God, for the restoration of Israel.'[21]

The Queen now needed to endorse the plan as well as both Houses of Parliament. Palmerston wrote to Queen Victoria on 21 July 1841 stating that as 'the Plan now proposed by the King of Prussia seems practicable' that he recommends that the Queen authorize 'to send out immediately Instructions to Lord Ponsonby to concur with the Prussian Minister at Constantinople the best means of endeavouring to carry this Plan into effect.'[22] The Queen recorded in her diary for 23 July 1841:

> ... saw Ld. Palmerston to whom I said I quite agreed & approved that we should consent to Bunsen's proposals, & Ld. Palmerston said they wished to send out a Protestant Bishop to Jerusalem, & that there was a man of the name of Alexander, who is at Cambridge, & who seems to unite all the qualities required. He is a Doctor of Divinity, a converted Jew, & a Prussian subject by birth ...'[23]

The initial *Memorandum* worked on by Bunsen, Shaftesbury and others, and known as the *Bunsen Memorandum*, and entitled 'The Church at Jerusalem,'[24] was completed and submitted to Palmerston on 25 July 1841. It adapted to this new twist concerning the Jewish nominee. Obviously there was no initial stipulation for sending out a Jewish Bishop, otherwise McCaul would not have been approached. Now, however, it seems that matters changed somewhat in orientation. In Bunsen's *Memorandum* Article I, it was stated 'that it must "appear in the highest order desirable" that the Bishop of Jerusalem should, in addition to the ordinary essentials of a Bishop, possess the following qualification:

1. Jewish descent.
2. Learning.
3. Membership of the ministry of the English Church.'[25]

This stipulation is of some importance. Before September 1813 it would be doubtful if such consideration would have been given. But thanks to the pioneering efforts particularly of Joseph Frey, two national churches now recognized that a Jewish follower of Jesus did not surrender his Jewish national identity upon entering into covenant relationship with Jesus.

The Ambassadors in Constantinople Informed.

21 Hodder, ibid, quoting Bunsen's Diary, p. 200.
22 Palmerston to Queen Victoria, 21 July 1841, A10/72, RA [Royal Archives], Windsor Palace.
23 Queen Victoria's Journal, 23 July 1841, RA [Royal Archives].
24 *Bunsen Memorandum*, Memo No 1, Count Plessen, 19 September 1884, FO 406/5460.
25 Baron Plessen, Memo No 2, 19 September 1884, FO 406/5460.

Palmerston informed Ambassador Ponsonby on 26 July 1841 that Her Majesty's Government 'adopts with great earnestness the plan proposed by the King of Prussia' and were deeply interested in the project.[26] He also wrote:

> Her Majesty's Government conceive that no special permission for this purpose will be required from the Porte.[27] This bishop will like any other British or Prussian subject have the right to reside in any part of the Turkish dominions, and the spiritual functions which he will exercise will in no way whatever interfere with the Mahometan subjects of the Sultan, and therefore they will be matters of which the Turkish Government will have no right to take any cognizance whatever.
>
> ... but you will make no communication on the subject to the Turkish Government till you receive instructions from the Secretary of State to do so. You will in fact consider this intimation as purely confidential, and intended solely for you as personal information.[28]

This *Instruction* is very revealing. Palmerston was keenly aware of the potential Turkish suspicion and opposition to the scheme, following so soon as it did after previous British and Prussian plans for post-War Palestine. No doubt the British and Prussian Ambassadors were aware of how it would be perceived in Constantinople – by both the Turkish authorities and the Ambassadors of the other Powers.

The Plan Ratified

The prelates and diplomats then completed some adjustments and modifications known as the *Addington Articles*, by 5 August 1841. The Archbishop then summoned a meeting with the Bishops to explain to them the plan. Apparently few responded.[29]

According to the arrangement the British Crown would be asked to authorize the consecration of a bishop for Jerusalem. As Bunsen informed the Prussian King, on 22 August 1841, the British and the Prussians would nominate the bishop alternately.[30] The Archbishop of Canterbury, though, would have the veto over the Prussian nomination. 'This arrangement', wrote Greaves, 'was to continue until a purely Prussian bishopric was set up at Bethlehem, when the Jerusalem see would become wholly English. Finally', Greaves continued, 'by a clause which was apparently kept secret at first, it was agreed that until the "restoration" of a Christian Jewish church, but not afterwards, the archbishop

---

26 Palmerston to Ponsonby, No 187, 26 July 1841, FO 78/429.
27 Another name used for the Turkish Governance.
28 Palmerston to Ponsonby, 27 September, 1841, FO 78/429.
29 Welch, ibid, p. 196.
30 Bunsen to King Frederick William IV, 22 August 1841, in Memo No 2 Baron Plessen, 19 Sept 1884, ibid.

of Canterbury should be the metropolitan of the new see.'[31]

The Bishop-elect, even when named by Prussia, had to be consecrated according to the Anglican rite, and conform to the Thirty-Nine Articles of the Anglican Confession of faith, which practically excluded members of the Evangelical German Church from being nominated.

There were some legal and financial complications however, in that the Jerusalem Bishopric could not fall into the category of the *Colonial Bishopric Fund (Act)*. Jerusalem was not a Crown Colony.

The Queen's advocate thereupon produced a bill in twenty-four hours. The *Foreign Bishoprics Act* (sometimes referred to as the *Jerusalem Bishopric Act*)[32] was introduced into the House of Lords on 30 August. It passed, and then also passed through the House of Commons, almost in silence.[33] Despite this, the new Prime Minister, Robert Peel still remained apprehensive of the whole venture, especially when Shaftesbury requested a British warship to transport the Bishop and his family to Jerusalem!

The second obstacle, financial, was also solved. To prove his personal interest in the project, the King of Prussia signed the Royal Prussian Deed of Endowment on 6 September 1841, promising the capital of 15,000 pounds, with the annual interest of 600 pounds going towards the Prussian contribution[34] for the bishop's stipend, paid yearly in advance.

The remainder, some 20,000 pounds was raised by general subscription in Britain, the interest from this, another 600 pounds, supplying the balance of the bishop's yearly stipend. The LJS gave 3,000 pounds towards the subscription, and the Archbishop of Canterbury and Bishop of London each gave 200 pounds towards it.[35] The two Archbishops and the Bishop of London would be the Trustees of the Fund.

Political opposition

Following the summer recess from Parliament, Ashley and Bunsen had to contend with growing opposition to the scheme, from various sections of the English Church who resented the concept of a Protestant Bishopric in Jerusalem (which they viewed as interfering in the jurisdiction of the ancient churches) and from the new Government, that took office at the end of August. This is evident in the outcome of an interview Bunsen had with Aberdeen, the new Foreign Secretary, who highlighted the dangers of the Bishopric:

---

31 Bunsen to Palmerston, 5 August 1841, FO 64/235, quoted in R.W Greaves, *ibid*, p. 342-343. Count Muntsert to Earl Granville, 17 July 1882, FO 406/5460.
32 Also officially known as the Foreigners Consecration Act Amendment Bill [see Welch, *ibid*, p. 195].
33 Greaves ,ibid, p. 344.
34 For full account, see Hechler, ibid, Documents section p. 46.
35 LJS General Committee Minutes, Vol. M, minute 2063, Bodleian, & Hechler, ibid, pp. 37-39, 179-181. The English fund was made formal in a deed dated 15 November 1841.

We shall excite the jealousy of Russia, Austria, France; they will demand more of the Porte, and so shall we; and thus we shall accelerate the downfall of the Turkish kingdom – it may…have been a good plan for the Conversion of the Jews, but I do not see that it would have answered for anything else…[36]

Ponsonby, in response to Palmerston's earlier directive, (which came not to Palmerston incidentally, but to his successor Aberdeen) was not in agreement with the Plan, stating that there was now a new regime in Constantinople[37] and that such a far-reaching Plan stood to endanger other specific British plans in the region, and especially permission to build the LJS church in Jerusalem.[38] The Prussian ambassador, Count de Koenigsmark, too, was not favourable, believing that the Porte[39] was suspicious of concealed ambitions by the British for gaining influence in the Levant.[40]

Once news of the impending Bishopric became public, opposition to it increased, prompting, so it seems, the Austrians to issue a formal protest at Constantinople.[41]

Ecclesiastical opposition

On 5 October Shaftesbury attended the first meeting of the *Ecclesiastical Commission*, and recorded:

Spoke to the Archbishop: found him almost totally changed…must take time to consider the propriety of a Jew for a Bishop; it would not, he was told, suit the Greek Christians; the Christian in the East would never acknowledge a Jew; the hatred of them was indelible, - that all these things should be considered.'[42]

Bishop Blomfield of London, received a terse letter from Pusey, leader of the Tractarian movement, a strong opponent, who stated 'it is now for the first time that the Church of England holds communion with those that are "without the Church."'[43]

This *Tractarian* movement was opposed to the concept of an evangelical bishopric associated with the non-episcopal Evangelical Prussian Church, established in an ancient see which belonged to the historic churches. Pusey wrote to his cousin Shaftesbury:

---

36 Ashley Diary, 23 September 1841, quoted in Orchard, ibid. pp. 224-5.
37 The sympathetic Reschid fell from power in March 1841.
38 Ponsonby to Aberdeen, no. 4, 29 September 1841; no 9, 6 October 1841; no 11, 7 October 184, FO 78/437, quoted in Greaves, ibid, p. 339.
39 Another term used for the Turkish governance.
40 Koenigsmark's report no 53, 6 October 1841, and forwarded by Bunsen to Aberdeen, 17 January 1842, in FO 64/241.
41 Finn, J. *Stirring Times,* (London, 1878) Volume I, p. 138.
42 Ashley Diary, 5 October 1841, Orchard, ibid. p. 226.
43 Ashley Diary, 12 October 1841, Orchard, ibid. p. 228.

> No one objects to the Bishopric of Jerusalem for what I imagine you value it – the sake of the Jews – but on account of the 'experimental church' (as it has been called) which they are going to make of Prussians …. Our Church was never brought into contact with the foreign reformation without suffering from it; and certainly that Reformation is not in a state now to do us less harm than heretofore, besides the grave injury of countenancing heresy …[44]

It was believed by Pusey and others that the episcopally based Anglican Church was incompatible with the non-episcopal Prussian Evangelical Church. One prominent Tractarian John Henry Newman later declared that it was this issue, the Protestant Bishopric, which 'was the third blow, which finally shattered my faith in the Anglican Church.'[45] He wrote again on 12 October 1841:

> We have not a single Anglican in Jerusalem; so we are sending a bishop to *make* a communion; not to govern our own people. Next, the excuse is, that there are converted Anglican Jews there who require a Bishop; I am told there are not a half-a-dozen. But for *them* the Bishop is sent out, and for them he is a Bishop of the *circumcision*…against the Epistle of the Galatians pretty nearly. Thirdly, for the sake of Prussia, he is to take under him all the foreign Protestants who will come; and the political advantages will be so great, from the influence of England, that there is no doubt they *will* come. They are to sign the Confession of Augsburg, and there is nothing to show that they hold the doctrine of Baptismal Regeneration.[46]

To officially register his opposition Newman wrote to the Archbishop, stating, that 'Lutheranism and Calvinism are heresies, repugnant to Scripture, springing up three centuries since, and anathematized by East as well as West.'[47] Another prominent opponent, Lord John Manners, wrote to William Gladstone:

> I don't at all like … the bishopric in the Holy Land…A spirit of insanity is abroad … The Jerusalem Bishopric is the sorest point of all; the Russian papers and the French Dissenters all look upon it as a flag of alliance held out to Zurich and Geneva from Lambeth; and have they not good reasons for so regarding it?

These opponents were basically concerned that the Church of England was allying herself, for the sake of a broader union of sorts, with Protestantism rather than with Rome. The Anglican Church by its essence was the *via media*, the middle ground of both Continental Protestantism and the Roman Church. There were those, especially Evangelicals, whose leanings were more towards

---

44 Quoted in Tibawi, ibid, p. 47.
45 Newman, ibid, p. 143.
46 Newman, ibid, p. 143.
47 Newman to Archbishop Howley, 11 November 1841, quoted in Newman, ibid, p. 145.

a union with Continental Protestantism, for whom a union with Rome was anathema. And likewise, there were those, primarily of the Anglo-Catholic or High Church persuasion (the *Tractarians*), whose allegiance was more towards Rome, for whom a union with Continental Protestantism was anathema.

The Protestant Bishopric offered the possibility of a common Protestant centre of reference in Jerusalem, instead of Canterbury (Anglicanism), Augsburg (Lutheranism) or Geneva (Reformed Christianity). For the Roman Catholics there was Rome, and for universal Protestantism, potentially, a restored Jerusalem.

In an effort to appease the opposition from the High Church and *Tractarian* parties, the Archbishop appointed Rev George Williams as Alexander's chaplain. Williams was a man of High Church tendencies and he was instructed to give attention to the Eastern Churches.[48]

The Archbishop also sent with Alexander a letter to the Patriarch of the Greek Orthodox Church. This letter, written in both English and Greek, informed the Orthodox Patriarch that it was sent 'in order to prevent any misunderstanding of this our purpose, we think it right to make known to you that we have charged the said Bishop, our brother, not to intermeddle in any way with the jurisdiction of the Prelates or other ecclesiastical Dignitaries bearing rule in the East.'

There was also opposition to the Plan in Prussia, especially from those opposed to episcopacy. Blake wrote of these opponents, 'They saw in Frederick William's action a covert plan to introduce Lutheran bishops into Prussian and perhaps other German states. Many Lutherans took an unfavourable view of any step in the direction of uniting them with a church as riven with dissension and as packed with antique abuses as the Church of England...Strict Lutherans regarded the united Church of England and Ireland with doubt and distrust, but they were a minority. In general Prussian opinion was relatively indifferent.'[49]

Influence upon permission for a Protestant Church in Jerusalem

While en-route for Jerusalem from Britain Nicolayson visited Constantinople in August 1841 where he made inquiries for gaining the necessary permits in order to build a church and expand the work. The new British ambassador, Lord Ponsonby, took up the cause most enthusiastically, especially concerning the official permit, or *Firman*, to build the church.

But he hit numerous obstacles. Ponsonby learned from the Turkish authorities that they could not permit the building of a new church in Jerusalem. Ponsonby proposed that Nicolayson 'procure the site of an ancient Church and erect the new Building thereon.' Nicolayson in turn approved of this plan, and assured Ponsonby that the area he purchased several years previously, had been a Chapel belonging to the Convent of Jacobius.

---

48 Greaves, ibid, p. 348. It seems that Williams was an adherent of Pusey. See above, footnote No 6.
49 Blake, R. *The Origins of the Jerusalem Bishopric*, p. 93.

Ponsonby then learned that the Porte only permitted new churches to be built on the site of existing ones, but those churches had to be either Catholic or Orthodox. He wrote to Palmerston, that, 'if the Porte could now be induced to grant to the Protestant Christians similar privileges, the Porte would have to contend against the opposition of the Clergy of the Catholick [sic] and Greek Churches whose influence will probably be exerted to the utmost to prevent the establishment in this Country of a Church considered by them to be a dangerous rival.'[50]

While Ponsonby now took upon himself the seemingly impossible task of obtaining a *Firman*, Nicolayson returned to Jerusalem to obtain further documentation he thought would assist with the task ahead. Then in September 1841, Ponsonby was able to gleefully write to Palmerston 'I expect to succeed in obtaining a Firman to authorize the erection of a Protestant Church at Jerusalem.' But in the same letter he acknowledges Palmerston's letter of 4 August 1841 which mentioned the King of Prussia's interest in the proposed church. Ponsonby sounded a warning to Palmerston, by stating that he had thus far negotiated the matter himself and didn't really need Prussian interference.[51]

Ponsonby's apprehension that Prussian involvement in British affairs in Constantinople would be detrimental, proved to be well-founded. As instructed, he met his Prussian counterpart, Count de Koenigsmark, in mid September concerning the establishment of 'Protestant Churches in this Country.'

In a communiqué sent to Palmerston on 15 September Ponsonby stated that the Ottoman Empire would give nothing more than 'unavowed permission' for 'us to build an English Church at Jerusalem, and a promise that they (the Ministers) will order the Turkish Authorities (including the Cadi at Jerusalem) not to oppose our erecting it' so long as it was 'modest and unostentatious in appearance and dimensions and not calculated to attract attention.' He concluded, 'The Porte will not, I fear, grant any Firman.'[52]

Although stating that no *Firman* would be issued, a 'tacit permission' to build the Church was a major breakthrough. Word of this 'promise' made its way to London, and from London to Jerusalem.

Unfortunately subsequent communiqués showed a deterioration in the situation – resulting, it would appear from Prussian interference. Ponsonby wrote on 15 September to Palmerston, 'The building of a Church is opposed in the Divan by the Ulema.'[53] Subsequent communiques from Ponsonby revealed that the Muslim jurists and legal scholars were furthering their opposition, and this as well as Prussian interference, was forcing Ponsonby on 6 October 1841

---

50 Ponsonby to Palmerston, 18 August 1841, No 270, p. 62, FO 78/437 and 2 September 1841, No 280, p. 161, FO 78/437.
51 Ponsonby to Palmerston, 8 September 1841. No 284, FO 78/437. Quoted in Hymson, ibid, p. 187.
52 Ponsonby to Palmerston, 15 September 1841, No 288, FO 78/437.
53 Ponsonby to Aberdeen, 29 September 1841, No 4, FO 78/437. *Ulema* were the Muslim jurists and legal scholars, who are experts in the *Sharia*, the Islamic Law.

'to insist upon the consent of the Sublime Porte to the building of a Church at Jerusalem for the performance of the rites of the Anglican Church'. A reply from Rifaat Pasha revealed the deep seated issues, which were:

> 'The Council refuses to grant permission for the erection of the Church because it is contrary to the religious law of the Turks.
> 'Because the Porte is not bound by any Treaty to grant that permission.
> 'Because the Franks[54] cannot possess any landed property in Turkey.
> 'Because the present is not the proper time to grant such permission owing to the state of minds in Syria.
> 'Because the Patriarch[55] will oppose the erection of a Protestant Church.
> 'Because the law of this Country being contrary to the demand, no foreign Government can find fault with the refusal given by the Sublime Porte …

Ponsonby also stated that Rifaat Pasha had reported that Count de Konigsmark had asked for permission for the Prussians to 'perform the rites of their religion in Turkey like other Nations, and Rifaat Pasha says that the Porte refuses to give such a Note.'[56] By October therefore, as the Bishopric Plan was being concluded in London, the environment was becoming noticeably uncomfortable in Constantinople for British designs in Jerusalem.

An official from the British Embassy met with Sarim Effendi at the Porte on 12 November 1841 and discussed the matter of Bishop Alexander. It was only too obvious that the Turks were very wary about this new British initiative.[57] In a subsequent communiqué to the Foreign Office, Ponsonby reiterated that the Turks were concerned about granting special privileges for Bishop Alexander.[58] Then in a response communiqué from Aberdeen, the new foreign secretary mentioned that he had sent to Constantinople the letter from Bunsen, showing that the idea of the Bishopric came from Prussia, and not from England!

This reveals an interesting bit of political jockeying. It appears that to take the heat off the British Embassy, and Ponsonby's endeavours to secure permission for the building of the church at Jerusalem, Aberdeen wanted to show that Britain was not solely responsible for both issues – the church in Jerusalem, and the Protestant Bishopric, but wanted some of the pressure to be transferred to the Prussians.[59]

Unbeknown to him, Bishop Michael Solomon Alexander was about to be caught up in the middle of some Eastern real-politik!

---

54 Franks was a general term applied to all foreigners within the Turkish Empire.
55 Refers to the Greek Orthodox Patriarch, either of Constantinople or of Jerusalem, who for the most part actually resided in Constantinople.
56 Ponsonby to Palmerston, 6 October 1841, No 9, p. 284, FO 78/437.
57 Ponsonby to Aberdeen, 22 January 1842, FO 78/473.
58 Ponsonby to Aberdeen, 24 February 1841, No 19, FO. 78/473 .
59 Aberdeen to Ponsonby, 24 March 1842, No 27, FO 78/473.

Widespread Support for the Bishopric.

Many Evangelicals were ecstatic about Alexander's appointment, and were seemingly unaffected by the intrigues and prospective complications in Constantinople. The LJS wrote: 'The appointment of a son of Abraham as Bishop of the United Church of England and Ireland at Jerusalem, forms a new era in the history of the Missionary labours among the Jews.'[60] Welch stated that 'Ashley and the Evangelical party saw in the Anglo-Prussian venture the blessed beginning of a restoration of Israel …'[61]

The *Christian Observer* wrote, in their November 1841 edition, that the establishment of the Protestant Bishopric would check the advancements of 'all-encroaching Popery' - as the real battle was with Rome.[62] Bunsen held his own personal opinions of this great venture, and wrote to a friend on 12 October 1841:

> This appearance of unity is only possible by forming a connection with an establishment already there, that of the English Jewish Missionary Society.
>
> The matter to be accomplished was the converting of this private establishment into a national and universal Christian foundation; and this could only be effected by the foundation of a Bishopric by the Church of England.
>
> To the Turks we must display unity; among ourselves we must maintain a brotherly understanding.
>
> Germany must assume an honourable and independent position in such a connection with the English establishment. We must acknowledge that establishment, and therefore also Episcopal authority.
>
> The English, on the other hand, must acknowledge our *Augsburg Confession*, and our German order of worship.[63]

Foreign Bishoprics Act (Jerusalem Bishopric Act)

The final political act was obtaining the Royal Assent, which the Queen gave on 5 October 1841, to what was commonly known as the '*Jerusalem Bishopric Act*.' Now all was accomplished, save the consecration of the new bishop, and his departure to his new See.

On 6 November 1841 Queen Victoria authorized the Archbishop of Canterbury to consecrate Rev Michael Solomon Alexander to be bishop over 'Syria, Chaldea, Egypt, and Abyssinia, as the limit within which the said Michael Solomon Alexander may exercise spiritual jurisdiction pursuant to the said Act, subject nevertheless to such alterations in the said limit as we from time to time may be pleased to assign.'[64]

---

60 *JI*, 1842, p. 3.
61 Welch, ibid, p. 195.
62 *Christian Observer*, November 1841, New Series, xlvii, p. 703. Quoted in Welch, ibid. p. 197.
63 Bunsen to Frederick Perthes, 12 October 1841, quoted in Hechler, ibid, p. 30.
64 Queens' license for Consecration, see Hechler, ibid, Documents section, p.60.

'BISHOPRIC OF THE CHURCH OF ST. JAMES AT JERUSALEM'

The full extent of the LJS's commitment to Alexander's task is revealed in a most profound statement emanating from their General Committee, and expounded in the November edition of their mouthpiece, the *Jewish Intelligence*. They wrote, under the title BISHOPRIC OF THE CHURCH OF ST. JAMES AT JERUSALEM. In referring to Bishop Alexander they stated:

> The Rev. Professor Alexander, himself a brother of St. James, both after the flesh and after the Spirit, has been nominated as BISHOP OF THE CHURCH OF ST. JAMES AT JERUSALEM; and Sunday, the 7th of November, is the day fixed for his consecration…It is unnecessary to urge the powerfully beneficial effect which an Anglican Bishop at Jerusalem may exercise over the Churches of the East, and how, without any intrusion, by example, by love, by meekness, he may do much towards the healing of the unhappy divisions, towards the correction of ancient errors, and the diffusion of the pure light of the Gospel. The friend of Israel need scarcely be told of the influence to be exercised by a Jewish Bishop over his brethren scattered through the world. In him the Church of the circumcision, 1700 years ago, rudely expelled from its holy habitation by heathen intolerance, will again find a centre of life and unity; in him the people of Israel may again behold a symbol of national resuscitation. In this most wonderful event, the mediator upon prophecy must recognize a sign that the time, the set time, to favour Zion is come …[65]

Consecration of Alexander

Michael Solomon Alexander was consecrated Bishop in Jerusalem on 7 November 1841 at Lambeth Palace. Among those officiating were Archbishop Benson, Bishop Howley, and the recently consecrated bishop of New Zealand, George Selwyn, who read from Acts 20, 'Now, behold, I go bound in the spirit unto Jerusalem, not knowing the things that shall befall me there.' New Zealand is the furthermost point on earth from Jerusalem, so there was something quite symbolic in this act of service.

Also present at this auspicious occasion were Shaftesbury, Mr. W.E. Gladstone (future Prime Minister of Britain), Bunsen, Sir George Rose (former British ambassador to Berlin, and whose son would soon meet Alexander in Beirut), Herr Abeken (Under-Secretary of Foreign Affairs at the King of Prussia's Court), Baron Schleinitz (the Prussian Charge d'Affaires), the Prussian Consul-General Hebeler, Sir Robert Inglis, Sir Thomas Baring (President of the LJS), Mr Arthur Guinness from Dublin, Sir Stratford Canning (British Ambassador designate to Constantinople), and others.[66] Alexander's daughter Deborah, many years later as Mrs. Ransom, wrote of this occasion that, 'After the Service,

---

65 BISHOPRIC OF THE CHURCH OF ST. JAMES AT JERUSALEM, *JI*, 1841, pp. 383-384.
66 Ransom, ibid, p. 7.

Lady Stratford Canning embraced Fanny so warmly that she broke Fanny's watch glass.'[67]

The sermon was preached by Alexander McCaul, from Isaiah 52:7, 'How beautiful on the mountains are the feet of those who bring good news, who proclaim peace, who bring good tidings, who proclaim salvation, who say to Zion, "Your God reigns!"'

McCaul concentrated upon the prophetic nature of the Bishopric. He emphasized that Jerusalem was an apt centre for the vital mission to the Jewish people, and that for those who genuinely believed Biblical prophecy, the stage was set in Jerusalem for the consummation of all things.

Bishop Alexander preached his farewell sermon at the Episcopal Jews Chapel on 8 November 1841, during which he made a very profound statement:

> Had it been said but a short time ago, that ere long this pulpit would be occupied by a humble member of the despised race of Israel, raised and consecrated to be the Bishop of the United Church of England and Ireland in Jerusalem, it would have been rejected as absurd, visionary, and altogether impossible; yet, brethren, here I stand a monument of the Divine sovereignty and power, a proof that nothing is too hard for the Lord, that with him all things are possible, and that his thoughts and ways are not ours…Surely, no one will now venture to doubt the possibility of the literal fulfillment of God's promises to Israel.[68]

That Alexander could make such a statement was due not to his achievements, but was due to the collective work and vision of many people over the previous three hundred years, and of late to the pioneer, Joseph Frey, and the testimony which emanated forth from the formation of the *Benei Abraham*.

Alexander then revealed how the Apostle Paul's journey to Jerusalem was a duty laid upon him, "Behold, I go bound in the Spirit unto Jerusalem." [69] He continued:

> The Christian course is one of great difficulty; it is indeed a warfare between light and darkness, a fighting against principalities and powers …
>
> And now brethren what shall I say respecting that ministry which I also have received of the Lord Jesus? "Behold, I also am bound in the Spirit to go to Jerusalem, there to testify of the Gospel to the grace of God; to preach to both Jews and Gentiles repentance towards God, and faith towards our Lord Jesus Christ." In the wonderful and mysterious providence of God … I am now set apart for one of the highest offices in the Church, destined to go to the land of my forefathers. I know not what shall befall me there,

---

67 Ransom, ibid, p. 7.
68 Farewell Sermon of Michael Solomon Alexander, (Wertheim, London, 1841), p. 5. Found in Alexander Papers, DS.3.a5, St. Anthony's.
69 Sermon, ibid, p. 10.

save that trials and afflictions abide me; but shall I thereby be discouraged from following the call of my Lord and master, who has done so much for me? God forbid! In holy confidence and in humble reliance on the mighty arm of the God of Jacob, I would say with the apostle, "I am persuaded that neither life, nor death, nor angels, nor principalities, nor powers, nor things present, nor things to come, nor height, nor depth, nor any other creature, shall be able to separate me from the love of God which is in Christ Jesus my Lord."[70]

Alexander then addressed the members of the LJS, exhorting them to persevere, and that there were promising signs that 'the time to favour Zion is at hand; that he who scattered Israel will gather him, and keep him as a shepherd doth his flock. You are God's chosen instruments to be the bearers of glad tidings unto Zion' and encouraged them that despite the numerous obstacles they would face, that 'the God of Israel will be faithful to his promise, "I will bless them that bless thee."'[71]

The LJS in summation wrote of the event:

> ... the consecration of a Jewish Christian to be a shepherd unto Israel is an event unheard of since the day that Jerusalem was delivered to be trodden down by the Gentiles, and forms an era in the history both of the Jewish nation and the Christian Church ... What the friends of Israel longed and prayed and laboured for was not simply the conversion of a few individuals, but the resuscitation of the Jewish people and the resurrection of the Jewish Church.[72]

Prussian Announcement and English Deed of Endowment

On 14 November the Prussian Minister of Spiritual Affairs, Karl Eichhorn, released a circular to inform the German populace of the Bishopric. This statement was very comprehensive, explaining the history of the how the Bishopric came into being, and the implications for Prussia. Eichhorn also indicated that there were to be further practical implications of the Bishopric scheme:

> Thus the ecclesiastical necessities of the new Bishopric may be considered as provided for. But, inasmuch as a Church community cannot have a growth rich in blessing, except in connexion with the instruction of youth, and the care of the sick, a still larger contribution is to be expected from the pious interest and beneficence of Evangelical Christians of Prussia and other German lands.
>
> Particularly important is the foundation of an Hospitum in which travelers,

---

70 Sermon, ibid, pp. 15-16.
71 Sermon, ibid, pp. 17-18.
72 *JI 1841*, pp. 390-1.

whom scientific research, ecclesiastical interest, or even other purposes, will probably bring to Jerusalem in increased numbers, may find a reception in case of need.[73]

Attached to this general letter was another circular calling for a special collection to raise funds for the establishment of such a Hospice for travellers, stating:

> The King's majesty has taken advantage of the opportunity afforded by his participation in the preservation of peace in the East, to procure for the Evangelical Church, for all future times, the same legal recognition in Turkey, which the Greek and Latin Churches have long since enjoyed in those countries ... In a very short time a Church for German Protestants will lift up its head in Jerusalem, and be opened for their worship according to their Confession and Liturgy ... [74]

For the Prussian authorities this scheme was not just about an ecclesiastical exercise, they saw this scheme as the practical beginning point of Prussian involvement in the East.

On 15 November 1841 the English Deed of Endowment for the Jerusalem Bishopric was signed and sealed. The Trustees for the Deed of Endowment were Lord Shaftesbury, Sir George Rose, Sir Thomas Baring, Sir Robert Inglis and John Labouchere.

A week later, on 23 November 1841 the LJS Committee met, and resolved that 'as the Bishop of Jerusalem is by virtue of his Lordship's office, ecclesiastical head of all the English clergy & the English Church at Jerusalem, so this Committee request his Lordship to take upon himself the direction and Governance of the Mission in the Holy Land & in the Province included in his Diocese.'[75]

There was a further Resolution requiring Nicolayson, Rev F.C Ewald and Dr George Macgowan, both of whom were to accompany Alexander as LJS workers, to submit to the ecclesiastical authority of Alexander.

So the Bishop's role as far as the British were concerned revolved around the LJS and involvement with the Jewish people. On the 16 November the *Prussian State Gazette* wrote, as the Prussian goals of the Bishopric; the need for securing legal recognition for Protestants in the east; to counter-balance in some form the political aspirations of the Russians, who protected the Orthodox, and the French, who protected the Catholics, and Prussia could only do this by joining with Britain.[76]

---

73 Berlin, 14 November 1841, quoted in Hechler, ibid, pp. 62-74.
74 Berlin, 14 November 1841, quoted in Hechler, ibid, pp. 62-74.
75 Letter from W Ayerst to J. Nicolayson, 25 November 1842. In 'Letters from Jerusalem 1834-1842', p. 222, Schick Library.
76 *Prussian State Gazette*, 16 November 1841. Quoted in F.D. Maurice, *Three Letters to the Rev. W. Palmer*, (London, 1842), pp. 45-6.

The Jewish Bishop was on his way to Jerusalem, and he was carrying on his shoulders the expectations, diverse goals and aspirations of two nations, of two ecclesiastical bodies, of both Jewish and Gentile followers of Jesus.

Would it all be too heavy a burden for one man to carry?

Chapter 27

Alexander to Jerusalem

Departure for Jerusalem

The Alexanders, minus son Robert who was to remain in England, made their way to Gosport (of Joseph Frey renown) and from there departed on 7 December 1842 aboard the ship *Devastation*. The Admiralty had previously offered the ship *Infernal* but Alexander did not think that name appropriate for such a voyage! The Admiralty complied and offered the other. 'The Admiralty's assistance', wrote Irwin, 'was supplemented by Mr Arthur Guinness, who in the first of his firm's timely benefactions to the Anglican church had provided without charge a supply of stout.'[1]

Accompanying Bishop Alexander and his family (Deborah advanced in pregnancy) and personal staff were Rev. George Williams, (Alexander's chaplain), Dr Edward Macgowan (the physician) and Rev. F.C. Ewald,` his wife and child.[2]

Arrival in the land of Israel

After stopping in Lisbon, Gibraltar and Malta the ship arrived in Beirut. Michael Solomon recorded, 'I cannot describe our feelings on getting the first sight of the land of our forefathers.'[3] Alexander's first duty was to notify the Consul-General, Colonel Hugh Rose[4], of his arrival, and shortly afterwards Rose came aboard. Later Alexander confirmed three young English sailors at the British Consulate.[5]

There had been conflict between the Maronites[6] and Druse[7], and ruthless actions against the Christians by Amer Pasha, but Rose was able to assure them that this conflict was over. Aberdeen had previously informed Ambassador Ponsonby, that 'Her Majesty's Government must hold the Porte responsible for any harm which befalls Bishop Alexander in consequence of the unwarranted proceedings of Amer Pasha.'[8]

---

1 Irwin, P. *Bishop Alexander and the Jews of Jerusalem*, p. 317.
2 Ransom, ibid, p. 10.
3 Alexander to LJS London, 17 January 1842, in *JI*, 1842, p. 127.
4 Son of Sir George Rose and afterwards Lord Strathnairne.
5 Ewald, F.C. *Journal of Missionary Labours in the City of Jerusalem*, (London 1846), p. 16.
6 The Maronite Christians are loyal to Rome. They gathered round Maron, a priest from Antioch in the 5th century and adhered to the beliefs of the Council of Chalcedon in 451.
7 The Druze are an off-shoot of Islam. Their faith is based largely on the beliefs of Hamzah ibn Ali ibn Ahmad, a minister of the Egyptian Fatimid Caliph al-Hakim in the 11th century.
8 Aberdeen to Ponsonby, 24 March 1842, FO 78/473, No 26.

Consul-General Rose accompanied the party on to Jaffa, where they arrived mid-afternoon on 19 January 1842. Rose later reported concerning Alexander that he was 'surprisingly in the dark as to the state of affairs in this and other countries, and totally unacquainted with the laws and rights of Turkey.'[9] His observation would basically prove correct.

Mrs. Ransom recalls of their arrival at Jaffa, 'Owing to its dangerous rocks and surf, we had to be carried ashore by Arabs, through the breakers. Mama was landed in a litter, made for her on board, of a hammock slung on two poles, and in that way she was carried to Jerusalem between 2 mules.'[10]

While in Jaffa the Turkish Governor (Pasha) and Muslim *Cadi*[11] paid their respects to the Bishop and Consul-General. Then the group began the journey to Jerusalem on 20 January meeting Nicolayson between Ramle and Jaffa. They stayed at the house of Nicolayson's friend, Abood Markos, in Ramle. Mrs. Ransom describes their experience here:

> We were the guests of the Pacha. Papa, Mr Williams and the other gentlemen were received into the Pacha's own Palace, but Mama and we feminines were banished to the Harem. Shall I ever forget that night of misery! We had to sleep on the divans, eat our meals on the floor, and it was past midnight before the ladies of the Harem left us alone. Skinny old hags, henna painted wives – girls, and little boys of 7 years old pawing us all over – tried on our clothes, especially corsets, and chattering, like monkeys and parrots. Oh, how tired we were, how we longed for rest, but not until our hosts chose to leave us, could we show signs of weariness, so sacred was the law of courtesy in the East.[12]

The following morning, Friday 21 January, the party continued on to Jerusalem, arriving in the late afternoon. Some distance from the City they were met by Mr. Johns, architect of the Church, and pro-consul (*locum tenens*) in the absence of Consul Young, and the American missionaries.[13] The *Times* correspondent later wrote that the Turkish *Pasha* sent a guard 'to compliment Colonel Rose on his arrival.'[14] It must have been an interesting spectacle, especially with Mrs. Alexander and her younger children, being conveyed in a *taterwan* or oriental litter, supported before and behind by mules.

---

9 Rose to Aberdeen, 4 February 1843, FO 78/535, No 11.
10 Ransom, *ibid*, p. 11.
11 Also spelt Kadi – religious leader.
12 Ransom, *ibid*, p. 13. *JI* 1842, p. 129.
13 Belonging to the *American Board of Commissioners for Foreign Missions*.
14 *The Times*, written in Jerusalem on 27 January, and printed 14 February 1842, pp. 2-5. Quoted in *JI*, 1842, pp. 131-132. Alexander later claimed that the Pasha had come out to meet the party, but had been forced to return to Jerusalem about 6 o'clock due to the damp. Tibawi however contends this, claiming that the Pasha would not be coming to greet Alexander, as Alexander, legally, had no official status, he was merely a British subject. See Tibawi, *ibid*, p.58 and notes 3 and 4.

The party then proceeded towards the Jaffa Gate, arriving at the same time as the Muslims were celebrating one of their main festivals, the *'Id Al-Adha*. Then as they entered through the gates, the 'guns thundered forth', wrote the *Times* correspondent 'the salute for the eve of Courban Bairam.'[15] Nicolayson described quite graphically this moment:

> The Pasha had himself been out at the gate waiting to receive his Lordship and the Consul-General till sunset; and when we arrived, the commander of the troops, with a detachment of cavalry, was still in waiting, and escorted us in. A body of soldiers were drawn up at the gate and presented arms, another again at the door of my house, where I had the honour and pleasure to entertain the whole party.[16]

First Days in Jerusalem

The Alexanders spent the first night at the home of John Nicolayson, but then later moved to the house where Consul Young had previously lived. Although the best available Michael Solomon remarked that 'It would be considered in England a miserable hovel. When I first came to see it, it gave me the idea of a dungeon, which seems to me here almost universally the appearance of the houses outside. I am happy to say Mrs. Alexander is quite satisfied, and so are the rest of the party.'[17]

Mrs. Alexander and the party may well have been satisfied, but daughter Deborah wasn't. Many years later she wrote of her recollections:

> The house which we first inhabited, down in the Turkish Quarter was very unhealthy. It was in full view of the Pool of Hezekiah, a stagnant tank of rain water, where frogs croaked, lizards and newts abounded, also there was a very noisy Turkish coffee shop close by, from which uproarious revels, much beating of tomtoms, clapping of hands, yellings and shouting made night hideous. Nearby was a tall and slender minaret from whose 4 sided gallery, four times a day, the blind Meuzzin in a powerful voice, called the Moslems to pray. Bells are not allowed by the Turks.[18]

On 22 January Colonel Rose accompanied Alexander to a formal meeting with Tahir Pasha, the Turkish Governor of Jerusalem, who must have been quite perplexed about how to meet this new resident.

The following day, being Sunday, Alexander preached his first message, probably in the temporary St. James chapel[19] from Isaiah 60:15, 'Whereas thou

---

15 *The Times,* quoted in *JI,* 1842, p. 132.
16 Nicolayson to LJS London, 24 January 1842, in *JI* 1842, p. 129. The *Times* added that the Pasha had sent a guard of honour and his *Janissaries,* guardians, to meet Colonel Rose.
17 Alexander to LJS London, 25 January 1825, *JI,* 1842, p. 128.
18 Ransom, ibid, p. 14.
19 More than likely the temporary chapel was located where the present Christ Church Centre dining room is located.

(alluding to Jerusalem and the Jews) hast been forsaken and hated, so that no man went through thee, I will make thee an eternal excellency, a joy of many generations.' The tendency of Alexander's discourse, wrote the *Times* correspondent, was to show that, although Jerusalem had endured, and might still endure, much suffering in the fulfillment of inspired prophecy, nevertheless brighter days were at hand.'[20]

In his sermon Alexander also referred to the Turkish government in the country as 'an usurped one' – a matter that led to a rebuke by Consul-General Rose. Alexander promised never again to speak in such terms.[21] Concerning the Bishop's relationship with the local inhabitants, Nicolayson recorded: 'I have just had evidence that the fact that his Lordship is nationally a member of the house of Judah, will make a strong impression on Moslems here, when it shall become generally known.'[22]

Opposition to Alexander's Presence.
Alexander's presence in Jerusalem, as a British bishop and as a Jewish bishop did however elicit opposition.[23] Israeli historian Professor Yehoshuah Ben Arieh wrote that Alexander's appointment 'sparked the interest of the Roman Catholics of Central Europe who demanded a counter balance to Western Protestant and Greek Orthodox activity. On 14th January 1842 the decision was made to appoint a Roman Catholic Bishop.'[24]

Indeed there was considerable opposition to the Protestant Bishopric, which is further highlighted in a letter by W. Ayerst to Nicolayson dated 19 February 1842:

> The public papers abound with rumours of difficulty in his way. These are chiefly taken from the French and Austrian papers, and we may well suppose that they endeavour to represent things as they wish to have them, and do not fail to look out for obstacles in the way of the execution of those plans which must tend to injure Popery.[25]

Yet the Bishop did not initially receive as much personal opposition in Jerusalem as could have been expected, a matter which both the *Morning Herald* and the *Times* papers commented upon.[26] In fact some very distorted stories were circulating in Europe, stating that the Bishop had been stoned while preaching in the open air, and more. Alexander was able to repudiate all such stories.

---

20 *Times*, quoted in *JI* 1842, p. 132.
21 Rose to Aberdeen, 15 February 1843, FO 78/535, No 19.
22 Nicolayson to LJS London, 24 January 1842, in *JI*, 1842, p. 131.
23 *Times*, quoted in *JI*, 1842, p. 132.
24 Ben Arieh, Y. *Jerusalem in the Nineteenth Century*, (Jerusalem, 1984), Vol. 1, p 231.
25 Ayerst, to Nicolayson 19 February 1842, in Letters from Jerusalem, 1834-1842, No 20, p. 224, Schick Library.
26 Articles from *Morning Herald* and *Times* quoted in *JI*, 1842, pp. 233-4.

Personal Trials & Official Duties

One of Alexander's first duties was to institute, in a more formal way, the daily Hebrew meeting at seven o'clock in the morning, and evening prayers in English. Nicolayson had been holding Hebrew prayers since 1839. Alexander wrote, 'We have now regular daily services in the temporary chapel: at seven in the morning in Hebrew, and at sunset in English; and though we are but a small band, yet I feel it peculiarly delightful thus daily to worship on Mount Zion.'[27]

Several weeks later, in early February, Mrs. Alexander bore a daughter, Louisa. Yet Alexander had to write on 26 February: '… it has pleased God to cause death to enter into our dwelling, by taking from us our dear infant on February 13, when just a fortnight old. This has been an unexpected additional severe trial to us, but our God is gracious, and enables us by his grace to acknowledge his fatherly hand in all things.'[28]

Further deaths consumed the Bishop's time and energy. In March seven British sailors from the war ship *Hatchet,* drowned near Jaffa. Alexander proceeded to Jaffa and purchased land for a burial ground for them.[29]

Such set-backs were partly compensated for by ministry opportunities. In the same week that Louisa Alexander died, two German missionaries associated with the CMS arrived from Egypt to receive ordination. Although encouraged, Michael Solomon had to confess, 'I should have been glad if Jewish missionaries of our Society had been the first to receive ordination from the first Hebrew Bishop of the Anglican Church in Jerusalem.'[30]

Foundations laid … for the physical Church

On 28 February 1842 Bishop Alexander placed the first stone underground for the new Hebrew-Protestant Church. Such an act so soon after his arrival was a major challenge to the Turkish Governor (*Pasha*) and Muslim authorities, as the building of a new church was a challenge to Islamic Law, the *Sharia*, which forbade the buildings of new churches.

Nicolayson and Alexander were oblivious to the intense battles then ensuing in Constantinople between the Turkish religious leaders, the *ulema*, and the British (and Prussian) Ambassadors. Alexander and Nicolayson based their authority to build upon the information provided by Palmerston to Shaftesbury in October 1841 which stated that Ambassador Ponsonby in Constantinople 'had obtained a positive promise' that instructions 'should be forthwith sent' to the Governor of Jerusalem granting permission for the Church to be built.[31]

In April, following a visit by the Governor-General of Syria, Mustapha Pasha, Alexander wrote to Bunsen that Mustapha 'has done or said nothing to impede

---

27 Alexander to LJS London, 26 February 1842, in *JI,* 1842, p. 161.
28 Alexander to LJS London, 26 February 1842, *JI,* 1842, p. 161.
29 *JI,* 1842, p. 192. Ewald, F.C. ibid, p. 82.
30 Alexander to LJS London, 26 February 1842, in *JI,* 1842, p. 161.
31 Tibawi, ibid, pp. 60-61.

our progress, as was generally feared, from the general impression, that he is not friendly disposed towards us, but from a circumstance which has transpired, it became evident that he took it for granted that we have a right to build the church.'[32]

Still, for the time being Alexander and Nicolayson continued with their plans.[33] On 7 August a master stonemason and several labourers left Malta en-route for Jerusalem to speed up construction on the Church.[34]

... and for the Spiritual Church

On 17 March Alexander ordained Mr. John Muhleisen of the CMS into deacons orders. Muhleisen was destined for service in Abyssinia. The service was joined by a number of visitors, including members of the Greek Church. In the same afternoon the newly ordained deacon read prayers at the German service.[35]

Macgowan was busy trying to re-establish the medical work alongside Melville Peter Bergheim, while Ewald was busy attempting to establish contacts with the Jewish people. The obstacles that he, and indeed Alexander, faced are summarized by the comment made by several Jewish men to Ewald, who stated, "We know that all of you have turned Christians for money; it is money that has induced you to forsake the faith of your fathers." It is often very difficult under such circumstances, Ewald wrote, 'to keep one's temper.'[36]

At this time three rabbis, who Mr. Pieritz (a former LJS worker) had previously befriended, were showing considerable interest in the message about Jesus, as too was a Jewish family, Mr A. L. Ducat and his wife Rose, who had recently arrived in Jerusalem. On 21 March, the family of John Meshullam arrived from Malta – boosting the numbers of the small Hebrew Christian-Protestant community.[37] Ewald was able to write on 25 March:

> Our small congregation of believing Jews on Mount Zion, consists at present of twenty-five souls. May the Lord soon add many, many more! Zion, with its small number of believing Jews, will still become a place of attraction to many sons of Abraham.[38]

Encouragements in England

Following the initial reports of Alexander's successful entry into Jerusalem and subsequent achievements, the supporters in England and Prussia became further enthused. Not surprisingly the issue of the Bishopric was one of the main matters at the LJS Annual Meeting, held on 6 May 1842, in London.

32 Alexander to Chevalier Bunsen, Easter Monday 1842, in *JI* 1842, p. 192.
33 Alexander to LJS London, 16 April 1842, in *JI*, 1842, p. 248.
34 *JI,* 1842, p. 353.
35 Ewald, ibid, p. 72.
36 Ewald, ibid, p. 89.
37 Ewald, ibid, p. 90. Ewald had befriended this family in Tunis, and they had later gone to Malta where they were baptized by Rev. Samuel Gobat of the CMS.
38 Ewald, ibid, p. 92.

Leading the charge was Shaftesbury. His statement emphasized again the tall expectations now placed upon the broad shoulders of Michael Solomon. Shaftesbury stated:

> ... the first Hebrew that for 1700 years was raised to the dignity of the Christian episcopate; was borne on one of her majesty's vessels, under the safeguard of the British flag ... and escorted by our gallant sailors ... to aid in the fulfillment of that august command, "Bring my sons from afar, and my daughters from the ends of the earth."

Then echoing the Evangelical language of the day he stated that all this would see 'that great and ultimate consummation when the usurped supremacy of Rome shall sink forever ... into the dust before the lawful supremacy of Jerusalem.'[39]

The anti-Rome sentiment was also echoed by Rev. Hugh Stowell, who stated, 'We do not marvel at Rome, and those who sympathize with her, being jealous of the appointment of a bishop to Jerusalem, for now who is the lawful Metropolitan of the Universal Church? Dr. Alexander, the Bishop of Jerusalem, where the first Christian Church was formed upon earth, and which the Saviour himself graced with his presence ... If, then, there be a Metropolitan Church on earth, that Church is the Church of Jerusalem; if there can be a Metropolitan on earth over the Universal Church, it is Bishop Alexander ... Therefore we cannot marvel that Rome is filled with jealousy, and mistrust, and apprehension, when she hears of a Bishop of Jerusalem.'[40]

Stowell was followed by Rev. Alexander McCaul. McCaul alluded to the prophetic nature of the Bishopric, stating:

> I would earnestly impress upon all the friends of the Jews one great truth, which is frequently lost sight of, - that is, that before the general conversion of the Jews, there is to be a select Church, a remnant according to the election of grace, to be restored and acknowledged as the first-fruits of the nation ... from Scripture it is clear that previous to the restoration of the Jews we are to have restoration of a remnant ... It is also necessary to remind you that the restoration of the Jews is in great part to be accomplished by human agency ... you will find in prophecy that human agency is to be employed.[41]

McCaul was followed to the rostrum by Alexander's old-time friend, Rev. William Marsh, who expressed the blessing which would fall upon their nation and Church. While alluding to Queen Victoria's habit of daily reading Scripture, Marsh remarked, 'for no one can read the sacred Scriptures with understanding and faith, and dependence upon God's Spirit, and be indifferent to the cause of Israel. There is not a passage in favour of that people which is not pregnant

---

39 Speech of Lord Shaftesbury, LJS AGM, 6 May 1842, in *JI*, 1842, pp. 178-179.
40 Speech of Rev. H Stowell, LJS AGM, 6 May 1842, in *JI*, 1842, pp. 182-183.
41 Speech of Rev. A McCaul, LJS AGM, 6 May 1842, in *JI*, 1842, pp. 185-187.

also with a blessing on those who bless the descendants of Abraham, Isaac and Jacob. Let Church and State show kindness to the Jews, and Church and State will receive a blessing.'[42]

Further ministry

In May the vibrant little community was able to observe the baptism of Mr. Ducat and his wife – the first Jewish people to enter into covenant with Jesus since Alexander arrived in the City.[43]

One area of ministry that Alexander seemed to enjoy and appreciate was the constant flow of overseas visitors. Amongst these were Lord Castlereagh, accompanied by his physician, Dr. George Fisk and Rev. H.M. Erskine. Fisk wrote that on Sunday 19th July he was invited by Alexander to read the prayers at the Morning service. The service, he wrote 'was conducted in a small temporary chapel – "upper room", in which some of the early efforts of Mr. Nicolayson were made. There was an air of primitive simplicity about it, according well with the position which we at present occupy in Jerusalem. It overlooks the site on which the new church is in process of erection. The congregation consisted of about thirty persons.'[44]

Fisk also related that Alexander invited him to attend the evening service at his own home, where it was usually conducted.[45] Quite often there was much merriment at these evening meetings. Music would be played and songs sung. Michael Solomon seems to have relished these opportunities to sing praises unto the Lord. Deborah the younger recorded, 'At our evening receptions, we always had much music. Papa kept open house on that day, as we could not hold service in the Church after sun down at that time. On one occasion we had 13 nationalities present.'[46] Of her father's music abilities, Deborah also wrote:

> Of all music Hebrew melodies are the most mournful. There is a touching pathos in the Jewish voice. Papa had a fine tenor voice and at such times as he would consent, and the occasions were very rare, to chant in Hebrew the Lamentations of Jeremiah, it was truly thrilling and would draw tears in some cases.[47]

Sickness and 'settlement' at Jifna

Michael Solomon and the entire family succumbed to sickness in July 1842. They all moved to the Georgian Monastery of the Cross several kilometers west of Jerusalem.[48] Unfortunately the Bishop was not able to fully recover

---

42 Speech of Rev. William Marsh, LJS AGM, 6 May 1842, in *JI*, 1842, pp. 187-190.
43 Ewald, ibid, pp. 98-99.
44 *JI*, 1844, p. 6.
45 *JI*, 1844, p. 6. Also Ewald, ibid, p. 106-107. Ewald wrote that the service took place in June.
46 Ransom, ibid, p. 21.
47 Ransom, ibid, p. 31.
48 Alexander to LJS London, 1 August 1842, in *JI*, 1842, p. 345.

at this location. Macgowan and for a time Bergheim, who had both also succumbed to sickness, had retired to the village of Giffna (Jifna) to the north of Jerusalem. Macgowan invited the Alexanders to enjoy this healthier site with him. Macgowan wrote:

> I wish that our friends in England could have had a peep at us in our encampment, living, like the patriarchs of old, in tents, surrounded by the richest plantations of olives and vines, pomegranates and fig-trees, laden with fruit; around were the beautiful hills covered with luxuriant vegetation, and above, the deep and cloudless serenity of the deep blue sky. We all enjoyed ourselves extremely, especially the children, who were quite delighted with the freedom and novelty of this new mode of life.[49]

Despite Macgowan's idyllic biblical picture of the camp at Jifna, this was not how the Greek Church, and its protector, Russia, viewed matters. They viewed the whole thing as a British settlement – *in Greek Christian territory*. It would seem that whatever Alexander did was sure to cause offense with one community or another. Alexander did manage, however, to recover from his bout of fever while there.[50]

Return to labours in Jerusalem

In September the Alexanders returned to their former house in Jerusalem. Soon afterwards they moved to the house belonging to Joseph Amzalak,[51] in which the American missionaries Mr. And Mrs. Whiting had been living. The Whitings were moving to Lebanon. Deborah the younger wrote that this was how, 'we occupied our nice house on Mount Zion, opposite the Castle of David, and near the Zion Gate. Our landlord was Rabbi Amstek, a splendid specimen of a Jew, with flowing beard, keen eye, and fine bearing.'[52]

On 12 August 1842 Mr. E. M. Tarkover arrived from England, with mail and goods from their friends there. Tarkover was to be trained for ordination. Then in early October eight Hebrew Christians and one Gentile Christian were confirmed. This occasion was indeed a high point of Alexander's first year, and prompted Nicolayson to write:

> Such was the depth of feeling with which he performed this truly affecting service, that when he began to lay his hands on the head of each candidate, and came to his own daughter, he was so completely overcome, that at first he could not proceed at all, and only gradually recovered firmness enough to go on.

49 Macgowan to LJS London, 31 August 1842, in *JI*, 1842, p. 379.
50 Alexander to Rev. William Wynne Willson, 28 September 1842, MSS 3393, [No f.61], Lambeth.
51 Amzalak was a British subject, originally from Gibraltar. He was quite unique in that being Jewish he had considerable contact with the British mission, and in particular with Nicolayson.
52 Ransom, ibid, p. 15. Deborah also mentions that later when Holman Hunt lived in Jerusalem he used Amzalek as one of his specimen Jewish men in some of his paintings.

> ... Our little chapel was quite crowded on this occasion, there being upwards of forty persons present, a large party having just come up from the Vesuvius steamer at Jaffa.[53]

Then the following week Alexander married two Jewish followers of Jesus, Peter Bergheim, the medical missionary, and Dorothy Rosenthal, a member of the Rosenthal family whom Nicolayson had baptized in 1839.

Ewald's outreach

In early March 1842 Ewald came into contact with one of three rabbis who had first heard about Jesus from Mr Pieritz and Nicolayson, but who had then been compelled to leave Jerusalem. Ewald then also re-established contact with the other rabbis. He asked them why they would not come out openly and confess faith in Jesus as Messiah, to which they replied that their wives and children would leave them.[54] This indeed was the reality facing many within the Jewish community. They were so dependent upon the rabbis, and the money they received from the *haluka*[55] distribution, that they dare not invoke the wrath of their leaders.

On another occasion Ewald relates the struggles that the secret Jewish disciples had to encounter:

> *June 4* – To-day I met outside the gate some of the believing Jews, who were sitting together in a lonely place reading the New Testament; they dare not take it to their houses for fear of the Jews and their own households; so they hide it in the rocks, and go as often as they can to read it together in secret and undisturbed by unbelieving Jews.[56]

Development of the Medical Work

Dr. Macgowan began his important work immediately upon arrival in Jerusalem. In his first report to London on 26 February, and stated that for several weeks past he had set in motion certain plans for improving the medical facilities. This report revealed that each day he met between twenty and thirty sick Jewish people. He concluded by impressing upon the Committee in London 'to lose no time in carrying into effect their plan of establishing a hospital in Jerusalem, in connexion with the mission.' He and Nicolayson had even located a suitable building, which they desired to secure.[57]

In his next report, on 1 July, Macgowan could state that he had fixed up

---

53 Nicolayson to LJS London, 1 November 1842, in *JI*, 1843, p. 16.
54 Ewald to LJS London, no date, in *JI*, 1842, p. 250.
55 *Halukah* is the Hebrew word for distribution, and is used to describe to system then operating in Palestine whereby alms were collected in Europe and then distributed by the rabbis amongst their co-religionists. This system was apt to be misused and abused.
56 Ewald, ibid, p. 103.
57 Macgowan to LJS London, 26 February 1842, in *JI*, 1842, pp. 162-165.

a suitable building for a new dispensary, where Bergheim spent much of his time, and a surgery. During this interim period, he said he had seen some 1,000 patients! There were times when so many people wanted to visit him that they sat on the steps outside.[58]

The London Committee was very favourable to Macgowan's plans for the hospital and he made preparations for leasing a suitable property. By November he had secured a suitable property on the edge of the Jewish Quarter, where he proposed having separated wards on two floors for men and women, as well as a separate ward for tourists and pilgrims, who would be expected to pay.

Macgowan's work stirred up opposition from those rabbis whose authority they felt was being undermined. Ewald reported in June, 'There is at present a great stir among the Jews here. The question, whether it be lawful for a Jew to ask for and receive medical advice and assistance from a Christian ... Several are of (the) opinion that it is not unlawful; and one has publicly expressed this opinion in a sermon.'[59]

When news of Macgowan's exertions reached the Jewish communities in Europe, many Jewish leaders, especially Sir Moses Montefiore in England became alarmed. Montefiore then set in motion the finding of a suitable Jewish doctor to come to Jerusalem to work on behalf of the Jewish community. This move marked one of the first signs of the break-up of the established *status quo* within the Jewish community of Jerusalem. The authority of the rabbis was being seriously challenged.

Political problems begin
Consul Young, who had gone to England in September 1841, returned to Jerusalem in May 1842 with fresh instructions from the new government. Foreign Secretary Aberdeen did not follow the same aspirations in the Eastern Mediterranean as his predecessor Palmerston. Aberdeen wished to appease the local authorities, and especially the Turks, as best he could.

Aberdeen wrote that Young was to offer Alexander 'no other degree of protection than that which all other British Subjects, of whatever profession or denomination they may be, are entitled to enjoy in the Dominions of the Sultan'. Also, that apart from offering Alexander official protection, Young was to 'carefully abstain from identifying yourself in any degree with his mission, and from assisting to promote any scheme of interference with the Jewish Subjects of the Porte, in which Bishop Alexander may possibly engage.'

Aberdeen impressed upon Young that he was not to interfere 'with the religious tenets of any class of the Sultan's Subjects.' This meant, particularly that he was not to afford 'persons who may associate themselves to Bishop Alexander's congregation any protection, as British Dependents, to which,

---

58 Macgowan to LJS London, 1 July 1842, in *JI*, 1842, pp. 316ff.
59 Ewald, ibid, p. 101.

under other circumstances, they could not properly lay claim.' It was, Aberdeen concluded, 'the express desire of Her Majesty's Government that the number of persons who receive British Protection shall be strictly limited to those who by birth are entitled to it, and also to those whom the capitulations to Turkey, construed in the strictest sense, permit to be withdrawn from the immediate control of the Turkish law.'[60]

These Instructions made it abundantly clear that, provided Consul Young abided by them, Alexander would have many difficulties in fulfilling his stated objectives in Jerusalem. It would be a matter of time before serious conflict between the two parties would arise.

Conflict Between Church and State – the Three Rabbis
Due to the very nature of the Bishopric, conflict was bound to occur with the other communities in Jerusalem living under the established *status quo*. Soon there was to be conflict between the British in Jerusalem, between Church and State, as represented by the Bishopric and Consulate.

On 4-5 October 1842 the three Jewish rabbis, Abraham Walphen, Eliezer Loria (or Luria) and Benjamin Bynes, who were serious about following Jesus as Lord and Messiah, called upon Ewald. They informed him that they and their families were intent on proceeding to Jaffa, where the rabbis could freely discuss with their wives 'their conviction of the truth of Christianity'.[61]

The other Jerusalem rabbis then heard of this, and informed the wives that a boat would pick them up in Jaffa, take them to London, where they would all become Christians, and then the husbands would send the wives away. Upon hearing this false story the wives refused to go to Jaffa. In accordance with this Ewald asked the inquiring rabbis to remain in his house, while he informed Alexander.[62]

The following morning a large gathering soon appeared at Ewald's house, including Alexander, Scott Calman, Tarkover, and Nicolayson, who recorded 'we found quite a number of the principal rabbies ... who seemed to be in warm discussion with "the three."'[63] Ewald adds:

> Then all the Jews left; but soon after the wives and children, and relatives of the converts came, and wept bitterly, entreating them, by all that was dear to them, to return. It was a most heart-rendering scene; but they also were obliged to go, without effecting what they desired...
>
> A few days after this had happened, I fell seriously ill; and during my illness all three returned home to their families.[64]

60 Aberdeen to Young, 3 May 1842, FO 78/501, No. 5.
61 Nicolayson to LJS London, 15 October 1842, in *JI*, 1843, p. 59.
62 Ewald, ibid, p. 133.
63 Nicolayson to LJS London, 15 October 1842, in *JI*, 1843, p. 60.
64 Ewald, ibid, pp. 133-134.

The matter quickly became very complicated. The rabbis were all Russian subjects, and accordingly the Russian consular agent in Jerusalem, Rabbi Yeshayahu [Rabbi Isaiah] Bordaki, proclaimed that these men were evading Russian consular jurisdiction, and demanded that the British mission surrender them.

Consul Young was asked to intervene, and then demanded that Alexander comply and surrender the three rabbis to the Russian consular-agent. Alexander refused, stating that the lives of the rabbis were in danger, and that the matter was religious and not political in nature.

Young then informed Alexander that Rabbi Isaiah had referred the matter to the Russian Consul, M. Marabuti, from Jaffa, who was then visiting Jerusalem. This being the case, the matter seemingly was now taken out of the hands of Rabbi Isaiah. If this was so the apprehension of physical violence against the three rabbis was now removed.

In a civil sense this simplified matters. But not for the three rabbis, who, Nicolayson wrote, 'evidently felt much discouraged and disappointed at this, having fully hoped that they would have had the countenance at least and influence of the British Consul in their favour, whereas they now felt (and the Jews boasted) that it was against them.'[65]

Alexander, Nicolayson and Consul Young then met the Russian Consul, on 7 October, to inform him of the peculiar nature of the case. Alexander and company claimed that the Jerusalem rabbinical authorities might bring charges against the three rabbis – in part due to the harm that news of three rabbis in Jerusalem following Jesus might have upon their authority over the Jewish community.[66]

Young wrote to Aberdeen on 11 October 1842 of his perspective on the affair, and stated that following the issuing of a second note to Alexander and the Bishop's reply ('that he anticipated no difficulty' in the matter) that he, Young 'began to apprehend serious difficulty might ensue.'[67] Alexander did not fully comprehend the political nature of the matter.

Rabbi Bordaki then sent a message to his superior Consul Marabuti. The Jerusalem rabbinical authorities feared that the three inquiring rabbis would be secreted off to Malta, so they placed guards at the City gates to forestall this from happening.

Consul Young then met Alexander personally. At this meeting Alexander and Young's different perspectives became apparent, as expressed in a letter from Young to Aberdeen in which he stated that Alexander, 'had been led to understand from all parties at home, that he was to have my assistance and co-operation in all of his attempts at conversion among the Jews, - at this I could

---

65 Nicolayson to LJS London, 15 October 1842, in *JI*, 1843, p. 61.
66 Nicolayson to LJS London, 15 October 1842, in *JI*, 1843, p. 61.
67 Young to Aberdeen, 11 October 1842, FO 78/501, No. 7.

not avoid expressing my surprise, as I assured the Bishop my Instructions from Your Lordship compelled me to adopt a line of conduct quite the reverse…'[68]

Young then had to inform Alexander that if the Russian Consul came to take these persons by force, then he, Young, would have to remain neutral, and allow this course of action. Alexander was still obstinately holding to his position – all the while placing Young in a delicate position. Young might have to act against British subjects in order to maintain integrity with his instructions – and the established *status quo*. This was evident when the Russian Vice-Consul called upon him. Marbuti said he had detained a messenger he was sending to Beirut with an account of the affair 'in hopes that matters would yet be accommodated through my intervention – otherwise it would go on to Constantinople and thence to St. Petersburg.'[69]

Such an undertaking would have been disastrous for all parties involved: it would have strongly jeopardized Alexander's right to remain in Jerusalem as it would have substantiated and confirmed Turkish apprehensions about the inappropriateness of his presence there in the first place; it would have provided the Russians, and other enemies at the Sultan's Court, be they French, Austrian or Turkish, with an opportunity to curtail British endeavours in the region; and it would have seriously harmed Young's authority in Jerusalem and credibility with the British Government.

Young, realizing the possible ramifications of this situation, assured Marbuti he would do his utmost to conclude the affair satisfactorily. Alexander soon afterwards seemed swayed – provided there was a guarantee that no harm would befall the three rabbis. In exchange he agreed to hand them over to the Russian Vice- Consul the following morning.

The following morning, however, Alexander was unsure, and asked Young to arrange a meeting with the Russian Vice-Consul himself. This was facilitated, and resulted in a mutual understanding between Alexander and the Russians. A fair trial was agreed to – in the presence of several of the Mission staff.

Then the unexpected happened. The three rabbis, under great duress from their families and the Jerusalem rabbinical authorities 'recanted, left the missionary's house and identified themselves with their Jewish Brethren.'[70]

There the matter seemed to rest – at least for the short-term. Young, in summarizing the affair to Aberdeen, stated, quite correctly, that 'The Bishop seems to regard the matter in a religious, rather than in a Civil point of view. It appeared to me to be a purely Civil case.' Young further stated that Alexander felt that by harbouring the rabbis in the home of the British missionaries they would be protected by the British Consul – which Young had stated was not to be the case. This was a difficult reality for Alexander to accept.

68 Young to Aberdeen, ibid.
69 Young to Aberdeen, ibid.
70 Young to Aberdeen, 11 October 1842, FO 78/501, No 7.

In conclusion Young provided a very sobering and realistic appraisal of the situation in Jerusalem:

> When a Jew in Jerusalem embraces the Christian faith many important considerations are involved. If the party is married a divorce takes place, until the wife becomes a convert also – The Children are also claimed by the Jews until they arrive at years of discretion. Their family and friends mourn for the convert as though he were dead, and the Widow and Children become dependent on the Congregation. The Rabbinical Law forbidding them to receive maintenance from a husband or father who has renounced his Faith…
>
> If a European Jew professes himself a convert (as in the recent case) his Government might prefer that he should unite himself to the Church recognized by his own Government rather than to one in connection with a Foreign State.
>
> It has been hitherto imagined in Jerusalem, that to be accepted a member of the mission to the Jews here, is to become an Englishman and entitled to English privileges. This seems to be Bishop Alexander's impression, as far as regards converted Jews – I have had to undeceive several Natives on this point, who wanting assistance in some difficulty have come to me saying they wish to become Protestant.[71]

Young's despatch to Aberdeen went initially to Rose in Beirut, who basically supported Young's stance. Later Lord Aberdeen himself sent a message to Young on 30 December 1842, stating, 'I have much satisfaction in expressing to you my entire approval of your proceedings in this matter and I have to instruct you to continue to act in the same judicious manner in any case of the kind which may hereafter occur.'[72]

Bishop Alexander must have been extremely perplexed. Only a year before he was being feted by the leaders and even the Queen herself in England, and conveyed to the Holy Land on a British warship. Now, it seemed, the British representative was working against him.

All the while the three rabbis remained ambivalent.[73] Although the position of Consul Young in this crisis disappointed the three rabbis, it was in fact a blessing in disguise for Alexander and the mission. In a way it helped to sort out the wheat from the tares. If anyone thought that by going to the British Mission meant automatically receiving British consular protection and an easy ride to success, they now had to think twice. If they wanted to be a follower of Jesus – it would be without such protection.

The three rabbis were soon to experience this reality themselves. In the period

71 Young to Aberdeen, ibid.
72 Aberdeen to Young, 30 December 1842, FO 78/501, No 5.
73 Nicolayson to LJS London, 16 October 1842, in *JI*, 1843, p. 64.

following the crisis of early October, they periodically met with Nicolayson (as Ewald was gravely sick). The Jewish leadership was aware of this. The situation erupted again on 27 October 1842. The leading rabbis pronounced a *cherem* or excommunication ban against the three in the synagogues, and, the three rabbis received ill-treatment from their fellow countrymen.

Upon hearing this Nicolayson proceeded immediately to see Alexander, but while there he was summoned home, and thereupon found two of the three rabbis, Abraham and Benjamin. Bergheim had brought them from the dispensary where he had treated them for their bruises. Alexander soon joined Nicolayson, as did Dr. Macgowan.

At Alexander's behest Macgowan and Nicolayson then went in search of the Russian Vice-Consul, but finding he had returned to Jaffa, they then turned to Consul Young, asking if he would implore upon Rabbi Yeshayahu to guarantee the protection of the three rabbis.

Two of the three rabbis, Abraham and Benjamin stayed with Nicolayson, while the third, Eliezer remained with his family for the present. But then on 31 October two of the rabbis, this time of their own accord, returned to the rabbinical fold. Although they claimed to be convinced of the truth of Jesus as Messiah, the pragmatic cost of such a decision was too much. Again there were threats of excommunication against all three. The wife of Benjamin refused to live with him again, and a divorce followed.

This episode like few before deeply upset the *status quo* of the Jewish community. The three rabbis were also compelled to supply the names of all secret inquirers, and the names of twenty-six were furnished to the rabbinical authorities. And to add insult to injury, the annual *haluka* portion was threatened to be withdrawn from those having contact with the missionaries. Herein lay the real power of the rabbinical authorities. Ewald met the Chief Rabbis and informed them that the British Government was presently concerned to protect the Jewish people of the Ottoman Empire – and it mattered not if the persecutors were Turks or fellow Jews![74]

Indeed the *status quo* was being rocked. This was further revealed when on 5 November a delegation of some senior rabbis came from Tiberias, to determine if 'the report they had heard was true, viz., that fourteen rabbis of Jerusalem had embraced Christianity.'[75]

Further foundations for the physical and spiritual Church

On 30 October 1842 Alexander bestowed deacon's orders upon E.M. Tarkover,[76] a Jewish follower of Jesus, and Mr. William Whitmarsh, a Gentile follower. The occasion prompted Nicolayson to write, somewhat prophetically:

---

74 Ewald to LJS London, 30 November 1842, in *JI*, 1843, p. 70.
75 Ewald, ibid, p. 142.
76 Tarkover soon after began a small school, 'which' Alexander wrote 'I trust will increase, and prove a blessing.' Alexander to LJS London, 30 November, 1842, in *JI*, 1843, p. 59.

> It is deeply interesting to observe that, by today's solemnities, the nucleus of a Hebrew Christian Church in this city is now complete in all its offices, as well as functions. There is now here a Bishop, a priest (Ewald), and a deacon also, all "Hebrew of Hebrews," a fact in the history of Jerusalem which had not been realized since its final destruction by Adrian (sic Hadrian) in the second century; and which thus completes also the chain of restored connexion between the first Hebrew church here…and its present, distant, yet genuine off-shoot. May it grow into a great tree of life, under whose branches the dispersed of Israel shall find shelter, and whose fruits shall be the healing of the nations![77]

All of this extra activity prompted Alexander to write that, 'through the instrumentality of the Society, a Hebrew-Christian congregation, in its complete form, is now established on Mount Zion! And before the completion of the one year we shall (d.v) have performed all the ordinances of the Church.'[78]

The timing of the above event was quite significant. For on 2 November 1842, *All Saints Day*, the foundation stone above ground for the new church, was laid. This event was important for the fledgling Hebrew Christian-Protestant community. Mrs. Alexander was given the honour of laying the foundation stone, and as there was no silver trowel available for the occasion, the Bishop offered his fish-slice.[79]

Another significant event was the arrival, on 4 November of a new Turkish governor, Izzet Pasha. Alexander, Nicolayson, Tarkover and Ewald were introduced to him by Consul Young.[80] Izzet Pasha soon afterwards set about determining the scene of his new domain. No doubt he was impressed (and concerned) by the events since Alexander's arrival – and the obvious challenge to the established *status quo*. This could only have been confirmed with the visit of the Jewish delegation from Tiberias on 5 November.[81] The new Pasha took great interest in the new church now being built.

End of the first calendar year
At the end of December eight Jewish people were baptized. This was a matter for Alexander to be truly grateful for, and he wrote in his first Circular letter from Jerusalem, that:

> Although the enemies have endeavoured, by every means, to oppose the establishment of the Jerusalem Bishopric in the first instance, and have subsequently even gone so far as to endeavour to ridicule it, by abominable and absurd inventions, I am happy to be able to state, that we have never

---

77 Nicolayson to LJS London, 1 November 1842, in *JI*, 1843, p. 17.
78 Alexander to LJS London, in *JI* 1842, p. 403.
79 Johns, J. *The Anglican Cathedral Church of St. James Jerusalem*. (London, 1844), pp. 5-6.
80 Ewald, ibid, p. 142.
81 Ironically the following day, 6 November, Alexander baptized another Jewish adult, Mr. Michael Weinkauff, a previous contact of Ewald.

been molested or disturbed in the least.

After stating the dangers and challenges confronting him and his work, Alexander concluded, 'But as it respects the future glory of Jerusalem, the restoration of the children, and the establishment of the Redeemer's kingdom, whilst these are sure to take place, according to the Divine promise, we must ever bear in mind, that the Lord has said, "For all this will I be enquired of." I beseech you therefore, brethren, for the Lord Jesus Christ's sake ... that ye strive together with me in your prayers to God for me, that my service which I have for Jerusalem may be accepted of him and be abundantly blessed."[82]

Indeed despite many trials and tribulations during the year, including the loss of a baby, Alexander did have much to be thankful for. He had every reason to suppose that abundant blessings awaited him in the coming year.

British Society and re-emergence of Frey

While Alexander was labouring alongside Nicolayson to establish the work of the LJS in Jerusalem, Rev. Dr. Burder, one of the pioneers of the initial Jewish work in the Missionary Society, chaired a meeting at the National Scotch Church in Regents Square on 7 November 1842.

Burder, together with other erstwhile supports of the Jewish cause from the Non-Conformist Churches, including Rev. Robert McCheyne from Dundee, founded the 'British Society for Promoting Christianity among the Jews'. The clock, it would seem, had turned back to 1805 when Joseph Frey began his work in London on behalf of the Non-Conformist Missionary Society. Indeed Joseph Frey was also recognized as the pioneer foundation layer of the British Jews Society, although its history after 1842 became synonymous with another esteemed Jewish follower of Jesus named Ridley Herschell.

Frey meanwhile was continuing his pioneering work in America. During the two years Frey ministered in New York he never stopped his involvement in the cause of Israel. On three occasions he attempted to get the Baptist ministers of New York to rally behind his vision of establishing an evangelistic work among the Jewish people. There was little response, which caused him to write:

> Notwithstanding this disappointment, I was not discouraged; having ascertained during my former preaching tours, that the church felt a deep interest in the conversion of the Jews, but that much more may be effected by visiting the churches than by mere addresses in the public papers. I therefore resolved to visit the churches and did so.[83]

The seemingly irrepressible Joseph Frey once again surrendered his pastorate to pursue a goal – that being to reach Jewish people with the message of

---

82 Letter from the Bishop of Jerusalem, 31 October 1842, in *JI,* 1843, p. 2.
83 *Hebrew Messenger*, January, 1846, quoted in Eichhorn, ibid, p. 108.

Jesus. Between the years 1841-1843 he visited some eight hundred churches throughout the United States, gaining so it would seem further support for his goal. Yet when he returned to New York City in 1843 his attempt to elicit the support there for such a ministry once again failed.[84]

Never one to accept defeat, Frey set out again in early 1844 on a second lecture tour, returning towards the end of the year. This time he persuaded a Baptist minister, Spencer Cone (the president of the New York Baptist Association) that it was imperative for the Baptists to be involved in ministry to the Jewish people. Cone in turn conveyed this perspective to others, and included in his communication the important information that recently three Jewish followers of Jesus had joined the Baptist movement in New York.[85]

Establishment of the *American Baptist Society for Evangelizing the Jews*

Frey's efforts finally paid off, for the American Baptist Society for Evangelizing the Jews was founded in New York on 9 December 1844. Rev. Cone was the president and Rev. Joseph Frey was the secretary and missionary. Frey thereafter held meetings in his own home for Jewish visitors, and a mid-week prayer meeting.

But once again Frey's efforts were plagued by the matter of finances, as the New York Baptists were inclined to see financial support coming also from the outlaying Baptist churches. This forced Frey to once again go on a speaking tour, which began in March 1845 and continued for seven months. During that period he visited five states in the south, and collected in excess of $1800.

It seemed that at last Frey, after numerous attempts, could see a ministry grow into maturity.

---

84 Eichhorn, ibid, p. 108.
85 Eichhorn, ibid, p. 108.

Chapter 28

Alexander in Jerusalem

Visit to Bethlehem and Hebron

In early 1843 Alexander and a party visited Bethlehem and Hebron. While in the area of Hebron Alexander held Divine Service near the famous Oak of Mamre, the traditional tree of Abraham. 'It was' Alexander wrote 'most affecting to us to have a service under that tree under such peculiar circumstances, a Hebrew Christian Bishop with three clergymen one of whom was likewise of the house of Israel.'[1]

The party remained in Hebron for several more days, visiting the Cave of the Machpelah, burial site of the Patriarchs. Alexander and Ewald in particular had more social interaction with the Jewish people. Alexander was quite moved by his visit to Hebron.[2]

Shortly after arriving back in Jerusalem Rabbis Eleazer and Benjamin rejoined Nicolayson, followed soon after by Rabbi Abraham.[3] The final break had been made. Ewald wrote, 'I went into the Jewish quarter. There was again a great excitement amongst the Jews…no one is permitted to speak to them, and they are given up by the Jews as lost.'[4] This was a high point for the infant Hebrew Christian community.

Church Construction Stopped.

This high point was soon after followed by a definite low point. On 14 January 1843 the Turkish Governor, Izzet Pasha, sent his *dragoman* (interpreter) to Nicolayson to inform him, that as neither he nor Consul Young had any orders concerning the building of the Church, that, construction was to stop 'till orders shall have been obtained from Constantinople.'[5]

Nicolayson immediately dispatched a letter to Young about the matter, to which Young responded that he had no authority to interfere, but would refer the matter to London, Constantinople and to the Consul-General in Beirut.[6] Alexander meanwhile wrote a letter immediately to Ambassador Stratford Canning in Constantinople.[7]

---

1 Bishop Alexander to Sir Richard Steele, 28 Feb 1843, Alexander Papers, St. Anthony's College, Oxford.
2 Bishop Alexander to Sir Richard Steele, 28 Feb 1843, Alexander papers, St. Anthony's College.
3 LJS Local Committee 17 January 1843, Minute 104. Journal 1842- 1867, p. 37, Schick Library.
4 Journal of F.C Ewald, in *JI*, 1843, p. 168.
5 LJS Local Committee 17 January 1843, Minute 104. Journal 1842- 1867, p. 34.
6 Young to Nicolayson, 14 January 1843 ibid, p. 36.
7 Alexander to Stratford Canning, 14 January 1843, MSS 3393, [No f.66], Alexander Papers, Lambeth Palace Archives.

Ironically the following day, 15 January, the two men sent out from London to construct the Church, Mr Habershon, and Mr Critchlow arrived in Jerusalem. Nicolayson met with the Pasha on 16 January and explained their situation, and also requested permission to continue until the necessary confirmation arrived from Constantinople. The Pasha, however, refused.[8] Bishop Alexander then planned to travel to Constantinople accompanied by Nicolayson.[9]

Trip to Beirut

Alexander and Nicolayson left for Constantinople via Beirut on 20 January – the same day it appears that the new Prussian Consul, Mr. Ernest Gustav Schultz, arrived in Jerusalem. Here was the proof that the King of Prussia was taking seriously his plan to further German interests in the land of Israel upon the LJS-Anglican foundation on 'Mount Zion.'[10]

While at Jaffa, Alexander sent a letter forward to Consul-General Rose proposing steps for resuming construction of the church building. At their subsequent meeting in Beirut, though, Rose produced materials he just received, a letter from Young and one from the Prussian Consul-General, von Wilderbruch. Young stated in his letter, 'I learnt today that there is a Firman from Constantinople to the Pasha on the subject of the building of the Church.' The Prussian Consul stated that he had just been informed by Young, that the Pasha 'acted in compliance with the Firman from Constantinople, which declares the ground on which the Church had been erected 'Wakef'[11], Mosque Property, and claims it as such.'[12]

Consul-General Rose stated in correspondence to Foreign Secretary Aberdeen that Alexander and Nicolayson continued to state they were justified in building the church due to the 'tacit permission' or positive information previously given to Nicolayson in 1841. Rose informed Alexander and Nicolayson though, that this was no guarantee of Government assistance, as Young himself had informed Nicolayson that the Turkish Government 'would not sanction the continuance of the building of the Church without a Firman.' Rose also stated that Nicolayson 'does not reply to this observation.'[13]

Despite the obvious non-compliance of Nicolayson and Alexander with the request of Young, Rose nevertheless felt that the Turkish authorities were dealing with this matter in an unfair manner. He informed Aberdeen that if the Turks were claiming this land as '*Wakf*', he would instruct Young to apply Article 24 of the Capitulations,[14] 'inasmuch as the ground is held in the name

---

8 Report of Visit 17 January 1843, in Journal, ibid, p. 36.
9 LJS Local Committee, 17 January 1843, Minute 105, ibid, p. 37.
10 Ewald, F.C. ibid, p. 149.
11 Also spelt *Wakf* – Muslim religious property.
12 Rose to Aberdeen, 26 January 1843, FO 78/535, No 9.
13 Rose to Aberdeen, 26 January 1843, PRO: FO 78/535, No 9.
14 Name given to stipulations in treaties between Turkey and the European Powers.

of the Rev. Mr. Nicolayson'. But, he added, such a proceeding would then be referred to Constantinople, which, he stated 'would probably never take place.' In other words this approach would get buried in Turkish bureaucracy. [15]

Rose asked Alexander not to proceed to Constantinople, where his presence would be a great embarrassment for the British[16]. Alexander agreed, and then wrote to Bunsen on 30 January describing the difficulties with the building and asking him to use his influence with the British Government on behalf of the project.[17]

Rose tried to assure Alexander that the British Government was not working against him, and also informed Aberdeen of the peculiar nature of the situation in the East, where the suspension of the 'British' church 'is considered as a slight, or proof of mistrust' of Britain.[18] Rose and von Wildenbruch then visited the Turkish Governor-General of Syria, Assad Pasha, asking him, that while the issue is being discussed in Constantinople, that he permit the building to continue.[19]

Unfortunately Assad Pasha related to Rose some false information from an individual about Roses' own involvement in this project, that the *Seraskier*[20] had demanded the cessation of the building, while he, Rose had urged its continuation. Assad stated 'that the Seraskier was right, as the Law of Empire forbids the erection of Foreign Churches.' Rose assured the Pasha that 'the statement of the person was entirely destitute of truth.' As the British and Prussian Consuls–General departed from this meeting, von Wildenbruch said to Rose, 'It is a Russian intrigue.'

Rose concluded from this discussion that Assad Pasha would not change the decision of Izzet Pasha (Governor of Jerusalem), and as von Wildenbruch had already concluded, that the work of the British in Jerusalem had the effect of causing 'jealousy and alarm' for the Russian Government, who 'would have wished that the Jews her subjects should have become Greeks, not Protestants.'[21]

Rose had also asked Alexander to accept the discontinuance of the building, to return immediately to Jerusalem (which Alexander did on 3 February), and to abide by the stipulations of the British Government.[22] In return Rose and his Prussian counterpart agreed to assist as best they could to gain the permit or *Firman* to continue the building. Alexander assured Rose that he would do his utmost in the future 'to make the wishes of Her Majesty's Government the Rule

---

15 Rose to Aberdeen, 26 January 1843, FO 78/535, No 9.
16 Rose to Aberdeen, 15 February 184 FO 78/535. No 193 .
17 Alexander to Bunsen, 30 January 1843, MSS 3393, Alexander Papers, Lambeth Palace Archives.
18 Rose to Aberdeen, 4 February 1843 FO 78/535, No 11 .
19 Rose to Aberdeen, 4 February 1843, FO 78/535. No 11.
20 A Turkish general, and in particular the commander-in-chief or Minister of War.
21 Rose to Aberdeen, 4 February 1843, FO 78.535. No 11.
22 Rose to Aberdeen, 15 February 1843, FO 78/535, No 19.

of his conduct.'[23]

Prior to leaving Beirut Alexander and Nicolayson did finally confess that it had been wrong for the Russian rabbis to seek protection in the home of a British subject. In this context Rose wrote:

> I then stated confidentially that I must previous to Bishop Alexander's departure relieve myself of responsibility by earnestly cautioning him, that if the Mission continued to adopt proceedings which could not be countenanced by Her Majesty's Servants and, which therefore must prove to the World that the members of it were deprived of that powerful aid, consequences might ensue, which would not only prejudice the cause of the Mission, but endanger the personal safety of those who composed it.
>
> I drew the attention of Bishop Alexander to the fact that the inhabitants of Jerusalem consisted of a variety of Sects, each remarkable for its blind attachment to its own creed, and aversion to those of its neighbours…that the proceedings of the Mission had indisposed the inhabitants of Jerusalem towards them, and awakened their watchful bigotry and caused suspicion, perhaps alarm to the Local Authorities.
>
> Finally the Porte would be too happy perhaps to urge that the presence of Bishop Alexander had produced disorder.[24]

This was indeed a sobering reprimand for Alexander. But Rose, in order to reveal the delicate position in which he found himself of trying to allay Turkish suspicion and opposition on the one hand, and upholding British interest on the other, wrote this profound statement to Aberdeen on 4 February:

> … if matters continue in their present state at Jerusalem, the influence of Her Majesty's Government in this Country, particularly in that City, will be materially hurt, and that unless a Firman, or permission, be obtained to resume the building of the Church, the position of Bishop Alexander will be anomalous, and the source of perpetual embarrassment to Her Majesty's Government and to himself.[25]

This entire episode, beginning with the controversy with the three rabbis, the stoppage of the church construction, and the resultant trip to Beirut, brought Alexander closer to an understanding of real politik in the Middle East.

The Peel-Aberdeen Government was much less sympathetic to his cause than was the previous government. And despite the power and prestige of Britain, and its involvement in helping Turkey regain control over the 'Holy Land' in 1840, the Law of the Empire and the Law of Islam were powerful obstacles.

---

23 Rose to Aberdeen, 4 February 1843, FO 78/535, No 11.
24 Rose to Aberdeen, 6 February 1843, FO 78/535, No 13.
25 Rose to Aberdeen, 4 February 1843, FO 78.535, No 11.

Prussian Activities

Meanwhile in Britain and Prussia Alexander's entrance into Jerusalem on 21 January was being remembered. The King of Prussia had issued an Edict 'making known the Royal permission to all clergy and congregations whose hearts moved them to remember Jerusalem, but leaving it perfectly free to others to abstain.'[26]

Due to inclement weather several different dates were available for the clergy to remember this occasion, and it seems that in Prussia alone, only sixteen clergy declined to remember it, while some 9,000 parishes did observe it. The same occurred in the provinces of Posen, Silesia, Pomerania, Saxony, Westphalia and the Rhine.

The LJS wrote (rather optimistically) of this occurrence

> In Prussia, 9,000 Protestant parishes, not one of which is Episcopalian, unite as one man to invoke blessings upon a Bishop and an Episcopal Mission, because, however they may differ in their views of Episcopacy, they are persuaded that the cause of Protestantism and the good of the Jewish people are at stake, and that in Jerusalem the first great step has been taken to unite the Protestant Churches of Europe, and to exhibit the purity of Protestant doctrine to the Churches of the East.'[27]

Difficulties and Complexities

In early 1843 difficulties associated with the three rabbis returned. They were living in Nicolayson's house, firmly resolved to follow Jesus and suffer the consequences. Tarkover had the task of teaching them English, while they were also preparing for baptism.

Their presence again with the 'British' created further difficulties, especially at the time when Constantine Basily, the Russian Consul-General in Beirut, was due to visit in March. The Jewish religious authorities were insisting that the rabbis (or at least two of them) divorce their wives and transfer the dowries to them. Thereafter the situation became very complicated, and involved the Russian, Prussian and British consuls![28]

Macgowan reported that Rabbi Eleazer was so affected by these events that he became quite ill, and wrote, 'Evil reports of the most cruel and unfounded nature have been raised against him, and in consequence of an appeal to the Russian Consul ... a successful attempt has been made to force him to divorce his wife, to whom he was much attached. The mental suffering produced by these distressing circumstances have weighed heavily on his spirits, and brought on an attack of illness ...'[29]

---

26 Editorial Note, *JI*, 1843, p. 270.
27 Editorial Note, *JI*, 1843, p. 274.
28 Young to Aberdeen, 31 March 1843, FO 78/540 (No 21).
29 Macgowan to LJS London, April 1843, in *JI*, 1843, p. 261.

Finally two rabbis, Eleazer (hereafter Christian Lazarus Luria) and Benjamin (hereafter John Benjamin Goldberg), were baptized on 21 May 1843, as Young stated, 'in the Hebrew Language.'[30] Two other 'Adult Israelites' Isaac Hirsch (hereafter Isaac Paul Herschon) and Simon Frankel (not to be confused with the Jewish doctor) were also baptized on that occasion. Alexander addressed the congregation in English, briefly explaining the history of the rabbis in particular. He then addressed the candidates in German, and then afterwards, Nicolayson wrote, 'the Bishop proceeded in his peculiarly solemn manner to administer to these four Israelites the sacrament of baptism in the holy tongue.'[31] Alexander on this occasion was able to conduct the proceedings in three languages – English, German and Hebrew.

Nicolayson stated of this event:

> It is not a small thing, that the apparently impenetrable phalanx of rabbinism at Jerusalem has thus actually been broken into; and two Jerusalem rabbies been incorporated into the restored Hebrew Christian Church on Mount Zion. How sore the Jews felt on this occasion you can easily conceive. They were, in fact, after all, taken by surprise, and felt sadly disappointed in having to yield up at last any lingering hope they might have had of their return.[32]

New Stations in Alexander's Diocese

The LJS had ordained that new stations be opened at Hebron, Beirut and Safed, and were dispatching Rev. C Schwartz from Constantinople to Hebron; Mr. Winbolt and Mr. A Davis to Beirut, and Mr. Sternchuss and Mr. Behrens to Safed.[33]

Hebron and Safed were two of the four Jewish Holy Cities, the others being Jerusalem and Tiberias. Except for a few small scattered communities, most of the Jewish population lived in these four cities. Tiberias was the fourth of the Holy Cities – and at this stage was outside the scope of the LJS operations, but would one day be filled by the Scottish Mission.

Although there was a small resident Jewish population there, Beirut's importance was also because it was a port for Jewish people travelling from Europe to the land of Israel, or for others coming from Antioch, Tripoli, Sidon, Aleppo and Damascus.

Alexander was to supervise the establishment of all these new centres. All of these men, except Schwartz, arrived in Jerusalem on 15 April, 1843[34] and began a period of orientation under Nicolayson and Alexander.

Rev Tarkover occupied the post at Beirut for a season until Winbolt was

---

30 Young to Aberdeen, 22 May 1843, FO 78/540 (No 26).
31 Nicolayson to LJS London, 27 May 1843, in *JI*, 1843, p. 281.
32 Nicolayson to LJS London, 27 May 1843, in *JI*, 1843, p. 281.
33 Minute 127, 7 March 1843, Minute Book, p. 41.
34 Minute 147, 19 April 1842, Minute Book, p. 48.

sufficiently prepared. Then when Tarkover was ordained priest by Alexander on 18 June 1843, he departed for Konigsberg in East Prussia.[35] Winbolt then took up this key position, and quickly instituted daily Hebrew morning and afternoon English services, a Hebrew Saturday service and a Sunday English service.

Media attention to Alexander's activities

Alexander's circular letter marking the first anniversary of his entrance into Jerusalem caused quite a deal of interest in Britain, Germany and elsewhere. The LJS dedicated three pages of commentary under the enlightening title ***Restoration of the Churches of Jerusalem and Judea.*** It offers no better summation of the expectations upon Alexander's shoulders from the support base in Britain:

> The restoration of the Jewish Church and Nation has long been an object of faith ... The letter of a Jewish Bishop, dated from the Holy City, and informing us that there is on the Mount Zion, besides a Jewish bishop, a Jewish priest, a Jewish deacon, and a congregation, though small, of Jewish believers, amongst whom the Gospel of Christ is faithfully preached, and all the rites of the Church administered in the last year, leads us to ask, whether the restoration of a Jewish Church is not now an object of sight and whether the glorious dawn of accomplishment has not begun to chase away the obscurity of prophecy unfulfilled ... The living Church in the Holy City appears small, and the other cities of Judea are still desolate, but Safet, Tiberias and Hebron will soon possess the elements of Christian congregations. The means of making them numerous and flourishing, exist abundantly in Europe, not now to speak of those who search after the truth in Palestine itself, and in other parts of Asia and Africa....in short, there is a great multitude of Jewish believers, who, if collected into churches, especially if reunited in their own holy land, would astonish the world by their numbers and convince the Rabbinist that they are not the only Jews in the world...
>
> What then is the difficulty? What is there to hinder the reunion of the true Israelites in the land of their fathers? On what does this happy consummation depend? So far as man is concerned, it depends on two things: first, the will of the Israelites themselves; and secondly, upon that of their friends.
>
> In the first place, believing Jews, scattered through England, Germany, etc, must remember their nation, their country, their promises, and their duty to God and the world, and love them better than worldly ease and comfort...But let those who have faith seek what God has promised, and where he has promised it, in the glory of all lands. Any considerable return of converted Israelites to the land of their fathers would infallibly draw a proportional number of their Talmudic brethren; for though Talmudism

---

35 Ewald, ibid, pp. 194-95.

itself has not sufficient life to lay hold on even the national promises of God, it has such a jealousy of Christianity…that it will imitate what it has not power to originate…The re-appearance of the Hebrew Churches of Jerusalem and Judea would be still more powerful in exciting attention and in drawing crowds of Jews to Judea, where they may find not only the material inheritance but the faith of Abraham.

…The most efficient means, indeed, the only means, for the national conversion of any people, is the rise of a visible Church of natives. All people are suspicious of a foreign religion and foreign teachers – the Jews peculiarly so … By the visibility of a national Church alone can this be removed; and where can the national Church of Israel command more attention, or find a more genial soil, than on the holy hill which 'is beautiful for situation, and the joy of the whole earth?' And be it remembered that this is no longer a mere vision or a theory. An infant Jewish Church already exists in that sacred locality…It is now a year since a Hebrew bishop again, after a lapse of many centuries, took up his seat in the Holy City … Why have the efforts of Christians not been concentrated upon that one spot, which prophecy, Providence, memory, hope and every sacred association, point out as the most important upon the earth's surface?[36]

This profound article concluded with an exhortation for the friends of Israel to further support this entity in Jerusalem. There is little doubt that this attitude was very much bound up with the presence of one man – Michael Solomon Alexander. It was he who exemplified the expectations of LJS, and even large sections of the British, German and world-wide Protestant communion.

To confirm that expectations upon Alexander spread further than just the LJS, a very prominent Church of England paper, the *Quarterly Review*, published a positive five-page article about Alexander and his Mission in its April 1843 edition, and it concluded:

A Bishop of the Hebrew race and a Bishop of Jerusalem, cannot but excite attention among the Jews, and if it lead to nothing farther than provoking to jealousy, in the first instance, even this is preparation for another step, whether that be for their gathering into the Christian Church, or reinstating them in that land which was so often promised to their fathers …[37]

Sir Moses Montefiore steps in – sends a Jewish Doctor

Another British newspaper, the *Morning Herald* newspaper carried an article on 3 February 1843 stating that Sir Moses Montefiore was establishing a dispensary in Jerusalem, at his own expense, and sending a young Prussian Jewish doctor,

---

36 *Restoration of the Churches of Jerusalem and Judea*. Quoted in *JI*, 1843 pp. 45-48.
37 *Church of England Quarterly Review*, April 1843, pp. 374-398. Quoted in *JI*, 1843, pp. 151-2.

Dr. Simon Frankel, to head up this dispensary, and in time to establish a hospital in Jerusalem.[38]

In addition the French based Rothschild family had donated 100,000 francs to the establishment of a Jewish hospital in Jerusalem. Dr. Frankel himself furthered this proposal, writing in the German *Allgemeine Zeitung des Judenthums* on 31 October 1843. :

> It is well-known to you that the Missionary Society strains every nerve to make proselytes; they leave nothing undone. They have erected a hospital in which none but Jews are to be admitted. No Jew, it is true, will enter it, if he can help it; but what shall the poor, unfortunate, sick, and houseless do? Who after all can blame him for it? And what is the consequence? Alas! A very sad one. (During the time I have been here, ten Jews have been baptized. On the 25th instant, a father, mother and daughter.) At any time a hospital would have administered relief to the sick and suffering; now, it will likewise counteract the efforts of the Mission – an object which, in my opinion, every one of our brethren should, and will keep in mind.[39]

Macgowan was pleased about Dr. Frankel's arrival. Frankel in fact very quickly sent his card to Macgowan, and 'I lost no time in calling upon him' Macgowan wrote, adding, 'I consider his arrival here as a real advantage to the immediate object we have in view which is' Macgowan continued 'to afford medical relief to the poor suffering Jews in Jerusalem.'[40]

The LJS was also pleased that the Jewish people were acting in this way, and wrote concerning the proposed new hospital: 'We hope that this will lead many to imitate the good example. It is indeed a matter of thankfulness that the Christian Church was permitted to lead the way in administering to the necessities of the afflicted and suffering sons and daughters of Abraham who now reside in the Holy City … Although so late, it is gratifying to find that the Jews themselves are willing to do something in this respect for their own nation.'[41]

Debate in Parliament.

A debate took place in the House of Commons on 11 April 1843 concerning Alexander and the Protestant cause in Jerusalem. Dr. (later Sir) John Bowring wanted the correspondence between the British Government and the Turkish Porte to be produced, so as to prove the ineligibility of the Bishopric and indeed of the Protestant presence in Jerusalem. Dr. Bowring made some stinging personal remarks about Alexander. Bowring 'thought that the circumstance of the Bishop being married was not calculated to serve him in the estimation

---

38 *Morning Herald*, 3 February 1843, quoted in *JI*, 1843, p. 90.
39 *Allgemeine Zeitung des Judenthums*, 31 October 1843, quoted in *JI*, 1844, pp. 134-35.
40 Macgowan to LJS London, April 1843, in *JI*, 1843, p. 260.
41 Editorial Note in *JI*, 1843, pp. 243-244.

of the people amongst whom he went. Amongst the whole east' Bowring continued 'it was impossible to connect the idea of sanctity with the Episcopal character, unless the individual had also the reputation of celibacy.' Dr. Bowring also saw fit to challenge the propriety of sending out a Jew as Bishop, and also slurred Alexander's academic qualifications.[42]

Sir Robert Inglis, a known LJS supporter, then arose and addressed these issues. Referring to Alexander's Jewish descent, Inglis rightly pointed out, 'Why, who was the first Bishop of Jerusalem – was he not a Jew? Was not the first Christian Church founded in Jerusalem by St. James?' Inglis further added that Alexander was a 'competent Hebrew scholar' and that he, Inglis, had been informed by good authorities that Alexander equipped himself well as Professor of Hebrew and Rabbinic Literature at Kings College.

Next it was the turn of Sir Robert Peel, the Prime Minister, to contend with Dr. Bowring's accusations. Lord Palmerston followed and challenged Dr. Bowring's tone and manner in which his raised his motion, and 'regretted that his Hon. Friend should have treated the subject with ridicule, but it was quite manifest that his Hon. Friend acted on misinformation.'

Dr. Bowring then apologized for having conveyed any idea of ridicule or levity, and stated his belief that the 'Government were not aware of the difficulties with which this Bishop had to contend.' He finally withdrew his motion.[43] The motion may have been withdrawn, but it did reveal the depth of feeling still within Britain concerning the presence of the *Jewish* Bishop Alexander in Jerusalem.

The Domestic Bishop

It would be all too easy to view Alexander as a man so immersed in his episcopal functions, and so caught up in all these debates about him and his presence in Jerusalem, that he had little or no family life. Alexander was very much the family man, spending time with them whenever possible, taking them for walks or rides, sometimes with Deborah his wife, and sometimes just with the elder children.

Young Deborah wrote of one such excursion:

> One of our walks was through the St. Stephen's gate, the reputed Via Dolorosa, the wretched Turkish burial ground, the brook Kedron, then dry, the garden of Gethsemane the Chapel of the Blessed Virgin Mary.
>
> The steep ascent of Mount Olivet, on whose brow, the Saviour wept over Jerusalem. Papa always felt this to be a hallowed spot. One night when camping there with Mr Rowlands, he was discovered at midnight kneeling on

---

[42] *Morning Post,* 12 April, 1843, in *JI*, 1843, p. 154. Bowring also raised the issue of the church in Jerusalem.
[43] *Morning Post,* 12 April, 1843, in *JI*, 1843, pp. 156-160.

the bare ground, in earnest prayer and weeping bitterly.⁴⁴

Deborah then described their daily schedule:

> Our daily life was regulated by the climate a good deal. A ride at sunrise, service in Church at 7. a.m. and 4. p.m. Lessons and meals until the cool of the day, when we used to ride out, frequently to what we called the ledge of rocks. This was a narrow, long ledge of rock, on the face of a steep hill in the valley of Jehoshaphat. To it the servant took out rugs, fruit, and afternoon tea, and at this delightful spot, truly a shelter in a weary land, we spent many happy days, only leaving it in time to reach Jerusalem before the City Gates were shut at sunset. Visitors often came out to call, which cause a pleasant diversion from the usual routine of reading, working and sketching.⁴⁵

The Alexander family, after all their trials and sicknesses since their arrival, especially the loss of their baby Louisa, as well as missing Robert, were able to greatly rejoice on 31 May 1843 with the arrival of another baby girl – Salome.

Repercussions from Previous Events

Due to the exposure which Alexander's presence in Jerusalem had generated, Foreign Secretary Aberdeen had no choice but to become more pro-active in these affairs. He sent a strong message to Ambassador Canning on 20 March, stating that the Foreign Office had been considering for some time information coming from the Consul-General in Syria and from the Consul in Jerusalem, '… respecting the conduct of Turkish Authorities at Jerusalem and Beyrout with regard to the Protestant Church at Jerusalem, the erection of which, after having been for some time tacitly permitted by the Turkish authorities has at length been abruptly and somewhat arbitrarily stopped.' Aberdeen then declared that:

> Although that building had certainly been commenced without the express authority of the Porte, which had always declined granting a formal permission for that object, yet, as it had been stated to Her Majesty's Government Ambassador at Constantinople (as appears from a Despatch, dated Sept 18 1841, no 288) that he had reason to suppose that, provided the fabrick should be modest and unostentatious in appearance and should form part of the Consular residence, no obstruction would be thrown by the Turkish Authorities in the way of its erection; as that building had not for many months been opposed or obstructed, Her Majesty's Government had certainly hoped that the further prosecution of it might and would have been allowed.
>
> Her Majesty's Government still entertain a hope that, on a temperate representation of their wishes being made to that effect, the Turkish

---

44 Ransom, ibid, p. 31.
45 Ransom, ibid, p. 22.

Government may be induced to permit the building to be recommenced and to continue without further interruption.

Aberdeen then instructed Canning to bring the matter to the attention of the appropriate Turkish minister.[46] Aberdeen was walking a diplomatic tightrope. He felt he had a right 'to demand' a political favour which Turkey owed Britain, but realized there would probably be a 'positive refusal' again to the proposal. Such an attitude is revealed in his further instructions to Consul Young vis-a-vis Alexander and the church building, whereby he informed the consul that he had acted properly in not getting involved in the church affair 'As the parties have acted without the declared sanction of the Porte.'[47]

However, Aberdeen also stated, should Turkey:

1) agree to the church being built he was to zealously assist,
2) if the works are only 'tacitly' allowed to be continued as heretofore he was to have nothing further to do in the matter than to employ his best efforts to induce the Pasha to give full extent to the 'tacit' permission of the Porte.
3) If the Turks refused permission for further construction of the church, then he must have nothing at all to do with it.

Aberdeen also informed Young that he perceived there were problems between him and Alexander 'which for the benefit of the public service' the Foreign Secretary stated 'ought to be corrected.' Aberdeen then provided Young with advice that, should Alexander contravene the Laws of Turkey '... in such a manner as wantonly to excite the hostility of the Turkish Authorities, you as British Consul have not the power to protect him, even if you were authorized by your Government to do so ...'[48]

Indeed the relationship between the two senior British representatives was strained, due mostly to the differing instructions both were operating under.[49] Relations between the two were so strained that in a communiqué to Aberdeen on 1 May 1843 Young wrote ten pages about their relationship, or lack of it! Young also claimed that both Alexander and Nicolayson had misrepresented him through reports which had subsequently appeared in the *Jewish Intelligence*.

Young had written to Alexander expressing his disappointment about this slandering of his name. Alexander had responded stating that in the matter of the three rabbis not receiving British protection Nicolayson was merely expressing what the three rabbis had felt, that is, disappointment at being handed over to

---

46 Aberdeen to Canning, 20 March 1843, FO 78/513, No 41.
47 Aberdeen to Young, 3 April 1843, FO 78/540.
48 Aberdeen to Young, 3 April 1843, FO 78/540.
49 Young to Aberdeen, 1 May 1843, FO 78/540, No 24.

the Russian Consul.[50] Despite such explanations, attempts to mediate by the Foreign Secretary and even Rose, and Alexander's promise to Rose in February to attempt and abide by British Government policies, it was going to be a huge challenge for Alexander to live and work in harmony with Young.

Despite their strained relationship Alexander presented Young, in May, a Memorandum to be delivered to Her Majesty's Government on behalf of Queen Victoria's birthday. The Memo stated amongst other things that Queen Victoria '… has been permitted to become a nursing Mother to Israel, not only in having her Consul in this long neglected and forsaken City and Country, but moreover by having been made instrumental in causing the pure worship of God to be established on Mount Zion in Jerusalem.' The Memo concluded, 'that her Majesty may be permitted to see 'the good of Jerusalem - all the days of her life' and that 'she may see her Children's Children and peace upon Israel.'[51]

Visit of Prince Albert of Prussia

In late April 1843 Prince Albert[52] (Albrecht in German) of Prussia visited Jerusalem. The Prince was the younger brother of the Prussian King, Frederick William IV.[53] Several days afterwards Alexander, Macgowan, Nicolayson and Ewald all had a visit with the Prince, who then in turn also inspected the LJS property and the plans for the Church building. This meeting was conducted in English – despite the fact that all with the exception of Macgowan were well acquainted with the German language.

The Prince attended the Protestant service on 4 May, where Alexander preached from Romans 11: 25-26: *I do not want you to be ignorant of this mystery, brothers, so that you may not be conceited: Israel has experienced a hardening in part until the full number of the Gentiles has come in. And so all Israel will be saved, as it is written; 'The deliverer will come from Zion; he will turn godlessness away from Jacob …*[54]

Several months later it was the turn of the King of Prussia himself to be remembered. On Sunday 15 October, the occasion of the King's birthday, Alexander preached a sermon in the morning service and made special reference to that fact. The Prussian Consul, Mr. Schultz actually attended the service in full Prussian uniform. Alexander again alluded to this occasion during the afternoon German service. The following day, 16 October, a delegation led by Bishop Alexander paid an official visit to Dr Schultz to 'congratulate him on

---

50 Young to Alexander, 13 April 1843 and Alexander to Young, 19 April, Young to Aberdeen, 1 May 1843, FO 78/540, No 24.
51 Memorandum from Bishop Alexander, 27 May 1843, FO 78/540. No 27.
52 Prince Albert was married to Princess Marianne of the Netherlands. They divorced in 1849, and the estranged princess then set off on a world tour, including Jerusalem and she was the first royal visitor to the newly completed Protestant Church, Christ Church, in 1850.
53 Nicolayson to LJS London, 1 May 1843, in *JI*, 1843, p. 258.
54 The passage concludes with verse 27: 'And this is my covenant with them when I take away their sins.'

this occasion.'[55]

Opening of the Hebrew College, Inquirers Home & School of Industry
In May 1843 the Bishop officially opened the Hebrew College. Part of the purpose of this College was to train the rabbis who had come to faith, but others also were to benefit from it. Alexander read from Psalms 132 and 133, and then addressed the students in English and German, during which he pointed out to them 'the nature, use, and blessings of such an institution, and the duties of those who may be received into the same.' The first students were Rabbi Eliezer, Rabbi Benjamin, Isaac Hirsch and Jonas.[56]

Rev. Williams, prior to his departure, was the first principal, and later he was followed by his successor, Rev Veitch. The subjects taught at the Hebrew College were Divinity, English, German, Hebrew, Arithmetic, Music and Translation from English into Hebrew. In September the Bishop examined the students.[57]

The Inquirers Home was opened in order to determine which of the prospective believers was genuine or not. This was an essential institution for the Jerusalem situation. For some, it would appear that the Protestants or British offered a better life than the narrow confines of the Jewish community. Someone could suppose they would feign 'belief' and get accepted into the Protestant community, and receive entrance into the Gentile world by undergoing baptism. This in fact was the accusation often levelled against the LJS. The object of this Institution was somehow to weed out these insincere believers. But it was not a complete guarantee that the objectives would succeed.

The 'inmates' or students were provided with board, lodging and clothes while undergoing training and observation. If they were deemed to be true disciples, they then graduated into either the Hebrew College or the House or School of Industry.

A very important adjunct to the LJS work was the School (or House) of Industry. Mr. Critchlow, the LJS clerk of works, initially supervised this work. Here the pupils were provided with board and keep, and were trained in various tasks that were useful for the daily operations of the Mission, as well as providing training for the pupils themselves. These included carpentry, joinery and general repairs.

This vocational training school, the very concept of Joseph Frey and before him the various German institutions, became renowned in later years, especially under the direction of the German Christian craftsman, Conrad Schick.

Relations with the French and Latins and the attack on Dr Macgowan
Ever since Britain opened her Consulate in 1838, and then dispatched the Protestant Bishop, France had become very wary of British involvement in

---

55 Ewald to LJS, 2 November 1843, in *JI* 1843, pp. 24-25.
56 Ewald, ibid, p. 190.
57 Ewald, ibid, pp. 212-213.

Jerusalem. The French therefore, in 1843, also established a Consulate in Jerusalem. And why not – for it was very clear from a geo-political perspective that Britain opened her Consulate in the first place in order to observe French (and Russian) activities in the region. The new French Consul, Gabriel de Lantivy, arrived in Jerusalem on 16 July 1843.[58]

Shortly after the French opened their Consulate Dr. Macgowan was accosted by Turkish soldiers in the market and very badly mistreated. Thankfully there were some Jewish people in the crowd who recognized Macgowan and who began to struggle with the soldiers trying to extricate Macgowan. 'I shall never forget' wrote Macgowan 'the courageous assistance they afforded me on that occasion, to which, in all probability, my preservation, humanly speaking, is owing.'[59] The Pasha took this matter very seriously and had the Turkish soldiers apprehended, and they were to be punished by flogging.

At that very time the French were in the process of hoisting their flag from the newly established consulate building. This act greatly provoked the local Muslims, and an infuriated mob then surrounded the consulate, forcing the French to abandon the raising of the flag.[60]

In the eyes of many of the Moslems there was no difference between the French and the British – they were all foreigners, *Franks*. Bishop Alexander's house was next door to the Consulate, and the enraged Muslim mob was on the point of seizing the two-year old Benny as hostage, he being the only available male. Fortunately the Bishop and Consul Young arrived on the scene in time and were able to appease the rioters, and 'Benny, all unconscious of his enormous importance, was left in peace.'[61] This was one occasion when Bishop and Consul did act together!

As a result of the impassioned state of the Muslim populace the Pasha requested that the anticipated flogging of the two Turkish, (Muslim) soldiers, should take place in Beirut and not in Jerusalem. Young wisely consented and Macgowan for his part was satisfied that justice had been carried out.

The French flag raising and Macgowan affairs brought to the surface simmering Muslim feelings and prejudices against the foreigners – *Franks*. The French flag incident also revealed the depth of French feelings of superiority and rivalry. Rose connected this French attitude with the establishment of the Anglo-Prussian presence, stating 'there can be but little doubt that the religious feeling of the Catholic States has been thereby alarmed.'[62] There is little doubt but that by performing this action the French Consul, 'sought to emphasize his country's preferred status as opposed to that of the other powers.'[63]

58 See Parfitt, T. *The Jews in Palestine 1800-1882*. (Woodbridge, Suffolk, 1987), p. 135.
59 Macgowan to LJS London, 29 July 1843, in *JI*, 1843, pp. 349-50.
60 Young to Rose, 24 July 1843, FO 78/540, No 28.
61 Corey, ibid, p. 73.
62 Rose to Aberdeen, 27 August 1843, FO 78/537, No 40.
63 Eliav, M. *Britain and the Holy Land 1838-1914*, (Jerusalem, 1997), p. 136.

The French Consul immediately reported to the French Ambassador at Constantinople about his loss of honour in this incident. Despite the fact that only a few years before the French had openly supported the Egyptians against the Turks, the French held a strong position in the Sublime Porte. Young received a call from de Lantivy on 29 September, and was informed by the French Consul that Rachid Pasha and five effendis had been banished from Jerusalem 'in consequence of his representations to the French Ambassador at Constantinople on the subject of the French Flag.'[64]

Both of these incidents reveal just how much the traditional *status* quo of Jerusalem was now being seriously challenged.

Ministry Events

The difficulties which many Jewish followers or inquirers underwent became apparent to Rabbi Abraham, one of the three rabbis. He returned to his wife, who, unfortunately then asked for a bill of divorce. According to the law, the party asking for the divorce is not entitled to the dowry. Rabbi Abraham reluctantly gave the bill of divorce— and then his wife presented him with her bill of dowry, and the rabbis sided with her and against her poor husband. 'All these things are done' Ewald stated 'to prevent others from coming in contact with us.'[65]

The opposition towards contact with the British Mission grew. Sir Moses Montefiore from London became so concerned that he gave an order to Rabbi Israel the printer to reprint the anti-Christian book *Chizuk Emunah*.[66] This book, 'Strengthening of Faith' was a polemic against the Christian message originally written by Rabbi Isaac of Troki.

Such negative factors were always balanced by positive ones. Mr. Whitmarsh was ordained on 20 August, and then on Wednesday 23 August following the early morning Hebrew service, Alexander confirmed Michael Weinkauf, who came up from Egypt for this important occasion.[67]

Shortly afterwards, on 24 September, Alexander baptized another Jewish person, or as the baptismal book states, 'an Adult Israelite' - Christian Willhelm Hanauer at the afternoon German service. 'Thus another son of Abraham' wrote Ewald 'has been added to our community on Mount Zion.'[68]

Rivalry with the Scottish Mission and a station at Safed

In 1839 the Presbyterian Church of Scotland dispatched a delegation to Palestine, headed by Robert McCheyne and Andrew Bonar. Their Report indicated that the area of Judea was occupied by the LJS, but that the Galilee

---

64 Young to Aberdeen, 2 October 1843, FO 78/540, No 41.
65 Ewald, ibid, p. 197.
66 Ewald, ibid, pp. 208-09.
67 Letter from Nicolayson, in *JI*, 1844, p. 377.
68 Ewald, ibid, p. 213. Hanauer later worked for the LJS while his son James Edward became one of the LJS's stalwarts.

was still an open field.

The Scottish Committee accordingly approached Palmerston in October 1840 to seek his approval for their plan to establish a missionary station in the Galilee, especially at Safed. But it took time for Palmerston to receive information back from his consular representatives in the region. In the meantime the Jerusalem Bishopric was established and Alexander was informed that the entire country was part of his diocese. Nevertheless one of the Scottish missionaries was sent to Palestine. Rose was instructed by Aberdeen to protect the Scottish missionary as best he could.[69] Soon afterwards Alexander was commissioned by the LJS to open a missionary station in Safed.

Consul-General Rose was quite aware of the dangers of a missionary presence in Safed, and recommended that such a settlement was 'attended with risk.' Consul Young in Jerusalem gave similar advice to Bishop Alexander. It seems though that neither Alexander nor the Scots were willing to listen to reason, and as a result a race began for establishing a permanent mission presence in Safed. During Alexander's visit to Beirut, Rose asked him 'to check a spirit of intolerance amongst some of his companions' towards the Scottish missionaries. Rose informed Aberdeen that such rivalry between the Protestant missions was no better than their accusations against the strife between the ancient churches.[70]

Meanwhile the two Hebrew Christians, P.H Sternschuss and A.I Behrens, who had been commissioned by the LJS for service in Safed, arrived in Jerusalem in March 1843. Alexander approached Young for these two, and two other newly arrived missionaries, to receive British consular protection. Young refused, stating that Sternschuss, an Austrian, had no passport, while Behrens had a passport from the Hanoverian Consulate in London.

Young stated that he could offer protection while they remained in Jerusalem, but he could not provide protection for them if they went to Safed, and informed Alexander 'of the difficulties of them establishing missionary stations in such remote places.' But, Young concluded, 'They seemed determined to proceed.' Young seemed to have a mature grasp on the issues at hand, and added:

> ... Their zeal on the present occasion is roused from the fact that the Scotch Presbyterian Church is about to establish a Mission to the Jews in Palestine, and that Saffat is one of the stations they have decided upon for the residence of one of their missionaries, who is already arrived in Beirut.
>
> The London Society is desirous of occupying the ground ... before the Scotch missionaries can enter the field ...[71]

---

69 Aberdeen to Rose 5 December 1842, FO 78/483.
70 Rose to Aberdeen, 15 February 1843 and 29 March 1843, FO 78/535.
71 Young to Aberdeen, 31 March 1843, FO 78/540, No 21. The Scottish endeavour failed and only many years later did they attempt again, at Tiberias (and later at Safed).

Sternschuss and Behrens, accompanied by Nicolayson, then travelled to Safed. On 16 June 1843, after having received certain Christian and even some Muslim visitors, Nicolayson, Behrens and Sternschuss 'commenced the regular course of daily Hebrew service, which the Bishop had directed the brethren to keep up among themselves … The next day, being first Sunday after Trinity, we had the full service in Hebrew.'[72]

The Jewish community then closed ranks against them – ostracizing any of their own people who had contact with these Hebrew Christian *apostates*, and even with-holding *haluka* funds.[73] Sternschuss wrote, 'The Jews here are complete slaves to the persons who have the management of the rent for distribution; and if anyone displeases them in the least, he is immediately threatened with the loss of the weekly and monthly charity-money.'[74]

The pressure continued to mount, and was also felt by the owner of the house they had rented. Alexander subsequently wrote a letter to Behrens and Sternschuss, 'encouraging them to persevere in it, unless the local Authorities should take upon themselves the responsibility of positively ordering them to quit the place.' Alexander also wrote to Rose and the Prussian Consul-General Von Wildenbruch asking for their assistance in this matter.[75] The two Consuls-General seemingly declined to get overly involved, and ultimately the LJS workers were forced to vacate Safed for a season.

Nicolayson to Constantinople

On 1 November 1843 Nicolayson left Jerusalem for Constantinople to present information to the British Ambassador relating to, Alexander wrote, 'a firman for our Church.'[76] Some time later Young communicated to Aberdeen, 'I learn indirectly that one of his objects is to obtain permission to purchase, if not my present dwelling, such property as will annex it to the Society's premises and thereby give to the whole the appearance of being part and parcel of the Consular Residence.'[77]

Young also stated that Nicolayson had failed to consult him of the trip.[78] In fact the initiative did not actually come from Alexander and Nicolayson, but from London. The LJS Committee, frustrated by the lack of action concerning the Church building, had requested the direct assistance of Bunsen.[79] Bunsen had stated that Nicolayson's presence in Constantinople to assist Canning was imperative. In addition the Prussian Ambassador Count Konigsmark, and his

---

72 Nicolayson to CMJ London, 28 June 1843, in *JI*, 1843, pp. 319-322.
73 Funds distributed to the Jewish residents – provided they remained under the authority of the rabbis.
74 P.H. Sternschuss to LJS London, [no date] in *JI*, 1843, p. 388.
75 LJS Jerusalem Local Committee, 46th Meeting 5 July 1843, Minute 174, Minute Book 1842-1867.
76 Alexander to Sir Robert Inglis, 21 December 1843, pp. 187-9. Lambeth Archives.
77 Young to Aberdeen, 2 January 1844, FO 78/581, p. 17. Also
78 Young to Aberdeen, 2 January 1844, FO 78/581, p. 17.
79 *Letters London to Nicolayson, 1843-1856*, No 46, 15 December 1844, Schick Library.

successor M. Le Coq, were both instructed by Berlin to support Canning in this quest.[80]

Although Nicolayson was instructed to accept Prussian support for this initiative, yet, Ayerst the secretary of the LJS wrote, 'you will do as far as may be to attend to <u>British</u> interests in arranging with the authorities. The more the <u>English</u> form and appearance our church and establishment & arrangements can wear the better.'[81]

A *Memorandum,* from Bunsen and LJS, was sent to Nicolayson at Constantinople, requiring him to urge Ambassador Canning 'to obtain the Firman' and to assist him in refuting the 'allegations contained in the hostile petition got up at Jerusalem & sent up to Constantinople.' The two allegations sent to Constantinople in a petition from the Muslim and Turkish authorities claimed a) that the purchase of the LJS property was illegal and invalid, and b) that there was no precedent for giving a *Firman* to build a new Church where there had not been an old one previously.[82] The Muslim leaders of Jerusalem were determined to halt construction of the Hebrew-Protestant Church.

As Nicolayson had purchased the property in 1838 he was the best able to answer any queries and accusations. Concerning the second accusation, the argument intended to be presented by the LJS, was that there had been a church on that property, albeit a Jacobite one. They were unsure, though, if this argument would succeed.

Realizing that the chances of being granted permission to build a church in its own right was very negligible, a new plan began to crystallize in late 1843. This was the idea to connect the proposed Church to Consul Young's residence, whereby the Church would merely be the Consul's chapel.[83]

In accordance with this new idea, Ayerst informed Nicolayson that Aberdeen's proposal, which had been adopted by the Prussians, was for 'building a Church for the Consul, or for the Consuls, of Gt. Brit & Prussia' and that the Church would not be an 'ostentatious building and will not have a prominent object' and would 'be contained within a square formed of dwellings - & school houses, enclosing the Church from all sides.'[84]

There was still uncertainty that the Turks would accept this proposal for a Consular chapel. The Prussians were actually prepared to fund the building of a house for their Consul, while the British Government was not prepared to do the same for their Consul. Ayerst stated though, that from the LJS and British

---

80 Ayerst to Nicolayson, 15 December 1843, in *Letters London to Nicolayson, 1843-1856,* No 46. Schick Library.
81 Ayerst to Nicolayson, in *Letters to Nicolayson 1843-1856,* No 46, 15 December 1843, Schick Library.
82 Memo to Nicolayson, in letter from Ayerst to Nicolayson, 15 December 1843, No 46 in *Letters London to Nicolayson.,* Schick Library.
83 Young to Aberdeen, 30 May 1844, FO 78/581, No 12.
84 Ayerst to Nicolayson, 15 December 1843, in *Letters London to Nicolayson 1843-1856,* No 46, Schick Library.

perspective, 'it may also seem desirable that the house of the Prussian Consul should <u>not form part of that square</u> but <u>rather be built behind the</u> Church near the Bishop's house or the Hospices.'

'The most desirable', Ayerst added, would be that the Consular residence 'will be near the Church.' He then concluded 'that a room or two in one of the houses forming the square be appointed for the Office (not residence) of the Consular Agents, to demonstrate the official nature of the Church in the eyes of the Turks.'[85] As noble and helpful a gesture as the Prussian offer was, it was potentially harmful to purely LJS and British interests. If the Prussians actually funded the building of a Consulate on LJS property, it could seriously complicate ownership issues later on.

While Nicolayson and Canning were trying to grasp these instructions, confusion was added when Ayerst wrote again soon afterwards, relaying the decisions of the LJS General Committee meeting on 26 December 1843, whereby they stated that it would be preferable to obtain permission for the Church as a Mission Church rather than as a Consular Church, and concluded, that if possible, 'let it be connected with the Bishop's residence.'[86]

Despite the high profile nature of the matter, Rose was not happy that Nicolayson had journeyed to Constantinople without having informed Young, violating an agreement they had previously made, and was also not pleased with Alexander, the head of the work in Jerusalem, who sanctioned this journey.[87]

Ending the year on a Positive Note

Despite the disappointment revolving around the Church, Alexander's final correspondence for the year was upbeat. On 29 December 1843 he wrote to Sir Robert Steele of what had just happened on Christmas Day:

> The same day, interesting everywhere to Christians, but particularly so in Jerusalem, was also marked by six Israelites being joined to our Church by Baptism[88], and by our having met for the first time in a new place of worship[89] which we have been obliged to fit up, as our former Church (an upper chamber) gave way after the late rains and is no longer safe for meeting in it. Our present one is much larger and more commodious, and if the Sultan should still persist in not granting a firman for the building of a new church, I shall be gratified if we are only allowed to go on as we are ... Individuals and families break through the shackles of rabbinism, and join themselves to our Church, and it is a really strikingly interesting fact that

---

85 Ayerst to Nicolayson, 15 December 1843, in *Letters London to Nicolayson, 1843-1856, No 46,* Schick Library.
86 Ayerst to Nicolayson, 4 January 1844, in *letters London to Nicolayson,* No 47, Schick Library. .
87 Rose to Aberdeen, 26 December 1843, FO 78/537, No 77.
88 Dr. Anton and Mrs. Marie Kiel and their daughter, Sophia; Mr. Max Ungar; Mr. Judah Levi and Miss Christina Ducat. In all some fifteen Jewish people had been baptized during the year.
89 The present day Alexander lounge at Christ Church Centre.

a very decent respectable Congregation of Protestant Christians now meet for divine worship on Mount Zion, composed chiefly of Christian Israelites. On Xmas Day we had 33 Communicants. This is surely a sign in addition to many others, that the 'set time is come.' May we all be found amongst God's servants, who take pleasure in the stones of Zion and favours the dust thereof.[90]

---

[90] Alexander to Sir Robert Steele, 29 December 1843, St. Anthony's and Bishop Alexander to CMJ London, 3 January 1844. in *JI,* 1844, p. 77. This building is the present ground floor of Alexander Building.

Chapter 29

Wolff returns to Bokhara

Events in Bokhara

While Alexander was ministering in Jerusalem and Joseph Frey in New York, Joseph Wolff was enjoying the sedentary life of a parish priest in Yorkshire. However, events in the East were soon to change that lifestyle.

The issue of the Eastern Question, which was instrumental in Alexander going to Jerusalem as the first Protestant bishop there, enveloped a larger region than just the Eastern Mediterranean. Britain was not only concerned about French and Russian designs upon the Eastern Mediterranean region, but she was equally concerned about Russian designs in that broader region to the north of India. Britain feared a Russian move south towards India. In the area to the north of India the Eastern Question was colloquially called 'the Great Game.'

Central in this 'Great Game' were the regions of Persia, Afghanistan and Bokhara. In the late 1830's the British felt that one of their best options to thwart any potential Russian move south, would be to establish geo-political relationships with the political entities between Russia and India. One of these was the Khanate of Bokhara.

In 1838 Colonel Charles Stoddart was sent to this region by the East India Company to inform the local Amirs (rulers and kings) that if Russia began to cause them trouble, they could call upon both Britain and the East India Company (which were often synonymous). The decision to send Stoddart, though, was an East India Company one, and not one from the British Government, so Stoddart had no official letter from Queen Victoria or any official notification.

When Stoddart came to Bokhara he seemingly behaved without proper respect towards the Amir, Nasrallah Khan, who was both a despotic ruler and a fanatical Muslim. Nasrallah Khan had Stoddart summarily imprisoned in a disgraceful dungeon. He barely survived this ordeal, and could only be released if he accepted Islam, which he did accordingly.[1] Stoddart was then placed under house arrest until due notification came from the Queen[2] - which never came.

Then in December 1840 Captain Arthur Conolly was sent to Bokhara to obtain his release from prison. Through Conolly's strong faith in Jesus, Stoddart renounced Islam and became a follower of Jesus. This decision put a seal upon

---

1 Wolff, *Travels*, p. 555.
2 Hopkins, ibid, p. 279.

his, and Conolly's lives and they were duly arrested in December 1841.[3] Their arrest though was not without a geo-political context.

Fearing a Russian move south a British force had invaded Afghanistan in 1839, in what became known as the First Afghan War. But in 1841 the Afghans rebelled against British control, and killed the British negotiating team in Kabul in December 1841. British forces were later defeated, and British prestige in the region deteriorated. Stoddart and Conolly were accused at this point of being British spies.

While in prison Conolly snuck out a note to his brother John in India, in which he stated among other things, 'Stoddart and I will comfort each other in every way till we die, when may our brotherhood be renewed in heaven through Jesus Christ our Saviour. Send this assurance to all our friends and do you, my dear John, stand on this faith. It is the only thing that can enable a man to bear up against the trials of this life and lead him to the noblest state of existence in the next. Farewell! Farewell!'[4]

The Amir of Bokhara, Nasrallah Khan then had both men publicly executed on 17 June 1842. No news of this act, however, was known outside of Bokhara. Despite a rumour, no one in Britain knew for certain whether they were alive or dead.

Wolff's next challenge

After five years of parish work Joseph Wolff in 1843 accepted a summer position as chaplain at Bruges in Belgium. The family left Yorkshire and went first to London to stay for a month with Sir Thomas Baring and then to Albury Park in Surrey the home of Henry Drummond.[5]

For some time now Wolff was concerned about the fate of his friend Conolly with whom he had enjoyed good fellowship in Cawnpore in 1833. In July 1843, without Georgiana's knowledge, he submitted an article to the newspapers aimed at British military officers, requesting financial assistance for him to make a journey to Bokhara with one companion in order to secure the release of the two imprisoned British officers.

Captain John Grover came to the fore, and met with Wolff at Albury Park. Together they worked out a basic plan. Then Joseph told Georgiana, who although initially opposed, then finally gave her consent. Grover then put together a support committee comprised of Sir Jeremiah Bryant, James Buckingham and Sir Edward Codrington, the Admiral of the British fleet at Navarino in 1827.[6]

Wolff also wrote to Lord Aberdeen the Secretary of State to offer his services

---

3 Hopkins, ibid, p. 280.
4 Hopkins, ibid, p. 280.
5 Wolff, *Travels*, p. 525.
6 Hopkins, ibid, p. 285.

to go to Bokhara in the capacity of a British citizen. Aberdeen replied that the government believed that Conolly and Stoddart were both dead, and they could not countenance Wolff going as he would probably suffer the same fate, but that if he did go the government would offer him whatever assistance they could. Wolff asked for and received official letters of recommendation to various leaders of the East, including to the Sultan of Turkey and the Shah of Persia.[7]

Wolff and his family then spent the summer on chaplaincy duties in the Anglican church in Bruges in Brussels, and then when they returned in October, Wolff set about preparing for his journey.

The journey

Wolff left Britain on 13 October 1843, headed for Constantinople, via Gibraltar, Malta (where he was happy to see again his friend Hookham Frere) and then Athens. In Athens he met the British Minister to Greece, Admiral Sir Edmund Lyons, who introduced him to the King and Queen of Greece.[8]

Wolff was enjoying the company so much in Athens that his ship, the *Iberia* left for Constantinople without him. Lyons and Captain James Stirling[9] came to the rescue, placing Wolff upon the *HMS Indus* which chased after the *Iberia,* and Wolff was ultimately reunited with the ship and his luggage. It was not for any citizen that Her Majesty's Navy would accord such favour![10]

The Turkish capital was reached in early November, and he very quickly made contact with Sir Stratford Canning the British Ambassador. At his invitation Wolff preached in the chapel at the British Embassy, to which many of the ambassadors attended. Later the Russian ambassador, Count Titow, informed Wolff that Czar Nicholas had informed their diplomats in Persia to give him all the help he required.

The British Ambassador's request to the Sultan for a letter was successful, and Wolff met with the Sultan's three leading advisors. The Foreign Secretary, Reis Effendi asked Wolff about his motive for making such a dangerous trip, to which Wolff replied:

> … being a disciple of Jesus, who laid down His life for mankind, he must also be ready to risk his life for the benefit of his fellow-creatures; and this was his motive for which he undertook that journey.[11]

After similar meetings with the other Turkish leaders, and despite their misgivings

---

7 Wolff, *Travels,* p. 525.
8 Wolff, *Travels,* p. 528.
9 Captain Sir James Stirling (1791-1865) formerly Governor of the Swan River Colony (Western Australia).
10 Wolff, *Travels,* p. 529.
11 Wolff, *Travels,* pp. 530-31.

about Wolff's safety, the Sultan Abdul Mejed personally wrote numerous letters to Islamic leaders, including to the King of Bokhara, Amir Nasrallah Khan.[12] All of these letters were then sewn into Wolff's coat by Lady Canning.

On 24 November 1843 Wolff caught a ship to Trebizond on the coast of the Black Sea, from where he began the journey overland to Erzerum on 1 December 1843. At this eastern city he preached to a small congregation on Christmas Day. While in Erzerum he also baptized a Jewish man.[13]

Wolff then set out through the snow for Khoy where he stayed with the Persian governor, and then proceeded on to Tabriz which was reached on 12 January 1844. From here he moved on to Teheran and arrived in the Persian capital on 3 February. The British envoy, Lieutenant Colonel Shiel[14] met Wolff, and informed him there were conflicting reports about the fate of Conolly and Stoddart, but that he himself felt they were both dead. Wolff at that point also sensed deeply that they were no longer alive, but he was resolved to continue with his journey nevertheless.[15]

While in Tehran Wolff preached in the chapel in the British Embassy, a service to which many visitors also participated. His mission was also taken seriously by other diplomatic envoys, and the Russian ambassador also gave him letters to the King of Bokhara. Wolff insisted though on meeting the Persian king, Shah Mohammed Mirza, which was arranged. The Shah reminisced with Wolff, said he admired Wolff's philanthropy, and after an hour provided him with a letter to the King of Bokhara.[16]

Wolff admitted to Colonel Shiel that he was concerned about travelling through Khorassan, as that was where he was so brutishly treated on his previous trip.[17] Nevertheless he left Tehran on 14 February 1844 and aimed towards Meshed (Mashhad) in north-east Persia, which was reached on 12 March 1844. Thereafter he was basically outside any form of British influence. It was here that he composed a letter to be sent ahead to the Amir of Bokhara.[18] His apprehensions about Khorassan though were unfounded, as now the name of a Briton was well-known there, thanks much to the recent war in Afghanistan, where men such as General Sir Charles Napier distinguished themselves.[19] He was very well treated there.

The oasis of Mowr was reached on 12 April whereupon he was warned by many, including the local ruler and the Jewish people, not to proceed on to Bokhara. They all informed Wolff that the two British prisoners had been

12 Wolff, *Travels*, p. 530.
13 Wolff, *Travels*, p. 539.
14 Lieut-Col Justin Shiel (1803-1871). Head of Mission and Envoy to Persia 1839-1854.
15 Wolff, *Travels*, p. 548.
16 Wolff, *Travels*, p. 549.
17 Wolff, *Travels*, p. 549.
18 Wolff, *Travels*, p. 558.
19 Wolff, *Travels*, p. 552.

executed, and that the Ameer (Amir) was a tyrant.[20] Wolff had no illusions of what awaited him. He knew that Amir Nasrallah was one of the most despotic rulers in the world, and that there was a good chance that he himself would be executed. He accordingly sent Georgiana and Henry a farewell letter.

After crossing the Oxus River and spending the night only some fifty kilometres from Bokhara, Wolff woke the next morning to find most of his crew had deserted him with the camels. He had no choice but to continue on foot. He hadn't gone too far when he was welcomed by three men on horseback – emissaries of the Amir Nasrallah.[21] Wolff entered Bokhara on 27 April 1844.

Imprisoned in Bokhara

Upon entry into the city Wolff was welcomed by the people, and the Amir's Master of Ceremonies, who asked him if he would 'submit to the etiquette observed at the court.' Wolff said that he would – in contrast to Stoddart.[22] The following day he was ushered into the King of Bokhara's palace, where, following the court formularies the Amir informed Wolff that the two British officers were dead.[23] Wolff was then quizzed as to the intent of his trip and if he came with the authority of the British Government; and why he wore the priests clothing that he did.

Thereafter Wolff was placed under house arrest, which provided the Amir time to decide Wolff's fate. Nasrallah Khan realized that if he also killed Wolff then he could incur the displeasure of Britain, and even Russia. Besides, Wolff also carried with him letters from both the Sultan and Shah.

Wolff had numerous interviews with the Amir, and also with some of his advisors, especially Abdul Samut Khan, who gave details of how Conolly and Stoddart died.[24] The Amir asked Wolff to write to Glover and to inform him of the deaths, and informed Wolff that he was allowed to leave on 9 May. Alas this did not happen, as the Amir changed his mind, something which occurred regularly during the following three months.[25]

It was during this time that Wolff attempted to escape, but was caught and brought before Abdul Samut Khan. At that point Wolff told Abdul Samut that he now understood that he was the one primarily responsible for the execution of Stoddart and Conolly. Abdul Samut Khan admitted that this was true, and

---

20 Wolff, *Travels*, p. 554.
21 Wolff, *Travels*, p. 559.
22 Wolff, *Travels*, p. 559. For this narrative I have relied primarily upon Wolff's own account as told in *Travels*, but where possible have alluded to Hopkins book for confirmation, as Hopkins also drew upon other of Wolff's accounts. There does appear to be some discrepancy between Wolff's chronology of some of the events of his imprisonment from Hopkins, but I do not think any such discrepancy is a hindrance to the overall narrative.
23 Wolff, *Travels*, p. 561.
24 Wolff, *Travels*, p. 568.
25 Hopkins, ibid, p. 308.

then added, "Yes, I am; I know how to handle you Englishmen; and I will pay you for insulting me at Peshawur."[26] The incident at Peshawar occurred during his long trip in 1832, in which Wolff had been warned about Abdul Samut. Wolff at this stage felt all hope was lost.

That evening when Wolff was still at Abdul Samut's house, he was tempted in the fashion of Joseph of old in Egypt, but Wolff saw immediately that it was a trap set to further the reason to have him executed. He sent the unveiled lady packing![27]

Shortly afterwards he was brought a letter by Abdul Samut's servants, purporting to be from Abdul Samut to one of his officers declaring that it was the King's intention to execute Wolff.[28] Thereafter Joseph virtually lost all hope and wrote a final letter to Georgiana and young Henry.[29]

During a period of some three months' incarceration Wolff's future fate was left suspended. On numerous occasions the chief chamberlain of the Amir would come and ask Wolff an assortment of questions. The Amir was then going on a military excursion to Khokand and Tashkand (Tashkent) in June 1844, but before departing some Jewish men asked for permission to visit with Wolff. The Amir gave permission, but stipulated that all conversations were not allowed in Hebrew, but only in Persian so that the attendants could understand.[30]

This order perturbed Wolff, as he wanted to know from the Jewish people more details about the fate of Stoddart and Conolly. To get around this stipulation he devised a way of communicating with the Jewish visitors, whereby he 'contrived a method of conversing with the Jews in Hebrew, in the presence of the Osbecks, without their knowing that he did converse in Hebrew …'[31] Wolff read the Scriptures in Hebrew but also conversed with his listeners at the same time. The Osbeck attendants thought they were merely reading the Bible, but they were actually carrying on a conversation in Hebrew! In this way he discovered the full details concerning the tragic end to the lives of Stoddart and Conolly.

While the Amir was away Wolff wrote a letter to all the monarchs of Europe.[32] Later the King received a letter from Lord Ellenborough, about Wolff, which infuriated him. He sent word that Wolff was to die. All now seemed lost for Wolff, and he wrote to Georgiana.

When the King returned from his campaign he sent a messenger who asked Wolff if he would become a Muslim. Wolff replied, "Tell the King, NEVER,

---

26 Wolff, *Travels*, p. 573.
27 Hopkins, ibid, p. 309.
28 Hopkins, ibid, p. 309.
29 Hopkins, ibid, p. 310.
30 Wolff, *Travels*, p. 574.
31 Wolff, *Travels*, p. 574.
32 Wolff, *Travels*, p. 577.

NEVER, NEVER."[33] A few hours later the executioner who had put Stoddart and Conolly to death came, and said to Wolff, "Joseph Wolff, to thee it shall happen as it did to Stoddart and Conolly …" Wolff at this stage prepared himself for death, and wrote in his Bible, "MY DEAREST GEORGIANA, - I have loved you unto death. Your affectionate husband J. Wolff, BOKHARA 1844."[34]

Wolff's last minute reprieve
When all hope of survival seemed lost for Wolff, help arrived in the person of the Persian ambassador, Abbas Kouli Khan.[35] Abbas carried with him a letter from the Persian Shah in which he stated that Persia and Britain had a good relationship which he did not want affected, and that if anything happened to Wolff he would be greatly upset.[36] In addition, he had been informed that Wolff had smuggled out a letter to the monarchs of Europe.

Not wanting to become the scorn of the great powers of Europe, Nasrallah Khan suddenly changed his disposition towards Wolff, and informed the Persian ambassador, "Well, I make a present to you of Joseph Wolff; he may go with you."[37]

On 3 August 1844 after one hundred days in suspense, Wolff left Bokhara accompanied by the Persian ambassador and a large caravan of camels. Before they left they were given a list of ten assassins in the caravan sent by the Amir to murder Wolff en-route. Once they crossed the border out of Bokhara Wolff exposed the would-be assassins.[38]

They rested up at Meshed, the capital of Khorassan, and then went onto Teheran where he was feted by the Shah of Persia. The return journey then took him back to Tabriz, by which time he was suffering from an attack of severe illness, and as they traversed the mountains of Armenia he again felt that his life could end at any time. But again he survived and continued the journey to Erzerum. By the time Wolff arrived at Erzerum he was lice infested, and for five days the British Consul, Colonel Williams tended and nursed him back to health, de-lousing him in the process.[39]

Then recovered and re-clothes, he continued onto to Trebizond, where he arrived on 9 February 1845, whereupon ten days later he boarded a steamship bound for Constantinople. Upon arrival he was again hosted by his close friend Ambassador Sir Stratford Canning.

Wolff arrived back in Southampton on 11 April 1845 where he was met by

33 Wolff, *Travels*, p. 578.
34 Wolff, *Travels*, p, 578.
35 Wolff, *Travels*, p. 578.
36 Hopkins, ibid, p. 310.
37 Wolff, *Travels*, pp. 578-79.
38 Wolff, *Travels*, p. 586.
39 Hopkins, ibid, p. 318.

Georgiana and young Henry. Back in London the first thing that Wolff did was to go to Holy Trinity Church and offer thanks to God for his miraculous escape from near certain death. Grover then organized a large meeting at Exeter Hall where he gave an account of his journey.[40]

Now without work and without income, Wolff set about writing out his memoirs, and by June 1845 his *Narrative of a Mission to Bokhara* had its first printing.

Mission accomplished?

Many would have asked the question if this second trip to Bokhara was successful, even justified. Wolff placed his own life at risk, while at the same time he brought much pressure on numerous other people, and much anguish to his wife and young son.

Was this trip really worth it? Although Wolff did minister to people the entire route, to the Jew, the Gentile and the Church, yet the purpose of this trip was not evangelistic in purpose.

If the British Government had no intention of being involved to ascertain the fate of two of its citizens, then it is hard to imagine any ordinary person would be willing to carry out such a dangerous task. Yet Joseph Wolff did.

The jury would probably be split in its verdict over whether it was all worth it. Yet if there is but one lesson that could be learnt from this episode it is the attitude of Joseph Wolff as expressed in his statement to the Sultan of Turkey's advisor:

"… being a disciple of Jesus, who laid down His life for mankind, he must also be ready to risk his life for the benefit of his fellow-creatures; and this was his motive for which he undertook that journey."[41]

Joseph Wolff left a legacy and a challenge to those who came after him, to both the Jewish and Gentile follower of Jesus, of what being a disciple of Jesus was all about.

---

40 Hopkins, ibid, p. 320.
41 Wolff, *Travels*, pp. 530-31.

CHAPTER 30

CONSOLIDATION IN JERUSALEM

Diplomatic and ecclesiastical opposition

Alexander wrote in his second anniversary letter that Jerusalem of late 'has become almost universally the object of attention …' His very presence and activities strongly contributed to the reason why the other European Powers, as well as the Turks and local Muslims, were giving more attention to the affairs of Jerusalem.

His observation concerning Jerusalem's stature was confirmed by Consul Young in a communiqué to Aberdeen on 20 January 1844, in which he wrote about agents of the French and Russian Governments operating in Jerusalem[1]. He also stated to Ambassador Canning in January 1844, 'Jerusalem is now become a central point of interest to France and Russia because both Governments have adopted, according to their respective creeds, the Character of Protectors of the native Christians …'[2]

This observation concerning the opposition of France to the Protestant endeavour was also made by one of Britain's most seasoned politicians of the time, Sir George Rose, former British Ambassador at Berlin, and Member of Parliament since 1818. Rose observed within the context of the problems facing the work in Jerusalem:

> … we have had to meet there difficulties arising out of the subtleties of our adversaries, and the emissaries of the Church of Rome – who, I know, had concerted their plans in Paris, where the utmost alarm at our enterprise prevailed.[3]

Despite the opposition Alexander continued firm in his belief about the necessity of the Bishopric in Jerusalem. He stated that, 'I feel daily more convinced that the establishment of a Protestant Bishopric in Jerusalem is the work of God; and as such we cannot be surprised at the opposition experienced during the past year. No Divine work has ever prospered without opposition, it is the very nature of things …'[4]

Journey to the Galilee

In February, following the Bishop's recovery from ill-health, the Alexanders,

---

1 Young to Aberdeen, 20 January 1844, FO 78/581, No 2.
2 Young to Canning, 8 January 1844, FO 78/581, No 1.
3 Speech of Sir George Rose at LJS AGM, 1844, quoted in *JI*, 1844, p. 169.
4 *Second Annual Letter from the Anglican Bishop of Jerusalem*, in *JI*, 1843, p. 2.

accompanied by Macgowan and his son journeyed north. On the second night they pitched their tent between Ramle and Haifa and Mrs. Alexander wrote in her diary, 'I was truly thankful to see how much my dear husband seemed to enjoy his ride and evidently looked forward with pleasure to our proposed journey.'[5]

That night Dr. Macgowan and his son visited the Alexanders in their tent and they conversed on numerous subjects, especially 'on the future prospects of the Jewish Nation.' They obviously dealt quite thoroughly with the subject as Mrs. Alexander commented on 'The absurdity of persons saying there was not sufficient space for them to dwell.'[6]

Their tour took in Haifa and Acre before they moved on to Nazareth, of which Alexander wrote, 'The situation of Nazareth is most striking and affecting to the Christian.' The next stop on their whistle stop tour was Tiberias. Alexander seemed to enjoy his experience in this city and wrote positively of visiting the hot springs and the splendid baths erected by Ibrahim Pasha[7] and the tour of the city which included the five synagogues. Alexander afterwards concluded: 'This assuredly would be a most important missionary station for the London Society, independent of Safet...The sea at Tiberias with all its associations, was almost overwhelming to us.'[8]

While the Macgowans journeyed to Damascus, Alexander and the remainder of the party headed on to Safed. Mrs Alexander wrote of the strenuous six-hour journey, 'The ride was most romantic, we had the lake with us for a long time, passed a little village called Migdal. Only one hour from Tiberias about a dozen houses in it. A great deal of rice grown here.'[9]

The Alexanders arrived in Safed in the evening of 22 February, catching Sternschuss and Behrens by surprise. Alexander wrote: '… it is with pleasure that I state that I was much gratified with all I heard and saw. It is impossible to describe the wretchedness of the place generally, and of their house in particular; but the brethren seemed contented, and quietly pursuing their work.'[10]

Sternschuss and Behrens were eager to join the party on their onward journey, and Alexander consented. They returned then to Acre, where the following day Alexander administered the Holy Communion and read the morning and evening lessons. Following this Alexander and his colleagues visited the synagogue, where, Sternschuss wrote, 'we found children reading the Scriptures, and examined them in the Hebrew language.'[11]

5 Alexander, Mrs. D, *Diary of a Journey to Mount Carmel,* MSS 3396, p. 4, Alexander Papers, Lambeth.
6 Alexander, Mrs. D, *Diary of a Journey to Mount Carmel,* MSS 3396, p. 5, Alexander Papers, Lambeth.
7 The step-son of Mehmet Ali, pasha of Egypt, who was Governor-General of the province of Syria during the period of Egyptian occupation.
8 Letter Alexander, circa February 1844, *JI* 1844, p. 141.
9 Alexander, Mrs. D, *Diary of a Journey to Mount Carmel,* MSS 3396, ibid. p. 22.
10 Letter Alexander, circa February 1844, *JI* 1844, p. 141.
11 Letter Sternschuss, 7 March 1844, *JI,* 1844, p. 146.

The party left Acre on 28 February 1844 and, after visiting both Tyre and Sidon briefly, arrived in Beirut on 1 March. The Alexanders resided with Dr. Kerns, while the other brethren stayed with the recently appointed LJS worker Rev Henry Winbolt. During their sojourn here Alexander was re-acquainted with Colonel Rose, and preached in the neat little Mission-house on two successive Sundays. The Bishop's activities were so intense that on one occasion he fainted - another indication of his frail health.

One engagement he had was with Mr. Whiting, the representative of the American Board of Commissioners for Foreign Missions.

Relations towards the American Mission

Throughout the 1820's and 30's there was generally a positive working relationship between the LJS workers and the Americans. With the establishment of the Bishopric this relationship slowly deteriorated, and in 1843 the American Board seriously considered relinquishing their Jerusalem station. Then in 1844 Rufus Anderson representing the American Board visited the Mediterranean and executed this decision, and the Americans then relocated to Beirut.[12] V. Lipman in her book *Americans and the Holy Land* concluded:

> The change in the 1840's from the close collaboration and unity of feeling between British and American missionaries in the Holy Land clearly dates from the establishment of the Anglican Bishopric and the arrival of a different type of British clergyman, more concerned with the specific traditions of the Church of England. George Williams, for instance, thought it unfortunate that the first representative of the English Church in Jerusalem had been the Danish Lutheran John Nicolayson.[13]

Rev. George Williams may indeed have been the main architect of this changed relationship having once written about Nicolayson (and the Americans), 'It was not to be expected ... that he should faithfully represent the distinctive nature of the Anglican doctrine. It was moreover very natural ... that the Lutheran minister and Congregational missionaries should meet together on a common footing.'[14]

The very nature of Alexander's position would have engendered a feeling of priority to those coming from Britain and Germany and fully submitting to the Bishopric. Be that as it may, the move of the American Board out of Jerusalem to Beirut provided the Americans with a much better base for their operations.

The overly religious and ecclesiastical nature of Jerusalem better suited the episcopally based Anglicans. For all of its faults the British and Bishopric

---

12 Field, James, A. *America and the Mediterranean World 1776-1882*, (Princeton, 1969), p. 204.
13 Lipman, V.D. *Americans and the Holy Land: Through British Eyes,* (Jerusalem & London, 1989), p. 84. See also Cresson, Warden. *Key of David* (Philadelphia, 1852), p. 201.
14 Williams, G. *Holy City,* (1849), pp. 579-80.

ventures were more assured of 'success' and acceptance amongst the locals, who were familiar with the episcopal form of Church government, while they were not so familiar with the non-Episcopal form of the American Non-Conformists. In addition, although America was growing in stature, its prestige was not comparable to that of Britain.

For all intents and purposes therefore when a local Arab considered accepting the Protestant message and leaving the security of his or her own *millet* (community) they would more than likely gravitate to the Anglican-British camp rather than to the American Non-Conformist camp. Nevertheless there is no doubt that the American Board did considerable work during its years in Jerusalem.

Beirut offered the Americans more scope and potential – without the envious interference of the various ecclesiastical authorities in Jerusalem. In fact in time the Americans played a very important role in developing the educational life of Lebanon, and even of shaping a future important political movement – the Arab nationalist movement.

Challenges in Constantinople

Throughout January Nicolayson continued his efforts in Constantinople, aided by both the British and Prussian Ambassadors. Despite Canning's best efforts it was now obvious that the Turkish officials were trying to bureaucratically bury this matter. Nicolayson in Constantinople and Alexander in Jerusalem – waited patiently.

Then a major crisis erupted in Constantinople. Several Turkish subjects had been executed for religious reasons, one being a Mohammedan who confessed faith in Jesus. Ambassador Canning had remonstrated with the Turkish Government over this. Nicolayson then wrote that both the British and French Ambassadors had stated to the Porte that the Turks must 'pledge themselves to put a stop to all persecution on account of religion' or the ambassadors 'Governments must withdraw from all Alliances with them.' 'The Turks,' Nicolayson concluded, 'in general are in the greatest alarm & perplexity ...'[15]

Nicolayson then stated that there were reports there could be significant changes in the Turkish administration, and that news had arrived that the Austrian Government had made the same demands as the other countries. This really was a crisis for the Turks - the Christian European Powers had challenged their authority to act on matters of religion.

'You will easily conceive' wrote Nicolayson 'that while such a crisis is pending all matters of minor importance must be in abeyance.' Nicolayson did not believe that Turkey would do anything that would prejudice its relationship with the Christian European Powers 'upon whose support the continuance of the

---

15 Nicolayson to LJS London, No 87, February 1844. In *Letters from Jerusalem to London, 1841-1844*. Conrad Schick Library, Alexander College, Christ Church, Jerusalem.

Empire depends.'[16]

Meanwhile Nicolayson was able to report that the supply of the plan and drawings of the LJS property in Jerusalem had given Canning the distinct idea of the church being attached with the Consulate.[17] Aberdeen's assistant, James Bidwell then sent Young a message on 16 March 1844 instructing him to send a sketch of the plan of Young's present dwelling 'showing how or in what manner the Premises now belonging to the Society ... could be made to appear as part and parcel of the Consular Residence.'[18] Herein lay the germ of an idea – the Hebrew-Protestant Church would become part of the British Consulate building.[19]

In late March the Turks finally made a compromise offer for the building of the Church, but 'in a form that the Ambassadors could not accept ... and therefore demanded an audience with the Sultan himself.' The Sultan was obviously prepared to issue a written order to the local authorities in Jerusalem to permit the building to restart.[20] However this was insufficient, as it was not a *Firman*, and therefore was not binding. Canning and the Prussian ambassador de Loq then pressed forth their requests again.[21]

Nicolayson finally concluded that there were really only two options left, 1) to leave the matter in the hand of the Ambassadors to secure a *Firman* or 2) to make do with a written order (not an *Imperial Firman* - decree) to the local authorities in Jerusalem to permit the building of the church to re-commence.[22] Frustrated and disappointed, Nicolayson left Constantinople and returned to Jerusalem on 7 June 1844.

The last official correspondence relating to this issue was contained in a dispatch sent by Canning to Aberdeen on 3 May in which 'it appeared that the consent of the Turkish Gov't to the resumption of the works would depend on the report which the Pasha of Saida had been called upon to furnish with reference to the Buildings proposed to be erected at Jerusalem for the accommodation of the British and Prussian Consulates, among which the Chapel was to be included.'[23]

Meanwhile back in Jerusalem plans were being considered for building an official home for Bishop Alexander adjacent to the unfinished Church. Then Mr Alison, the Secretary of Legation at the British Embassy in Constantinople, arrived in late June, to see for himself the situation and report back to Canning, as well as report to Young what Canning was proposing. He gave an optimistic

16 Nicolayson to LJS London, No 87, February 1844. In *Letters from Jerusalem to London, 1841-1844*. Conrad Schick Library, Alexander College, Christ Church, Jerusalem.
17 Nicolayson to London, No 87, 26 February 1844. In *Letters from Jerusalem to London, 1841-1844*. Conrad Schick Library, Alexander College, Christ Church, Jerusalem.
18 Bidwell to Young, 16 March 1844, FO 78/581, No 2.
19 Young to Aberdeen, 30 May 1844, FO 78/581, No 12 .
20 See Nicolayson to London 26 April 1844, No 91. In *Letters from Jerusalem to London, 1841-1844*.
21 Nicolayson to London, No 90, 27 March 1844. In *Letters from Jerusalem to London, 1841-1844*.
22 Nicolayson to London 26 April 1844, No 91. In *Letters from Jerusalem to London, 1841-1844*.
23 Aberdeen to Canning, 20 March 1845, FO 78/592, [No 32].

report that upon his return to Constantinople, permission would be forthcoming.

In view of this news, the Jerusalem Local Committee requested the Committee in London to furnish a definite plan so that building could recommence once permission was granted.[24] The architect Mr Habershon was in London and presented fresh plans, which were accepted, although the General Committee recommended some minor modifications.[25]

Alexander was now expectant that one of the major objectives of his tenure, the construction of the Hebrew-Protestant Church, would soon be a reality.

Opening of Book Depot.
Shortly after returning from his long trip to the north Alexander had the pleasure of opening the Book Shop or Depot. This institution was located close to the Bishop's house, and was headed up initially by Rabbi Judah Levi [Lyons].

The Book Depot was opened to make available the Scriptures in Hebrew, Arabic, Greek, Italian, French, German, and Spanish. It also supplied numerous other materials including Alexander McCaul's *Old Paths,* as well as Bunyan's *Pilgrim's Progress* in Hebrew. The Book of Common Prayer in Hebrew, which Alexander had played a significant role in compiling, was also available.

The opening of this institution was of great importance for Jerusalem. It now permitted those Jewish people (and others) who were bold enough to enter, to quietly seek after the message the LJS workers were proclaiming. This in itself was a provocation to the rabbinical authorities, who soon afterwards were very vigilant in hindering and stopping would-be seekers from entering this institution.

Further additions to the Protestant-Hebrew Christian community
On Good Friday 1844 four of the Jewish disciples baptized on Christmas Day were confirmed. At the Easter Sunday service two days later there were forty people receiving Communion – twenty of whom were Jewish followers of Jesus. On that same day, Rabbi Judah Levi [henceforth Lyons] was baptized in the afternoon German service.[26]

These inspiring events were followed shortly after, on 6 May, with the confirmation of Rabbi Judah Levi Lyons, Max Ungar, and Christina Ducat, all of whom had been adequately prepared by Ewald.[27] Then the two intrepid workers from Safed, Sternschuss and Behrens came to Jerusalem and on 2 June were ordained into Anglican orders.

On 13 July Alexander baptized another Hebrew Christian, Moses Epstein at the Hebrew service. Epstein was a student at the House of Industry.[28] The

---

24 LJS Jerusalem 58th Meeting, 25 June 1844, Minute 213.LJS Local Committee 1842-1867.
25 LJS Jerusalem 63rd meeting, 30 July 1844, Minute 227. LJS Local Committee 1842-1867.
26 Ewald, ibid, p. 246
27 Ewald, ibid, p. 254.
28 Ewald, ibid, p. 257.

following day, 14 July, Murray Vicars and Henry Aaron Stern were both ordained by Alexander in preparation for further work in the mission field.

Shortly after Alexander sent C.W. Hanauer to Jaffa where he opened a small Bible Depot. This moved was followed in September 1844 when Vicars, Stern and Sternschuss left Jerusalem for Chaldea – to open a station in Baghdad. This must have been a site to behold, as they travelled via Damascus as part of a caravan of 450 camels!

Another of Alexander's charges had now been fulfilled – although the venture in Baghdad did not meet with initial success.

Further Jewish Reactions
The initiatives of the LJS were causing considerable reaction within the Jewish community as too were the initiatives of Montefiore. Ewald recorded in May:

> There has been a considerable commotion among the three Jewish communities here, viz., the Sephardim, Ashkenazim and Chasidim, on account of Sir Moses Montefiore's proposal to establish a school, manufactories, and a hospital in the Holy City. Most of the chief rabbies and leaders are decidedly opposed to that generous offer.
>
> On the 8th of May the leading members of the three congregations met together to consider these matters. A warm correspondence has been carried on between those who have most influence here, and those in Europe on that subject.[29]

In a circular the Rabbis sent to their brethren in Europe the following was stated: 'We, the seed of Israel, the holy nation, have nothing to do with foreign sciences, wisdoms, works, thoughts, and medicines, and such like, which would destroy our chief occupation.'[30]

The peace between the various congregations, in opposition to the modernizing proposals of Montefiore, was short lived, and Ewald wrote in July that the German congregations were prepared to listen to reason and were preparing a house to become some form of a hospital.[31]

Undoubtedly it was the exertions of Dr. Frankel that assisted with this undertaking. Frankel had written a letter to the major European Jewish newspaper *Allgemaine Zeitung des Judenthums*, which was printed on 4 March. Frankel stated:

> It is well-known to you that the Missionary Society strains every nerve to make proselytes; they leave nothing undone. Thus they have erected a hospital in which none but Jews are to be admitted. No Jew, it is true will enter it, if he can help it: but what shall the poor, unfortunate, sick, and houseless do?

29 Ewald, ibid, p. 252.
30 Ewald, ibid, p. 257.
31 Ewald, ibid, p. 259.

Who, after all, can blame him for it? And what is the consequence? Alas! A very sad one. (During the time I have been here, ten Jews have been baptized. On the 25th instant, a father, mother, and daughter.) At any time a hospital would have administered relief to the sick and suffering; now it will likewise counteract the efforts of the Mission – an object which, in my opinion[32], every one of our brethren should, and will keep in view.'

Shortly afterwards Ewald, the faithful co-worker of Alexander since the very beginning, was forced to return to England. Since the untimely death of his wife, Ewald had not been able to successfully combine his domestic and work responsibilities. His departure was a severe blow to the fledgling Hebrew Christian-Protestant community.

Domestic

The one constant concern for the Alexander family was sickness. On 25 July Mrs. Alexander wrote to Rev John Coleman, 'Both the Bishop and myself have suffered during this month from fever of which we are but slowly recovering. The heat is intense ...'[33]

Towards the end of the year Alexander was again confronted with worrying health problems for his family. He informed Coleman that he postponed his anticipated trip to Egypt 'when two of my children were attacked with a dangerous fever.'[34]

Macgowan went even further and stated that Deborah and her younger sister, Annie, 'were both seized with feverish symptoms' and 'presented symptoms of high fever and delirium, and required the most active treatment.'[35]

Yet despite all these sicknesses, and particularly with Mrs. Alexander, at the end of the year they were able to rejoice together. The Bishop wrote to Rev. Coleman in December, 'In the midst of all, Mrs A was confined ... on the 18th (adding another daughter to our number) but a day or two after she was attacked with the fever which made us ... very anxious about her safety.[36] Thankfully Mrs. Alexander recovered from her fever and the family could rejoice at the arrival of young Emily Alexander.

Disturbed State of the Country

At that time the province of Syria was divided into *pashalicks*, each governed by a Turkish *pasha* or governor, although the *pashas* only really ruled within the main towns – while the local Arab chieftains ruled elsewhere.

'The Arabs' Ewald wrote just prior to his departure from Jerusalem in

---

32 *Allgemeine Zeitung des Judenthums,* 4 March 1844. Quoted in *JI* 1844, pp. 134-135.
33 Lambeth Palace, Alexander Papers, MSS 3393, Mrs. Alexander to Rev John Coleman, (f.92)
34 Lambeth Palace, Alexander papers, Alexander to Rev. John Coleman, 30 December 1844.
35 Macgowan to London, 4 November, 1844, in *JI,* 1845, p. 22.
36 Alexander to Rev. John Coleman, 30 December 1844, MSS 3397, Lambeth.

October 'are constantly in arms against each other.'[37] According to a report in the *Jewish Intelligence,* the pashas of Jaffa and Lydda were murdered on their way to Jerusalem, by Sheikh Abu Ghosh.[38] The Pasha of Jerusalem then went to Jaffa, which was in theory under his control. The Turkish soldiers in Jaffa, however, who had not received their salaries for some time, besieged him in the Castle in Jaffa until they received their dues. Then, upon his return to Jerusalem the same thing happened there as well. When the Pasha did not respond positively to their request for back-pay, they took over the Citadel or Castle of David (which overlooked the LJS property) and threatened to fire on the town.

As invariably occurred in such situations, the various Christian convents and the Jewish people were commanded to provide the money – a demand they collectively refused. The situation then deteriorated into near anarchy. On 18 October 1844 Alexander received information from the French Consul Lantivy 'warning them of the danger of going outside the City and recommending to have their houses well guarded at night.' The Pasha had in fact informed Lantivy 'that the Sheikhs were in open revolt, that he had no troops, and that it was not unlikely he might be compelled to abandon the City and to seek refuge for himself and his people in the castle.'[39]

Young consulted with Alexander and the leading British subjects, and it was collectively agreed 'that we should show (as) little symptoms of alarm as possible but rather wait patiently and see the development of affairs.' Young then informed Rose in Beirut that a British warship off Jaffa would be beneficial,[40] while also suggesting to Alexander that they all retire to the coast, 'until sufficient measures are taken by the Turkish Government to render to secure the life and property of her majesty's subjects in case of popular tumult.'[41] When remembering the outburst of feeling toward the *Franks* only a year before, this advice was perhaps quite considerate.

Alexander thanked Young for all of his endeavours and advice, but informed the Consul, 'I sincerely trust that whilst there is evident cause of alarm He who rules and guides all the affairs of men, will overrule everything for the good of this Land and of His people.'[42] All concern was soon alleviated as Rose quickly responded to Young's request, and on 29 October 1844 Captain Glascock anchored *HMS Tyne* off Jaffa, and sent word to Young in Jerusalem.[43] Young happily was able to respond to Captain Glascock that two battalions of Turkish troops had entered Jerusalem on 3 November, and that all now seemed well.[44]

37 Ewald to LJS London, 31 July, 1844, in *JI* 1844, p. 327.
38 *JI*, 1845, p. 4.
39 Young to Rose, 19 October, 1844, FO 78/581, No 32.
40 Young to Rose, 19 October, 1844, FO 78/581, No 32.
41 Young to Aberdeen, 23 October 1844, FO 78/581, No 37.
42 Alexander to Young, 22 October 1844, FO 78/581, p. 229.
43 Captain Glascock to Young, 29 October 1844, FO 78/581, No 32.
44 Young to Captain Glascock, 4 November 1844, FO 78/581, p. 257.

Although it was a relief for all foreigners to see those Turkish troops arriving no-one was more relieved than Alexander. He had taken a 'gamble' by not accepting Young's advice to leave for Jaffa and therefore had the welfare of his own family and the members of his community to worry about.

When those Turkish troops marched into Jerusalem they were headed by none other than Sheikh Abu Ghosh! This provided little comfort to many of the citizens, and it was stated that one Karaite Jewish man was murdered and his head severed from his body, while his wife was savagely ravaged, to the point where her life was endangered.[45]

The security in Jerusalem was still somewhat dubious – but the dispatch of the British warship was a clear sign to any would-be troublemakers to be wary of harming British subjects. How accurate were those forecasts of the LJS pioneer workers, Lewis, Dalton and Nicolayson, who saw the need of a resident British Consul in Jerusalem.

Opening of the Hospital

The small Hebrew-Protestant community barely had time to catch its breath before the next major event. On 12 December 1844 the LJS hospital, Jerusalem's first *modern* hospital, was opened.

Although the success of this venture is rightfully attributed to Dr. Macgowan, a fair degree of credit must also be given to Alexander. This was one of the important issues in his initial instructions. He encouraged and supported the medical work fully during his almost three years in the Holy City.

Nicolayson recorded that there was opposition to its opening by the Sephardim rabbis. He also stated that the Ashkenazim, in their efforts to oppose the Hospital, opened through the efforts of Rabbi Isaiah Bak a 'hospital' of their own, through the generosity of Sir Moses Montefiore. But, Nicolayson wrote, 'The order and comfort of ours is so much superior, and the confidence felt in Dr. Macgowan's experienced skill so much more influential, that it is quite full already.'[46]

Opening of station at Hebron

Bishop Alexander's next major project was establishing a station in Hebron. Veitch and Mr. Keavus set out there in December 1844. Young opposed such an endeavor, and wrote to Rose that 'I pointed out to Mr. Veitch the violent and fanatical character of the people of Hebron, and also the danger of opposition from the Jerusalem Jews, who would probably influence their brethren at Hebron to view Mr Keavus' movements with suspicion, added to this I thought the closeness with which our movements generally are watched here by Foreign Agents, was another cause for caution in extending the Society's efforts in this neighbourhood at the present juncture, when the question of the Church is still

---

45 *JI*, 1843, pp. 4-5.
46 Nicolayson to London, 31 December, 1844, in *JI*, 1845, p. 89.

a subject of Sir Stratford Canning's solicitude at Constantinople.'[47]

Young was able to report to Aberdeen, on 20 December, quite thankfully, that both Veitch and Keavus had returned from Hebron, and that the venture had been abandoned.

French Reactions to Anglicans Initiatives

Young's comment about 'the closeness with which our movements generally are watched here by Foreign Agents' was an accurate description of the affairs in the 'Holy Land.' The British in particular were concerned with French ambitions in the region, and the Peel-Aberdeen administration therefore purposed to avoid any possible conflict with France.

But the French were very concerned with British ambitions. The French Consul, de Lantivy, Alexander's neighbour, had for a year now observed the British-Anglican endeavours. Through correspondence to Baron Rothschild, and in particular to his Foreign Minister in Paris, he proposed to counter this British activity through increased French cultural activity – and even of offering more consular support to the Jewish people.

Tudor Parfitt stated that 'The time was ripe, thought de Lantivy, to extend the scope of French influence and to increase the scale of French cultural activity.'[48] In a long communication to the French Foreign Minister, de Lantivy summarized Anglican activity, highlighting that they 'had a doctor, architect and chemist working for them as well as a well-equipped hospital.'[49]

To highlight that this was a British initiative, including both Anglicans and Jewish endeavours, he also included the present initiatives of Sir Moses Montefiore. De Lantivy concluded that the French had to increase their activities in order 'contrebalancer les influences rivales des Anglicans et des Russo-Grecs.'[50]

Young wanted to ensure there was no cause of major conflict with the French over issues developing in his sphere of operation. This caution also hints, again, of the cross purposes of Consul Young, and Bishop Alexander. Young had in view the 'bigger geo-political' picture. Alexander had in view the 'bigger Kingdom of God' picture. Young viewed each of Alexander's moves as to how it affected Britain's relationship with Turkey, and the other European powers, all of whom looked at each of these missionary moves as an initiative of the British Government.

It seems that one matter only precipitated Alexander's decisions and moves – to introduce Jesus to Jewish people wherever they lived in his area of episcopal authority.

---

47 Young to Rose, 17 December 1844 , FO 78/625.
48 Parfitt, T. *The Jews in Palestine 1800-1882*, p. 143.
49 Parfitt, T. *The Jews in Palestine 1800-1882*, p. 144.
50 A.E., Dir. Pol. 75 (188), de Lantivy to Minister, Jerusalem, 28 July 1844. Quoted in Parfitt, T. *The Jews in Palestine 1800-1882*, p. 144.

Chapter 31

A Hebrew Protestant 'Church' for Jerusalem

Optimism and opposition

Bishop Alexander's annual circular letter written to commemorate his entry into Jerusalem, was full of his usual optimism and he reiterated that his main objective for being in Jerusalem continued to be connected with 'that people who are still beloved for their father's sake, who are to obtain mercy through the mercy of the Gentile Churches (Romans xi), and who are destined again "To blossom and bud and fill the face of the world with fruit." (Isaiah xxvii.6)'[1]

In a letter to Sir Thomas Baring in early January 1845 Alexander mentioned how 'in a paper which the Jews (I ought to say the Rabbis, for the people are differently minded) have lately printed for general circulation among their Brethren throughout Europe they actually call upon their European Brothers' who have influence with the Governments to use every effort <u>to get us removed</u>.'[2]

It wasn't long before more efforts were made to get rid of the Anglicans. On 21 January 1845 a Jewish patient died in the hospital. When informed, the Chief Rabbi refused him a Jewish burial. The Sephardi and Ashkenazi Chief Rabbis then sent a note to Dr Macgowan, stating 'that unless I shall promise to dismiss all the Hebrew servants from the hospital, and like-wise the patients who are actually in the hospital, and moreover unless I shall engage not to receive any more Jews into the hospital in the future, that they the Rabbis will not allow the internment of the patient who died this morning in the hospital.'[3]

As no steps had been taken by the Chief Rabbis for burial by the next day, the body was interned in the British burial ground near the upper or Mamilla pool.[4]

Within a few days both the Sephardi and Ashkenazi Chief Rabbis had issued very severe *cherems* or excommunication bans against the English Hospital, and the patients were induced to leave. The rabbis then issued statements which were dispatched to Europe, casting a very negative light on the activities of Alexander's mission. This was the most severe test the small Protestant community had had to endure since the crisis with the three rabbis in 1842.[5]

This crisis was followed shortly afterwards by a serious situation in Safed

---

1 *Third Annual Letter from the Anglican Bishop in Jerusalem*, in *JI*, 1845, p. 1.
2 Letter Alexander to Sir Thomas Baring, 1845. St. Anthony's College, Oxford.
3 Note from Chief Rabbis to Dr. Macgowan, FO 78/625.
4 Macgowan to Young, 22 January 1845, FO 78/625.
5 Letter Alexander to Sir Thomas Baring, 1845. St. Anthony's.

which necessitated a brief curtailment of the work there.⁶ This was another challenging period for Alexander, as it also involved a conflict of interests with Consul Young's instructions, with Alexander desiring British consular protection for his staff in Safed while Young stated that he was not able to fully comply with this request.⁷

Petition to Lord Aberdeen

These problems were in addition to the ongoing saga concerning the building of the Church – which in its unfinished state was becoming an embarrassment to Alexander, to the LJS and even to the British Government.

Despite all the efforts of Ambassadors Ponsonby and Canning, there was just no breakthrough in gaining a *firman* for building the Church. In the beginning of 1845 the LJS engineered a nationwide petition. They obtained the signatures of the Archbishop of Canterbury, the Bishop of London, other bishops, many nobility and dignitaries in the Church, some 1400 clergy and over 14,000 other citizens. It was an amazing achievement.

Led by Lord Shaftesbury, the delegation presented the petition to Lord Aberdeen on 18 March 1845. Although primarily requesting permission to build the Church, the delegation also requested the granting of official recognition to the Protestant Bishop in Jerusalem, and for those professing the Protestant faith.

The heart of the petition is found in these words:

> ... the Society most deeply regret, that whilst the Greeks, Roman Catholics, Armenians, and other minor sects of Christians, enjoy the permission to worship God in their respective temples, and whilst no privilege is withheld on the representations of French and Russian diplomacy, - the pure Reformed religion of the British nation, to whom, under God, Turkey is indebted for the recovery of Syria, should be alone proscribed, and her Protestant children alone denied the possession of a consecrated building for the service of God, and especially that recognition of the Protestant faith which is indispensable to ensure protection.⁸

Aberdeen sent a copy of the Memorial to Ambassador Canning on 20 March 1845, and stated in his letter the British Government's eagerness to obtain permission for the Protestant Church to be built.⁹

The matter had now been expressed, very forthrightly, from the highest authority in Britain. The public voice in Britain had forced the Government to take heed of the groundswell of interest in having a Hebrew-Protestant Church

---

6 Various correspondence relating to the subject, FO 78/625.
7 Young to Alexander, 8 February 1845, FO 78/625.
8 *Presentation of a Memorial from the Society to Lord Aberdeen*, in *JI*, 1845, pp. 125-127.
9 Aberdeen to Canning, 20 March 1845, FO 78/592, No 32.

in Jerusalem.

Visit to Damascus

In mid-April Alexander and a party travelled to Damascus via Beirut.[10] Not only did Alexander enjoy visiting the various sites of Damascus, but also interaction with many Jewish people with whom he entered freely into conversation on matters of faith. To many of these he was able to give copies of the Hebrew New Testament.[11]

On one occasion Alexander and the party, which included Mr Wood, as well as a Druze prince with one of the Chief Rabbis as guide, was able to visit a small village near to Damascus, the site of a cave in which it is believed Elijah the prophet dwelt. Alexander recorded of this visit:

> We found the synagogue full of Jews. One of the Chachamim sat on a low stool, surrounded by a large group of hearers, to whom he was said to preach. They all immediately rose, and made us sit down before the Ark. The book which the Chacham[12] had in his hand was entitled 'Words of the Covenant.' This led me to ask them whether it referred to the old or to the new Covenant? The question startled them, and at once gave me an opportunity of referring to Jeremiah xxxi.; explaining to them the nature of the new Covenant. They took out of a special Ark a very beautiful MS. of the whole of the Old Testament, which was written in the twelfth century, and is greatly prized by them. We read in the same the passage in Jeremiah, and some others connected with it; all the others listening most attentively to a long and interesting conversation carried on under such remarkable circumstances, in a Jewish synagogue, near Damascus, and which I hope has not been in vain. There were at least 200 present.[13]

When reading of this account it is easy to recollect the incident in a stage coach in Germany in 1798 when a young Jewish German man also heard the words of Jeremiah's New Covenant and whose life was changed as a result thereof.

The return trip back to Jerusalem after this exciting visit was itself also full of excitement - and crisis. On one occasion a large snake crawled into Fanny Alexander's tent. Luckily it was spotted and killed - and then found its way into a bottle and became part of Mr. Veitch's snake collection. The crisis occurred when the Bishop became very unwell at Djebail, and was in a poor state of health for several days.[14]

---

10 Veitch to London, 4 June 1845, in *JI*, 1845, p. 292.
11 Alexander to London, 6 May 1845, in *JI*, 1845, p. 260.
12 Learned one, or rabbi.
13 Alexander to London, 6 May 1845, in *JI*, 1845, p. 260.
14 Veitch to London, 4 June 1845, in *JI*, 1845, pp. 331-332.

Special visitors

As these were the days before Cook's Tours, fewer people visited Jerusalem than in later decades, and most of those who did were people of means and renown. The Alexanders continued to open their house to them, and Michael Solomon was always on call. Of this part of his ministry Deborah the younger wrote:

> Papa had to show hospitality extensively in Jerusalem as there were no hotels and resorts for travelers there at that time, except the Convents. Travellers in those days were of a high class. People of culture – of wealth – and many of high birth brought letters of introduction to Papa ... During the months of January, February and March our house was full of pleasant visitors. Among many may be mentioned Dr Lepsius, the German Egyptologist, Dr Strauss, Dr Abeken, Under Secretary for Foreign Affairs at the Court of Berlin, Count Pourtenberg, Count von Wildenbrook, the Marquis of Sligo, Lord Eastnor, W.F Makepeace Thackeray, Eliot Warburton, Eastlake, author of Eothen, also that marvelous man Arthur Kavanagh who, with neither arms or legs, was able to ride fearlessly.[15]

In June a very special German visitor was Rev. Dr. Heinrich Abeken, who had served as chaplain of the Prussian legation at Rome with Bunsen some years before, as well as assisting Bunsen in the deliberations to establish the Bishopric. Abeken confided some of his impressions of Alexander back to Bunsen in a letter on 7 July:

> ... You cannot imagine how difficult it is to form and keep together a congregation consisting of Germans, English, and Jews; and if all these three had not been united in the person of the Bishop, it would never have been done. As the three nations are mixed here, there has hitherto been no proper cordiality between them. It is the Bishop who feels equal love towards all of them. Daily do I discover some new admirable quality in this man, when seeing as I do with what a candid but dignified manner, with what faithfulness and perseverance, what circumspection and discretion, and above all, with what cheerful courage, such as only genuine Christian love can inspire, he passes through all difficulties, of which there are not a few, both great and small.[16]

No clearer affirmation of the character of Bishop Michael Solomon Alexander, and his important role in Jerusalem could have been stated.

Finally – a *Firman* for the Church.

Sir Stratford Canning had an important audience with the Sultan of Turkey on 25 August 1845, a meeting in which a high principle of Islamic law was about to

---

15 Ransom, ibid, p. 21a.
16 Rev. Dr Abeken to Chevalier Bunsen, 7 July 1845, in *JI*, 1845, p. 375.

be overturned. Canning recorded for posterity:

> His Highness took occasion to confirm what His Minister for Foreign Affairs had previously announced to me, namely, that he consented to issue an Imperial Firman for the completion of the Protestant Church at Jerusalem and other suspended buildings with which that sacred edifice is connected. I have much pleasure in adding that His Highness particularly requested me to represent this concession as a mark of the cordial satisfaction which he felt in complying with Her Majesty's wishes.
>
> I cannot but gratify Your Lordship to learn that in every thing which fell from the Sultan's lips at this Audience there was a marked expression of good-will towards the British Crown and Nation, as well as of the most friendly consideration for Her Majesty's person, and confidence in the policy of Her Majesty's Government towards this Empire.[17]

Canning received a translation of a special Memorandum from the Porte on 2 September. Then on 4 October Aberdeen wrote to Shaftesbury, stating, that in response to his Memorial presented in March on behalf of the LJS, he was pleased to announce that at long last an Imperial *Firman* had been 'obtained from the Sultan by Her Majesty's Ambassador at Constantinople, by which permission is granted for the erection of the desired building within the precincts of the British Consulate.'[18]

The Imperial Turkish Decree, or *Firman*, stated:

> *It has been represented, both now and before, on the part of the British Embassy residing at my Court, that British and Prussian Protestant subjects visiting Jerusalem, meet with difficulties and obstructions, owing to their not possessing a place of worship for the observance of Protestant rites, and it has been requested that permission should be given to erect, for the first time, a special Protestant place of worship, within the British Consular residence at Jerusalem.*
>
> *Whereas, it is in accordance with the perfect amity and cordial relations existing between the Government of Great Britain and my Sublime Porte, that the requests of that Government shall be complied with as far as possible; and whereas, moreover, the aforesaid place of worship is to be within the Consular residence, my Royal permission is therefore granted for the erection of the aforesaid special place of worship, within the aforesaid Consular residence. And my Imperial order having been issued for that purpose, the present decree, containing permission, has been specially given from my Imperial Divan.*

This document was one of the most significant to have been issued by the Turkish Sultan and was perhaps the most tangible expression given of the *Hatti Sherif of Gulhane* of 1839. It was, in effect, a violation of Islamic principles.

---

17 Canning to Aberdeen, 25 August, 1845, in FO 78/600,No199.
18 Aberdeen to Lord Ashley, 4 October 1845, in *JI*, 1845, p. 369.

The Sultan was forced to make this compromise for political expediency – but he knew others elsewhere would not understand real-politik. Hence the *Firman* continued:

> *When, therefore, it becomes known unto you, Vallee of Said, Governor of Jerusalem, and others aforesaid, that our Royal permission has been granted for the erection in the manner above stated, of the aforesaid place of worship, you will be careful that no person do in any manner oppose the erection of the aforesaid place of worship in the manner stated. And you will not act in contravention hereof. For which purpose my Imperial Firman is issued.*
>
> *On its arrival you will act in accordance with my Imperial Firman, issued for this purpose in the manner aforesaid; be it thus known unto you, giving full faith to the Imperial cipher.*[19]

A New Consul and Delivery of the *Firman*

Consul Young resigned in 1845, and James Finn was chosen to replace him. Finn, a LJS Committee member, a previous acquaintance of Bishop Alexander, and an author of several books on Jewish subjects, had recently married Elizabeth Ann, daughter of Alexander's long-term friend Alexander McCaul. The signs were there for a promising future between Bishop and Consul. Both men were committed to the Jewish cause.

Until Finn's arrival the position was temporarily held by Henry Newbolt, who arrived in Jerusalem on 12 October 1845, with the *Firman*. The instructions given to Newbolt were very specific. In order to uphold the terms of the *Firman* it was imperative that the British Consulate be as close to the proposed Church as possible – efforts at securing Young's residence having failed. Accordingly on 16 October the Archives of the British Consulate were transferred from Young's house to 'a building adjoining the present Protestant place of Worship in the immediate vicinity of the new Anglican church.'[20]

Immediately following the transferal of the archives, Newbolt, Consul Young and the Prussian Consul Mr. Schultz presented the *Imperial Firman* to Ali Pasha, Governor of Jerusalem, together with an order from the Turkish Governor-General of Syria.

The Governor read the *Firman*, 'but objected' wrote Newbolt 'to the continuation of the building of the present church on the premises of the Society on the plea that it is not within the British Consular Residence as specified in the Firman of the Sultan.'[21] Newbolt contended that in fact the

---

19 Sultan of Turkey to British Government, 10 September 1845, in *JI*, 1845, p. 370. Afterwards the LJS stated to its supporters that the stipulation of the Church being the private chapel of the Consulate did not impinge upon the LJS's ownership rights over the 'Chapel' and property.
20 Newbolt to Aberdeen, 4 November 1845, FO 78/626, No 186. This building, henceforth also known as the *Cancelleria*, is where the present Conrad Schick Library & Archive is locate, which itself is attached to the Alexander Lounge, location of the 'Protestant place of Worship' or St. James Chapel, in November 1845.
21 Newbolt to Aberdeen, 4 November 1845, FO 78/626, No 186.

British Cancelleria was on the same premises as the Protestant Church to be built and actually adjoining the proposed Church building. The Pasha then agreed to visit the proposed Church building.

On 18 October the Pasha with a large entourage visited the site of the proposed Church and closely inspected the premises. Newbolt wrote of the Pasha's conclusion:

> Although on this occasion His Excellency could not refuse to acknowledge the present Cancelleria as the British Consulate, he still argued that the Firman did not authorize the continuation of the present Church, but a new place of worship for British and Prussian Protestant subjects within the Consulate, that the Consulate never having been on the premises before, he could not consider the continuation of the present church as agreeing with the order of the Firman.[22]

Newbolt endeavoured to explain to the Governor that he could no longer refer to Consul Young's house as the British Consulate, but that he, Newbolt, had specifically set up the British Consulate on the LJS premises in order to act in accordance with the specifications of the *Firman*. But all to no avail. Newbolt continued, 'he further requested (there being at the time laborers employed preparing for the foundation of a house for Bishop Alexander) that the people then employed on the premises should be stopped...'[23] Nicolayson's analysis of this hindrance was:

> The wording of the Firman gave the local authorities here the advantage of founding their opposition at once on the alleged inapplicability of that document, to the resuming of the building previously commenced, as not being "within the Consulate" and the Pasha persisted in demanding a delay till the matter could be referred to Beyrout...We are fully aware, both of the source of this opposition, and of its extent and object. In order to render the present Firman unavailing for our purposes, a counter-memorial has been addressed by a powerful party here, to the Sublime Porte.[24]

The technicality pounced on by the Pasha and opponents to the scheme was that the office of the British Consul at that time was a small room adjacent to the temporary chapel and a few metres away from the unfinished Church building. This then did not permit, according to the Pasha, the literal wording of the *Firman* to be fulfilled – that the Church had to be constructed *within* that premise, not atop the foundations of the Church already begun.

Alexander in his exuberance after receiving word of the *Firman*, had ordered

---

22 Newbolt to Aberdeen, 4 November 1845, FO 78/626, No 187.
23 Newbolt to Aberdeen, 4 November 1845, FO 78/626, No 187.
24 Nicolayson to LJS London, 1 November, 1845, in *JI*, 1846, pp. 26-27.

construction to be restarted, and in particular upon his proposed house attached to the Church. Consul Newbolt, after consulting with the Governor, informed Alexander on 18 October:

> His Excellency then requested that the workmen who are now employed and at work on the grounds might be stopped, giving as his reasons, that the arrival of the new Consul with the Firman was fully known in the City, and that the feeling against building a Protestant Church was so strong that he apprehended difficulties should workmen be seen employed in the immediate vicinity of the church.[25]

Newbolt implored the Bishop to desist from upsetting the *status quo*, while he referred the matter back to Consul-General Rose. Alexander responded immediately, 'I shall of course in compliance with His Excellency's request give directions to suspend that work.'[26] One could imagine Alexander's annoyance by this new obstacle, but, having had such a poor relationship with Young, it would appear that he was determined to work alongside the new, albeit temporary, Consul.

But such temperance was obviously not felt by Alexander's associates. After confiding with them, Alexander wrote the following day to Newbolt, 'I find there is a strong feeling in the Mission against being again stopped proceeding with any work on the Premises of the Church, and I would beg of you to submit to His Excellency the Pasha that what is now being done, is only in a small preparatory manner, and cannot possibly lead to any realization of the Pasha's fears.'[27]

Consul Newbolt was quickly thrust into the middle of what was potentially an explosive situation. Yet he stuck to his convictions, and responded to Alexander, that he would pursue his endeavours to meet with the Pasha and further discuss this issue, but in the meantime he stated, 'I hope you will not resume the work on the premises of the Society, or if so, I cannot be responsible for any consequences.'[28] Alexander, by now more than aware of the explosive nature of Jerusalem, replied that he would stop any further construction work.[29]

Newbolt finally met with the Pasha on 20 October, and laid before him the Bishop's requests. The Governor was unmoved, and requested Newbolt to desist from any further building until the messengers had returned from Beirut – a reply from Consul-General Rose and the Turkish Governor-General there.[30] He explained to Newbolt that although he anticipated no disturbance, yet 'the people here were hasty, and easily excited, and … there would still be great

25 Consul Newbolt to Bishop Alexander, 18 October, 1845, FO 78/626, No 190.
26 Bishop Alexander to Consul Newbolt, 18 October, 1845, FO 78/626, No 191.
27 Alexander to Newbolt, 19 October 1845, FO 78/626, No 192.
28 Consul Newbolt to Bishop Alexander, 19 October, 1845, FO 78/626, No 192.
29 Bishop Alexander to Consul Newbolt, 19 October, 1845, FO 78/626, No 192.
30 Newbolt to Alexander, 20 October 1845, FO 78/626, No 193.

talk about the English building a church, that (on) this reaching the ears of his superiors, he would be blamed for allowing the work without being certain that he was right in so doing.'[31]

The Governor knew that opposition from the local Muslim sheikhs could easily lead to civil unrest. Such were the sensitivities of the local, especially Muslim population of Jerusalem. Alexander did well to listen to this sound advice – as frustrating as it was for him.

Rose's reply reached Newbolt on 2 November – a mere five days before Alexander was due to begin his trip to Egypt and England. Rose stated that he had 'failed in his endeavours' with the Turkish Governor-General 'for the execution of the Firman, but obtained a letter from him, directing Ali Pasha to cause no hindrance to the work that he had stopped on the premises, unless there could be assigned some legal and regular obstacle for his hindrance of such work…' The work being referred to here was not on the construction of the Church itself – the subject of the counter complaint sent to Constantinople, but the work on Bishop Alexander's private house adjacent to the Church.

Newbolt again met with Ali Pasha, who again stated that the order did not permit Bishop Alexander 'to build on the premises of the Church, or, that he was allowed to build a new house…'[32] Newbolt remonstrated and asked for the objections to be placed in writing. Ali Pasha complied – but they were in Turkish, which Newbolt had no facility in Jerusalem to adequately translate. These were then sent back to Rose in Beirut. It all seemed to be another attempt to bury the matter in Turkish bureaucracy.[33]

It was a frustrating period as Newbolt stated to Aberdeen, 'In all my interviews with Ali Pasha on the subject of the Firman there appears to me to have been predetermined opposition…'[34] Indeed there was – and had been from the very outset of the building, and even of Alexander's entrance into the City. Alexander meanwhile was waiting anxiously. He desperately desired to have the issue settled before leaving for England.

Consul-General Rose failed in his attempts to get the suspension of building rescinded, so he informed Newbolt to demand written information from Ali Pasha as to his reasons for not carrying out the wishes of the *Firman*.[35] Newbolt accordingly wrote to Ali Pasha on 24 November requesting written reasons so he could transmit them 'to Her Majesty's Consul General for the information of His Excellency Her Britannic Majesty's Ambassador at Constantinople, and

---

31 Newbolt to Alexander, 20 October 1845, FO 78/626, No 193.
32 Newbolt to Aberdeen, 4 November, 1845, FO 78/626, No 186.
33 Newbolt to Aberdeen, 4 November 1845, FO 78/626, No 188.
34 Newbolt to Aberdeen, 4 November 1845, FO 78/626, No 188.
35 Newbolt to Aberdeen, 5 December 1845, FO 78/626, [201]. Shortly after issuing this suspension order, Ali Pasha was transferred to Damascus, and he was succeeded by Mahamet, former pasha of Acre.

Her Britannic Majesty's Government.'[36]

The letter from Ali Pasha reiterated the claim that the Church was not within the Consular residence, and that as Alexander's house immediately adjoined the proposed Church, it was seen to be contiguous with it – work could not be continued with. But what was especially galling in the letter, translated from the Turkish, was the claim that the area where the Church was to be built was in fact '*the property of Wafk*[37] and was adjoining a Muslim place of worship.'[38]

The Muslim opponents in Jerusalem were persevering in their opposition, this time attempting to claim that the LJS property was actually Islamic *Wakf* property!

The matter returned to Ambassador Canning, who, as much as anyone else, was annoyed by this further hindrance, and immediately set about clarifying the wording of the *Firman*.

The Bishop's Fourth Annual Letter – 30 October 1845

Bishop Alexander's *Annual Letter* was written from Jerusalem on 30 October 1845. As could be expected it was of great excitement and optimism. He wrote of having received the *Firman* and of the associated complications, and concluded:

> ... however much opposition may, and still will, be raised against the carrying of the same into effect, it cannot and must not be looked upon otherwise, than as an additional sign of the further development of the Divine purposes of mercy to Zion.
>
> The Protestant Episcopal Church[39] of England will now have "a local inhabitation" as well as "a name," on the rock of Jerusalem ..."[40]

The granting of the *Firman* was gratifying to both Nicolayson, the representative Gentile in the Hebrew-Christian-Protestant community and to Alexander, the representative Israelite at Jerusalem in that same community. For Alexander this was one of the main objectives in his coming to Jerusalem. Additionally, in the East, a leader was associated with the prestige of his position. Mosques, Synagogues and other Churches abounded in the Holy City. An Imam, Rabbi or Patriarch could point to a physical edifice as representing the community to which he belonged.

Alexander, Bishop of the Protestant Church, and therefore in the eyes of

---

36 Translation of letter from Newbolt to Ali Pasha, Governor of Jerusalem, 24 November 1845, FO 78/626, No 203.
37 Italics mine.
38 Translation of letter from Ali Pasha to Consul Newbolt, FO 78/626, No 204-5.
39 This seems to have been the initial name given to the proposed new Church. Johns in his ill-advised publication named it the 'Cathedral Church of St. James'. However it does not seem that this was the intended name for the new Church. The proposed Church was also referred to as the 'Hebrew-Protestant Church.'
40 Alexander to LJS London, in *JI*, 1846, p. 3.

the Eastern peoples the representative of both Britain and the Protestant movement, could only point to an unfinished building, while both France and Russia could point to edifices representing Roman and Greek Christianity.

This decision, encompassed in the Imperial *Firman* – was a high point, perhaps the high point of Alexander's four years in Jerusalem. In the Bishop's last letter to London, dated 4 November, before setting off on a journey to Egypt and England, he stated:

> The Firman has been presented to the authorities here … It is quite evident that there are parties still working against us; but they cannot succeed, although impediments may still be thrown in our way. The fact of a Firman having been granted, after all the anxiety and trouble, must be viewed as a cause of thanksgiving: and I doubt not that everything will soon be satisfactorily arranged.[41]

---

41 Alexander to LJS London, 4 November, 1845, in *JI*, 1846. p. 23.

CHAPTER 32

THE DEATHS OF ALEXANDER, FREY AND WOLFF

Alexander's trip to Egypt

On 7 November 1845 Alexander and a party comprising Mrs. Alexander, Miss Fanny Alexander, Rev. Veitch, and Rev. Dr Abeken, set out from Jerusalem to visit Egypt. They would spend one week in Cairo, during which time he would participate in certain activities associated with the CMS operation, and then proceed onto Alexandria and partake of similar work there, before departing for England on 10 December 1845.[1]

Concerning their time in the Sinai desert Mrs. Alexander recalled:

> On setting out through the Desert, each day my beloved husband and myself rode our own horses; we generally were in advance of the caravan, and we used regularly to chant some of our Hebrew chants, and sung the following hymns: "Children of the Heavenly King:" "Long has the Harp of Judah hung:" cxith Psalm; "Glorious things of thee are spoken:" all out of our own hymn-book: and never did his warm and tender heart overflow so fully, as when he spoke of Israel's future restoration. When I spoke to him about his duties in England, he answered, "I hope, if invited, to preach my first sermon in England at the Episcopal Jews' Chapel ..."[2]

On the evening of Friday 21 November the party had arrived at Abou Suwyreh, whereupon heavy rain fell during the night, and the following day the entire area outside the tents was drenched. At this point Michael Solomon 'complained of indisposition' Veitch wrote and 'of pain in the chest and shoulders'[3] a similar feeling, Veitch recalled that he suffered at the conclusion of his Damascus trip.[4] On that previous trip Dr. Kerns had advised that this discomfort was caused by 'the strain of the muscles, from riding for so many hours on consecutive days, augmented in its bad effects by the damp of the preceding night.'[5]

So during the day Alexander opted out of riding his horse and rode instead in the litter on the camel. As the weather had cleared up by mid-morning they were

---

1 Mrs Lieder to Rev. J. Blackburn, 4 December 1845, in *JI*, 1845, p. 36.
2 Communication by Mrs. Alexander, in *JI*, 1846, p. 35.
3 Rev W.D Veitch to LJS London, 2 January 1846, in *JI*, 1846, p. 92.
4 Rev. W.D Veitch to LJS London, 26 November, 1845, in *JI*, 1846, p. 1.
5 Rev. W.D Veitch, to LJS London, 2 January 1846, in *JI*, 1846, p. 93.

able to stop, light a fire, and enjoy breakfast. Michael Solomon, however, was 'seized with sickness and vomited immediately after breakfast' Veitch recalled, adding 'but still I confess I felt no serious alarm, as he speedily recovered, and we proceeded.'[6] That evening they arrived at the village of Ras Ovaddi on the eastern branch of the Nile, the area known as Ras el Wady (Head of the Valley) and Alexander was feeling better.

During the evening meal in Veitch's tent, Alexander insisted he was well, and seeing as they would not travel the following day that he would be able to recover. Following the evening meal he retired to his tent, declaring to his beloved wife 'how exceedingly comfortable he felt'[7] then 'prayed most sweetly with his wife and daughter, and then laid down upon his bed, which was placed on the sand.'[8]

Mrs. Alexander then went to bed, and then 'she was first awoke by the bellowing of a camel, and then by a groan which proceeded from her husband. She thought it strange, and instantly got up, when she saw him sitting up in his bed, with his eyes closed and apparently dead. She spoke to him, but received no answer – she touched him, but had no reply – when she gave the alarm.'[9]

Veitch then describes how, 'I was aroused by some exclamations from Mrs Alexander; I ran instantly into his tent, and saw at once that all was over. We tried all we could think of…[but] Death had taken place in a moment.'[10] He then wrote of what followed, 'It was truly a heart-rendering scene … to see the widowed wife and fatherless daughter, bending over the lowly pallet, on which were stretched the lifeless remains. Never shall I forget the harrowing scene, or the fortitude with which so awful bereavement was endured.'[11]

The sad party set out the following morning for Cairo where they were met by Mr. Lieder and other members of the CMS station in Cairo, who had been warned already of the Bishop's death.

An autopsy was carried out soon afterwards, of which Mrs Lieder wrote: 'The immediate cause of death was the rupture of one of the largest blood-vessels near the heart; but the whole of the lungs, liver, and heart, were found in an exceedingly diseased state; and had been so for a length of time.' The doctors however clearly stated that Alexander's death was not due to fatigue from the trip across the desert, which by accounts was actually a wonderfully enjoyable and stress-less journey, but 'it was a complaint that he might, in like manner, have been called away in Jerusalem.'[12]

Mrs Lieder, in describing the results of the autopsy, also stated, 'the

6 Rev. W.D Veitch, to LJS London, 2 January 1846, in *JI*, 1846, p. 93.
7 Rev. W.D Veitch, to LJS London, 2 January 1846, in *JI*, 1846, p. 93.
8 Mrs Lieder to Rev. J. Blackburn, 4 December 1845, in *JI*, 1845, p. 36.
9 Mrs Lieder to Rev. J. Blackburn, 4 December 1845, in *JI*, 1845, p. 36.
10 Rev. W.D Veitch to LJS London, 26 November, 1845, in *JI*, 1846, pp. 1-2.
11 Rev. W.D. Veitch to LJS London, 26 November, 1845, in *JI*, 1846, p. 2.
12 Mrs. Lieder to Rev. J. Blackburn, 4 December 1845, in *JI*, 1846. p. 36.

accelerating cause, doubtless, was great and continued anxiety – such as the Bishopric of Jerusalem and its cares can best account for. I heard it said on this occasion that had his Lordship not come into the East, he might possibly have lived to a good old age; but the mitre of Jerusalem, like the wreath of our blessed Lord, has been to him a crown of thorns.'[13]

Several pressing matters now weighed upon Mrs. Alexander - whether or not to continue her journey to England, wait in Egypt for her children to join her, or return to Jerusalem. She finally opted to continue to England.

The other matter concerned where to bury the Bishop. The CMS people desired for the Bishop's body to be interred in their new graveyard. Consul-General Barnett and Consul Young (who was then in Cairo) thought Jerusalem, as this was Alexander's wish.[14] Mrs. Alexander then concurred with the opinions of Her Majesty's envoys.

The Memorial Service was held on Sunday 30 November. A very sizeable congregation gathered, including the British and Russian Consuls-General, the wife of the French Consul-General, many dignitaries of the local Churches, and all of the English residents. Rev. Veitch preached the sermon, from Deuteronomy 34:5, 'So Moses, the servant of the Lord, died there in the Land of Moab, according to the word of the Lord.'[15]

The bitter and the sweet
Nicolayson was entrusted with the difficult task of informing family and friends in Jerusalem of the Bishop's death. Deborah the younger describes how the news came to her:

> One afternoon ... very hurriedly Mr. Nicolayson arrived at our home and without taking notice of me, went into the drawing room to interview Miss Cecil. I was eventually sent for and saw that something was wrong and asked at once if any news had come of Mama. She was the one I naturally expected might be ill. I was told that a messenger had just come from Egypt and that Papa had been taken very ill, before they reached Cairo. Later on, the sad – and most overwhelming event of his death in his sleep – was broken to me. I was simply stunned. I tried to cry but tears are never my relief in sorrow. I was roused by a fearful commotion in the nursery where I found all my dear little sisters and brother in floods of tears, and Margaret, our English nurse, in hysterics on the floor. I threw a glass of cold water over her, and then tried to comfort the dear little ones.[16]

---

13 Mrs. Lieder to Rev. J. Blackburn, 4 December 1845, in *JI*, 1846. p. 36.
14 Mrs. Lieder to Rev. J. Blackburn, 4 December 1845, in *JI*, 1846. p. 37.
15 Mrs. Lieder to Rev. J. Blackburn, 4 December 1845, in *JI*, 1846. p. 38.
16 Ransom, ibid, p. 35.

Nicolayson also stated:

> How deeply and tenderly the departed was beloved as well as revered by all here, the effect of the painful announcement I had to make, in the opening of my sermon on the Sunday morning after its receipt, most affectingly showed. Scarcely any present who was not dissolved in tears.
>
> I may mention that, having waited yesterday on both the patriarchs here, the Armenian and the Greek, to make the melancholy announcement to them, they both expressed their deep sympathy, particularly for the afflicted widow and orphans; and the former (the Armenian patriarch), sent the Bishop Procurator, and the Dragoman of the convent, to my house to-day to express still more emphatically his sincere condolence. He was personally much attached to our late beloved Bishop, who, indeed, was universally esteemed by all who knew him personally.[17]

In one of those bittersweet ironies of history two Tartar messengers arrived at sunset on 9 December 1845 bearing fresh dispatches from Constantinople which contained 'fresh, most explicit, and peremptory orders to our new Pasha here,' wrote Nicolayson 'for the instant removal of all impediment to "resuming the erection of the English Protestant Church already commenced here," and of other buildings.[18]

Bishop Alexander's last journey

About eleven in the morning of 6 December, Bishop Alexander's coffin, draped in black and carried on the *tatarwan* between two camels, left the CMS home, for the long journey back to Jerusalem accompanied by Rev. Veitch and his servant. Mrs. Lieder wrote these words concerning the occasion:

> I cannot help comparing the present position of our excellent friend, Mr. Veitch, to that of Joseph, when he took the bones of good old Jacob through the same identical wilderness of Shur; for Jacob prayed them not to bury him in Egypt, for, he said, "I will lie with my fathers, and thou shalt carry me out of Egypt, and shalt bury me in their burying-place." – (Genesis xlvii. 20).[19]

Veitch was concerned about the upcoming journey, and wrote:

> My fear was that if a party of Arabs ... should come upon us, they would break open the coffin in the hope of obtaining plunder. All we had met had eyed it most wistfully, and we had overheard their speculations as to the

---

17 Nicolayson to LJS London, 9 December 1845, in *JI*, 1846, p. 97.
18 Nicolayson to LJS London, 9 December 1845, in *JI*, 1846, p. 97.
19 Mrs. Lieder to Rev. J. Blackburn, 4 December 1845, in *JI*, 1846. p. 38.

value of its contents, and it is very unlikely that here, where truth is a thing unknown, they would have credited any assurance of ours on the matter.[20]

Thankfully the party travelled through the Sinai unmolested. At El Arish his letters of recommendation from Mehmet Ali were of great assistance – and the Turkish governor provided him with nine soldiers for the onward journey to Gaza. From this location to Jerusalem Veitch and his special cargo was accompanied by several Albanian soldiers. 'The name of the redoubted Pasha of Egypt' wrote Veitch 'worked wonders.'[21]

Several days later Nicolayson came out to the Tombs of the Kings, outside the city walls where Veitch and his party had already arrived, 'attended by crowds of people of all classes from town.' Nicolayson wrote:

> The coffin fastened on two long poles, and carried between two camels, was now covered with the pall, and all belonging to the mission walked as mourners, after it, until near the burial-ground, where it was taken off the camels and carried on men's shoulders. I then met it in the surplice at the limit of the cemetery, and preceded it, reading the sentences, to the grave broken into the rock, and regularly built up with masonry. It was now quite dark, and we had only the light afforded by a few lanthorns. I therefore only read that part of the service which is appointed to be read at the grave, and thus we had the last melancholy satisfaction of committing the mortal remains of the *first* Anglican Bishop of Jerusalem to their resting place, in "sure and certain hope of the resurrection of eternal life." The next morning I preached from 2 Corinthians v.1, &., on the glorious hope of immortality set forth in living reality in Christ.
>
> We now indeed all feel like orphans, yet we continue to pursue our work, as far as possible, in all respects as before.[22]

Indeed as the small Hebrew Christian-Protestant community contemplated upon what they had just witnessed, they were a stunned group, and one could well understand Nicolayson's sentiment that they felt like orphans. They were not unlike, in a small sense, a similar group of people some 1800 years before, also in Jerusalem, when their leader, also a Jew, had just been buried in a borrowed tomb.

The Immediate Shock
Alexander's death was announced to the LJS Committee on 23 December

---

20 Rev. W.D Veitch, to LJS London, 2 January 1846, in *JI*, 1846, p. 94.
21 Rev. W.D Veitch, to LJS London, 2 January 1846, in *JI*, 1846, p. 95.
22 Nicolayson to LJS London, 31 December 1845, in *JI*, 1846, p. 96.

1845.²³ They were deeply shocked. Shaftesbury himself recorded the event in his diary for 15 December:

> I would rather have heard many fearful things than this sad event; it buries at once half my hopes for the speedy welfare of our Church, our nation, and the children of Israel! What an overthrow to our plans! What a humbling to our foresight! What a trial to our faith! Alas! This bright spot, on which my eyes, amidst all the surrounding darkness, confusion, and terrors of England, have long been reposing, is now apparently bedimmed.
>
> I am quite dismayed ... We were rejoicing in his expected arrival in England to aid our efforts, and advance the cause; he is cut down as suddenly as a flower by the scythe!
>
> But what is our condition? Have we run counter to the will of God? Have we conceived a merely human project, and then imagined it to be a decree of the Almighty, when we erected a bishopric in Jerusalem, and appointed a Hebrew to exercise the functions? Have we vainly and presumptuously attempted to define 'the times and seasons which the Father hath put in His own power?' God, who knows our hearts, alone can tell. It seemed to us that we acted in faith for the honour of His name, and in the love of His ancient people; but now it would appear that the thing was amiss, and not according to God's wisdom and pleasure.
>
> And yet. Short-sighted, feeble creatures as we are, all this may be merely a means to a speedier and ampler glory! ²⁴

While Shaftesbury was looking at Alexander as the representative to herald Israel's full restoration, Dr. Macgowan summated the feelings of many who knew Bishop Alexander as their leader, their shepherd, their personal friend:

> To those Christian friends who take part or feel interested in those efforts which have been made of late years for the spiritual regeneration of God's ancient people, the removal of the first bishop of the Protestant Church in Jerusalem, himself a Hebrew, and thus forming a connecting link with the primitive Hebrew Christian Church, this must be considered as a public calamity. But to us, who have enjoyed the privilege of being under his pastoral care, of sharing his intimacy, and of appreciating his kind nature and simple-hearted piety, the loss is attended with deeper and more personal feelings ... His ear, his heart, his purse, were open at all times to every application for the furtherance of the object dearest to his heart. He was indeed an Israelite in whom was no guile.²⁵

---

23 See LJS General Committee Minute Book Vol. O, 23 December 1845, Bodleian.
24 Quoted in Earl of Shaftesbury, K.G., *The Jerusalem Bishopric,* (London, 1887), p. 13.
25 Macgowan to LJS London, December and January Reports, in *JI*, 1846, p. 114.

These sentiments were richly reinforced by thirty-one Jewish followers of Jesus in Jerusalem, who on 27 December wrote a Memorial to Mrs. Alexander:

> Madam – We, the undersigned, members of the House of Israel, and brethren after the flesh and Spirit to yourself and our much beloved, highly revered, and deeply lamented Bishop, with the loss of who it has pleased the mysterious and inscrutable providence of God to afflict us all, beg leave to express to you our sentiments of the most sincere and heartfelt sympathy in your late bereavement. We will not attempt to comfort you under your severe affliction, for we need ourselves to be comforted; but we will rather pray to the God of all consolation, who has graciously pledged himself never to leave nor to forsake his own, that he may verify in you the precious promises of the Gospel, so that it may become your privilege to realize all those blessings, which to bestow is the sole prerogative of Him, who is emphatically called the Comforter.
>
> Next to yourself and your dear family, we consider *ourselves the chief mourners*; for we feel both collectively and individually that we have lost not only a *true father in Christ*, but also a loving brother and a most kind friend. The *suavity and benignity of his manner*, which so greatly endeared him to all, and which gained him the highest and most entire filial confidence of every one of us, tends much to increase the keen sense we feel of our loss. *The affectionate love he bore to Israel*, which peculiarly characterised him, could not fail to render him beloved by every one who had the privilege of being acquainted with him: while his exalted piety, and most exemplary life and conversation, inspired the highest reverential esteem. He was a burning and a shining light; and when he was raised to the highest dignity in the Church, he conferred the most conspicuous honour on our whole nation, but especially on the little band of Jewish believers. With him captive Judah's brightest earthly star has set, and the top-stone has been taken away from the rising Hebrew church. But shall we repine at God's dispensations, because they are trying and painful to us? We know that we dare not, and all we can do now is, that we implore the Father of all mercies to grant us grace to glorify him, by a dutiful submission and calm resignation to his holy will and pleasure.
>
> Our greatest consolation is, the firm conviction and blessed assurance we feel, that our beloved Bishop is with Christ: he had, indeed, fought the good fight of faith, and come off more than conqueror through Him who loved us, and gave himself for us: may we have grace given to us, so to follow his good example, that when we shall have finished our earthly course, we may together with him be made partakers of Christ's heavenly kingdom.
>
> As an apology for thus obtruding on your attention, we beg to state, in conclusion, that reluctant as we feel by this means to remind you of your

great loss, we think it but due to yourself and our dear Bishop, - whose memory will always be very dear to us, and a small tribute of the sympathy we feel, - thus to express our sentiments with regard to the event which has at once made us mourners and orphans.

That the Lord may be pleased to shower down upon you and your dear family the rich fullness of his choicest blessings, will be the constant prayer of, Madam, your like afflicted and sympathizing servants.[26]

Further accolades poured in from many quarters, Anglican, Lutheran, non-Episcopal, British, Prussian, other nationalities, former friends and yes even foes. The *Times* newspaper, when referring to an accusation that Alexander's appointment was due to political intrigue, stated of Alexander:

But any man more completely the reverse of an intriguer than the late Bishop of Jerusalem can scarcely be conceived. He was indeed an Israelite without guile. If he had a fault it was that, incapable of evil himself, he was too slow to see it in others.'[27]

Immediate Consequences
Scott Calman was entrusted with caring for the Bishop's children who remained in Jerusalem. He wrote soon afterwards to Mrs. Alexander:

The Jerusalem Mission has lost much in my estimation and judgement of what is really true and valuable, by the removal of the Bishop your late husband who acted as a connected link between Jew and Gentile. Since that event, I am sorry to say, everything here has assumed a form of isolation and separation, every one seeking his own.[28]

You lost in him a faithful husband, the children a dutiful parent, and I a much revered friend, the removal of whom left a vacant void in Jerusalem that nothing earthly can fill it up.[29]

Joseph Frey's last years
While the Evangelical community in Britain and Prussia were mourning the loss of Bishop Alexander, Joseph Frey returned to his home at the end of 1845 buoyed with the success of the long speaking tour. He was so encouraged that in January 1846 he printed the first of a new magazine entitled *The Hebrew Messenger*.

Several months later, in May 1846, the new *American Baptist Society for*

---

26 Testimonial to Mrs. Alexander, 27 December 1845, in *JI*, 1846, pp. 127-128.
27 *Times, d*ated 5 December 1845, in *JI* 1846, pp. 38-39..
28 Lambeth Palace, Alexander Papers. MSS 3393, [f. 139] Scott Calman to Mrs. Alexander 4 August 1846, p. 202.
29 Lambeth Palace, Alexander Papers. MSS 3397, [f. 139] Scott Calman to Mrs. Alexander 4 August 1846, p. 204

Evangelizing the Jews held its first annual general meeting, which was presided over by Rev. Cone. Frey must have been reminded of the annual general meetings of the two Evangelical societies he worked with in London.

Unfortunately the life and vitality of the American Baptist Society soon dried up, as it had not the finances required to continue. Frey yet again was forced to travel and lecture in order to raise the necessary funds. On this occasion he ventured to the north and central states, where, for some reason, the giving was much less than expected.[30]

Due to the lack of financial support the *American Baptist Society for Evangelizing the Jews* folded up in early 1847. Once more Joseph Frey was cast away from a child he had helped to birth.

Frey now moved away from the east coast to Pontiac in Michigan. There, so it seems, he taught Hebrew – just as he had all those years before in Germany. Joseph Frey died in Pontiac on 5 June 1850 at the age of seventy-eight.

Joseph Wolff's final years

Following his return from Bokhara, recovery from the stresses and then associated speaking, Joseph Wolff was offered a small parish in Isle Brewers in Somerset by General Sir John Michael in 1847. He accepted this position and continued to live there for the next fifteen years side by side with Georgiana, while young Henry grew into a man of repute, a diplomat in time, even in Persia itself.

Although sometimes unsettled Wolff nevertheless during these years managed to build a parsonage for Georgiana and himself – which would then also be for his successors; a school, and then by 1860, a new church building.

Wolff's life was drastically changed when Georgiana died on 16 January 1859. In his time of bereavement he dictated his life story to Mrs Margaret Gatty, wife of Rev. Alfred Gatty, and their daughters. The life story, *Travels and Adventures* was printed in 1861.[31]

Margaret Gatty once said of Wolff, 'Anyone who undertakes you must have the strength of a horse, the wit of an elephant, the patience of an ass and the cheerfulness of a lark.'[32]

Apart from Georgiana there was one other woman with just those qualities, one Louisa King. Wolff married Louisa on 14 May 1861. But their marriage lasted just less than one year, for on 2 May 1862 at the age of sixty-six, Joseph Wolff died in Somerset.

With Wolff's death the last of the three sons of Abraham had been removed to their eternal reward.

---

30 Eichhorn, ibid, p. 109.
31 Hopkins, ibid, p. 334.
32 Hopkins, ibid, p. 335.

Chapter 33

The legacy of Frey, Wolff and Alexander

Joseph Frey's legacy
Joseph Frey was the pioneer, the foundation layer. In fulfilling this role he endured almost unceasing struggles, challenges and conflicts, and was invariably the underdog, the one who had to prove himself and adapt to changing circumstances – as a Jew, as a German, and as a Non-Conformist.

There seems little doubt that the foundation he laid greatly assisted Wolff and Alexander, as well as numerous other Jewish followers of Jesus thereafter.

No individual or institution is perfect. Yet despite the imperfections of Frey, the London Jews Society and the *Benei Abraham*, institutions and movements were built upon those foundations. The London Jews Society in time established bases in some forty locations world-wide in order to introduce Jewish people to Jesus. Today, there are numerous other organisations in Britain and the world which are dedicated to introducing Jewish people to Jesus. The LJS (today known as CMJ) is still a viable organisation operating in several countries, and particularly so in Israel.

One other Society which owns Frey as its founder is the British Society for Promoting Christianity among the Jews (today CWI), which was formed in 1842 by the Non-Conformists.

In addition, the small *Benei Abraham*, although lying dormant following Frey's departure to America, never died and vanished. That foundation was slowly built upon and in time developed into the Hebrew Christian Alliance in Britain in 1866, which, itself in time grew into a world-wide formation. This Hebrew Christian movement has developed into the Messianic Jewish movement, so that today one can see the Hebrew Christian-Messianic Jewish movement spread right across the globe.

The beginnings and development of the Hebrew Christian-Messianic Jewish movement, the London Jews Society (today CMJ) and the British Jews Society, are not attributed solely to Joseph Frey by any means. But Frey most certainly is one of their fathers.

But what of Frey's life in North America, did he also leave a legacy there? George Berlin wrote:

> To be sure, Frey enjoyed little success in his missionary endeavors in America and he seems to have made only a modest impact on the small American Jewish community. Frey's significance lies, rather, in the impact he made on

Christian America.¹

This impact is best expressed in the words, again of Berlin, who wrote:

> Frey became a well-known personality during his nearly three decade long career in America. His many lectures often drew large audiences and his books were widely read. *Joseph and Benjamin*, the most popular of his books aside from his autobiographical writings, went through nine editions by 1842. It is instructive that this was Frey's most successful work. Frey claimed that *Joseph and Benjamin* had "proved that every doctrine which I believe as a Christian, was revealed in the Old Testament, and was believed by the ancient Jews, which I proved from their own writings." It was highly praised by Christian reviewers not only as an able refutation of Judaism to be used in polemics against Jews, but also as a valuable summary of Christian doctrine that should be used by ministers and Sabbath school teachers. *Joseph and Benjamin* confirmed Christians in their own faith and strengthened their traditional view of the Jews and their belief that the latter would ultimately recognize the truth of Christianity. Through *Joseph and Benjamin* and his other works, Frey made an impact upon American thinking concerning the Jews and gave a new impetus to the American missionary impulse. His portrayal of Jewish life and belief appealed to American reform and millenarian sentiments and reinforced American Christian ideas of the time.
>
> ... Frey the converted Jew who optimistically preached that the Jews should and could be converted, and that free and liberal minded Americans should be especially interested in the cause, strengthened the belief of Americans that they could play a significant role in the unfolding of God's plan for history.²

If Berlin's assessment is correct, then we can conclude that Joseph Frey was also a foundation layer of a Christian interest and awareness of the Jewish people in North America as well.

Another who wrote of Frey's contribution to North America was George H. Genzer, who stated in the *Dictionary of American Biography*:

> At heart he probably remained a Jew, his frequent changes of doctrine and abode being so many attempts to escape from his inner misery.³

On one matter Genzer was clear, Frey most definitely remained a Jew: but a

---

1 Berlin, G.L. "Joseph S.C.F. Frey, The Jews, and early Nineteenth Century Millenarianism", in *Journal of the Early Republic*, Vol. I, No. I (Spring, 1981), p. 31.
2 Berlin, ibid, p. 49.
3 Genzer, G.H. *Dictionary of American Biography*, New York, 1931, Vol. VII, p. 29, quoted by Berlin, ibid, footnote 9, p. 30.

Jew who was a follower of Jesus. What Genzer's comment may focus upon is that throughout his life as a follower of Jesus, Frey lacked the deep assurance that he was accepted just as he was. It seems that wherever he went he carried that underdog label with him: whether in Germany, Britain or America. He was most probably often regarded as an oddity – this Jew who follows Jesus. Being such an oddity, he most probably was never accepted as an equal by some, perhaps by many. Such though is often the way it is with pioneers and foundation layers.

The Hebrew Christian-Messianic Jewish movement and even the world-wide Church both owe a great debt of gratitude to Joseph Frey.

The legacy of Joseph Wolff

One could surmise that Joseph Wolff was nothing more than a nomadic Jew who essentially never changed his lifestyle once he became a follower of Jesus. That assessment is true to a degree.

But Joseph Wolff, it would seem, was always seeking after the truth. When he finally discovered the truth embodied in Jesus, then his greatest desire was to share this truth with others.

An argument could then be sustained that he was very unorthodox in how he went about this task. But if Wolff stuck to so-called British evangelical orthodoxy, far fewer people, both Jew and Gentile, would have heard about and been introduced to Jesus. It was exactly because Joseph Wolff was unorthodox and nomadic that the message of Jesus spread as far and as wide as it did. It was due to his initial explorations that the LJS later established works in various locations in the East.

Perhaps one of the greatest legacies to come to us from the exotic lifestyle of Joseph Wolff is from his only non-missionary journey. It comes to us via the words he said to the Turkish official who asked why he was risking life and limb to travel to Bohkara in 1844. Those words of Wolff's were:

> … being a disciple of Jesus, who laid down His life for mankind, he must also be ready to risk his life for the benefit of his fellow-creatures; and this was his motive for which he undertook that journey.[4]

There is nothing unorthodox about this statement. It seems to me, even from only a cursory reading of some of his numerous journals and writings, and even allowing for any inaccuracies and editor's exaggerations contained within those writings, that one thing really motivated Joseph Wolff: knowing the truth, and then proclaiming that truth as it is in Jesus to all and sundry.

---

4 Wolff, *Travels*, pp. 530-31.

The legacy of Michael Solomon Alexander

It was very difficult for both the Restorationist-minded Evangelicals in Britain and Europe, and the flock of Jewish and Gentile disciples of Jesus in Jerusalem, to fill the void left by Alexander's death.

It is very clear that everything that was expected of Alexander was not fulfilled – there was no Jewish restoration, and there was, at least in 1845, no world-wide Protestant union with Jerusalem as its centre.

If Alexander had survived, certainly things would have gone differently. Whether or not those plans, ambitions and visions of Shaftesbury, the Restorationists and of King Frederick William and Bunsen would have been fulfilled is difficult to surmise.

But what is clear is that Alexander, together with Nicolayson, laid a foundation in Jerusalem and the land of Israel upon which many have built.

Alexander's replacement as bishop was Samuel Gobat. Gobat had worked mostly among non-Jewish people, and did not desire to work exclusively among Jewish people as Alexander had done. Thus, during his tenure of some thirty-three years (1846-1879), he also reached out to the Arab peoples of Palestine, the land of Israel.

Under Gobat, German interests also grew tremendously. Geo-politically the Jerusalem Protestant Bishopric provided Prussia (and later Germany) with the ideal launching pad for German penetration into the region. It was not by any means the only avenue for such German penetration, but it was the main one.

In 1842 Prussia was the smallest of the European great powers, and needed a back on which to climb. Britain, the Anglican Church, and the LJS, provided that back. But by the 1880's Prussia had been replaced by the ambitious German Empire of the Kaiser and of Otto von Bismark.

This German Empire was seeking penetration into the Turkish Empire, primarily through cultural and economic connections. By the end of the 19th century while Germany was seeking expansion, Turkey was seeking a new, and more trustworthy, European ally. Germany and Turkey saw each other as fulfilling the needs of the other.

Michael Solomon Alexander expended much of his energy on one major project while in Jerusalem for those four years – the building of a Protestant Church. When this Church, named Christ Church, was finally completed in 1849 it not only violated Islamic law, but was also a focal point of national interest for the Germans as well as for the British. It provided a cover under which to shelter – and expand.

But with the new Germany, those wings were no longer big enough to shelter two nations, two ecclesiastical bodies – two visions. The Germans came to view Christ Church as the British Church, the British national emblem in Jerusalem. It was time for Germany to branch out and establish her own independent cover. The growing relationship between Germany and Turkey facilitated this desire for growth.

So the Germans obtained through the generosity of the Turkish Sultan property adjacent to the Church of the Holy Sepulchre in 1869, whereupon they laid the foundations for a large complex.

Gobat's successor, Joseph Barclay, was nominated by the British. Barclay, however, died prematurely in 1881. Thereafter the German Government desired to cancel the 1841 Agreement. This was now the time of German expansionism. Indeed by 1888 that initial agreement had been annulled, and now Germany went its own way in Jerusalem and the land of Israel.[5]

In 1898 the German Emperor, or Kaiser, visited the Turkish Empire, was feted by the Sultan, and then journeyed to Jerusalem to officially open the new German Church of the Redeemer. To consolidate the growing German-Turkish geo-political connection, the Sultan permitted a readjustment of Jaffa Gate, the entrance way into the Old City in order to facilitate the entrance of the Kaiser and his grand entourage.

On the same trip the Kaiser met several times with Theodore Herzl, the leader of the newly founded Jewish nationalist group, known henceforth as the Zionist movement. The Zionists had fully anticipated that Germany would be the modern day Cyrus who would facilitate the return of the Jewish people to the land of Israel. It was Germany they turned to in order to elicit a grant from the Turkish Sultan to permit a Jewish 'homeland' or national entity to develop in *Eretz Ha-Kodesh* - the Holy Land.

However the German Kaiser understood real politik all too well. He understood that to adopt or support such a movement would jeopardize his standing with the Sultan, who was also the Caliph of Islam. The Turks had no desire to surrender any of their Empire to a minority nationalist movement.

The Zionists were rebuffed, and thereupon turned to the only nation which historically had shown commitment to this hoped for Jewish restoration – Britain. It was Britain which had harboured the interest in Israel's restoration, and which in 1840 had proposed just such a plan to the Turkish Government. Although Turkey refused, yet it was this environment of interest in 1840 which precipitated the King of Prussia's move for having the Protestant Bishopric established.

Israel's physical restoration to the land, though, did not occur in 1840. In fact it could not occur while Britain was politically allied to Turkey. But in 1914 Turkey opted to fight alongside Germany – against Britain. So in 1917 when British and Anzac (Australian and New Zealand) troops conquered Turkish Palestine and this time ousted the Turks, the opportunity arose for the plan of

---

5 Munster to Earl Granville, 17 July 1882, *Correspondence respecting the Protestant Bishopric at Jerusalem*, FO 406/5460.

1840 to be implemented.

On the day that British and Anzac troops captured Beersheba (31 October 1917), the British Government agreed to establish a Jewish national home in Palestine; a promise thereafter known as the Balfour Declaration. Then General Allenby representing the Allied nations, entered the Old City of Jerusalem on 11 December 1917 and ascended the steps leading into the Citadel or Fortress of Jerusalem. The closest buildings to him were those of Christ Church, the Hebrew-Protestant Church which Alexander had laboured to see built.

One very common adage used in 1917 was that Britain was doing for the Jewish people the same that Cyrus the Emperor of Persia had done for them some 2500 years before – restoring them to their homeland. Indeed as the historical record reveals, this was very much the case. But this event of 1917 was presaged by that of 1840, and 1917 was followed by the event on 14 May 1948 when the State of Israel was formed, an important step in the restoration of Israel, but by no means the final step. There still remains a time when 'all Israel shall be saved.'

One very important component of the Cyrus event was the introduction into Jerusalem of a reformed Israelite faith system. Alexander and his colleagues around the period of 1840 were involved in a similar undertaking. This undertaking is no better described than by Alexander's very good friend, Alexander McCaul, who wrote at this time:

> SALVATION IS OF THE JEWS. Amongst all the religious systems in the world, there are two deserving of attentive consideration, and they are both of Jewish origin, and were once exclusively confined to the Jewish nation. They are now known by the names of Judaism and Christianity; but it must never be forgotten that the latter is as entirely Jewish as the former. The author of Christianity was a Jew. The first preachers of Christianity were all Jews. The first Christians were all Jews; so that, in discussing the truth of these respective systems, we are not opposing a Gentile religion to a Jewish religion, but comparing one Jewish creed with another Jewish creed. Neither, in defending Christianity, do we wish to diminish aught from the privileges of the Jewish people; on the contrary, we candidly acknowledge that we are disciples of the Jews, converts to Jewish doctrines, partakers of the Jewish hope, and advocates of that truth which the Jews have taught us. We are fully persuaded that the Jews whom we follow were in the right – that they have pointed out to us 'the old paths', 'the good way', and 'we have found rest to our souls'. And we, therefore, conscientiously believe that those Jews who follow the opposite system are as wrong as their forefathers, who, when God commanded them to walk in the good old way, replied, 'We will not walk therein.'[6]

6 McCaul, A. *The Old Paths*, (London, 1846), p. 1.

The heart's desire of Michael Solomon Alexander, as too of Joseph Frey and Joseph Wolff, was nothing other than to point their fellow Jewish people to the 'good old way,' just like those Jewish followers of Jesus did in Jerusalem some 1700 years before them.

Patrick Irwin, wrote of Alexander's legacy:

> For the Church Alexander had created something of lasting worth. His modest and hard-won success so beset by controversy in establishing a Hebrew Christian congregation in Jerusalem ensured that Christian Jewry would have a share in the development of the Holy Land. He had established foundations on which others could build. Mission to the Jews would no longer be the principal activity of the Anglican bishopric, but Alexander's episcopate had bound it securely to the Anglican church.
>
> The Jews of Jerusalem too were Alexander's debtors. In his encouragement of the medical mission he had demonstrated that his love for the Jews was not dependent upon their accepting Christianity. Alexander can with justice take his place among the Jews of the nineteenth century who sought to raise up the Jews of Jerusalem from their state of degradation. The activities of these Jewish philanthropists can indeed be regarded as a response to the challenge provided by the pioneer Christian enterprises of Alexander's episcopate.
>
> Thus as Christian pastor and Jerusalem pioneer Alexander has two distinct claims on posterity's regard. They have survived the evaporation of the unrealistic expectations of 1841. The restoration of Israel was delayed and the link with Prussia faded, but Alexander's modest achievements remain. Perhaps most appealing, though, is Alexander the man, the convert with a passionate concern for the Jewish people that transcended all difficulties. An innocent abroad he may have been, but his generosity of spirit is singularly refreshing. The Holy City has never lacked energetic defenders of the faith. Alexander was something rarer in Jerusalem, a tolerant divine.[7]

Today

Today there are close to ten thousand Jewish followers of Jesus in Israel, worshipping God in more than seventy mostly Hebrew speaking congregations. Although their appearance is distinctly different from those Jewish followers of Bishop Alexander's time, yet they are a legacy of his efforts and the efforts of others such as John Nicolayson.

There are today upwards of one hundred thousand Jewish followers of Jesus spread throughout the world; worshipping in Messianic synagogues, Messianic congregations and within numerous denominational settings. They display their Jewishness to varying degrees, but they for the most part express unashamedly the fact that they are *Jews who follow Jesus*.

---

7 Irwin, Patrick. *Bishop Alexander and the Jews of Jerusalem*. pp. 326-7.

For this they can thank people such as Joseph Frey, Joseph Wolff, Michael Solomon Alexander, those other forty Jewish disciples who formed the original *Benei Abraham* – and many others.

These three representative Jewish followers of Jesus played a huge role in the whole plan of restoration: they have helped to restore the Jewish dynamic back into the world-wide Church. Today, the world-wide Church can no longer say it is the Gentile Church. Today the world-wide Church is being challenged to seriously consider its true foundations, and the root from which it has come.

These three sons of Abraham, as indeed the other Jewish pioneers, have given a particular flavour to that river which came together by the confluence of the Puritan, Pietist, Moravian and Evangelical streams. When streams converge thereafter it is difficult to differentiate those original streams as they all flow together.

When Jewish followers of Jesus join together with Gentile-background followers of Jesus then those profound words of Paul become real:

> For He Himself is our peace, who made both groups into one, and broke down the barrier of the dividing wall, by abolishing in His flesh the enmity, which is the Law of commandments contained in ordinances, that in Himself He might make the two into one new man, thus establishing peace, and might reconcile them both in one body to God through the cross, by it having put to death the enmity.
>
> And He came and preached peace to you who were far away, and peace to those who were near; for through Him we both have access in one Spirit to the Father. (Ephesians 2: 14-18, NAS)

Selected Bibliography

Books

Alexander, Mrs. D. *Autobiography*, unpublished manuscript, Alexander Papers, Lambeth Palace Archives, London.

Alexander, Mrs. D. *Diary of a Journey to Mount Carmel*, (Lambeth Palace Archives).

Ariel, Y. *Evangelizing the Chosen People: Missions to the Jews in American, 1880-2000*, (University of North Carolina, 2000).

Battiscombe, G. *Shaftesbury : A biography of the Seventh Earl 1801-1885*, (London, 1974).

Bebbington, D.W. *Evangelicalism in Modern Britain*, (London, 1979).

Ben Arieh, Y. *Jerusalem in the Nineteenth Century*, (Jerusalem, 1984), Volume 1.

Bicheno, J. *The Signs of the Times: or, The Overthrow of the Papal Tyranny in France, the Prelude of Destruction to Popery and Despotism; but of Peace to Mankind*, (London, 1793).

Bicheno, J. *The Restoration of the Jews, And the Crisis of all Nations*, (London, 1800).

Brown, M. *Our Hands are Stained with Blood*, (Harrisburg, 1990).

Bunsen, F. *Memoirs*, I, (London, 1868).

Callenberg, J. *A short account of an Essay to bring the Jewish nation to the Knowledge and Practise of the Truth of the Gospel, etc*, (Halle, 1734).

Clark, Christopher. *The Politics of Conversion*, (Oxford, 1995).

Corey, M. *From Rabbi to Bishop*, (London, 1956).

Cresson, Warden. *Key of David*, (Philadelphia, 1852).

Dunlop, Rev J. *Memories of Gospel Triumphs amongst the Jews*, (London, 1894).

Eichhorn, D. *Evangelizing the American Jew*, (New York, 1978).

Eliav, M. *Britain and the Holy Land, 1838-1914*: Selected Documents from the British Consulate of Jerusalem, (Jerusalem, 1997).

Eliav, M. *Eretz Israel and its Yishuv in the Nineteenth century (1777-1917)*, (Jerusalem, 1978) [Hebrew].

Endelman, T. *The Jews of Britain*, (Berkely, 2002).

Ewald, Rev. F.C. *Journal of Missionary Labours in the City of Jerusalem,* (London, 1846).

Field, J. *America and the Mediterranean World 1776-1882,* (Princeton, 1969).

Finn, E.A. *Reminiscences of Mrs. Finn,* (London & Edinburgh, 1930).

Finn, J. *Stirring Times,* ((London, 1878).

Frey, J. *Judah and Israel, or The Restoration and Conversion of the Jews and the Ten Tribes* (London, 1837).

Frey, J. *Narrative of the Reverend Joseph Samuel C. F. Frey*, (London, 1809).

Friedmann, I. *The Question of Palestine,* (New Brunswick, 1992).

Gidney, W. *The History of the London Society for Promoting Christianity among the Jews,* (London, 1908).

Hatchard, J. *The Predictions and Promises of God Respecting Israel, (Appendix),* (London, 1825).

Hearnshaw F.J.C. *The Centenary History of King's College London,* (London, 1929).

Hechler, W.H. *The Jerusalem Bishopric,* (London, 1883).

Hodder, E. *The Life and Work of the Seventh Earl of Shaftesbury,* (London, 1887).

Hole, C. *Early History of the Church Missionary Society,*(London, 1896).

Hopkins, H. *Sublime Vagabond,* (Worthing, 1984).

Hyamson, A. *British Consulate in Jerusalem in relation to the Jews of Palestine 1838-1914,* (London, 1939).

Johns, J.W. *The Anglican Cathedral Church of St. James Jerusalem,* (London, 1844).

Jurieu, P. *The Accomplishment of the Scripture Prophecies,* (London, 1687).

Kobler, F. *The Vision was There,* (London, 1956).

Kobler, F. *Napoleon and the Jews,* (Jerusalem, 1975).

Lieber, S. *Mystics and Missionaries, The Jews in Palestine, 1799-1840,* (Salt Lake City, 1992).

Lipman, V.D. *Americans and the Holy Land: Through British Eyes,* (Hebrew University, Jerusalem & London, 1989).

Lovett, R. *History of the London Missionary Society,* 1795-1895, (London, 1899).

Maurice, F. *Three Letters to the Rev. W. Palmer,* (London, 1842).

Milton, J. *Paradise Regained,* (1671).

Mizrachi, E. *Two Americans Within the Gates*, (Hagerstown, 1995).

Murray, I. *The Puritan Hope*, (Edinburgh, 1971).

Newman, J.H. *Apologia Pro Vita Sua*, (London, 1890).

Orchard, Stephen. *English Evangelical Eschatology 1790-1850*, unpublished thesis, (Cambridge, 1992).

Parfitt, T. *The Jews in Palestine 1800-1882*, (Woodbridge, Suffolk, 1987).

Parkes, J. *The Conflict of the Church and the Synagogue*, (Cleveland, 1964).

Parry, Yarom. *British Mission to the Jews in Nineteenth Century Palestine*, (London, 2003).

Pragai, M. *Faith and Fulfilment: Christians and the Return to the Promised Land*, (London, 1985).

Ransom, D. *Life of Mrs. Ransom*, Unpublished manuscript, (London, 1913).

Ridley, J. *Lord Palmerston*, (New York, 1971).

Schwarzfuchs, S. *Napoleon the Jews and the Sanhedrin*, (London, 1979).

Scult, M. *Millennial Expectations and Jewish Liberties*, (Leiden, 1978).

Sizer, S. *Christian Zionism: Road-map to Armaggedon?*, (Leicester, 2004).

Sobel, B.Z. *Hebrew Christianity: The Thirteenth Tribe*, (New York, 1974).

Spangenberg, A. *The Life of Count Zinzendorf*, (London, 1838).

Stirling, A. *The Ways of Yesterday*, (London, 1930).

Tibawi, A. L. *British Interests in Palestine 1800-1901*, (Oxford, 1961).

Trevelyan, G.M. *The History of England*, (London, 1948).

Tuchman, B. *Bible and Sword*, (New York, 1956).

Wilkinson, P. *For Zion's Sake*, (Paternoster, 2010).

Williams, G. *Holy City*, (1849).

Wilson, M. *Our Father Abraham*, (Grand Rapids, 1989).

Wolff, J. *Sketch of the Life and Journal of the Rev. J. Wolff, Missionary to Palestine and Persia*, (Norwich, 1827).

Wolff, J. *Travels and Adventures of the Rev. Joseph Wolff*, (1860).

Wolf, L. *Notes on the Diplomatic History of the Jewish Question*, (London, 1919).

Yeats, J. *The Rise of British Missions to the Jews 1808-1818*, (unpublished dissertation, Southwestern Baptist Theological Seminary, no date).

Archives

Bodleian Library, Oxford.

British National Archives, Kew, London.

Conrad Schick Library & Archive, Christ Church, Jerusalem.

King's College Archive, the Strand, London.

Lambeth Palace Archive, London.

RCB Library, Dublin.

School of Oriental and Asian Studies (SOAS), London.

St. Anthony's Library, Oxford.

Yad Ben Zvi Archives, Jerusalem.

Articles

Berlin, G. "Joseph S.C.F. Frey, The Jews, and early Nineteenth Century Millenarianism", in *Journal of the Early Republic,* Vol. I, No. I (Spring, 1981).

Blake, Robert. *The Origins of the Jerusalem Bishopric,* in Church State and Society in the 19th Century, (Munchen, 1984), pp. 87-95.

Brown, F. *The Fathers of the Victorians: The Age of Wilberforce,* (University Press, Cambridge, 1961).

Brown, Malcolm. *The Jews of Norfolk and Suffolk before 1840* in Jewish Historical Studies. Transactions of The Jewish Historical Society of England, Vol. 32, 1990-92.

Carmel, A. 'Activities of the European Powers in Palestine 1799-1914', in *Asian and African Studies,* 19 (1985).

Detzler, Wayne. A. Seeds of Missiology in the German *Erwecking* (1815-1848). In *JETS* 38/2 (June 1995), pp. 231-239.

Ehrlich, Richard A. *Michael Solomon Alexander, The First Evangelical Bishop in Jerusalem,* in AJR Information, April 1963, London.

Greaves, R.W. *The Jerusalem Bishopric 1841,* English Historical Review 1949 LXIV.

Irwin, Patrick. *Bishop Alexander and the Jews of Jerusalem* in Studies in Church History, Vol. 21: Persecution and Toleration, ed. W.J.Shields, (Oxford 1984).

Miller, G. *Bibliographical Society of America,* Vol. XXX, 1936.

Skinner, James. *The Three Anglican Bishops in Jerusalem,* in Church Quarterly

www.christianhistoryinstitute.org. Frank A James III, 'Augustine's Millenial Views' in *Christian History Institute*, Issue 15.

www.thriceholy.net. Aurelius Augustine, *City of God*, Book 20, Chapter 7.

www.jewishencyclopedia.com. Jewish Encyclopaedia, (1906), *Host: Desecration of*.

www.humanitas-international.org. Luther, M. *On the Jews and their Lies*, (1543, Translated by Martin H. Bertram, 1971), Section XI.

www.yashanet.com. Excerpt from "Ad Quaelstiones et Objecta Juaei Cuiusdam Responsio," (*A Response To Questions and Objections of a Certain Jew*) by John Calvin; The Jew in Christian Theology, Gerhard Falk, McFarland and Company, Inc., Jefferson, NC and London, 1931.

www.wikipedia.johncalvin. *Calvin's Commentaries*. Grand Rapids, MI: Eerdmans, 1948, quoted in Lange van Ravenswaay 2009, p. 146.

www.the-highway.com. Masselink, W. *The History of Chiliasm*.

www.kettmiller.mysite.wanadoo-members.co.uk/Page7.html.

www.conservativeonline.org/journals/01_03_journal/1997v1n3_id01.htmThomas Brightman, *A Revelation of the Revelation,* Leyden, 1616, pp. 557-9; 851-2; 932-3.

www.exlibris.org/nonconform/engdis/fifthmonarchists.html

www.presbyterianreformed.org/worship.htm.

www.ccel.org/ccel/hutton/moravian.html

www.chi.gospelcom.net/GLIMPSEF/Glimpses/glmps163.shtml

www.smu.edu/bidwell/html/Manuscript Collection.htm#Thaweis. Thomas Haweis Collection.

www.olivercowdrey.com. *American Society for Meliorating the Condition of the Jews*, Oliver Cowdrey.

PAMPHLETS

Callenberg, J. *A Short account of an essay to bring the Jewish nation to the Knowledge and Practise of the Truth of the Gospel, etc,* (Halle, 1734). Quoted in *Jewish Repository*, January 1813.

The Jerusalem Bishopric, (London, 1856).

review, July 1884.

Sarna, J. 'The American Jewish Response to Nineteenth Century Christian Missions', in *Journal of American History*, Vol. 68, No. 1.

Taylor, B. *Alexander's Apostasy: First Steps to Jerusalem*, in *Christianity and Judaism*, Ecclesiastical Historical Society, (Oxford, 1992).

Verete, M. *A Plan for the Internationalization of Jerusalem* in 'From Palmerston to Balfour: Collected Essays of Mayir Verete,' (Frank Cass, London).

Verete, M. *The Restoration of the Jews in English Protestant Thought 1790-1840;* in Middle Eastern Studies, January 1972, (Frank Cass, London).

Welch, P.J. *Anglican Churchmen and the establishment of the Jerusalem Bishopric*, in Journal of Ecclesiastical History, Vol. 8, No 2, 1957.

JOURNALS AND PERIODICALS

Evangelical Magazine, 1793, 1795, 1796.

Jewish Repository.

Jewish Intelligence.

Jewish Monthly Intelligence.

LJS Annual Reports.

Missionary Society Reports.

Report of the Directors to the Fourteenth General Meeting of *The Missionary Society*, May 12, 1808, (London, 1808).

WEBSITES

www.wikipedia.

www.earlychristianwritings.com. Justin Martyr, *Dialogue with Trypho the Jew*, Chapter 29.

www.preteristarchive.com. John Chrysostom, *Adversus Iudaeos*, ('Homilies against the Jews').

www.newadvent.org/fathers. Augustine, *Contra Faustum*, Book 12. 12.

www.patheos.com. Thomas McDonald, *St Augustine and the Jews*.

www.bmcr.brynmawr.edu . Robert McEachnie, University of Florida, review of Paula Fredriksen, *Augustine and the Jews: A Christian Defense of Jews and Judaism*, (New Haven/London: Yale University Press, 2010).

www.newadvent.org/fathers. Augustine, *City of God*, Book 18, Chapter 46.